THE CREATIVE FIGHT

CREATE YOUR BEST WORK AND LIVE THE LIFE YOU IMAGINE

CHRIS ORWIG

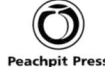

Peachpit Press

THE CREATIVE FIGHT:
CREATE YOUR BEST WORK AND LIVE THE LIFE YOU IMAGINE
Chris Orwig

Peachpit Press
www.peachpit.com

To report errors, please send a note to errata@peachpit.com
Peachpit Press is a division of Pearson Education.

Project Editor: Valerie Witte
Production Editor: David Van Ness
Copy Editor: Scout Festa
Proofreader: Liz Welch
Composition: Kim Scott, Bumpy Design
Indexer: James Minkin
Cover Image: John Kelsey / Chris Orwig
Cover Design: Cybele Grandjean
Interior Design: Cybele Grandjean

ISBN-13: 978-0-134-07848-9
ISBN-10:   0-134-07848-9

9 8 7 6 5 4 3 2
Printed and bound in the United States of America

For my father,
who taught me how to fight the good fight
and live for a higher ideal.

TABLE OF CONTENTS

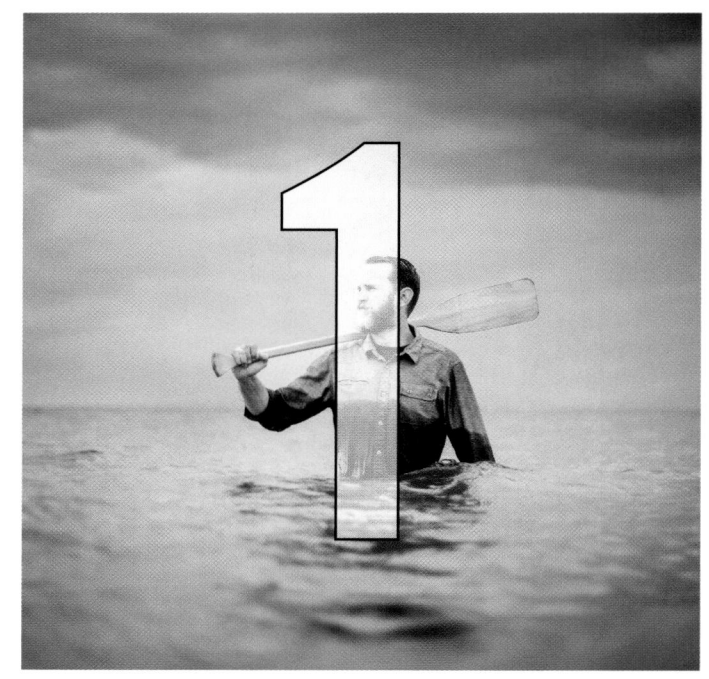

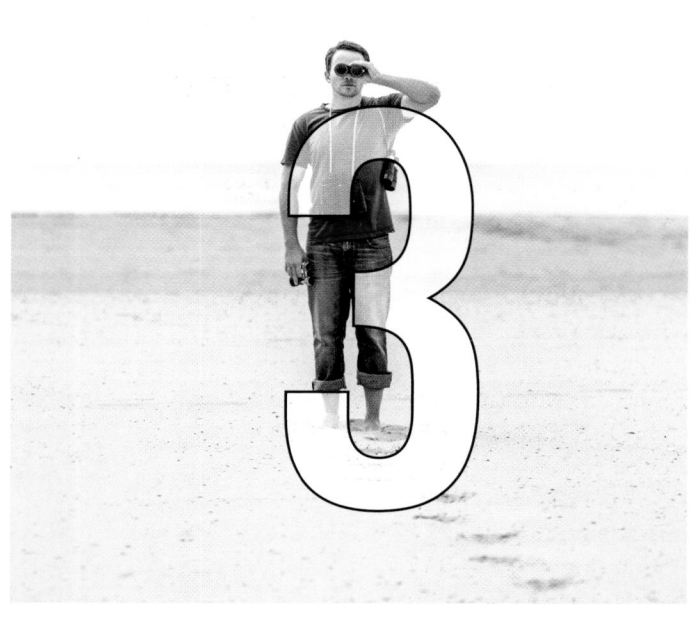

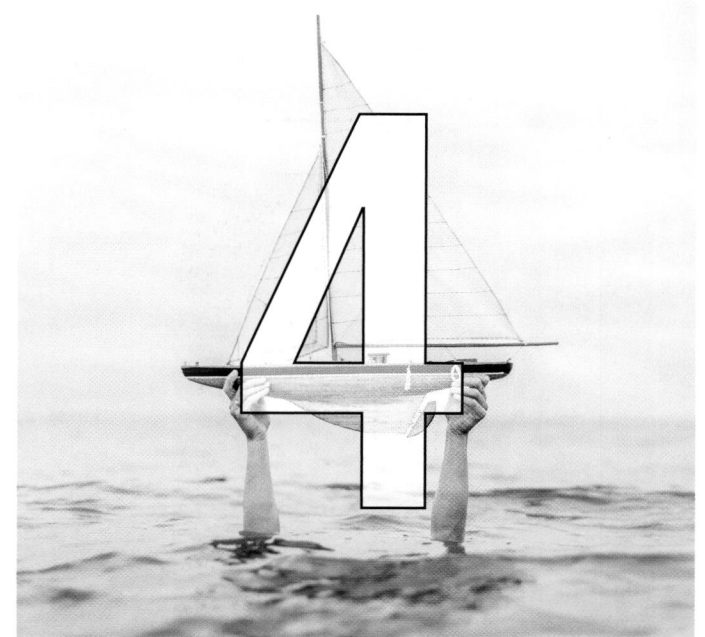

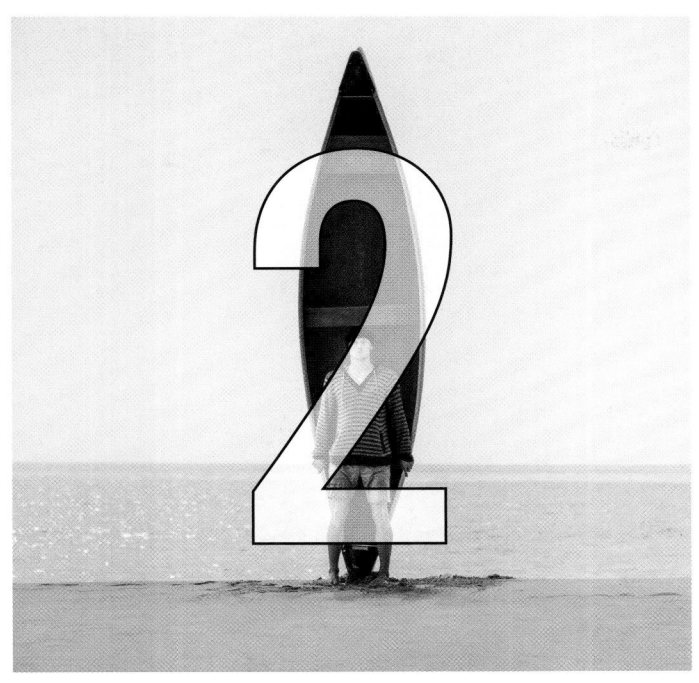

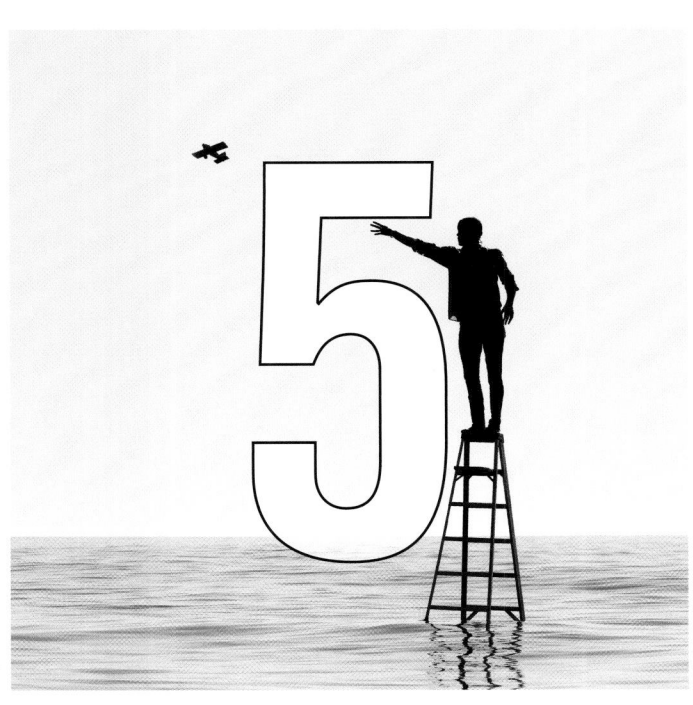

INTRODUCTION

"I am writing this book because we are all going to die." — Jack Kerouac. I suppose that's why all books are written. Books, whether the study of seashells or Shakespearean verse, help us to live. Books deepen our appreciation, awaken our senses, and strengthen our resolve to live in a meaningful way. This book is my attempt.

All creative acts, especially books, begin with uncertainty and risk. The lack of certainty provides a clearing for the creative impulse to grow. Free from the restraint of self-assured confidence, curiosity kicks in and we begin to wonder "What if?" and "Why?" It's here that the creative spirit revs up and asks, "What can I do?" and "How can I make the most with what I have?"

Such questions help us grow. And the best part of writing this book is how it has shaped who I am. By narrowing my own focus on creativity it has enriched my life and clarified who I want to become. That's what creativity does and that's my hope for you—that it enlivens your soul and inspires you to live the life for which you are designed.

We are all born with natural capacities to create, and we all have creative potential of which we are unaware. Everyone, including you, has untapped potential that is patiently waiting inside. Yet the creative spark can easily get snuffed out. It must be tended to like a campfire on a cold and rainy day. Neglect it and it will quietly dwindle, dissipate, and die. Keep it alive and you will thrive. This book will point the way.

For starters, creativity isn't something we passively receive. You have to go after it to claim its prize. Creativity requires fight. When we were young we were willing to take the risk and put in the time. Unfettered by self-doubt we created on demand. Now older, we've lost what we once had, unless we make the choice to change. It begins with deciding to stop waiting for inspiration and start taking action ourselves. When we begin the fight it's like steel striking flint, and it deeply affects what we create, how we see, and who we are. And when we begin pursuing living life as if it were a work of art, our creativity swells.

At first glance, riding this swell seems simple, easy, and fun. But this thinking falls short—the creative spark is a much more complex and unpredictable force. And the pursuit of creativity is a much more interesting and adventurous ride. To become more creative we need to unlearn old ideas—like the idea that creativity is a gift for an elite few or the myth that inspiration comes while we sit around. And we need to be reminded of what we easily forget, like the idea that creativity requires guts, confidence, and hard work and that creativity isn't a gift but a life force that courses through our veins.

Creativity fuels a drive to live the life for which we were designed. It despises those who live half-hearted and half-lived lives. Creativity reaches for good, provokes change, and calls us to strive, stretch, and try. Yet such creative efforts require risk. Afraid of failure and uncertain how to move ahead, most of us have forgotten what to do. We want to become more creative, but we don't know where to begin. Or worse, when inspired we don't know how to keep the spark alive. This book can help.

This book will show you that becoming more creative isn't just about thinking happy thoughts or using colorful crayons; the path to creativity is a much wider trail. As Plutarch wrote in the first century, "Music, to create harmony, must investigate discord." And to help you become more creative, this book will investigate a range of topics, from climbing ladders to tenacity, grit, and death. The goal is to find melody amidst discord and to rekindle your fire for creating your best work and making the most of your time.

As nice as that sounds, this isn't a book about thinking your way to happiness or wishing your way to a more fulfilled life. It is about effort and fight. The secrets to becoming more creative are always accompanied by habit, practice, and work. As Theodore Roosevelt, an exemplar of the creative fight, once said, "I may be an average man but by George I work harder at it than the average man." Average to excellent is up to you and it's less about talent and more about drive.

So this book is written for those of us who are driven to live a better life. And it's a guide for igniting and sustaining the spark no matter what you do or who you are. Yet this book can't do anything by itself. It relies on you to take the lead. To give you a nudge, at the end of each chapter you'll find exercises that provide reflection questions and practical steps. Use these questions as a springboard to create your own. Think of these as small sparks that can be used to ignite big flames.

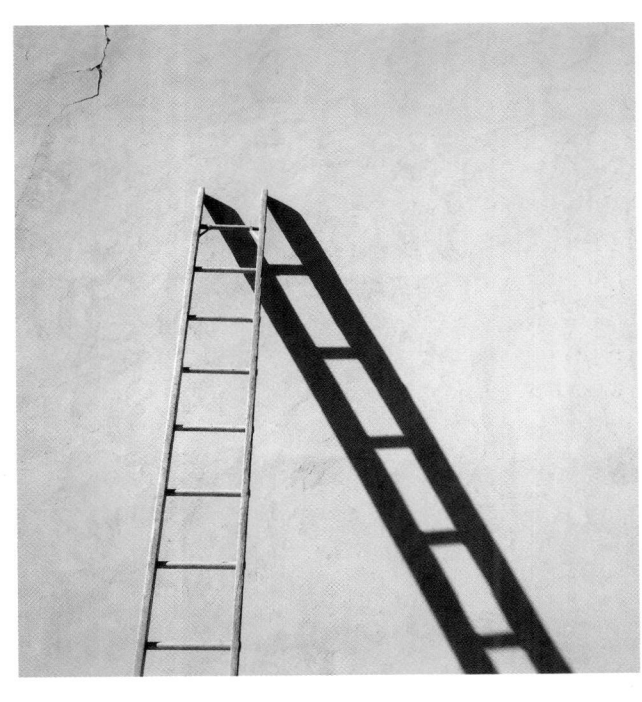

Most importantly, this book will work only if you take action and respond. Read passively and the book will diminish to an interesting collection of stories and ideas. Overanalyze and you'll miss the point. Creativity is not a problem to be solved but a practice to be enjoyed. Like a good travel book, it will become better when you take the journey yourself. The book invites you to join in.

And the best books are those that rarely stay pristine. Rather, they are worn thin from reading on the train and parched from being read in the sun. After some time these books resemble a vessel that has traveled far from home. Such books become marked up and taken over by the readers so that it is no longer the author's work but their own. That is my hope whether you're reading this in digital or print form. This book is my gift to you. No longer mine, it's now yours.

As you read, you'll discover that the book isn't a foolproof formula or a promise of increased creativity by following seven simple steps. The creative fight is more fluid, flexible, and open than that—sometimes suggesting quiet and other times being loud; sometimes asking you to go slow and other times to sprint. Distrust anyone who tells you that creativity can be figured out. Creativity is a wild elusive force. You can't trap it in a cage, but you can learn how to harness its strength. This book is your guide.

While you read, don't hesitate to drop me a line. I would love to hear about your story and learn about the wisdom you have. You can send me a note (and find more resources) at the book companion site: thecreativefight.com. Lastly, I hope that someday we cross paths so that we can compare notes and share what we have learned since this adventure began. Either way, let's keep in touch.

Finally, I'm humbled and honored that you have picked up this book. May it be one that brings change and helps you find the ladder that leads to a more creative and meaningful life and emboldens you to accomplish your dreams.

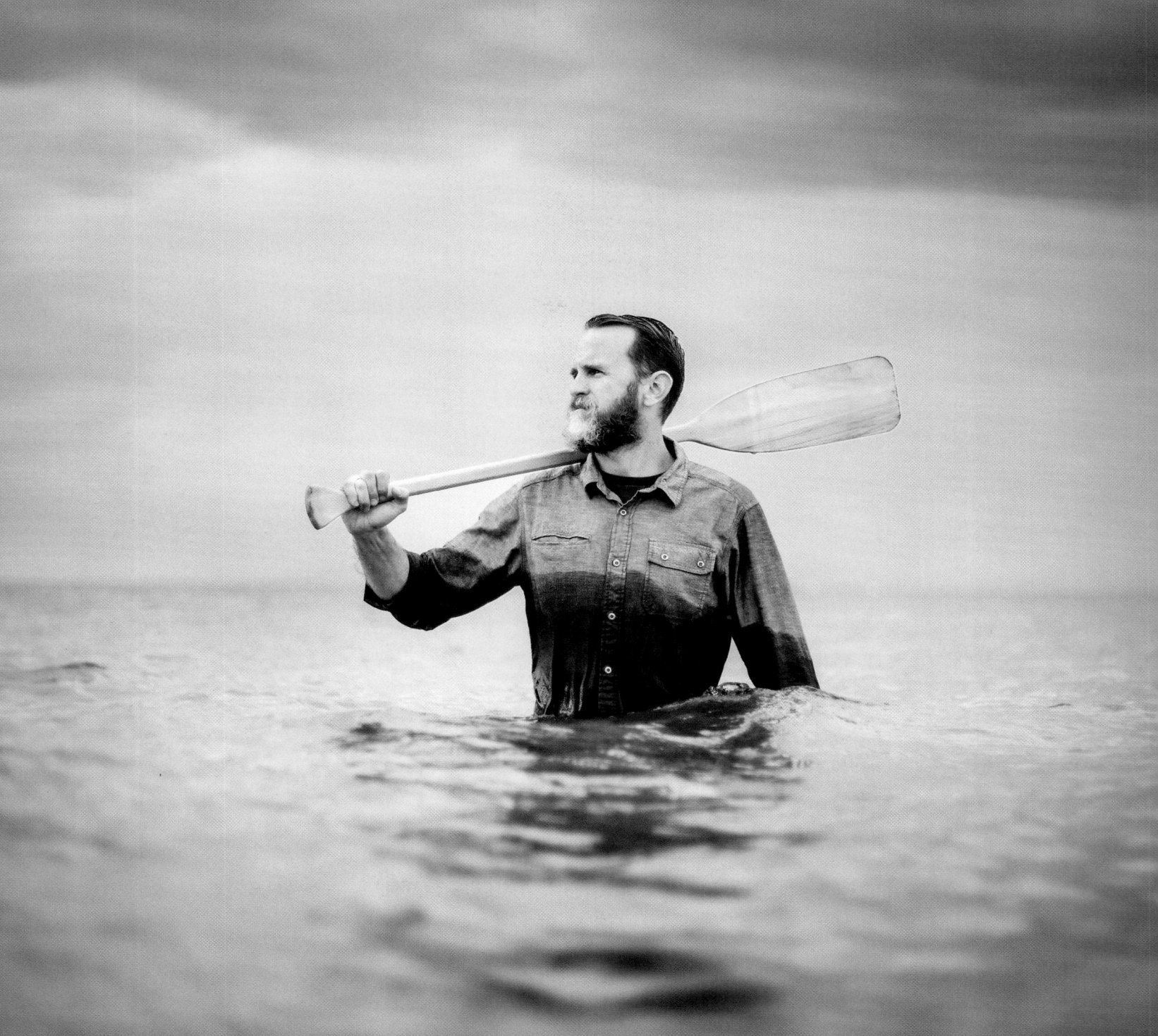

PART ONE: BEGIN

ALL JOURNEYS HAVE SECRET DESTINATIONS OF WHICH THE TRAVELER IS UNAWARE.

— MARTIN BUBER

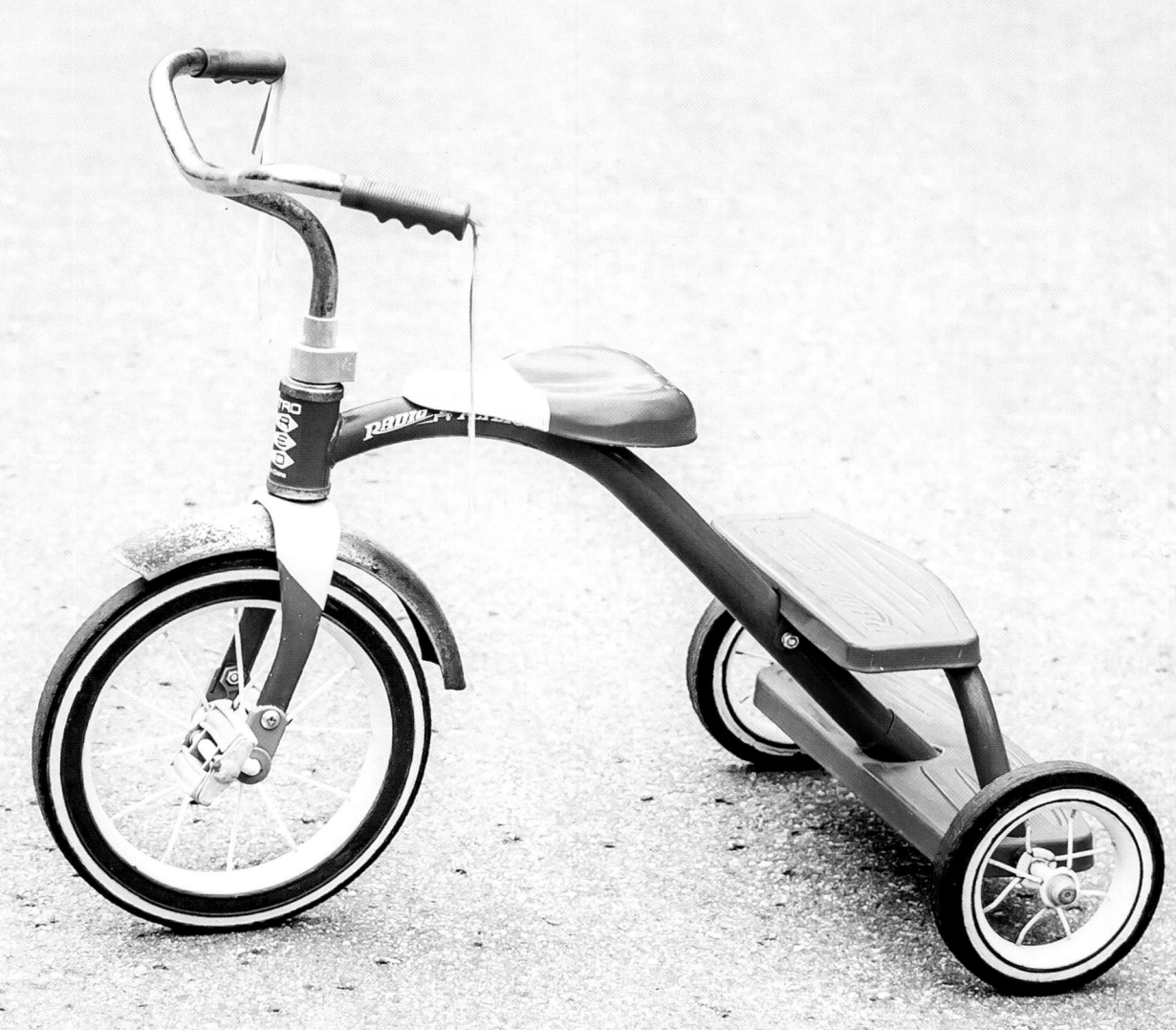

CHAPTER ONE

NOT WHAT IT SEEMS

Andrew was born without a hand. It was a shock to his parents, but nothing they couldn't embrace. Andrew didn't really know any different, and he was a happy little guy who made the most with what he had. The whole family pitched in whenever they could. Yet at preschool all the other kids raced around the playground on trikes. Andrew tried to keep up with his pals, but he couldn't steer with just one hand. It was disappointing to see him limited in this way.

So the parents and the occupational therapists put their minds together. There had to be a some way to help Andrew take part in the fun. The early ideas for solving this problem were awkward, expensive, and just wouldn't work. Frustrated and exhausted, they were about ready to give up. But great parents don't surrender without a fight. They started to try out different ideas, and with a little divergent thinking and some duct tape, a potential solution was found.

NEVER GIVE UP An idea surfaced to use duct tape and a plastic cup to create a hand grip that Andrew could use. They used duct tape to attach a hard plastic cup to the handlebars right where you would normally put your hand. Then Andrew could stick his arm into the cup and steer. They showed Andrew the modified bike, and without hesitation he hopped on and raced away.

Can you imagine the smile that spread across Andrew's face as he pedaled around with his friends? True creativity is contagious in the best way. Andrew's success will lead to other kids being able to do the same. Or maybe this story will inspire you like it's inspired me. Maybe it will make you grateful for something you have, like both of your hands or parents who believed in you even when life was bleak. When we witness creativity, it gives us courage to be creative ourselves. It unlocks something that has been buried deep.

The reason Andrew was able to eventually bike is because his parents were upset. Their disappointment was the fuel for creative success. Those who think creativity is just cute are completely wrong. Creativity is more than drawing with crayons and finding shapes in the clouds. And creativity isn't just for animators and people who do modern dance. Creativity is raw energy for life. It is unpredictable and fierce. It is wild, elusive, and untamed. It's the force that helps the starving child survive. It's the strength that pushes the underdog to succeed. It's the drive that keeps our dreams alive. It's the core of businesses that thrive. It's the secret of strong relationships. It's the key to a meaningful life. Yet creativity is a chameleon that can easily go unnoticed and is often overlooked. Once you learn how to find and befriend creativity, you will discover that it gives you an edge that cannot be denied. So where is it?

CREATIVITY ISN'T CUTE Creativity is ubiquitous. It isn't found only in Hollywood, in Silicon Valley, or on the top of the mountains in Nepal. It isn't tied to age, gender, or race. It's not something special that only a few people have. Creativity is a gift from the divine, but it isn't limited to a specialized group. Creativity isn't elitist or proud. It isn't tethered to one type of vocation or career. Whether you are aware of it or not, creativity courses through our veins. Even now it races as you read these words. Your mind, heart, and soul are creativity machines. Creativity is woven into the twists and turns of your double helix strands. We are all born with innate capacities to create, and we all have creative potential that is concealed. Unfortunately, creativity doesn't grow on its own—it takes effort and fight. Neglect to nourish your creative spirit and it will wither and die.

Creativity isn't just an internal trait; it's all around. Look around you now. Is there anything you can see that came to be without a creative impulse or act? Coffee is creative and so is sex. What about the watch strapped to your wrist or the color of the paint on the wall, the design of your desk, the computer nearby, and the shoes on your feet? There is nothing separate from creativity's reach.

Creativity has given us romance, recovery, culture, cuisine, music, motocross, fables, fashion, and sports. Deep creativity stirs our soul. It reminds us of something we once knew but have since forgotten. Creativity awakens life, like the taste of those cookies brings back your grandmother's face or that one song reminds you of being 16. We not only watch and witness creativity, we take part in it ourselves. And the most creative act of all is living life to the fullest degree. Without creativity by your side, it's impossible to live a rich and meaningful life.

CREATIVITY ISN'T WEAK Creativity is essential to life. It's like the oxygen that gives us life and the sunshine that provides growth. Creativity is like an electric current to illuminate our path. It is a fire that reinvigorates our resolve to do what matters most. Creativity is hope when all seems lost. It sustains us so that we can thrive. When the creative juices flow, we become more productive and alive. We move forward and accomplish impossible tasks. When the creative flow stops, we get irrationally stuck. Why?

Creativity is a powerful yet fickle force. It can't be summoned like a butler or turned on with the flip of a switch. The secrets to creativity are complex, yet here are a few keys. You

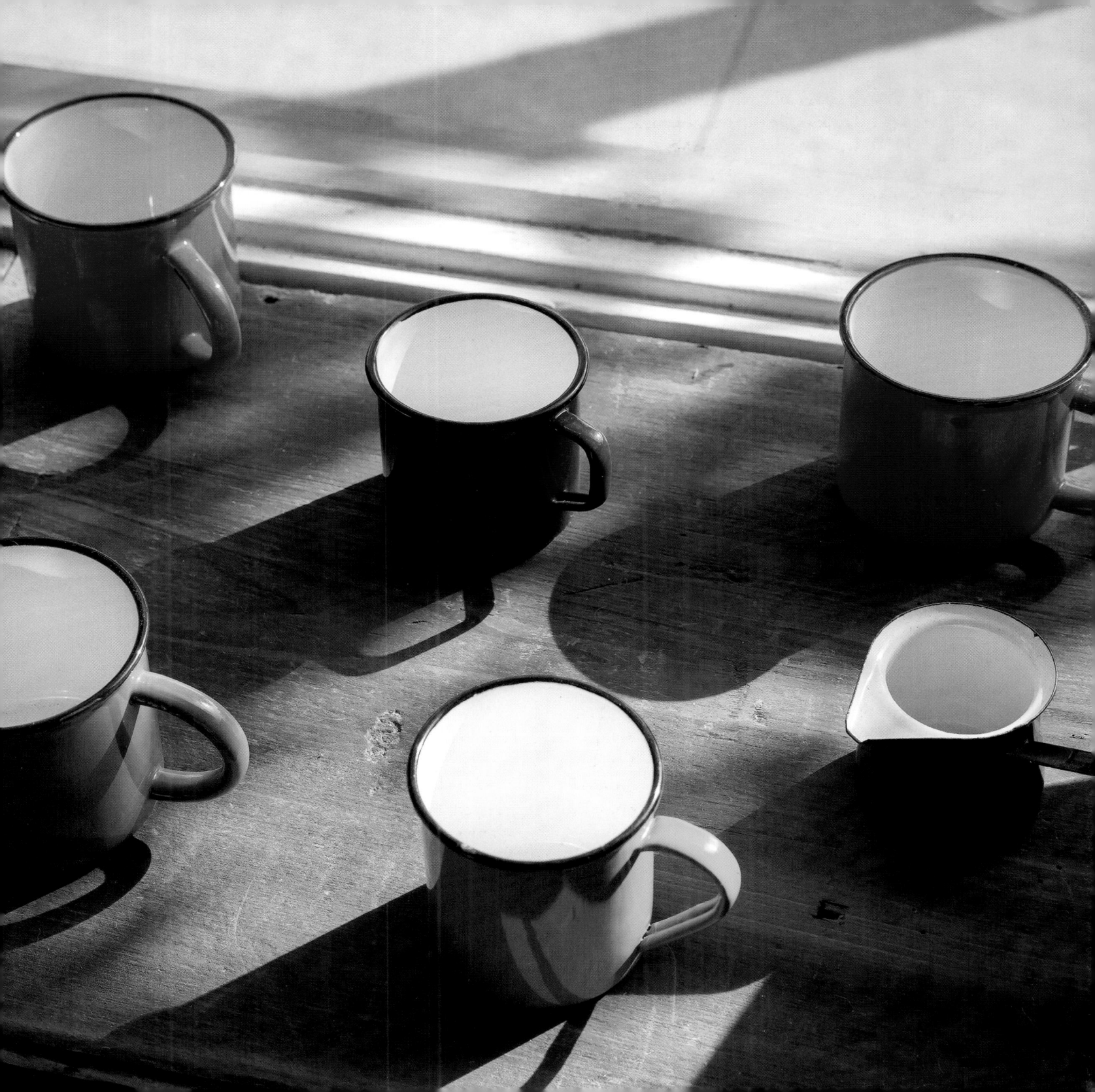

will find those scattered throughout the pages of this book. Yet first you must know that creativity rarely grows without resistance trying to knock it down. Like Wendell Berry said, "The impeded stream is the one that sings." The obstacle gives creativity its song. Without resistance, creativity doesn't take root. Without struggle, creativity doesn't grow tall.

The most important struggle of your life is discovering how to make the most of your time. Too often we neglect this fight. We are too busy checking our phones to notice how time slips by. The creative spirit begs you to stop living in such a boring way. It calls you to look up and to stop being a spectator of your own life. Life is too short to passively let it go. Ignite the armchair. Get the hell out. That could be one of the most creative acts you will ever take. It's time to stand on your own two feet and use your creative muscle to make the most of what you have. Every invention, business idea, song, movie, and poem is a result of one man, woman, or child fighting to do just that. Creativity isn't just a nice idea; it is a weapon of change and a tool that generates life. And creativity flows in the good times and shines the brightest when everything seems bleak. Creativity never gives up hope. The caged birds sings for freedom but also to make the most of what she has.

Creativity doesn't hinge on getting everything right. Creativity thrives when stuff goes wrong. When Miguel de Cervantes was wrongly imprisoned, he wrote *Don Quixote*, one of the greatest pieces of literature of all time. In spite of being deaf and blind, Helen Keller learned to use her voice to change the world. Do you get what I'm saying? Creativity flourishes when times get tough. The tougher the times, the more creativity grows. The obstacle gives birth to new ideas. Creativity and fight are the key—that's what makes the ordinary become something else. But to make that happen you have to unlearn what you have been taught.

THE FIGHT BEGINS Creativity isn't only for kids or people who have creative jobs. Creativity is for accountants, dentists, and the widow who lost her true love. And it's time to silence the liar who said that you aren't that creative after all. Whether

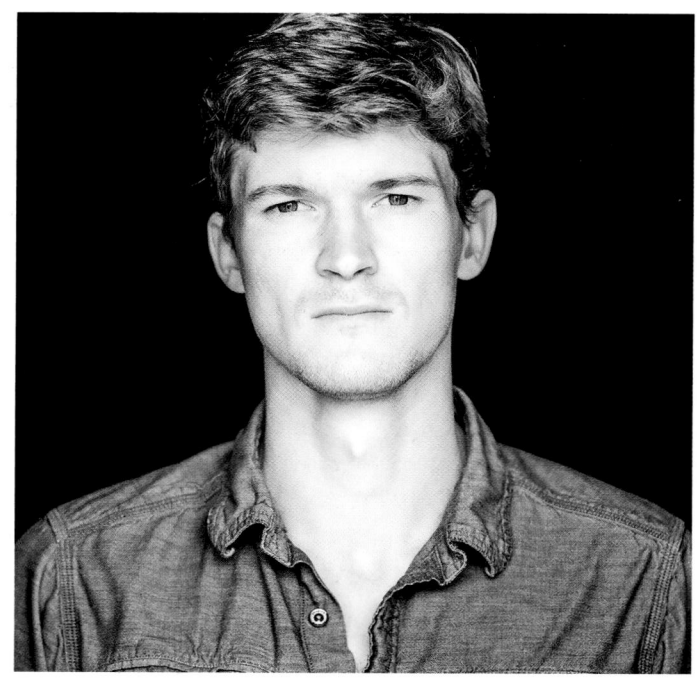

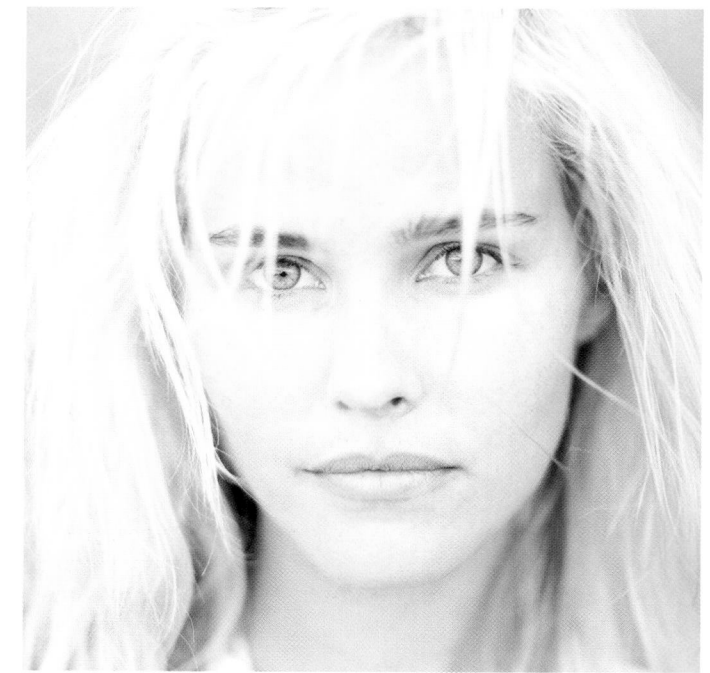

6

it was a teacher, a bully, a friend, or just a voice in your head, it's time to ditch that untruth. And the fool who keeps saying that creativity is only the domain of certain professions was wrong. Creativity isn't limited to drawing and dance. There is an art to creativity, just as there is an art to living life to the fullest degree. And creativity doesn't mystically appear when you passively sit by. The creative muse shows up when you get to work. You have to take action if you want sparks to fly.

The challenge with creativity is to keep it alive as time marches on. Neglect creativity and it will seem like it's gone. But it's always there, like wildflower seeds buried beneath dry ground. If you're in a drought, consider this book a storm. It may not be easy, but it will be good. Creating your best work and living the life of your dreams will require fighting your way through the wind, rain, sleet, and snow. Becoming more creative always requires immense effort and skill.

Those who take up the fight reap benefits in unexpected ways. Creativity is contagious. Become creative in one area of your life and it will affect the other areas as well. Like an incoming tide, it lifts every boat from the ocean floor.

An adventure lies ahead that will change who you are. It will refine your strengths and challenge your faults. It will improve your work, deepen your appreciation of life, awaken senses, open your eyes, and rekindle your sense of awe. It will make you a better spouse, lover, parent, or friend. It will reveal how you can contribute in great ways. It will add variety, significance, esteem, and connection to your life. Most importantly, it will begin to illuminate your life's deeper call. All of this of course hinges upon your willingness to join the cause. Creativity won't come knocking on your door—"You have to go after creativity with a club," as Jack London said. Are you ready to begin?

TOO MUCH SANITY MAY BE MADNESS AND THE MADDEST OF ALL, TO SEE LIFE AS IT IS AND NOT AS IT SHOULD BE.
—MIGUEL DE CERVANTES

EXERCISE

STEP 1
Think of a few problems that you are facing and write them down in your journal.

STEP 2
Think of small, simple, and sideways solutions that might help.
Imagine you were hired as a creative consultant; what recommendations would you provide?

STEP 3
When it comes to designing a more ideal life, what might you change?
Is there anything in particular you would like to add or remove?
How can creativity help you to live a life that is more aligned with who you want to become?

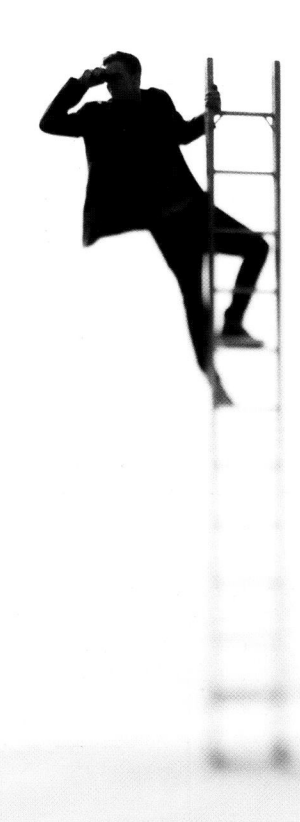

CHAPTER TWO

DEFINING THE FIGHT

The creative fight is less about conquest and more about a discovery within. It's more John Muir and less Atila the Hun. Rather than crush, kill, and destroy, this is a fight about finding why you are here.

Reflecting on his youth, John Muir wrote, "I was on the world. But was I in it?" He desperately wanted to belong and find the reason for which he was alive. Muir explained, "I was tormented with soul hunger." He was driven to find out why.

Then in 1868 he found himself standing on the edge of the Yosemite Valley for the first time. This changed everything. After a 10-day visit he needed to return. As he famously said, "The mountains are calling and I must go."

When you discover your life's calling, it ignites a creative drive. A year later, John Muir's passion burned strong. He found a way to return to Yosemite by accepting a job as a sheep herder in the mountains nearby.

DON'T QUIT YOUR DAY JOB It was a "day job" John Muir came to despise, but it got him where he needed to be. This job gave him access to explore the grandeur of the mountains every day. As long as you keep climbing, day jobs can make perfect ladders regardless of how rudimentary they are.

Muir's time in Yosemite brought him back to life. The mountains revved his soul and brought a sparkle to his eyes. His ensuing charisma and energy were contagious. One visitor, Theresa Yelverton, wrote, "His face shone with pure and holy enthusiasm… he was like a mountain goat jumping from boulder to boulder with a joyous, ringing laugh rhapsodizing about the wonders of God." The world needs more people like that—people who have become quiet enough to hear the call, and then bold enough to respond.

Muir would later draw the boundaries for Yosemite National Park and convince Theodore Roosevelt to federally protect that place. Because of his efforts, Muir is considered the "father of the National Parks." If you have ever been to a National Park, you have John Muir to thank. The creative fight is not self-absorbed. It's always looking for ways to spread good. John Muir's fight enlivened his soul and enabled him to change the world. Muir soaked up the glory of the mountains and invited others to do the same, "Climb the mountains and get their good tidings. Nature's peace will flow into you as sunshine into tree."

THE POWER OF IMAGINATION MAKES US INFINITE.

— JOHN MUIR

EXERCISE

STEP 1. John Muir recognized an inner stirring when he stood in Yosemite for the first time. List a few experiences when you have felt that curious tug that makes you wonder why you are here.

1. ....

2. ....

STEP 2. Pay attention to the people and things that make you come alive, and they can be a magnetic force that guides your creative growth. What makes you come alive? What are your favorite things? Using the categories below, write out a few responses of your own. The more specific the better.

Music	Cinema	Travel
Geography	Food	Animals
Literature	Outdoors	Faith
Magazines	Athletics	Weather
Friends	Inspiration	Art

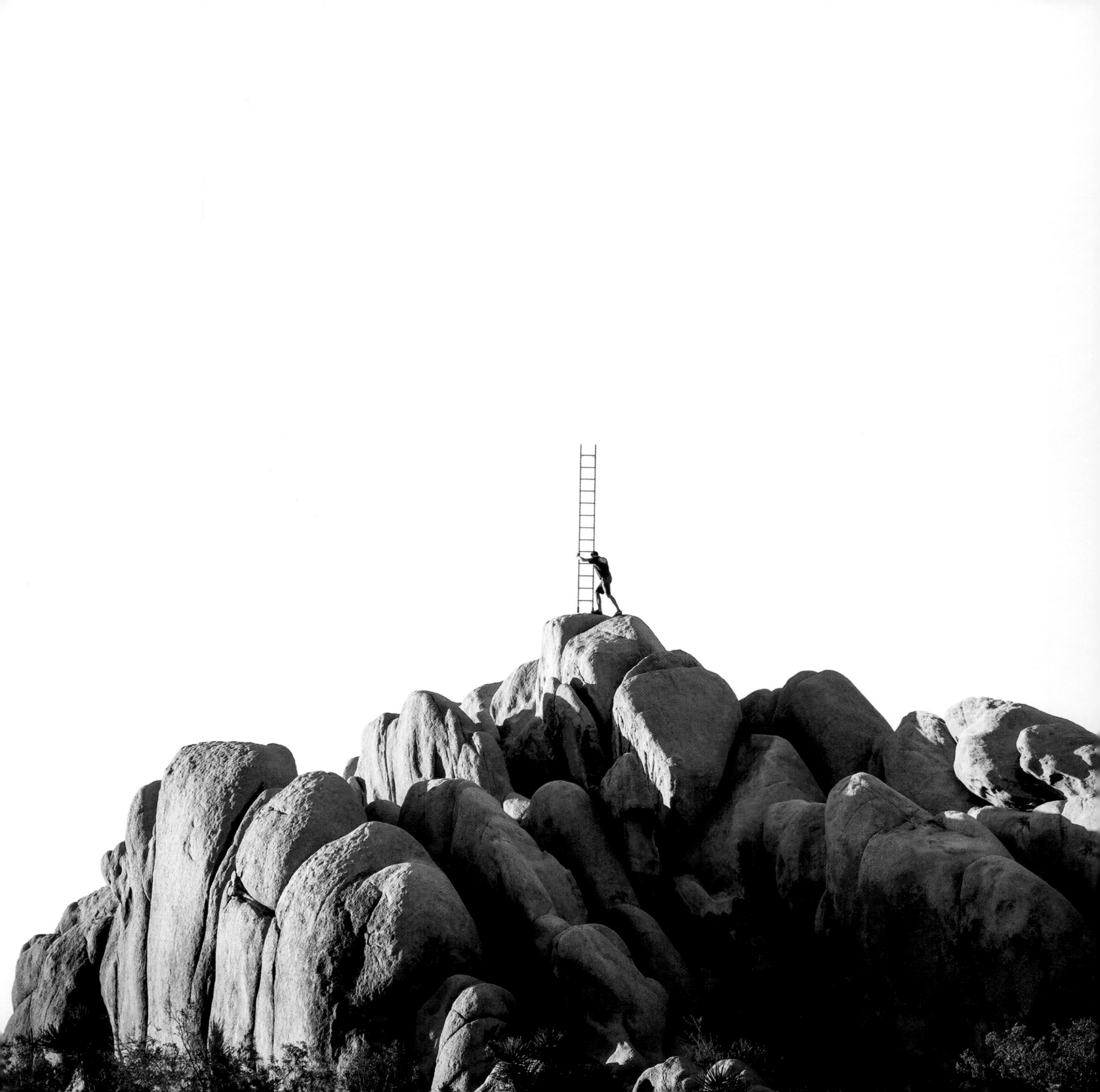

CHAPTER THREE

THE LADDER

Too often in life, we climb the ladder of success only to get to the top and realize that the ladder is leaning against the wrong tree (to paraphrase Thomas Merton). Or worse, it isn't leaning against anything at all.

This book is about finding the right ladder and getting to the top. I'm a photographer by trade, but this book isn't limited to that. It's about creating your best work whatever you do. As you'll discover, *The Creative Fight* isn't for a select few. At its core, the fight is about living life to the fullest degree. And the best way to achieve this goal isn't simply fighting harder, but fighting in the right way. Too often we climb the ladder without looking up. It's not just the effort we expend but the work itself that makes the journey worthwhile. As Theodore Roosevelt said, "Far and away the best prize that life has to offer is the chance to work hard at work worth doing." The challenge is to discover what the work is.

REACHING FOR A RUNG Ladders are incredibly creative tools. They break up impossible heights into a series of simple steps. Ladders lead to success. When I was a kid, every summer my family would visit nearby farms that allowed us to pick our own fruit. Without a ladder, the best apricots, cherries, peaches, and plums were out of reach. And ladders have been part of our culture since ancient times. Ten thousand years ago, someone painted a scene with a ladder in the Spider Caves in Spain. The scene depicts a human using a ladder to climb to a wild honeybee nest. Getting honey any other way would be an impossible task. Yet climbing up to a beehive doesn't sound like the greatest idea, unless you're prepared.

I'm a backyard beekeeper, and my friend Tony and I have climbed many ladders in pursuit of catching a swarm so that we can establish a hive. The best time of day to do this is at night, when the bees are huddled together in a clump. Usually a swarm will consist of tens of thousands of bees. When dealing with something like that, preparation and patience are key. Without a ladder, catching a swarm would be a lost cause. With the wrong ladder, like the time we used a rickety old piece of junk, things can really go wrong. Accidentally losing your step and knocking into a clump of twenty thousand bees makes quite a buzz.

Sometimes we climb ladders to reach for our dreams. Other times we climb to see what's on the other side of the wall. Too often we choose a ladder simply because it's nearby. Yet the closest and easiest ladder may not be the best one to climb.

You may be halfway up the wrong ladder right now. Or maybe your mistake is something else. The most common blunder is to use a ladder that is too short. To make a short ladder taller, we ignore the "Do not stand on the top step" warning and step up—that's how ladder fatalities happen every year. Or maybe your ladder isn't resting on even ground. Or you might be climbing a ladder that leads to a swarm of angry bees. Or your ladder might be leaning against a dead-end wall. Regardless, this book is about how we can find the right ladder and climb all the way up. It's never enough to imagine and dream. This may help you find the ladder, but you still have to make the climb.

RECOVERING WHAT IS LOST The pursuit in this book is discovering how to recover lost creativity. Creativity doesn't come easily, and it's impossible to achieve without some help. Yet there are some strategies that we can take in order to improve our odds. Much of the approach involves rethinking what we already know.

Let's revisit the idea of success. It bothers me that the business world has hijacked this term. Success isn't just power and wealth. And it isn't bigger, better, and more. Success isn't a house and it isn't a car. Corporate America has got it wrong. Worse are websites like successories.com, which promote a diluted form of success with their traditional motivational kitsch. On the website, you can buy motivational clichés on posters or a sleek geometric Plexiglas trophy that reads, "Success is reaching the highest peak then exceeding above it." When you think about it, that doesn't even really make sense. Are you supposed to climb to the top of Mount Everest and then take a rocket ship into outer space?

Yvon Chouinard, the famous mountaineer, put it best: "How you climb a mountain is more important than reaching the top." Success isn't planting your flag at the top of a peak. It's embracing the challenge and enjoying the view. Success isn't only external results but an internal reward. Chouinard said, "We do not climb mountains to get to the top. We climb mountains so that we can be changed." Chouinard's idea provides us with a different way to approach success. This shift in focus has saved my career.

I was ten thousand hours and ten years into my career when I hit the wall. I was a "successful" photographer and was gaining momentum in my craft. I taught at a prestigious photography school, spoke at conferences, and had written a few photography books. Yet I felt disconnected and dull. My career seemed great from the outside, but I was feeling trapped. So I took some time off and started to reflect.

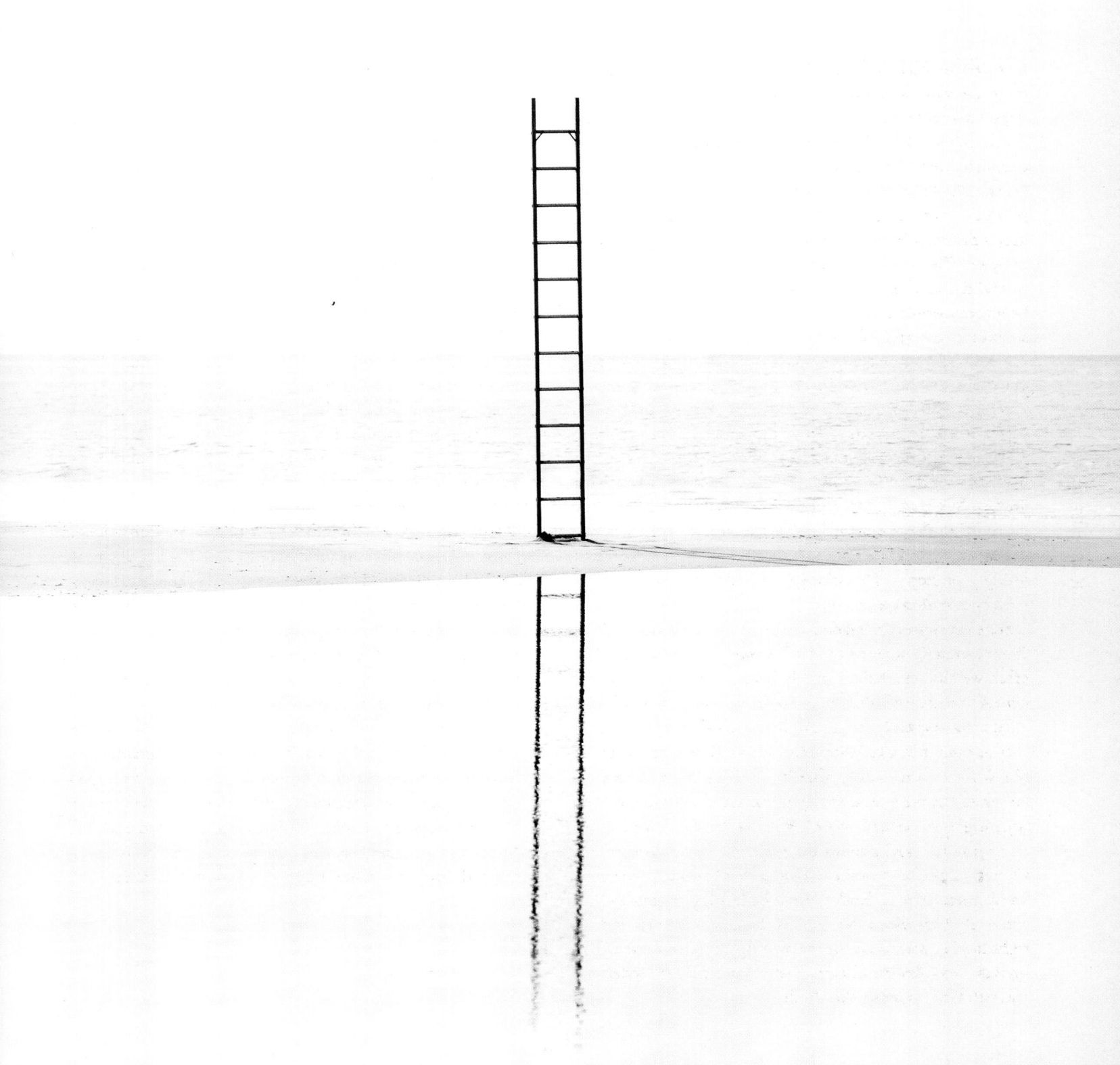

FINDING WHAT IS REAL Plato said, "The unexamined life isn't worth living." That wasn't going to be me. I began to fill my journal with pages of thoughts and ideas. I talked with mentors and friends. After some time, it became clear that my problem wasn't photography, it was me. I had fallen into the trap of misunderstanding my success. I was reading my own press and got caught up in the externals of photography rather than nurturing my own internal drive. One day in my office, this realization set in and I started to cry. The fuzziness of the tears helped everything to become clear. For me, photography wasn't about the camera and lens. It was about pursuit to savor life, to encourage others, and to grow and to be changed. My photographs weren't plastic trophies, but journal entries of how my soul had grown. This realization freed me from the trap I was in.

The way the world defines success doesn't work. It's time we take this term back. Success is more than a list of accomplishments and it's definitely more than stuff. Success is leading a fulfilling life, spending time with family, and connecting with friends. To be successful we have to fight, but we have to fight in the right way. Success isn't just calling attention to yourself. David McCullough, a junior high English teacher, said it well: "Climb the mountain so you can see the world, not so the world can see you." The biggest success isn't just about you, but about accomplishing dreams and inspiring others to do the same. True success is a reciprocal force.

To be fair, the business world doesn't have it completely wrong. Successful business can be a huge force for good. The real problem is whether or not we let something or someone else define what we should define ourselves. Achieving success is less about blame and more about taking a stand. It's a really difficult term to define. So most of us default to the definition that is trending at the time. That's where I went wrong. That's where we all go wrong. The way we experience success evolves and changes throughout life, so it's easy to get it wrong. What might have been success five years ago isn't success today.

EXERCISE

STEP 1
What ladder are you climbing and do you like where it leads?

Vocation/Career
....

Relationships
....

Creative Expression
....

STEP 2
What ladder would you like to climb?

Vocation/Career
....

Relationships
....

Creative Expression
....

STEP 3
Create and articulate your own definition of success.

....

....

....

....

....

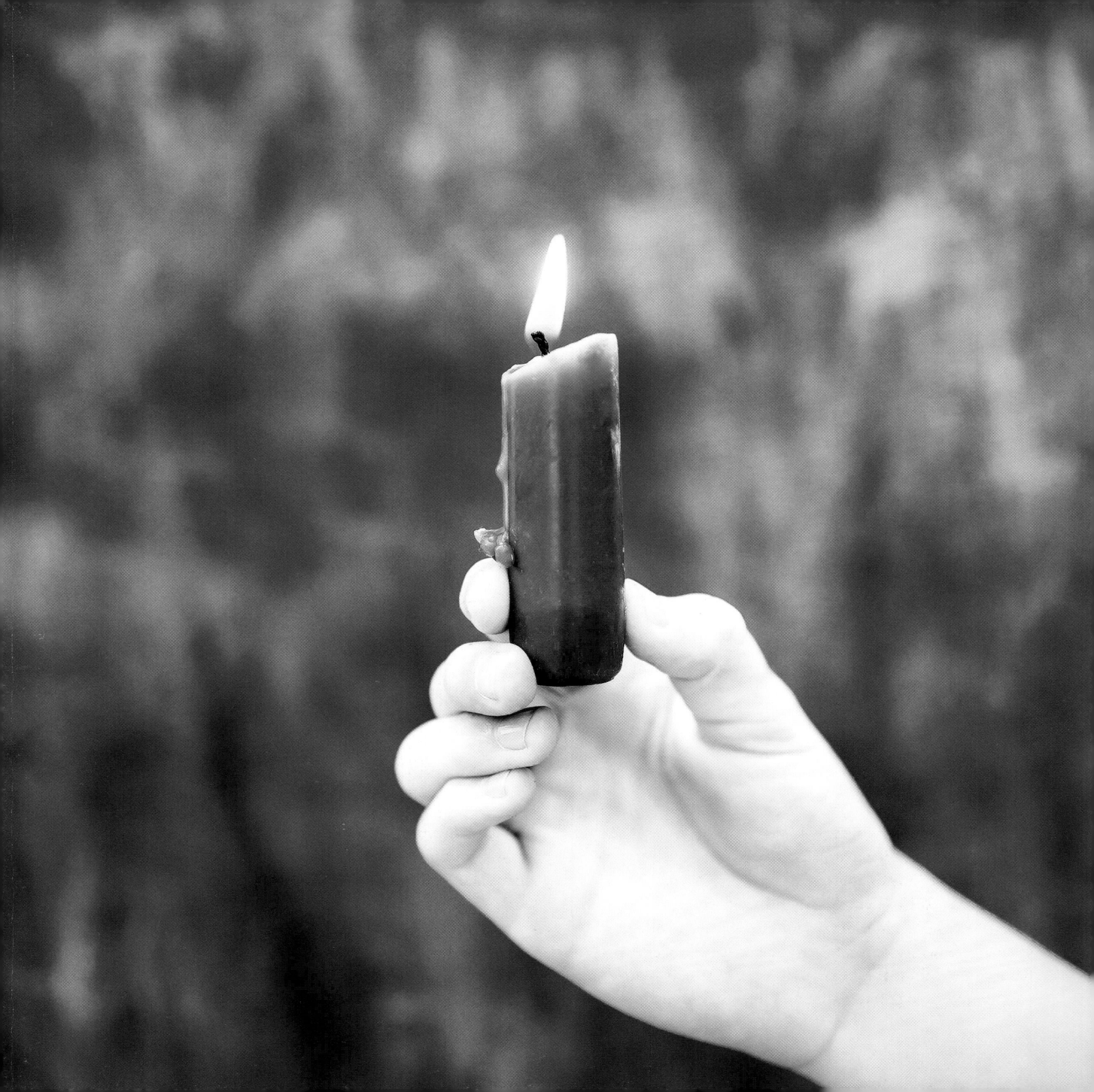

CHAPTER FOUR

CREATIVITY IN SPITE OF AGE

"Life is a jar full of darkness, without a candle that is." With a mixture of curiosity and pride, my 10-year-old daughter Annika showed me the journal entry where she had penned those words. What a wonderful and creative heart she has; Annika is candlelight to my world. Her journal is filled with so many drawings, doodles, and ideas. Annika's creativity has a natural flow. Her two sisters are creative as well. The youngest loves to paint, and the middle sister loves to cook.

All kids are creative in their own way—sometimes out of necessity and other times just because. That's what makes being around kids so much fun. Each year, I like to visit my daughters' elementary school classes to see the kids' creativity firsthand. I find some reason to help out, and when I'm there I like to ask the group, "How many of you can draw?" Every time, each and every hand is raised high into the air. Next I ask, "How many of you can sing?" Again, all the hands shoot up into the air and many of the students start to sing. Their uninhibited creativity is a breath of fresh air. In contrast, when I ask the same questions to students at the college where I have been teaching for the last 12 years, the response is dismal—only a few raise their hands. Regardless of the group, year after year the results are consistently the same. After a few years, I started to wonder why.

The elementary students heard the questions in a straightforward way, while the college students heard the question with strings attached. The college students heard something like this, "How many of you can draw or sing…. *well?*" As we get older we learn to compare. We compare ourselves with others and dwell on where we fall short. The college students thought to themselves, "I can't draw that well, so I shouldn't raise my hand." This comparative logic is extra baggage that devalues and decreases any creativity we once had.

SCHOOLS KILL CREATIVITY In one of the most viewed TED talks in the world, Sir Ken Robinson argues that mass education is at fault. Instead of fanning the flame, it snuffs it out. "Schools kill creativity" is the title of his talk. He makes a solid case for the need to change education. The 30+ million views reveal that these are not just good ideas but something that resonates deep. I once heard Ken speak at a small gathering and was moved by his passion on and off the stage. He is a champion of *The Creative Fight*. Ken reminds us that what makes human life so interesting, diverse, and dynamic is the inherent creative drive that we all possess.

After hearing him speak, I was inspired to go back to my classroom to implement what I heard. Yet I also started to wonder about creativity from a more specific point of view. Ken is driven to change the big broad system of education, but what about those who are stuck in school? Or what about those who already have their college degree? These questions awakened a desire in me to help individuals reignite the creativity that has been lost. While Ken is leading an upper-level fight, I want to contribute at the

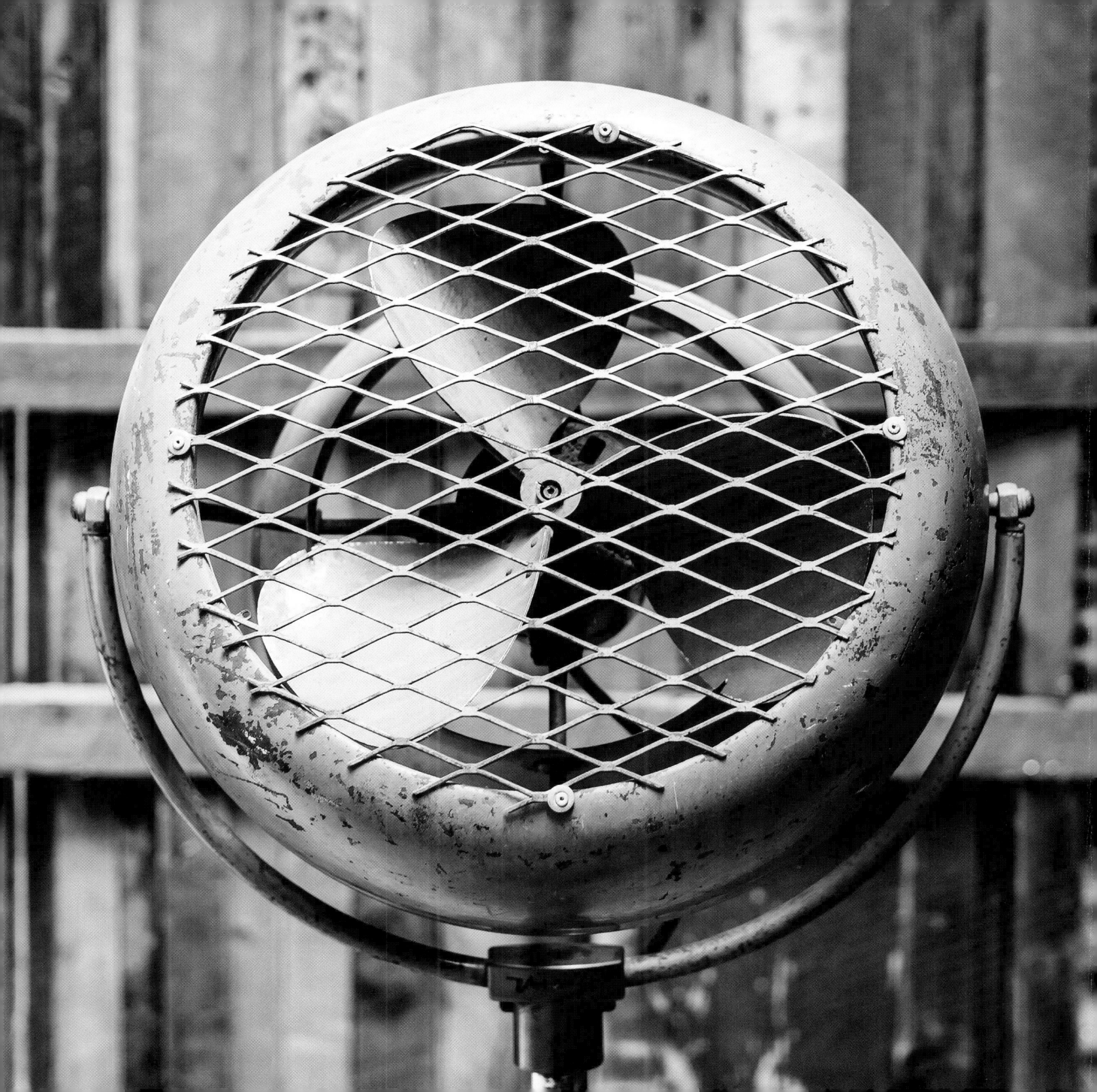

grassroots. I want to create a new approach for those in the trenches and on the front lines. If education has failed, I want to create something that would help people succeed. Ken's talk is powerful, but if you aren't careful, it kind of lets you off the hook. It's easy to find fault in a system that has gone wrong. It's difficult to search for a solution within yourself.

CREATIVITY AND GETTING OLD

For most people, creativity diminishes as we grow old, but this decline isn't inevitable. With conscious effort, our creativity can grow and flourish in unexpected ways. The sculptor Louise Bourgeois created some of her most famous pieces after she was 80 years old. When asked whether she could have made her works earlier she replied, "Absolutely not. I was not sophisticated enough." Frank Lloyd Wright's masterpiece, the Guggenheim Museum, was completed just six months before he died, at the age of 92. And it isn't just the famous who keep their creativity alive.

My aunt Cack (that's her nickname) recently retired from decades of work in the social services helping kids. Her retirement was well earned. While talking about retirement, a colleague started to bemoan the misery of getting old and hitting retirement age. With dignity and grace Aunt Cack responded, "Getting old is a gift that many don't get to enjoy." It's true. Plenty throughout history died too young—Anne Frank, at 15; Martin Luther King Jr., at 39; or Aunt Cack's sister (my mother-in-law), who died at 62. Whatever your age, your life is a gift and you better start treating it that way. Taking this gift seriously requires creative chops—aging isn't easy, so you have to continually adapt.

Ben Franklin is an exemplar in keeping the creative edge. In his old age, he needed glasses to see things far away and up close. He got tired of switching between two types of glasses, so he invented bifocals at the age of 78. Franklin didn't stop creating when he was old but continued to innovate what would have been impossible at an earlier time. That's exactly what my aunt Cack has done with her life. Rather than withering away, she has more enthusiasm than ever and is enjoying retirement to the utmost degree.

UNLEARNING HELPLESSNESS

The first step to becoming more creative (regardless of your age) is to stop blaming ourselves and to take action. Even if you think that you aren't very creative, it doesn't mean you can't change. You might just need some practice, or you might need to let go of the resentment against that mean teacher who criticized your lack of skill. Like Roald Dahl, the author of *Charlie and the Chocolate Factory* and countless other great books, whose teacher wrote this note on his report card when he was 15: "A persistent muddler. Vocabulary negligible, sentences malconstructed. He reminds me of a camel." Roald Dahl wasn't the sharpest kid, but he channeled all of that into plot lines, characters, and words. That is what makes his writing so much fun. Here's a part of one poem to prove the point:

"My teacher wasn't half as nice as yours seems to be. He'd twist and twist and twist you by the ear and twist it more and more. Until at last the ear came off and landed on the floor."

The garden of creativity will not grow by itself. Leave it alone and the weeds will run amok. One of the most persistent weeds is a psychological condition that was discovered in animals in 1967 by Martin Seligman, and has since been proven to wreak havoc on human lives. In an initial study, an animal was put in a cage and exposed to pain (for example, an electric shock) without the ability to escape. (As a side note, I know this is cruel, but I didn't make this up.) Eventually the animal would stop trying to avoid the pain. Next, the scientists unlocked and opened the cage. Then a shock was administered, and surprisingly the animal wouldn't budge. Conditioned by their previous helplessness, they didn't even try.

This condition was termed "learned helplessness," and it happens with humans as well—such as the students Ken Robinson fights for whose creativity was crushed in school, or my college students who were told they couldn't draw. This extra baggage is tough to set down. The antidote for learned helplessness is to act, move, create. Passivity leads to continued pain, whereas creativity leads to a better life. What prevents forward momentum is fear—the electric shock isn't easy to forget. The best way to overcome the fear is to take small steps; that's what my new dentist did.

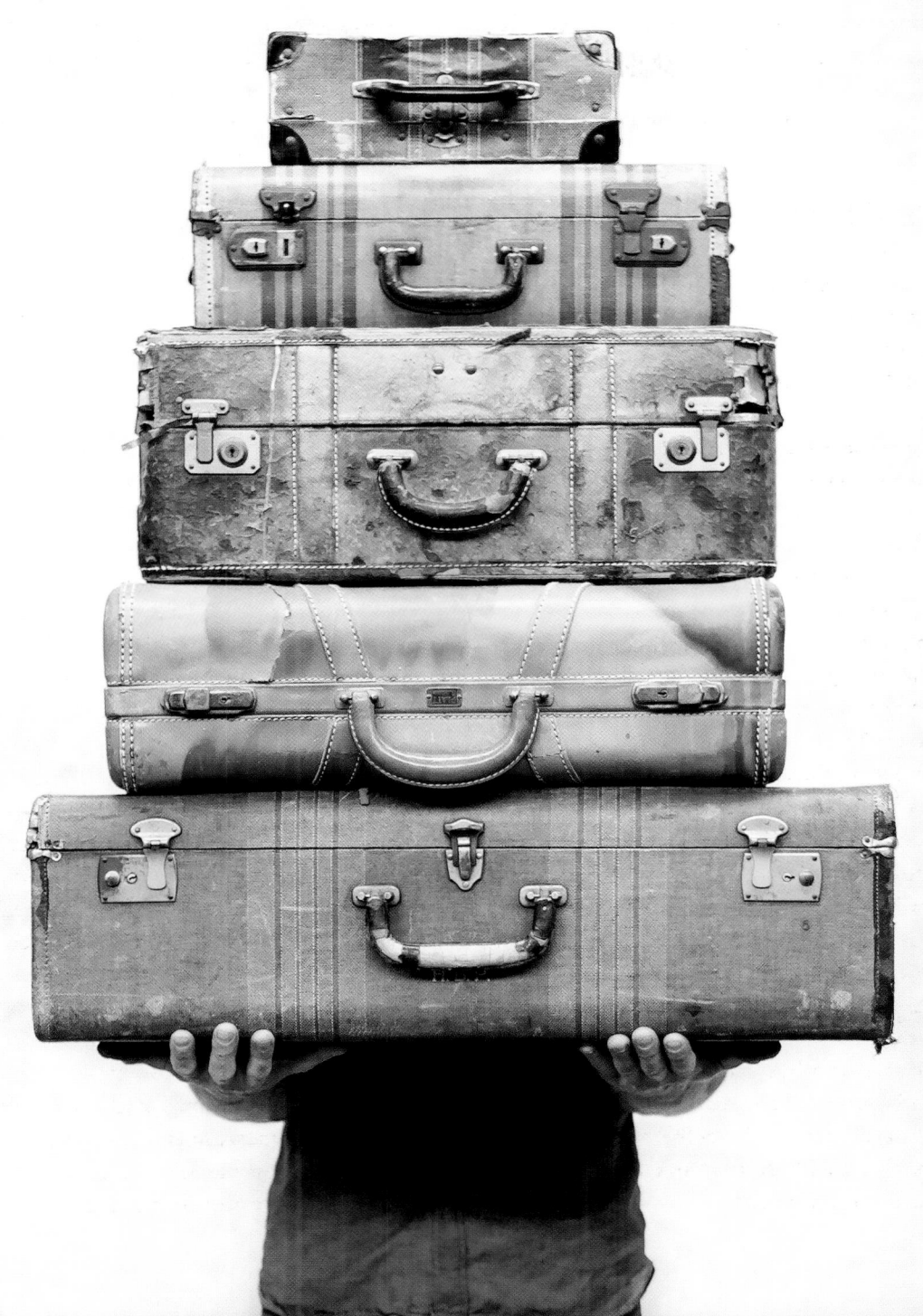

THE CREATIVE DENTIST My old dentist retired and his practice was taken over by a recent graduate from a prestigious dental school. The new dentist revamped the whole office, starting with new paint and then furniture and tools. One time when I went in to get my teeth cleaned, I sat down in the dentist chair and the dental hygienist greeted me by name. This had never happened before. Just as the teeth cleaning was about to begin, someone walked in and asked in a pleasant tone, "Would you like a complimentary foot massage today?" Of course I said yes!

I sat there getting my feet massaged and my dental work done, and I thought, "Wow, that's a creative way to help put someone at ease." The new dentist's tactics worked, and I've been going back for years. The best part is that the dentist didn't stop with those initial ideas. He continued to refine and improve himself, his office, and his staff. Now it's a world-class practice, and it all started with a few small creative acts.

Creativity doesn't have to be elaborate or wild. My dentist is the most clean-cut and conservative guy you'll meet. Yet he's creative in how he has developed his career. If he started dressing up like a clown, all of his patients would leave. The best type of creativity is authentic. My dentist doesn't pretend to be someone else. And if a dentist can be creative, then so can you.

The best way to ignite the creative spark isn't to impersonate someone else. Everyone's creativity is unique—that's what makes it such a specialized skill. And don't overdo your early attempts, but keep it simple, like lifting weights for the first time. Too much too fast, and you will injure yourself—confirming the fear that your critics were right and, worse, putting yourself back in the cage. Even great artists begin small. Picasso sketched before he put paint on his brush. Martha Graham stretched before she attempted to leap across the stage. Yo-Yo Ma begins each day by playing the same tune. So let's try a few simple exercises ourselves to get the creative juices to flow.

**YOU ARE UNIQUE, AND IF THAT IS NOT FULFILLED,
THEN SOMETHING HAS BEEN LOST.**

—MARTHA GRAHAM

AND ABOVE ALL, WATCH WITH GLITTERING EYES
THE WHOLE WORLD AROUND YOU BECAUSE THE GREATEST SECRETS
ARE ALWAYS HIDDEN IN THE MOST UNLIKELY PLACES.
THOSE WHO DON'T BELIEVE IN MAGIC WILL NEVER FIND IT.

— **ROALD DAHL**

EXERCISE

STEP 1. DOODLE AND DRAW

Begin small by drawing a stick figure story. Don't worry about how the drawing looks. Simply draw a narrative scene using a stick figure as a way to get the creative juices to flow. Your scene might include a stick figure floating in a hot air balloon or a stick figure skiing off a mountaintop. The key is to take the pressure off and to come up with simple ways to get started. Creativity doesn't have to be elaborate and grand. Often it's the little ideas that lead somewhere else.

STEP 2. DAILY PRACTICE

Creative people aren't creative only when the spotlight turns on. So finding ways to practice creativity on a daily basis can provide a huge boost. Think through your day and ask yourself if there is some way you can stretch your creative muscles with small tasks. Here are a few ideas: cut up toast in a different pattern, drive home from work taking a different route, listen to one song that is outside your normal mix, handwrite one message to a colleague or friend, or take one photograph of a stranger each day. Choose an idea that won't stress you out, and try it for the next week.

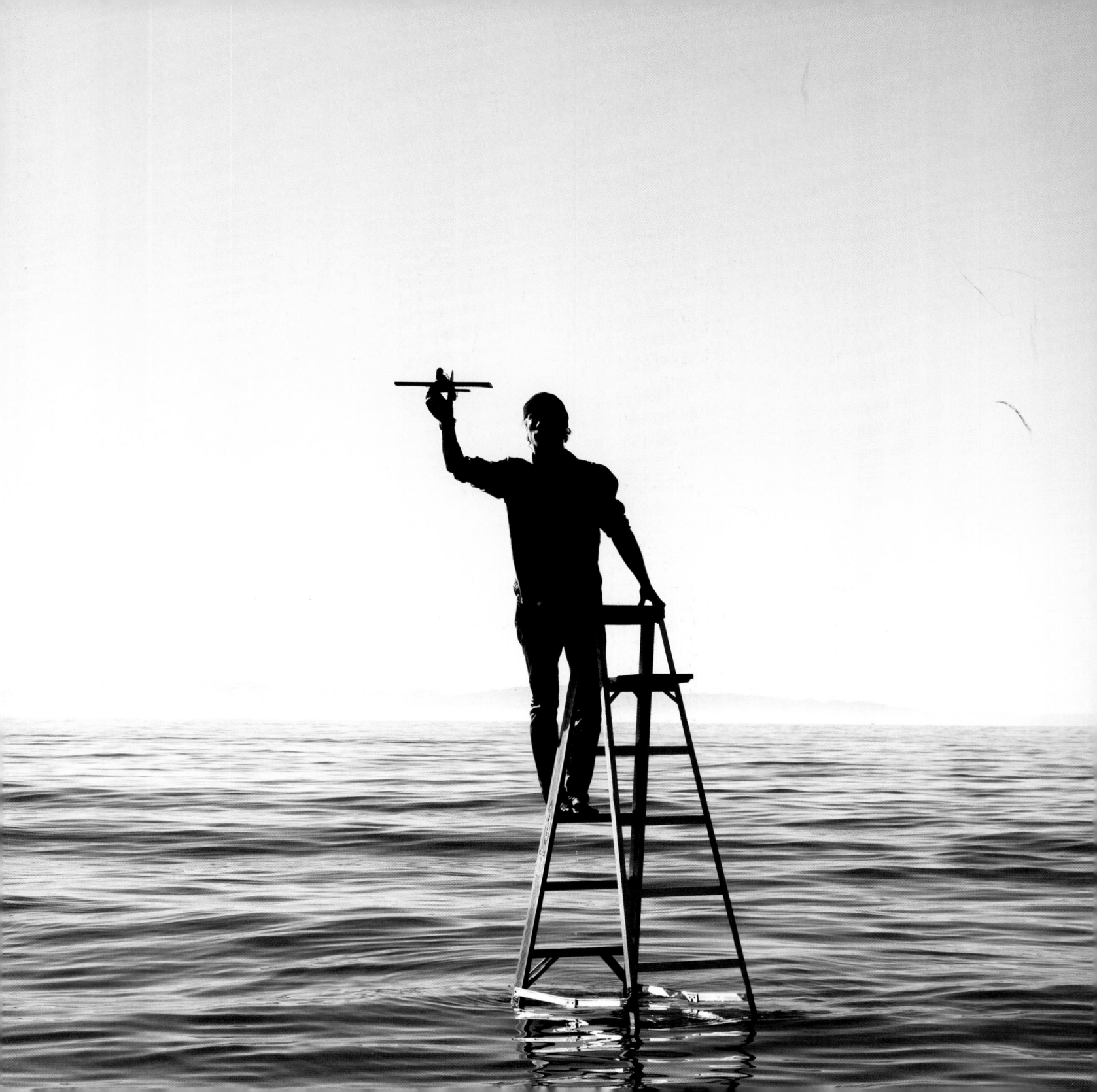

CHAPTER FIVE

CREATIVITY AND SLICED BREAD

Creativity isn't something that stands on its own. It's part of a larger process that involves at least these four parts: 1. Information 2. Imagination 3. Creativity 4. Innovation. These steps are connected like four corners on a single piece of sliced bread.

The first corner is information. Information is where it all begins. It is knowledge, data, input, and ideas. Information is raw like a piece of unfinished wood or a straightforward fact. Without information we have nowhere to go.

The second corner is imagination. Imagination is the ability to call to mind something that doesn't yet exist or that isn't present right now. You can imagine a unicorn flying across the sky or the look of surprise on your sister's face when she opens her gift. Imagination is wild, free, and fun. Imagination is naive and it doesn't like to conform. Imagination is made up of ideals, but it doesn't mind breaking the rules. Imagination feels empathy for a stranger. Imagination can be

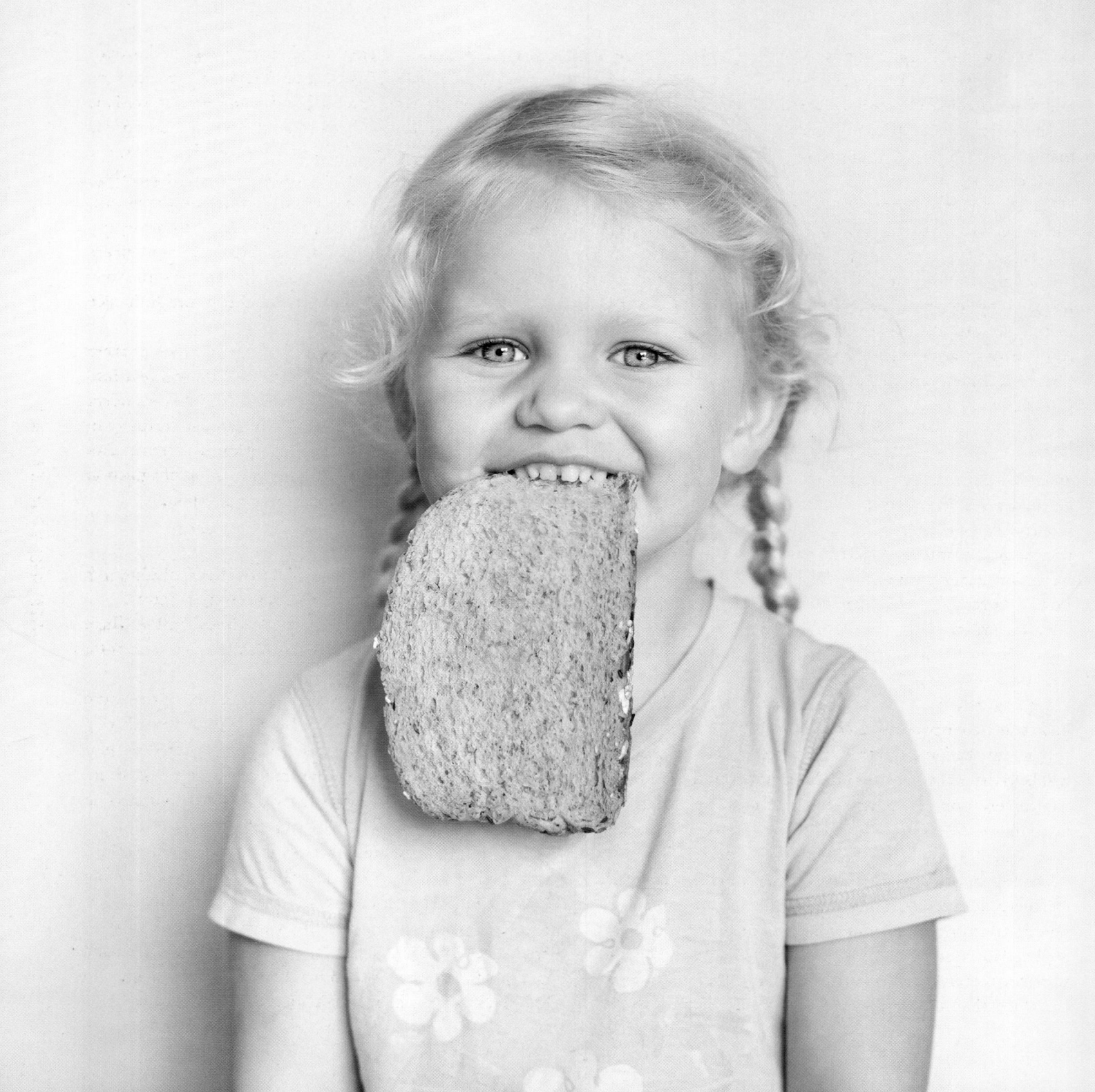

twisted or weird. Imagination is up in the clouds and under the sea. Imagination has no boundaries at all. As Einstein said, "Imagination encircles the world." And you don't have to be Einstein to know that imagination is more important than knowledge. Imagination is where knowledge is let out of the cage.

The third corner is creativity. Creativity is where imagination gets to work. Creativity requires that we roll up our sleeves. John Lennon imagined world peace, yet it was an act of creativity to write and perform the song. Creativity is where we get things done. To create is to make. We all do that, no matter our jobs. Yet the creative flow can dwindle or thrive. And creativity always has a forward positive lean. Creativity likes to ask questions and look for ways to add value to life. It isn't elitist, arrogant, or proud. Creativity is down to earth and real. It likes to have fun but also works hard.

Creativity has many friends, like curiosity, craftsmanship, and contribution. One of creativity's closest friends is art. Creativity is similar to art but at the same time distinct—like fraternal twins who were born on the same day but with distinctive genetic strands. All art is creative but not all creativity is art. Sometimes creativity creates beauty or value, but other times it falls short. Yet creativity always aims for good.

At its core, creativity is about taking the ordinary and making it more. It's about making the best with the situation and materials at hand. It's about seeing what has been seen but doing so with a new lens. Creativity helps us thrive. It makes us better parents, citizens, and friends. Creativity is contagious. Become creative in one area of your life and it will help the other areas as well. Most importantly, creativity requires exertion, power, and force. The creative juices rarely flow while you passively watch. Creativity beckons us to leave our spectator's mind-set, to start and to get something done.

The fourth corner is innovation. Innovation is born when creativity produces something of value that affects more than one. Innovation is a new idea, device, or process. It is the application of creativity in a particular way. Art is innovative. Art is creativity that has reached a higher goal. There are innovations that improve global communications or the way we make shoes. There is art that has changed the world. Innovations include things like antibiotics, fiber optics, or biofuels. The airplane, Internet, and phone are innovations too. Innovations always rely on creative work. Yet some of the biggest innovations came about as the result of the pursuit of something else. Innovation almost always comes as a celebratory surprise. And new innovations lead to new knowledge, information, and ideas, just as the best art self-propagates, gives birth to new ideas, expands the imagination, and makes others want to create their own art. In this way, the four corners are inseparable and baked together in this little slice of bread.

The four corners are clearly distinct, yet not one of them can stand alone. Remove one corner and you will tear into another element as well. The magic is in the interdependent combination of the whole. So while we'll pursue creativity in this book, it's critical to keep this larger picture in mind. Creativity isn't self-contained. And it isn't just about imagination or fun; it's also about information and innovation.

THE CREATIVE PROCESS IN ACTION Let's take a quick look at how this process works in more concrete terms.

Information is seeing a picture of a treehouse online. There it is. This is the beginning of an idea. Whether or not the idea will survive depends on the next step.

Imagination is conjuring up an image of what a treehouse might look like in your backyard. Imagination is remembering the treehouse you wished you had. Imagination is letting your mind wander to think about how much fun your kids would have. Imagination gets carried away and starts to dream up a treehouse that will cost $15k to build.

Like the proverbial voice of wisdom, information reminds imagination that the cost is too high. Information likes to stop imagination from getting out of control. Sometimes imagination will comply, and other times it will rebel. Imagination bounces around like a Super Ball thrown indoors. Imagination is unpredictable and fun. But it likes to change shape. No longer a bouncing ball, imagination turns into a flood.

A TREE HOUSE, A FREE HOUSE, A SECRET YOU AND ME HOUSE,
A HIGH UP IN THE LEAFY BRANCHES COZY AS CAN BE HOUSE.
A STREET HOUSE, A NEAT HOUSE, BE SURE TO WIPE YOUR FEET HOUSE
IS NOT MY KIND OF HOUSE AT ALL—LET'S GO LIVE IN A TREE HOUSE.

— SHEL SILVERSTEIN

The combined force of information and imagination is a current that can sweep you away or get you to act. Sometimes imagination can provoke you to search endlessly for new ideas.

Creativity calls you to fight the tide and to gather your ideas onto one Pinterest board. This creative act fuels and focuses your imagination even more. Next comes the creative step of sketching a treehouse idea during a dull meeting at work. Then you decide to stop by the lumberyard to think about supplies. With each stride, your creative muscles become stronger. Still, imagination tempts you to stop. You have to fight off imagination's pull if you're actually going to build.

The moment the first nail secures wood to the tree, the creative fight begins to win. No longer the domain of dreams, the treehouse is becoming real. With tenacity and drive, the odds for the project's success increase.

During the construction phase, if the treehouse builder discovers a new building technique and posts online to rave reviews, innovation has been achieved. If the treehouse is so well designed that it's referred to as a work of art, then maybe it is. When the treehouse is complete, it stands as a testament to the creative fight and it becomes a gift to the kids and to the neighbors who now want to build one themselves. This treehouse story isn't just a fictional tale. This is my story (minus the part about being a work of art). We now have two treehouses in our backyard, and they inspired three other tree forts that have since been built by neighborhood friends.

EXERCISE

STEP 1

In order to identify the flow of the creative process, reflect back on something
you accomplished and write out what was involved in each step. If you
didn't achieve the final step, that's OK. When it comes to adding value in an innovative way,
write out what you strove for. Creativity always reaches for good.

Information ....

Imagination ....

Creativity ....

Innovation ....

STEP 2

Creative accomplishment rarely happens on its own. Creating a roadmap can help.
Write out a creative project you want to achieve and the steps needed to get there.

Creative Project ....

Information ....

Imagination ....

Creativity ....

Innovation ....

STEP 3

Take a moment to let your imagination roam free. If you had the chance to become a better artist,
what field would you pursue? On a scratch sheet of paper, write down a few ideas.

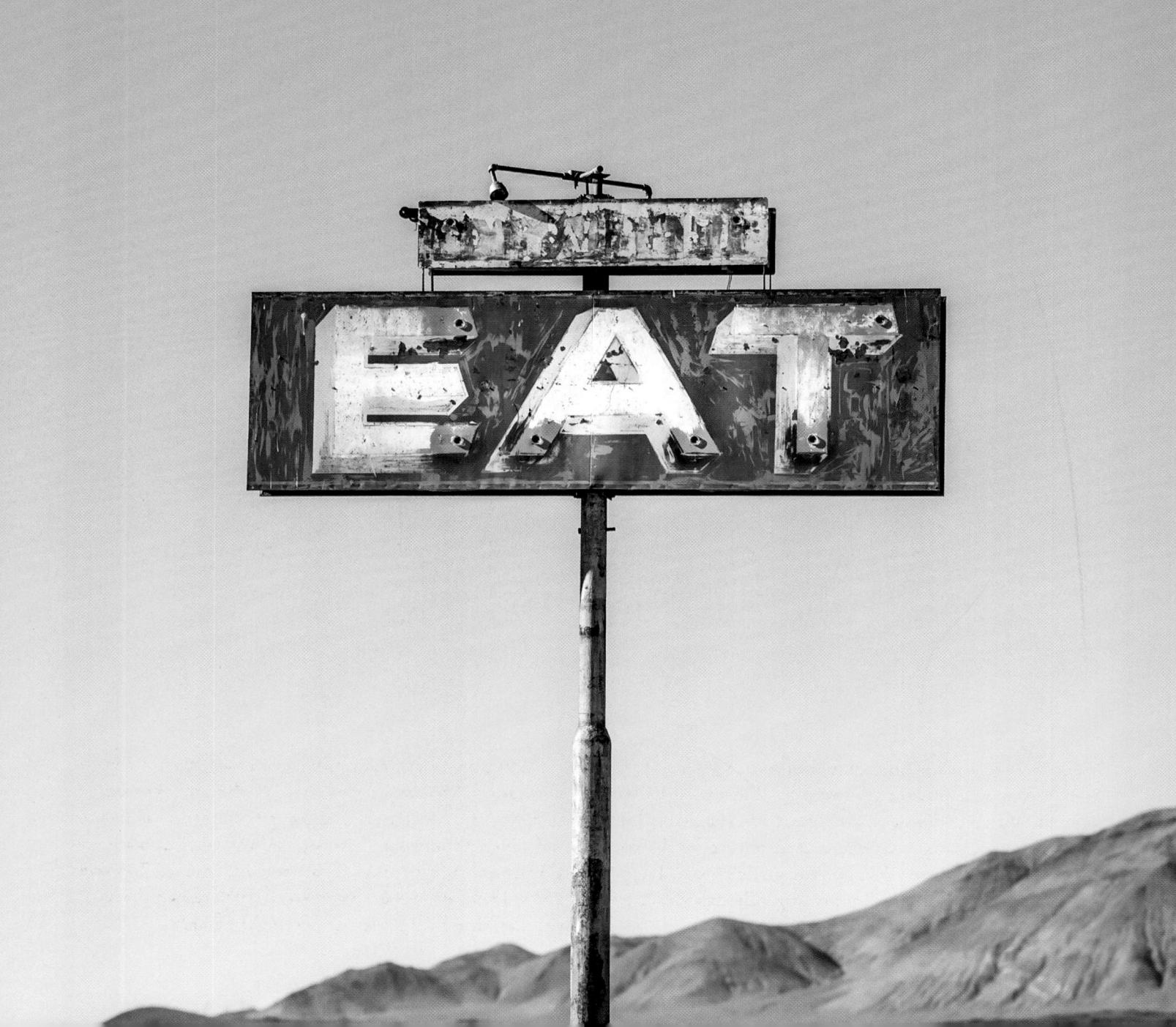

CHAPTER SIX

TWINKIES, A FROG, AND GRAPES

My brother, my sister, and I stared in awe as we watched the marvel of mass production sweep by. There we stood as thousands of Hostess Twinkies marched past. The tour guide asked if anyone wanted a sample, and before the words had left her mouth our hands shot up. The guide said, "OK, go ahead and pick one to eat." I'll never forget the experience of that warm and fresh baked good.

During my childhood summer vacations, my mom would take my brother, my sister, and me to visit factories to see how food was made. At the time we thought that's what all families did. On these factory visits, we had the chance to see how licorice, pasta, sourdough bread, fortune cookies, Twinkies, and animal cookies were made. My favorite factory tours were the ones where we got to eat fresh baked goods.

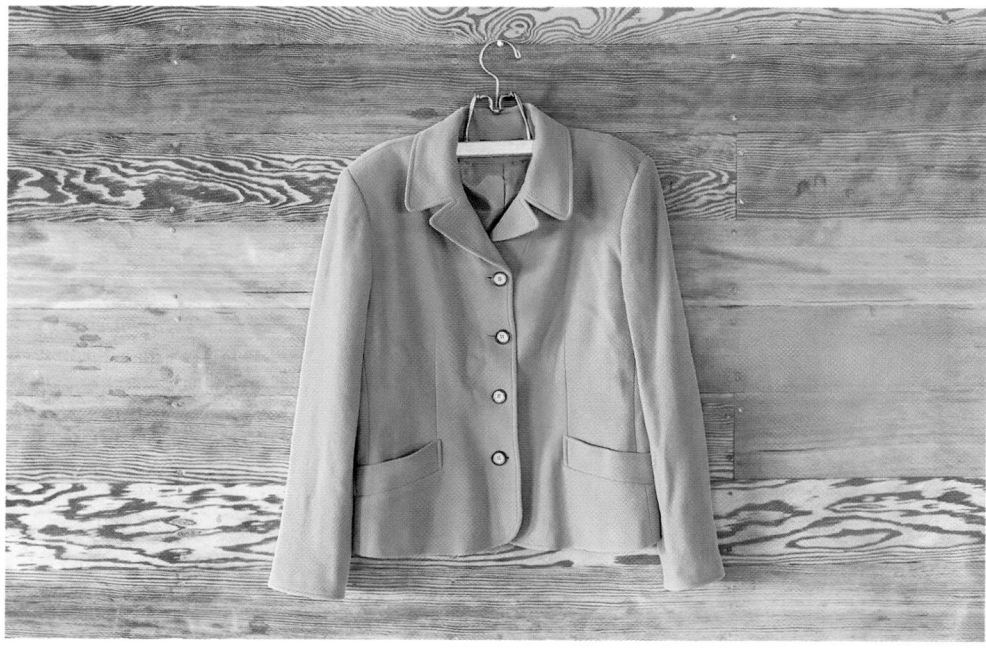

THE ESSENCE OF CREATIVITY The delightful smells and the delicious tastes are deeply embedded in my brain. What I know now that I didn't know then was that these trips were my mom's way to teach us about the essence of the creative arts. And this wasn't something we just witnessed; it was something we ate. This was a lesson about what we could understand. We digested creativity and it became a part of who we were. Those factory visits taught us to never underestimate the power of transforming ordinary ingredients into something more.

Creativity almost always begins with the combination of ordinary things. As a kid, I learned this from those factories and from my mom. She was an artist. I watched in curiosity as she mixed paints to create new colors for the pictures she made. I watched in awe as she mixed flour, sugar, and eggs to create a birthday cake in the shape of a hamburger or a racecar. Ordinary ingredients become extraordinary when we combine, stir, mix, and bake. Great ideas come never from thin air but from the mismatch of what's nearby. That's exactly what happened for Jim and John.

SORRY, MOM Jim was a freshman in college and noticed his mom's old green coat. He picked up a pair of scissors and wondered if his mom would mind. There was something about the felt fabric that he liked. Jim was working on a school project and he was running late. So he tossed aside his worries about his mom's reaction and began to cut and slice. Soon he had a green shape, and what remained of the jacket was just the sleeves. Then, Jim took some thread and stitched together the sides. Next he found a ping-pong ball and sliced it in half. With a little bit of glue and a black marker, the two halves made perfect eyes. After a bit more work, Jim held up his creation and thought to himself, It really does look like a frog. And it was then that Kermit the Frog was born. As a teenager, Jim Henson had created one of the most well-loved puppets from ordinary stuff lying around his house.

Whether in a modern factory or in ancient times, creativity has always been about making the most of what you have. Sometimes creativity thrives when you are having fun, and other times it flourishes when you have your back against the

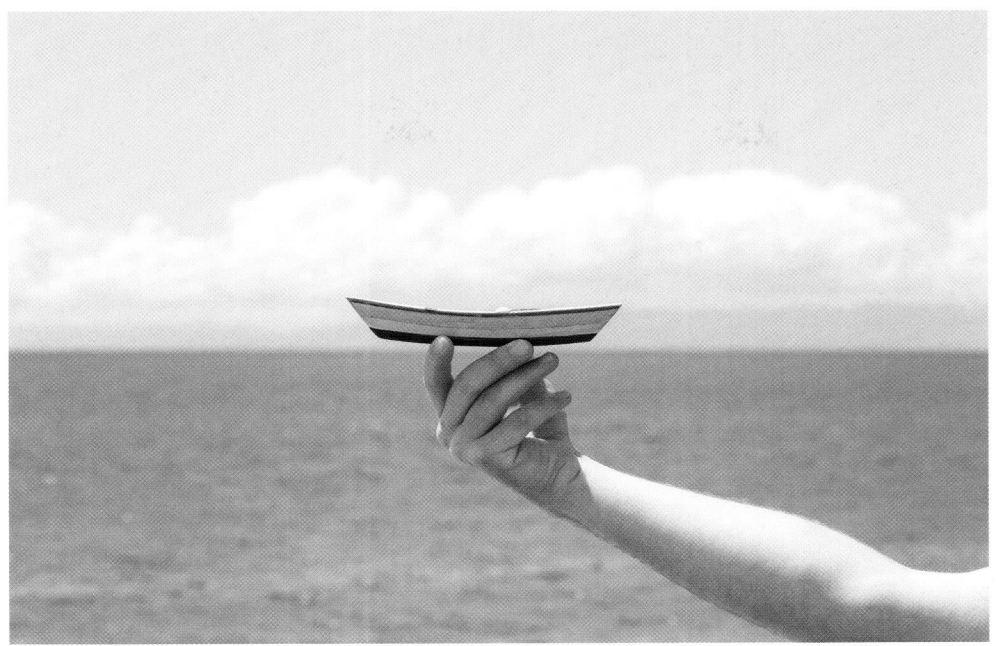

wall. The latter was the case with a young man named John who lived in Medieval times.

HOLY MIRRORS AND WINE John was ambitious but he was also short on funds. Investors had helped him make "holy mirrors" for religious pilgrims to buy. When the mirror was held up to a relic, it supposedly captured and reflected the glory of God. The target market was the horde of devout pilgrims that were soon to arrive. Unfortunately, a severe flood delayed the pilgrimage until the following year. John was buried in mirror inventory and swimming in debt. The investors were upset. Fortunately, the financial pressure didn't crush his spirit but instead ignited a creative spark.

John lived in a region known for its production of wine. As a result, he was familiar with the process of turning grapes into wine. John bought an old wine press that had been used for squishing juice out of grapes. With a few modifications, he transformed the press from making juice to printing words.

And it was then that he, John (Johannes) Gutenberg, invented the printing press that changed the course of the world.

Creativity is never about wishing that you had better fabric or lived in a different region of the world. Creatives don't use "if only" as an excuse. If only focuses on what might have been. Creatives focus on making the most of the raw materials that they have. Taking these materials and combining them into something new is where creativity becomes art.

And the most creative among us don't shy away from this ideal. Gutenberg's own words reflect this truth: "Yes, it is a press, certainly, but a press from which shall flow in inexhaustible streams, the most abundant and most marvelous liquor that has ever flowed to relieve the thirst of men! Through it, God will spread His Word. A spring of truth shall flow from it: like a new star it shall scatter the darkness of ignorance, and cause a light heretofore unknown to shine amongst men."

Whatever your creative pursuit, the quickest way to set sail is to use the boat that you have and to reach for the clouds. Combine ordinary ingredients but strive for great things.

EXERCISE

If creativity is the mixing of the ordinary into something new, like converting a winepress into a letterpress, it helps to become strangely familiar with what is ordinary to us. Artists, inventors, and creatives are those who can see the ordinary as something new. Here's an exercise to help you do just that.

STEP 1

Write down words that reflect your interests, who you are, where you live, and what you do. Don't worry about grammar or being exhaustive. This list is only for you.

Here's the start of my list to give you some ideas:
Santa Barbara, Surfer, Bee Keeper, Hiker, Biker, Dad, Photographer, Harmonica, Piano, Guitar, Ukulele, Teacher, California, Skateboard, Farmers' Market, Camping.

STEP 2

Select a few words to combine. Again, here's my example: Santa Barbara + Surfer + Photography. Strange as it may sound, it took me years before I found this combo because it was so obvious. Once I found it, my photography career blossomed in a whole new way. Consider how Gutenberg did the same when he combined a winepress and type. Then write down a few of your own combinations below.

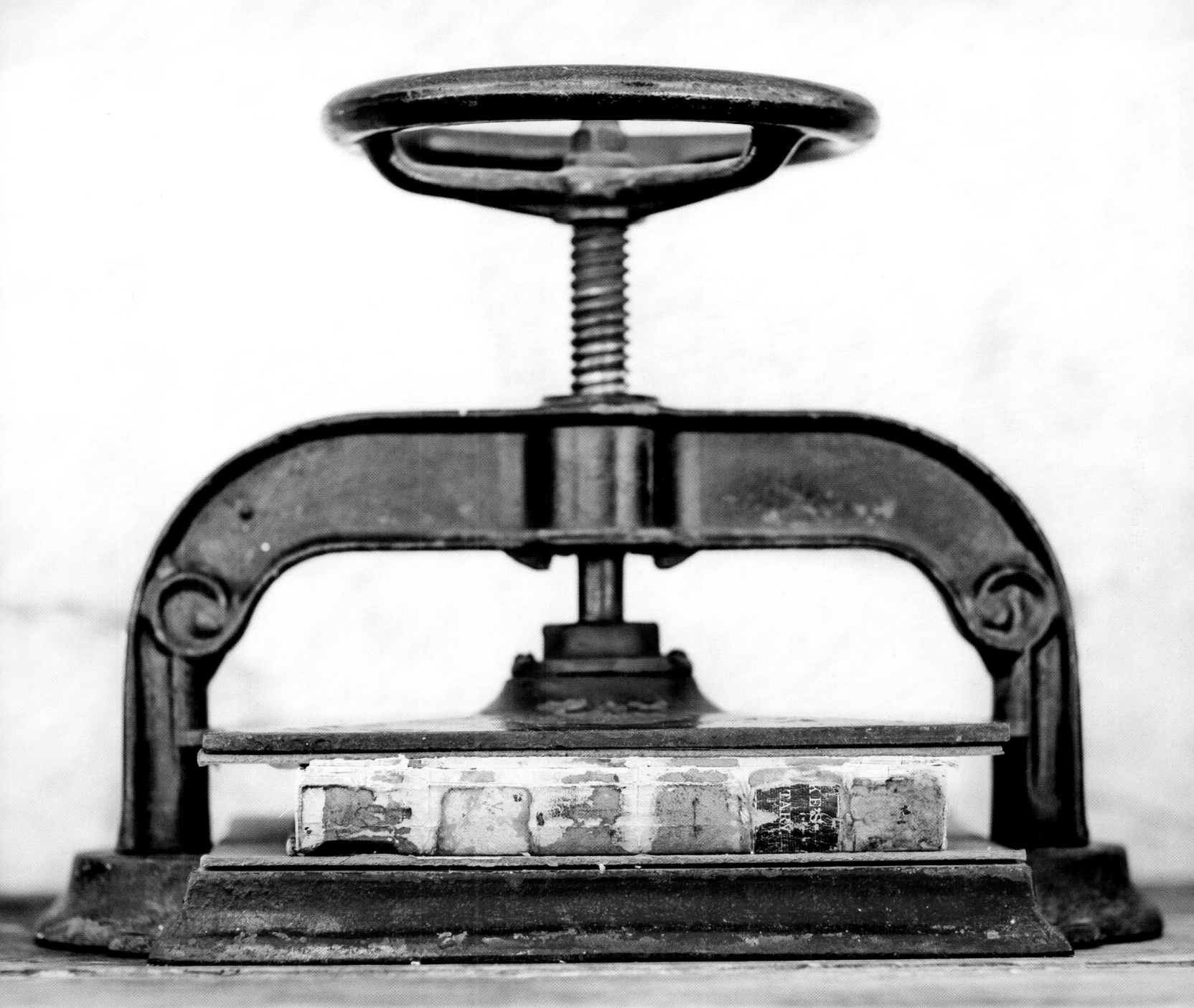

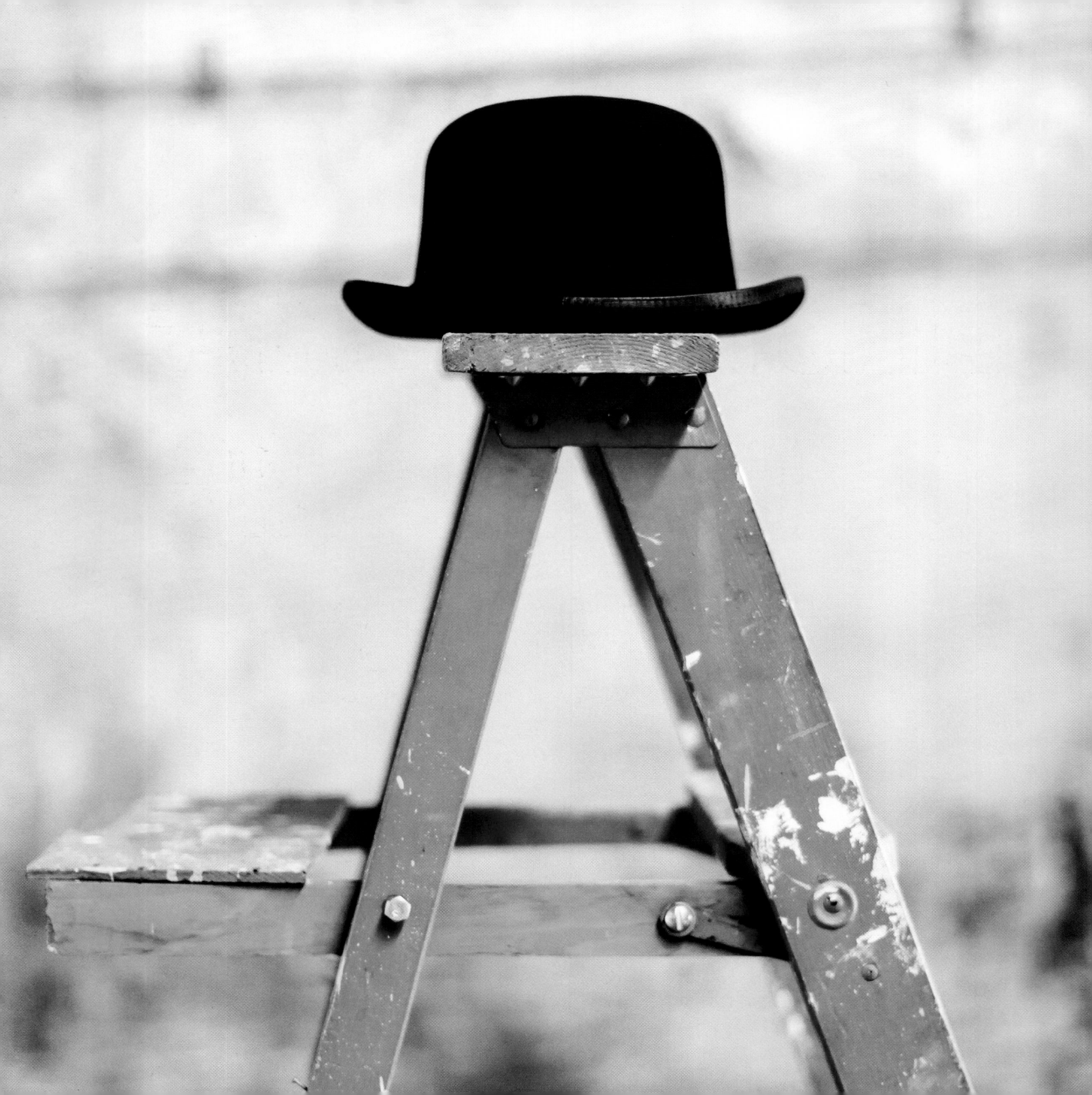

CHAPTER SEVEN

EINSTEIN'S GAME OF CONNECTING THE DOTS

How is it that some people come up with such creative ideas while others fall flat? Imagine if you could ask Einstein his thoughts. He might respond by saying, "The secret to creativity is what I call 'combinatory play.'" Einstein often explained that this was the cornerstone of all that he did. Einstein based his scientific method on the approach of playfully combining unrelated thoughts, topics, and disciplines to create new ideas. The most famous example of this was his combination of energy, mass, and the speed of light ($E=mc^2$), which gave us the ability to understand the universe in a new way. But it doesn't take a genius to know that combination is the secret to good ideas. We all take part in this type of creativity on a daily basis when we decide what combination of clothes to wear or what spread to put on our toast.

39

Mihaly Csikszentmihalyi, in his landmark book *Creativity*, explains that creative breakthroughs come from linking information that is not usually thought to be related. Think of this as like putting peanut butter and jelly on a slice of bread. Peanuts and berries aren't related but work well when they are linked. This is the secret of some of the most creative minds of all time. It sounds too simple to be true, but an essential aspect of creativity is connecting the dots.

THE WORLD'S WORST COMPUTER NAME "Executec" was almost one of the most successful computer companies in the world. But the founders didn't like that name so they thought about "Personal Computers Inc." instead. Fortunately, neither of those names stuck. They needed something that took the geeky computer edge off. They wanted something that was unintimidating and more down to earth. One of the founders was on a fruitarian diet and had just returned from working on a Gravenstein apple farm in Oregon. He liked apples and thought the name Apple sounded fun. Today, it's impossible to imagine the company named anything else. Could you imagine owning an Executec iPad? It just doesn't have the same ring.

Steve Jobs said, "Creativity is just connecting things. When you ask creative people how they did something, they feel a little guilty because they didn't really do it, they just saw something. It seemed obvious to them after a while. That's because they were able to connect experiences they've had and synthesize new things." Jobs is famous for inventing the new, but his inventions always came from somewhere else. Jobs's talent lay not in conjuring up ideas from thin air but from combining unlikely ideas into something that made sense.

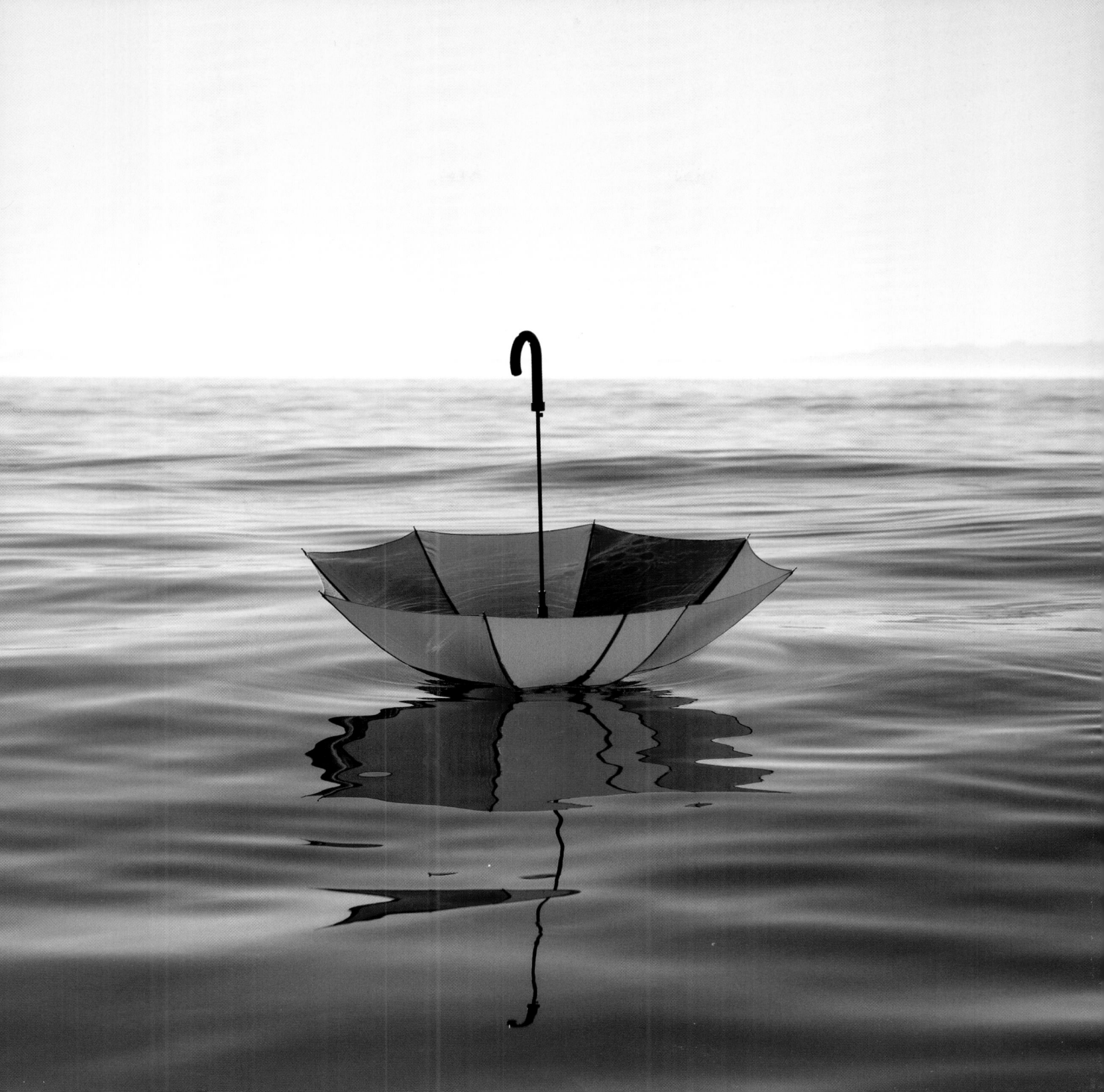

INVENTOR OR SPONGE? YOU DECIDE The story of the invention of the light bulb is the same. The invention is attributed to Thomas Edison having a moment of insight and success. Yet even Edison, who was a master of marketing and spin, deferred this idea and said, "Innovation is ninety-nine percent perspiration and one percent inspiration." The innovation of the light bulb took years and was the accumulation of connecting many small dots. Even when it did finally work, it didn't work that well—it could only burn for five minutes. So when they invited the press to come take a look, they only let them stay for three or four minutes before it went dark. When asked how long the bulbs would last, Edison said, "Forever, almost."

In his book about innovation, Steven Johnson said, "There was no light bulb moment in the story of the light bulb." Even Edison described himself as "Less of an innovator and more of a sponge." Just as with Steve Jobs, who didn't invent the iPod but made it widespread, Edison didn't invent the light bulb but came up with a light bulb that was a commercial success. Edison absorbed ideas and built a team with complementary skills. This, and perspiration, was the secret of his success.

Becoming a master at combinatory play requires letting down your guard. Most of us have become too serious to consider our work as play. Imagine if you were starting a computer company today, would you consider naming it after fruit or something else that you liked? Why not? And it's not just the name but also how we think about the thing itself. Steve Jobs thought of computing in an atypical way. In an era when computers were the domain of geeks, he considered computers "the equivalent of a bicycle for the mind." Such comparisons—apples and bikes—aren't perfect, but when you are just playing that's OK. When we play, we engage in activity for enjoyment and recreation rather than a serious or practical purpose. When we play we relax, and this state can allow for synapses to form. Let's try it for ourselves.

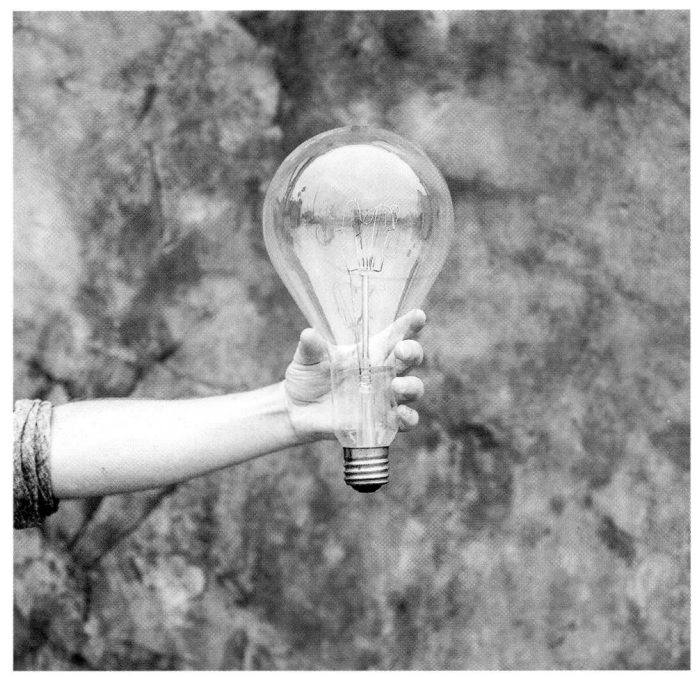

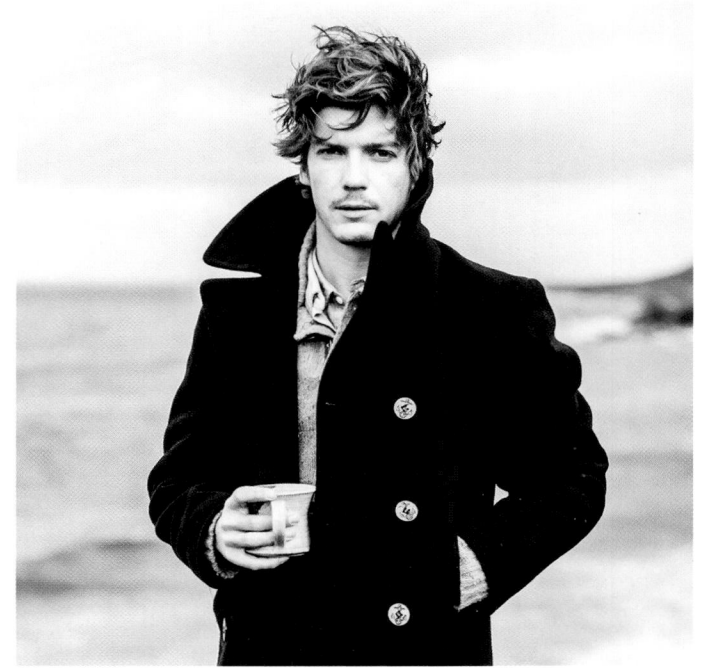

EXERCISE

Down at the beach one day, I asked a friend to hold a red umbrella over his head so I could capture a photograph. A gust of wind blew the umbrella out of his hand and it fell into the sea. The accident became one of the best shots of the day (it's the image in the previous spread). When you play, you discover what you may have otherwise overlooked.

STEP 1

Choose a creative practice you enjoy (drawing, writing, playing piano, creating photographs, cooking desserts, and so on), and veer from your normal routine and try out some crazy ideas. Play the piano with your eyes closed, shoot some photographs using silly props, and so on. Most importantly, stop worrying about the results and cut yourself some slack. Stop stifling the creative process with such a strong grip. As the poet Sharon Olds puts it, "When we give our pen some free will we may surprise ourselves."

STEP 2

After you have finished the task, reflect on using a more open approach. How did you feel? What were the results? Were you more or less effective? What might you try next?

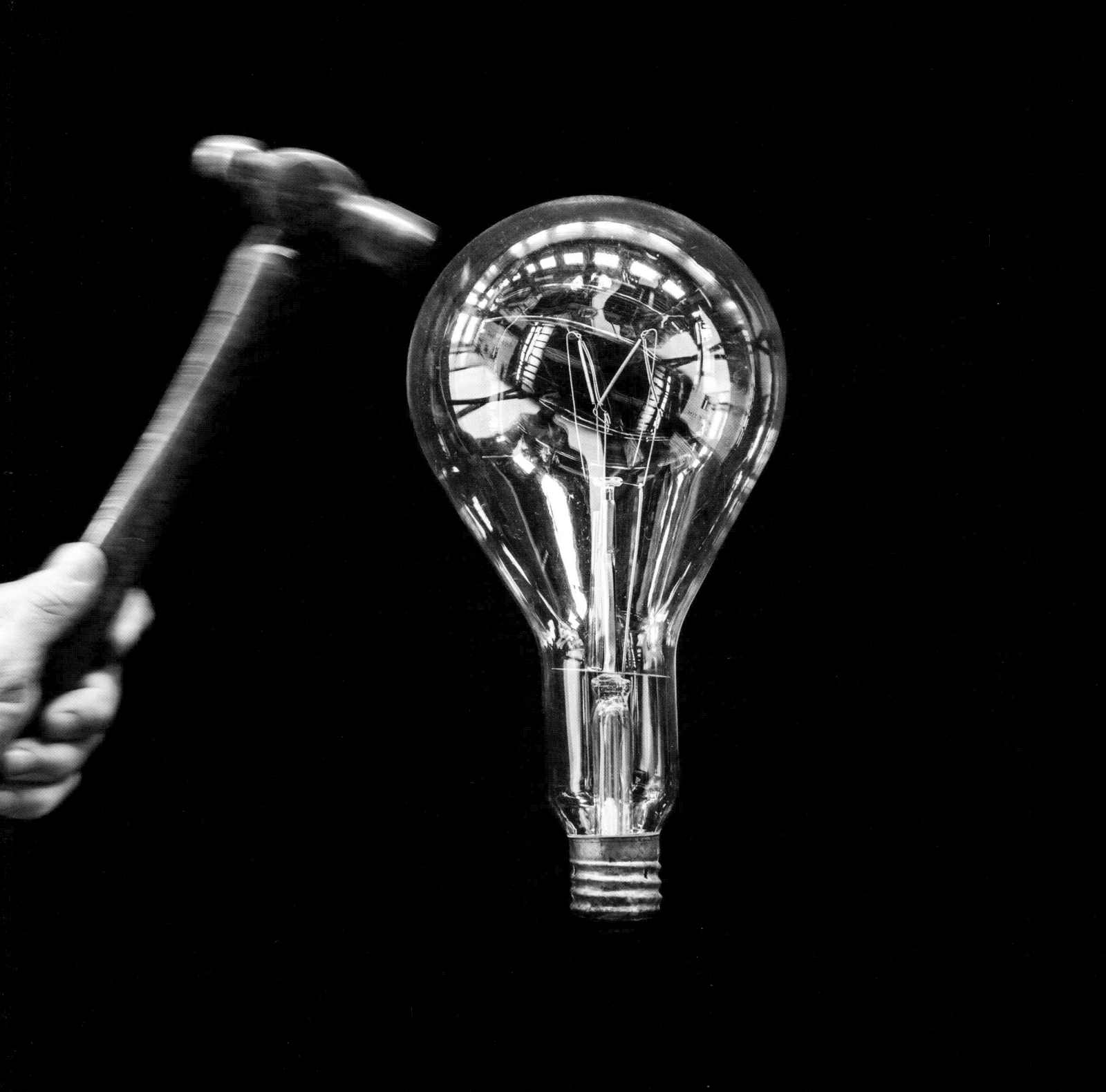

CHAPTER EIGHT

CRITICAL CREATIVITY

The creative spirit may be fierce, but it's also fragile—and the quickest way to crush it is with cold-hearted critique. Yet it's both impossible and inadvisable to live in a world without criticism. Even though it can stifle us, criticism isn't inherently bad. It can be corrosive, but it can also sharpen the edge. And critique is indispensable to creative growth. Without critique, the quality of one's creative output can

collapse. That's what happened when the office of the "Devil's Advocate" was phased out.

In the late 1500s, Pope Sixtus V established a new position in the Roman Catholic church to help determine who should become a saint. Only the most faithful and respected were considered for the job of *Promotor Fidei* (Promoter of the Faith) or *Advocatus Diaboli* (Devil's Advocate).

THE DEMISE OF THE DEVIL'S ADVOCATE The office of the Devil's Advocate protected the sainthood from being watered down. Over the next four centuries, this role helped to uphold the integrity of the canonization of saints. That was until 1983, when the office was dissolved. Up until that point, only 98 people had been canonized as saints. After the position was eliminated, 500 were quickly canonized. Some argue that the fast-tracking of the sainthood led to its demise. The point for us isn't one of religious tradition and faith. The point is to start thinking about the role of critique in a new way. For everyone, whether you are an artist or an accountant, critical feedback can help. Too much critique and it will crush, but just enough and the pressure can refine, strengthen, and be a catalyst for growth.

My friend Travis runs a highly successful fashion brand. In order to keep his company on course, once a year he brings in devil's advocates to identify weakness and blind spots. Travis explains, "Critique can distract, but it can also clarify. For us, listening to critique provides a healthy tension that strengthens the brand." The type of people that Travis brings in are those he trusts. We all know that getting critique from any old stray dog brings with it rabies and fleas. So Travis chooses reputable people that have his best interests in mind. His annual sessions with the devil's advocates generate growth.

Sometimes it's worthwhile to invite the critics over for dinner, and other times to fight against them tooth and nail. My mind flooded with criticism as I prepared to write this book. So I hastily wrote out my thoughts: "*&%#! the critics. Let them feel smug because they were able to find someone else's faults. And I will know full well that I have given it my best to make my life, relationships, vocation, and this book works of art." It was cathartic to lash out at the invisible critics who were holding me back.

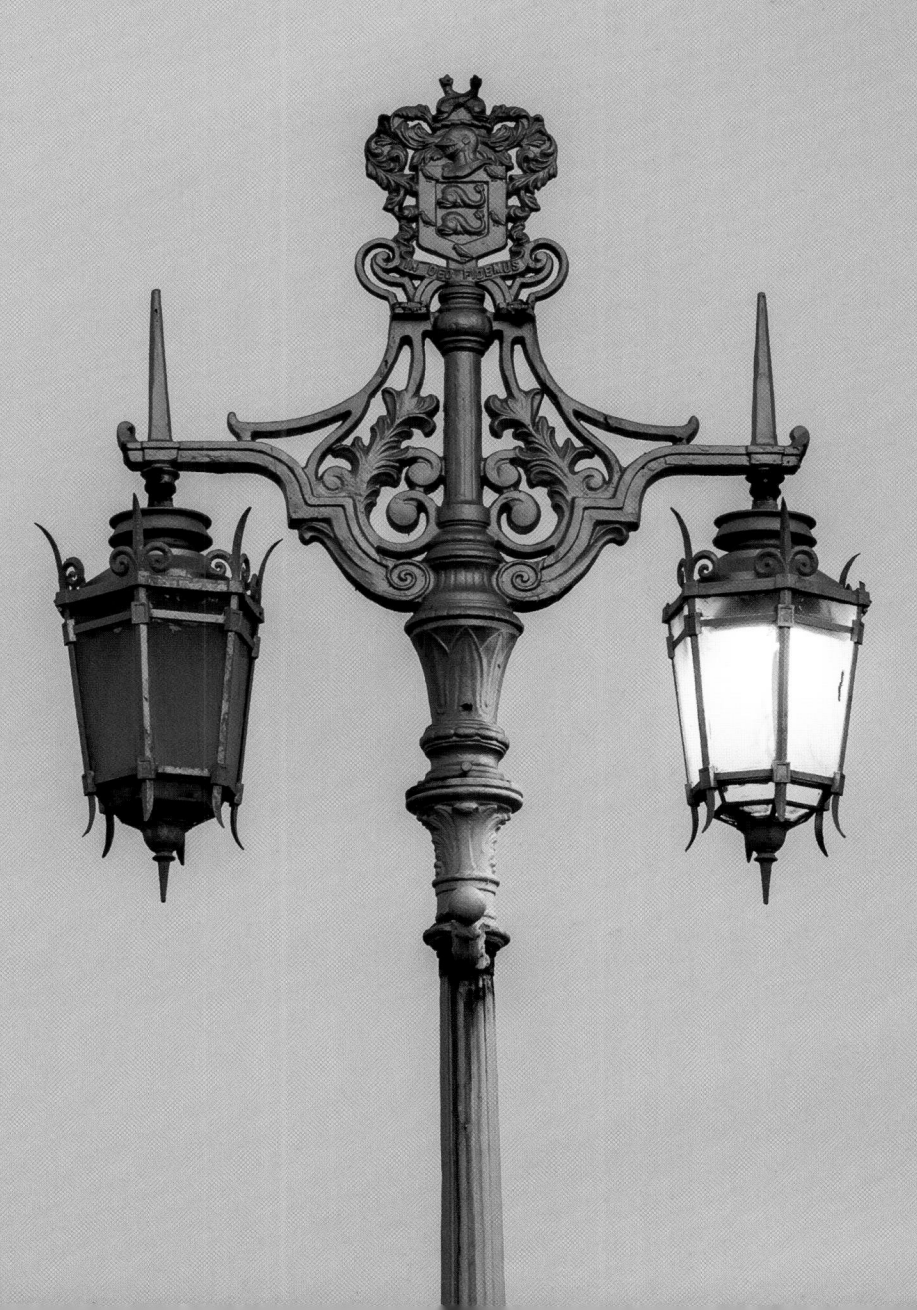

Next, I turned to one of my literary heroes, Jack London, and reread what was said about him. His biographer Earl Labor wrote, "Because he wrote so clearly that anybody with a good basic education could understand what he was saying, Jack put the critics out of business." The critics were confused because his literary greatness was down-to-earth and anchored in the reality of living with the same ferocity and tenacity with which he wrote. As one literary critic wrote, "The greatest story Jack London ever wrote was the story he lived." This was a turning point for me—writing isn't about words but about life. My creative project (this book) wasn't going to be theoretical and fake, but anchored in who I am and how I live.

London lived with such a fierce passion that it was not his work but the life he lived that was the true story—almost as if his work and life were one and the same. In London's own words, "I would rather be ashes than dust! I would rather that my spark should burn out in a brilliant blaze than it should be stifled by dry-rot. I would rather be a superb meteor, every atom of me in magnificent glow, than a sleepy and permanent planet. The function of man is to live, not to exist. I shall not waste my days trying to prolong them. I shall use my time." Those words were a credo that guided his life and kept the critics far away.

The problem with most of us is that we have recruited the wrong critics. Unknowingly, we have accepted the critical voices that we carry around in our heads. These voices distract, scratch, bite, and nag—whether it's your mom's disappointment, or the judgment of a colleague or friend. The number one reason that we don't take creative risks? Because we are afraid. We're afraid that these voices might be right. We're afraid that we aren't very good. We're afraid that we'll look like a fool. So we give these voices more credit than they deserve. One way to stop the voices from from stealing your dreams is to create a paradigm and a plan.

DEFINE A PARADIGM The Brazilian novelist Paulo Coelho has sold millions of copies of his books, but still there are critics who tear his work to shreds. When asked, "Do the critics

hurt you?" he said, "No. Writers are lampposts and critics are dogs." Coelho has adopted a paradigm that safeguards his creative role. A paradigm is a framework through which we can understand our world. His paradigm is one of standing tall and shining light. Rather than getting angry or fighting back, he directs his energy to doing what he does best. Every creative act begets criticism. If you want to become more creative, you have to adopt a paradigm that accepts, but doesn't overinflate, this truth.

Another paradigm is to see critique as a catalyst for change. Travis, my friend with the fashion brand, has adopted this paradigm—rather than being afraid of critique, he encourages it. This doesn't happen every day, as too much critique would decrease morale. He does this once or twice a year. This paradigm can also be helpful when critique comes in an unexpected way. When famed architect Frank Gehry took his first architecture course at USC, he failed miserably. The instructor told him to drop out of the major and never take another architecture class. Gehry saw this as a challenge and enrolled in the class again and got an A. It is this type of tenacity that has marked his world-famous career. His path is defined by what other people say can't be done. For Gehry, critique isn't an enemy but a friend.

Jack London's paradigm was one in which he mostly ignored the critics and threw himself into the adventure of living life—from learning to surf in Honolulu to sailing around the world. Jack was aware when the critics didn't like his work, but he didn't let that hold him back.

DEVELOP A PLAN After defining your paradigm, it's time to develop a plan. The author Brené Brown shared her plan in the wildly popular TED talk "I carry a small sheet of paper in my wallet that has written on it the names of people whose opinions of me matter." In another talk, "Why your critics aren't the ones who count," she cuts to the chase: "If you're not in the arena, also getting your ass kicked, I'm not interested in your feedback." Your plan needs to define who matters and how you are going to handle and process critique.

When it comes to selecting promoters of the faith or devil's advocates, my list is short. I have a handful of colleagues and friends that I can trust. I'm confident that these people have my best interests in mind and that they can handle my uncertainty, successes, and mistakes. I learned long ago that you can't bear your soul to certain friends. That's OK. Being open and vulnerable isn't being dumb. But when it comes to inviting people to evaluate and reflect on what you have done, fewer is best. I suggest no more than five.

Next, when it comes to asking someone to evaluate your work, how you ask for critique will determine the response. Ben Decker, a global communications expert who coaches business leaders like Charles Schwab, explains that critique must always be complemented with encouraging words. Decker encourages a 3x3 approach: three positives and three areas for improvement. Whether you are asking for feedback or giving it out, this approach makes the more difficult messages easier to hear.

Another important strategy to have in place is one that deals with the unsolicited feedback that catches you off guard. Such unfiltered critique can have a toxic effect. You need to decide how to handle and process the negative comments you are bound to get. I like to think of these messages as suspicious-looking packages that arrive at your front door. I set them aside and then deal with them after the rush. After opening the package, I review the message and consider the source.

A well-known photographer and colleague of mine doesn't like my photography at all. And I don't like his. So whenever he makes a critical comment about my work, I write it off. I can do this with confidence because I've thought about the source. You can't listen to every comment with equal weight. As an artist, the goal isn't to be liked by all. You have to choose where you are going to stand and then shine your light. Complying with every critical word will make your head spin. As Anne Lamott put it, "Lighthouses don't go running all over an island looking for boats to save; they just stand there shining." With your feet firmly planted, you have to decide what to shine and where to stand.

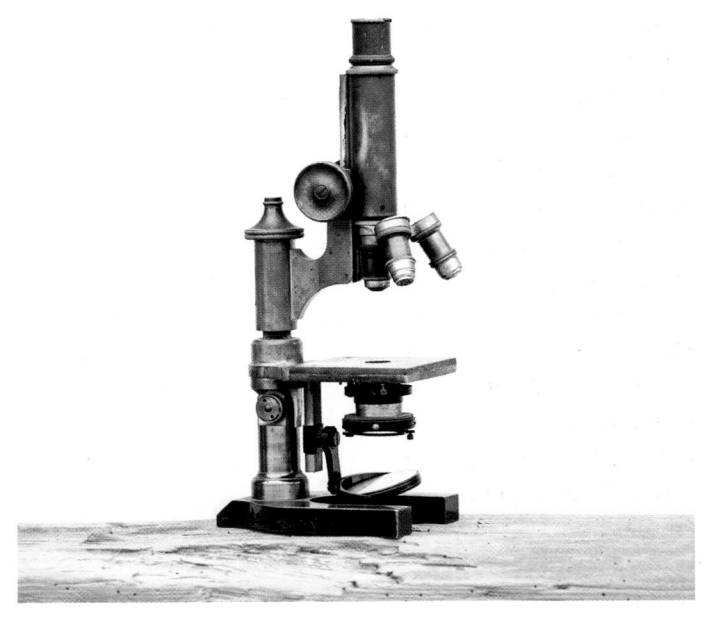

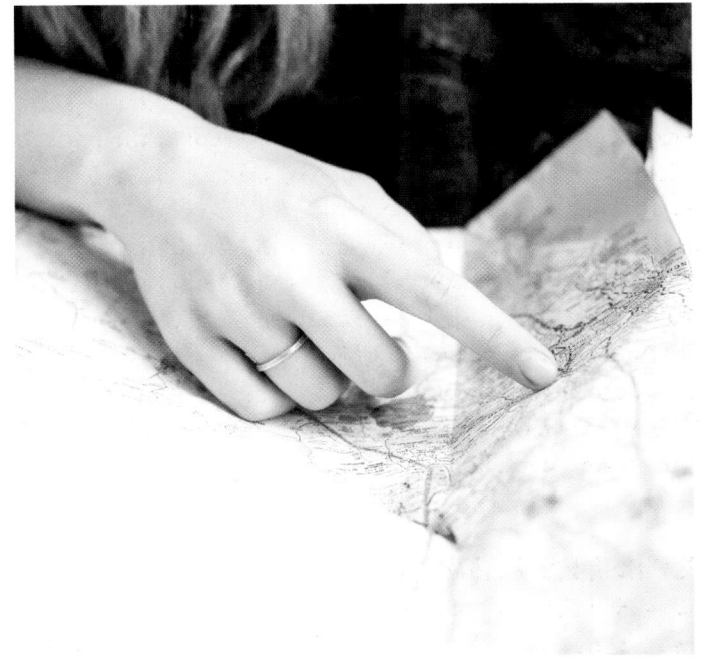

Another time I received a lackluster review for one of my photography books. I had poured my heart and soul into that project, so this critique hurt. After reading the review, I Googled the guy who made the negative remarks. It turned out that the review came from a retired lawyer who was a mediocre photographer at best. Ha! I thought to myself. Then I dug deeper to find that the quality and accuracy of his book reviews was good. So I read the review again and discovered that his critique was not about me but about the structure and form of the book. He wasn't being unfair; his words were right on the mark. So I decided to take to heart what he had to say. The result was some advice that has helped me advance my writing career.

The most scathing letter I have ever received came from a client. After reading the letter, I was shocked, embarrassed, ashamed, and confused. A few days later, the swelling still hadn't gone down, so I forwarded it to Dane, one of my trusted colleagues and friends. Dane responded with a one-page letter that began with the words "This is *poison*." His response was salve to my wounds. We all need friendships like this. Without them the poison settles in, but with them it lessens the sting.

Dealing with critique in private makes it worse. When you are seriously wounded, it's nearly impossible to operate on yourself. If you don't have someone to talk to about your battle wounds, it's time to make a change. Find a friend, mentor, colleague, therapist, religious leader, or relative who can help you make sense of the mistakes you are bound to make. Start with a small issue to test how this person will respond. Then share more only if you sense respect and thoughtfulness in the way they respond.

HE HAS A RIGHT TO CRITICIZE, WHO HAS A HEART TO HELP.

— ABRAHAM LINCOLN

EXERCISE

STEP 1
Create a new paradigm for understanding critique.

Begin by asking someone you respect or admire,
"How do you mentally process critique?"

Next, take a stab at writing out your own paradigm in a journal.
Consider using imagery like "lampposts and dogs" or simple statements that
put critique in its place. Don't worry about getting it perfect. Think of this more as a
rough draft to test out some ideas.

STEP 2
Come up with a plan for fielding and processing critique.
Here are a few ideas: Choose the people you trust.
Consider the source. Solicit criticism in a more thoughtful way. Save positive feedback.

Follow the steps below to begin to write out your own plan.

1. Write down three to five names of people whose opinion matters to you.

2. Craft your own unique strategy for dealing with criticism.

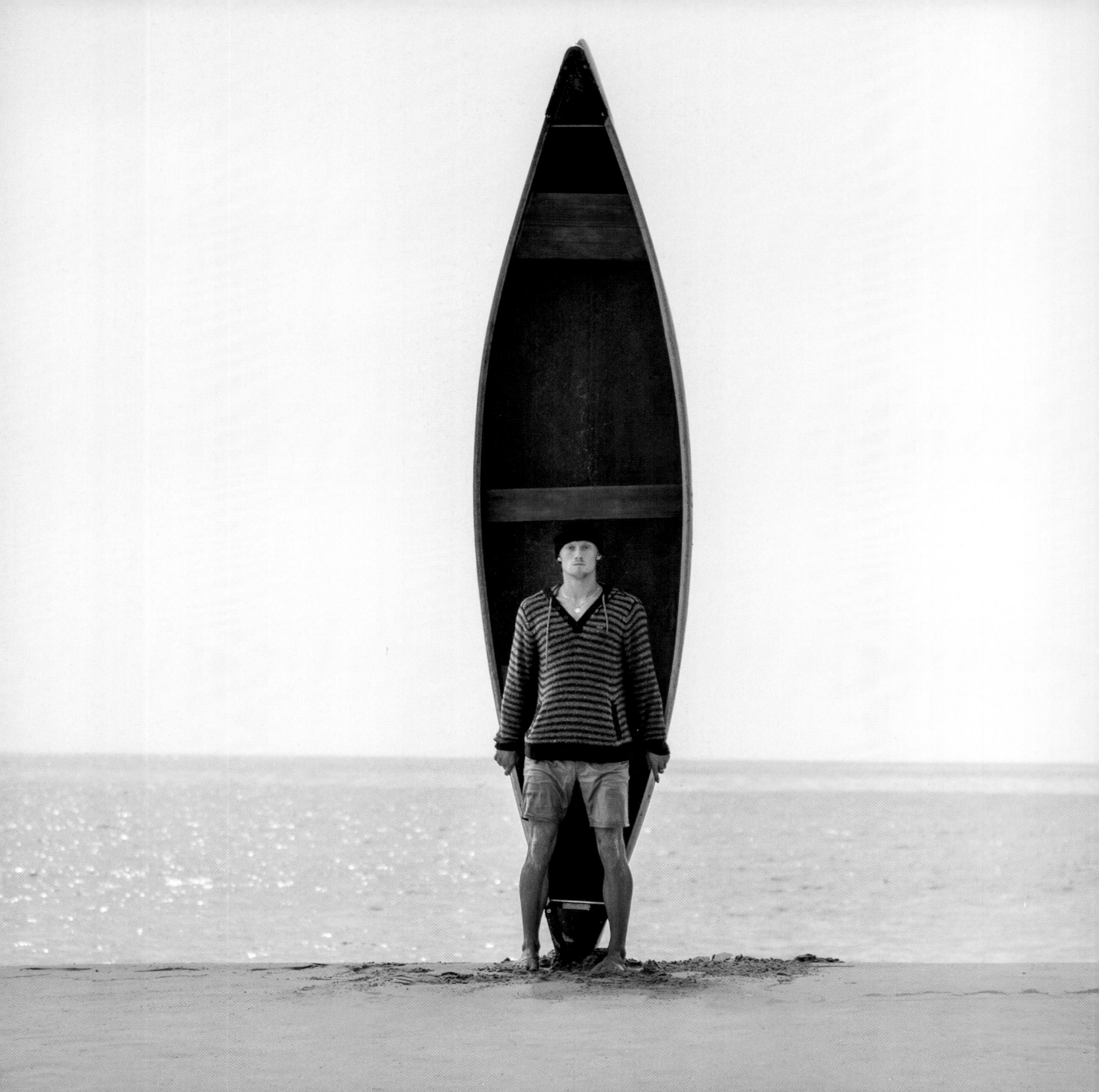

PART TWO: THE JOURNEY

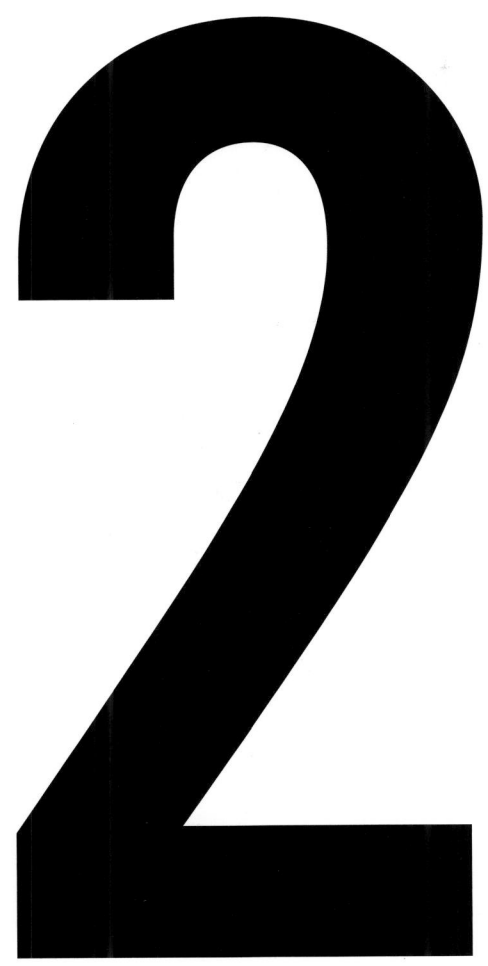

IT IS NOT DEATH THAT MAN SHOULD FEAR,
BUT HE SHOULD FEAR NEVER BEGINNING TO LIVE.
— MARCUS AURELIUS

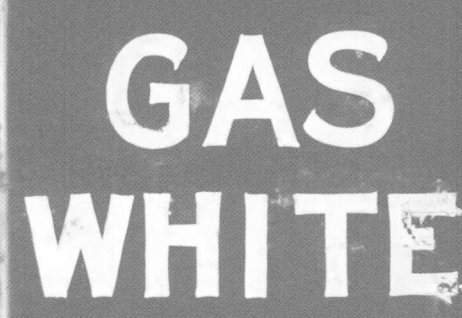

CHAPTER NINE

BLIND PASSION

When ignited, passion is a wild and untamed force. That's why following your passions isn't always good advice. We've all witnessed the train wreck when someone blindly followed their passions and it wrecked their career and hurt both family and friends. Benjamin Franklin called it out years ago: "If passion drives you, let reason hold the reins."

The passion, success, and creativity of people like Steve Jobs, Albert Einstein, and Pablo Picasso are impossible to overstate. Who they were and what they did transcends the genre that they represent. Their influence is relevant not only to computing, science, and art, but to anyone who wants to contribute in the highest way. For many, they have become archetypes for living a more creative life, yet their passion wasn't without its blind spots.

MIND BEFORE HEART Steve Jobs was a brilliant rule breaker who cared deeply about making his mark. His passion was like high-octane fuel. He didn't just think differently, he acted differently. When it came to bringing innovation to this world, such rule-breaking made the world a better place. For Jobs, the normal rules didn't apply. He was a force to be reckoned with, and sometimes this force was good and other times it was cruel. Consider how he consistently parked in handicap parking spots without an ounce of shame. Dig around a bit and you'll find other examples similar to this. Jobs did break the rules, but often it was at the expense of people who got in the way. He was creative in many ways, but in other ways he wasn't exactly a saint. Too often for the sake of inspiration, we oversimplify the past.

Even Einstein, "the most intelligent mind of his time," wasn't free of stupid mistakes. When his marriage to Mileva was falling apart, he wrote her a letter declaring a list of conditions that she must fulfill for the marriage to stay intact. Here's a brief sample of what he wrote: "1) You will not expect any intimacy from me, nor will you reproach me in any way. 2) You will stop talking to me if I request it. 3) You will leave my bedroom or study immediately without protest if I request it." Einstein may have been smart, but writing that letter was just plain dumb.

Then there is Picasso, one of the most popular guys in this group. His art is a gift to humanity, that cannot be denied. Yet Picasso didn't exactly treat women in the most dignified way. He once said, "For me there are only two kinds of women, goddesses and doormats." Picasso was married twice and had numerous love affairs throughout his life. His relationships were all over the map—one of his lovers was 40 years younger and underage. Out of the seven women that he stayed with the longest, two killed themselves and two went mad. If Picasso knocked on my front door asking to date one of my daughters, I would get out a baseball bat and tell him to leave.

Jobs, Einstein, and Picasso are some of the most often quoted, referenced, and celebrated people in the creative space. They have been inducted into the creativity Hall of Fame, and

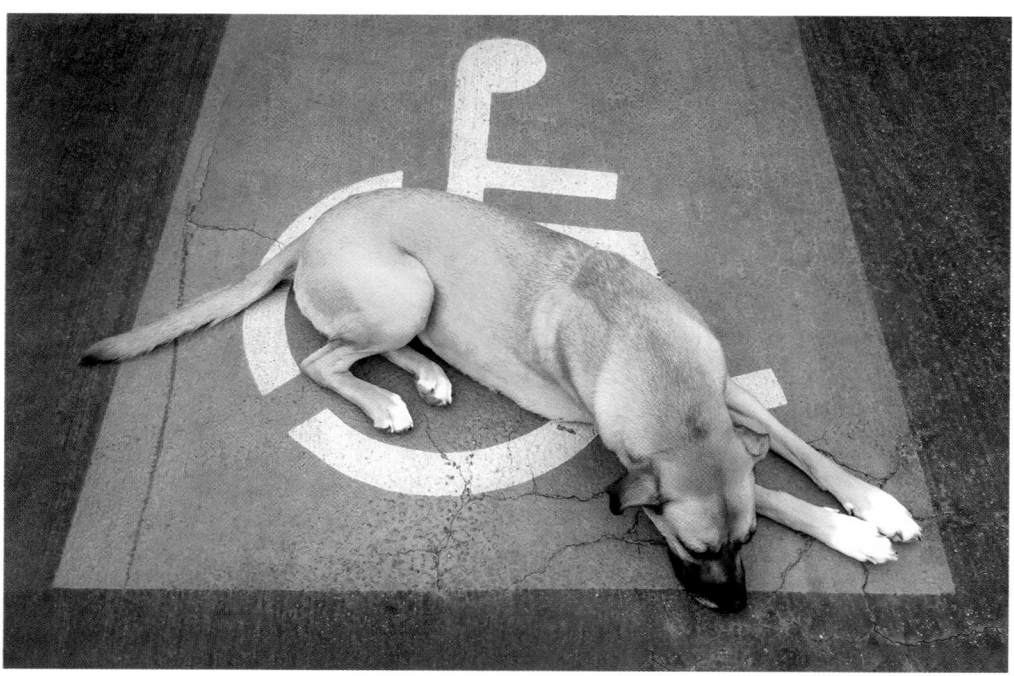

their statues are made of gold. So what's the point? Why bring up the darkness, and does the darkness diminish the light?

The point isn't to say that we are better than they were. As Abe Lincoln said of his enemies in the South during the Civil War, "Don't critique: they are just what we would be under similar circumstances." We are all human and we have no idea how we would have handled life in their shoes. More importantly, indulging in self-righteous judgment doesn't bring about change, but neither does glossing over the truth.

Honest assessment, humble awareness, and resolute determination to not make the same mistakes, that's where change is born. We study history to learn from success, failures, and mistakes. That's why a dishonest view of history isn't much help. A more realistic view helps you craft our own life, rather than blindly following someone else. Learn from the legends, but ultimately you need to make your own path. The world doesn't need another Picasso or Steve Jobs. The world needs you.

Rather than follow, it's time to take on the identity of a pioneer. That is the core thread of what made those men great. They led the way into uncharted land. They made mistakes along the way, but that doesn't delete the good that they found. Take the good and discard the wrong.

EXERCISE

Take a few minutes to reflect on who inspires you most. Think about people from the near and distant past. Think about family and friends. Think about colleagues and peers. Then list five to ten people who are at the top of your list. Identify what they taught you and why. Below are a few examples to get you started.

PERSON	TEACHING
Theodore Roosevelt	Tenacity
Albert Einstein	Creativity is combination

CHAPTER TEN

MAGNETIC NORTH

Creativity beckons you to break out of the mold, but it isn't a license to do whatever you want. The end doesn't justify the means no matter how deep your passion swells. Mark Twain famously said, "Twenty years from now you will be more disappointed by the things that you didn't do than by the ones you did do." These are great words to put on a motivational coffee mug, but they aren't entirely true. They ignite a spark, but the fire might be burning the wrong stuff—like the patio furniture instead of chopped wood.

Nothing epitomizes the creative fight more than turning tragedy into triumph, and that's what Lance Armstrong had done. The world rallied for him as he neared the finish line of the Tour de France. His passion burned bright. The way he overcame the odds inspired us to do the same.

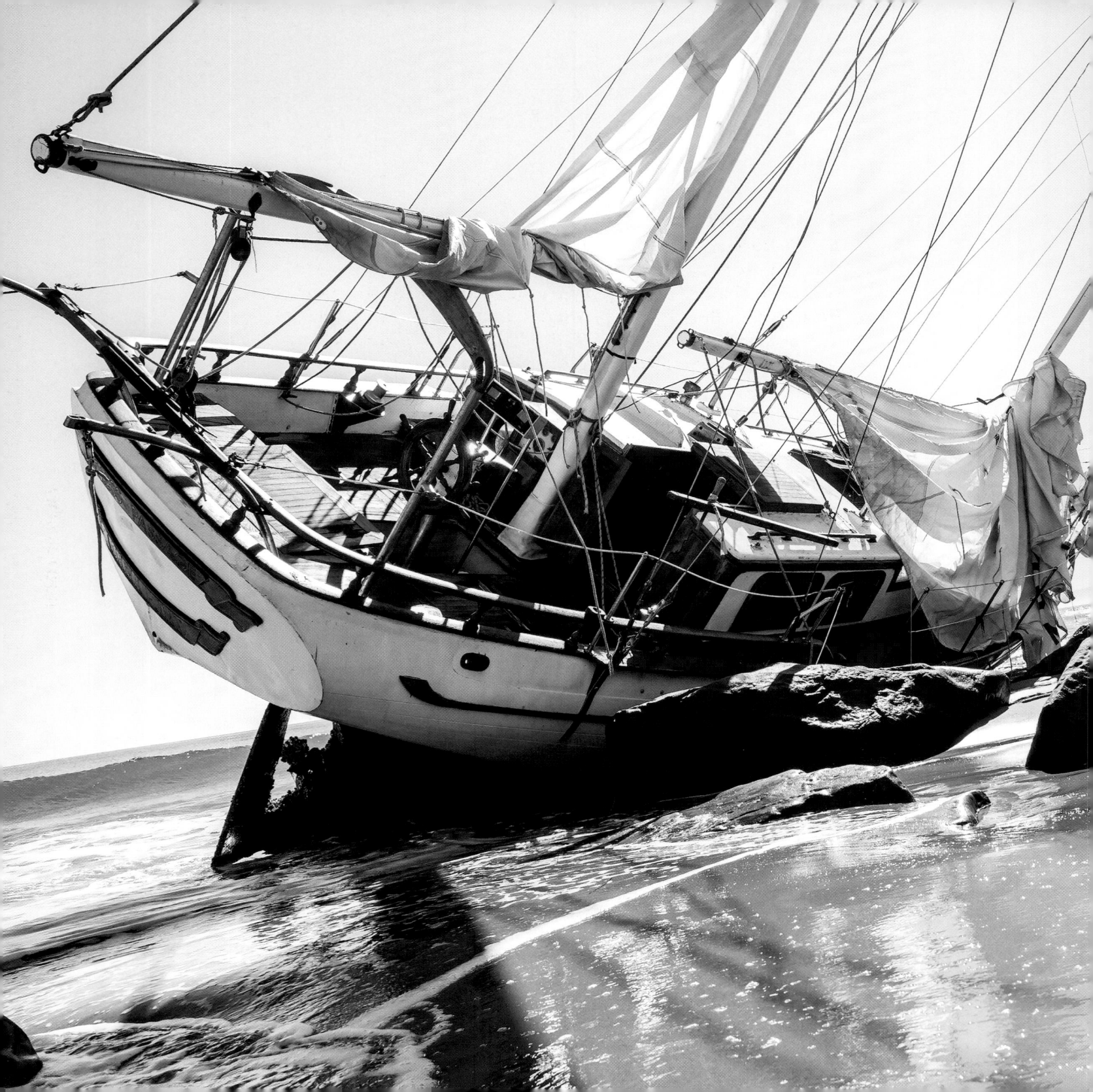

DREAM, DISCOVER, AND DIE I was facing health issues of my own, and Lance's determination gave me the courage to fight. Then we discovered that Armstrong's victory was unfairly won. It wasn't a creative fight but a cheater's lie. The betrayal stung. Twenty years from now, Armstrong will still be living in the shadow of his mistake. Armstrong doesn't stand alone; there are countless others who took their creative license too far. Creativity isn't carte blanche to do whatever you please.

Mark Twain loved to stir people up. He wrote with an intellect and wit that got people out of their seats. Since the beginning of his writing days, he was rallying people to "Throw off the bowlines. Sail away from the safe harbor. Catch the trade winds in your sails. Explore. Dream. Discover." These words will never go out of style. We will always need to be reminded to leave safety behind for the pursuit of our dreams. Yet such advice is naively incomplete. You can't just run out the door, jump on a ship, and hope to survive. Without proper understanding of nautical navigation, you will die. Incurable optimism is valuable, but when it comes to taking a journey so is planning ahead.

REGRET Dreams float in the clouds, but true creativity is always rooted in dirt. What gives creativity its strength is the pursuit of a magnetic north. The combination of heart, mind, and soul create this magnetic pull. Lance Armstrong was driven by power and his passion to succeed. Blinded by passion, he neglected his mind and soul. And this isn't just about Lance, Einstein, Picasso, or Steve Jobs. Celebrities are easy to notice and to blame. When they fall it makes us feel better about ourselves. Yet we have all made mistakes big and small. Speaking for myself, I have made mistakes in my life for which I am ashamed. I'm guessing you may be in the same boat. We have all fallen short.

MISTAKE Passion transfers energy to your creative pursuits. It gives you the gumption to bounce back even when you fall down. Yet too much passion can get out of control. One horrible day, I followed my passions and made one of the biggest mistakes of my career. I was crushed by the weight of what I had done. I was immobilized by guilt and shame. I knew I needed help, so I sought the counsel of a pro.

HELP After a few weeks my therapist's advice began to sink in: "Shame paralyzes, while regret helps you to move." Regret transforms. It doesn't belittle or lessen the consequences of mistakes, but it does build resolve to make amends and to lead a better life. Shame is self-hatred, while regret is rooted in love. The strongest love is grace—which literally means unmerited or undeserved love. That was all I had. This force helped me own up to my mistake, seek amends, and change. Creativity is looking at a situation in a new way, and that's exactly what grace helped me to do.

E. M. Forster once said, "One person with passion is better than forty people merely interested." Sure, that's true as long as the passion is standing on solid ground. The key to living without regret isn't to live with passion and blindly follow Mark Twain's advice. Passion by itself isn't enough. Without the sure footing that strong values provide, pursuing your dreams can be an icy slope. Clearly defining your values and sticking to them is like putting on metal crampons that give you grip.

PASSION, THOUGH A BAD REGULATOR, IS A POWERFUL SPRING.

—RALPH WALDO EMERSON

EXERCISE

STEP 1

Select three core values that describe you and three core values that you aspire to have.
Write these down on an empty page in your journal. Let the words float in the middle of the page.
Come up with your own core values, or select from the words below:

Honesty. Authenticity. Creativity. Kindness. Generosity. Frugality. Moderation.
Justice. Integrity. Curiosity. Charity. Adventure. Loyalty. Serenity. Drive.
Humor. Income. Family. Nutrition. Exercise. Faith. Friendship. Community. Innovation. Prayer.
Meditation. Patience. Temperance. Silence. Resolution. Humility. Boldness.

STEP 2

Create three sentences that spell out how you would like to implement your values.
For example, if you selected family as a core value, write out a sentence to further articulate what
you mean. One sentence might be, "Because family is important to me, I am committed
to stop working on nights and weekends." Or you might write, "I so deeply value time with my wife
and kids that for the next three weeks I will turn off my laptop and phone as soon as I
get home." Or, "I miss my extended family and am going to plan a visit within the next year."
Most importantly, make it specific to you.

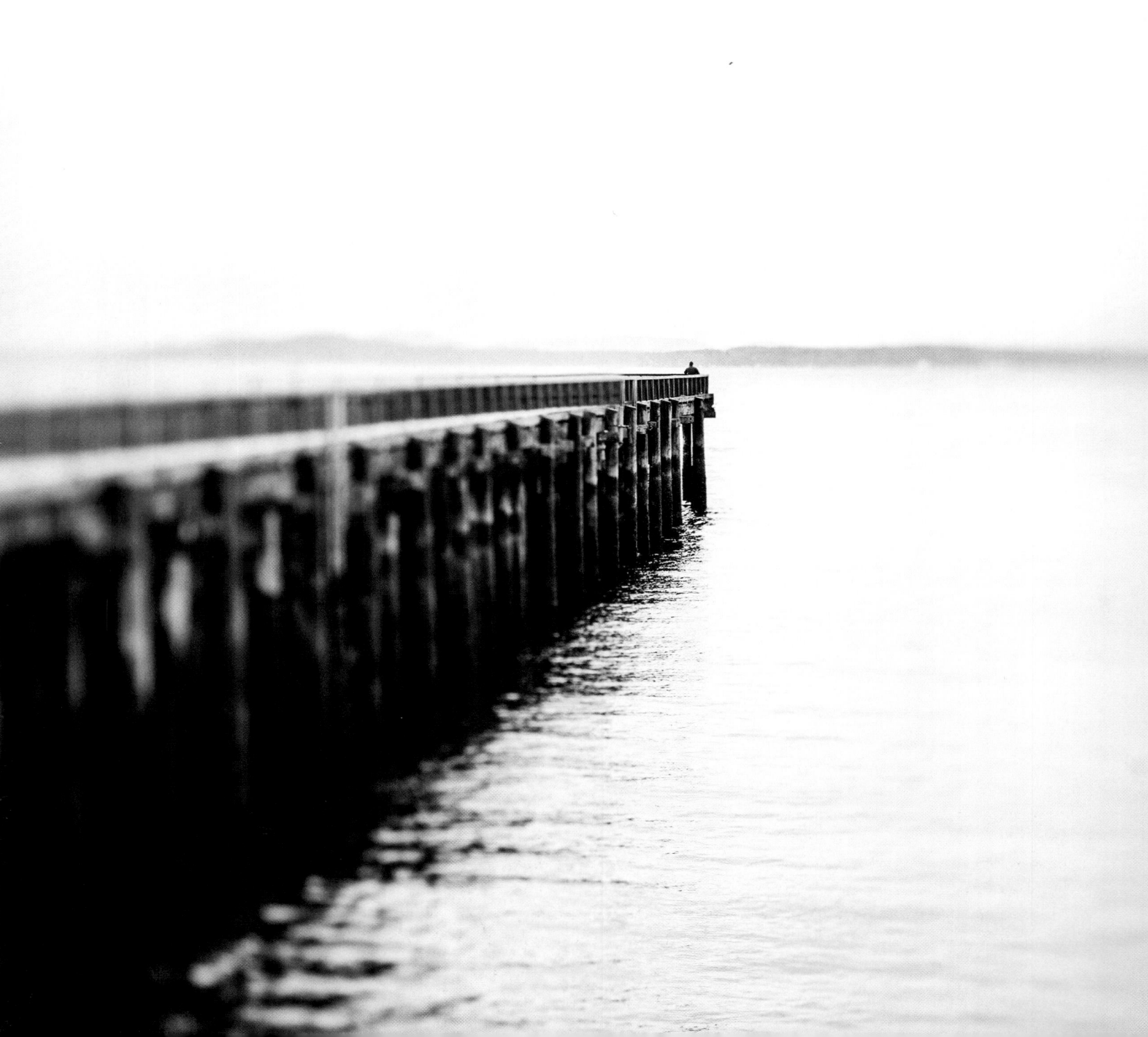

CHAPTER ELEVEN

THE VOW

In 1964, Donald Rusk Currey accidentally killed the oldest living tree. He didn't realize it until he started counting its rings—over 4900 of them. Imagine the numb shock and sadness as he discovered what he had done. Was it on ring number 3857 that the truth set in? This was a mistake that couldn't be undone. The dead tree was lying on the ground. Fortunately, neglecting our own creativity isn't like taking an axe to a tree. Most people abandon the creativity of their youth because they are afraid—afraid that what they create isn't very good. And that this might mean they aren't any good either. But the creative spark can't die, even when we turn our back on it for years—the creative life force is much more powerful than that. It's been alive since the beginning of time, and with some effort it can be rekindled.

THE SONGLESS MAN The older we get, the more we tie our identity to what we can and cannot do, and the louder the self-critical voices in our heads. Nothing stops the creative flow quicker than a few critical words—which is what happened to my friend Jeff. He was a creative and talented young kid. He was fearless and brave, and like most kids he loved to sing. That was, until his voice started to change. The laughter and ridicule from his peers stung. Embarrassed and hurt, he vowed, "I will never sing in front of another human again." The singing stopped.

For 42 years, Jeff kept his vow. Then one evening Jeff went to a friend's for dinner. The gathering took place on a backyard deck perched above a small canyon and surrounded by gigantic trees. The sun had set and the candles glowed. Before we sat down to eat, our host (who is a bit of a free spirit) invited us to sing a traditional Thanksgiving song. She sang first and then we all joined in. We then sat down to homemade soup and fresh-baked bread.

As we broke the bread, Jeff told us that it was the first time he had sung in a very long time. With glassy eyes, he told us about the vow. We quietly listened. What an honor to witness such risk. Jeff's face glowed. He was free.

IMAGINE FINALLY BEING ABLE TO SING Jeff's risk made me want to take my own. Creative risks are always contagious in that way. Even now, it makes me want to slam my fist on the table and say, "Enough!" It's time for me to proclaim my own vow: "I will be who I am, come what may!" We all wrongly hold ourselves back without even really knowing what we've done. It's not until we count the tree rings that we realize how much life has been taken away. Life has never been about singing with perfect pitch. It's always better to sing off key than to quietly hold ourselves back. Authenticity trumps perfection every time. Perfection may impress, but rarely does it truly shine.

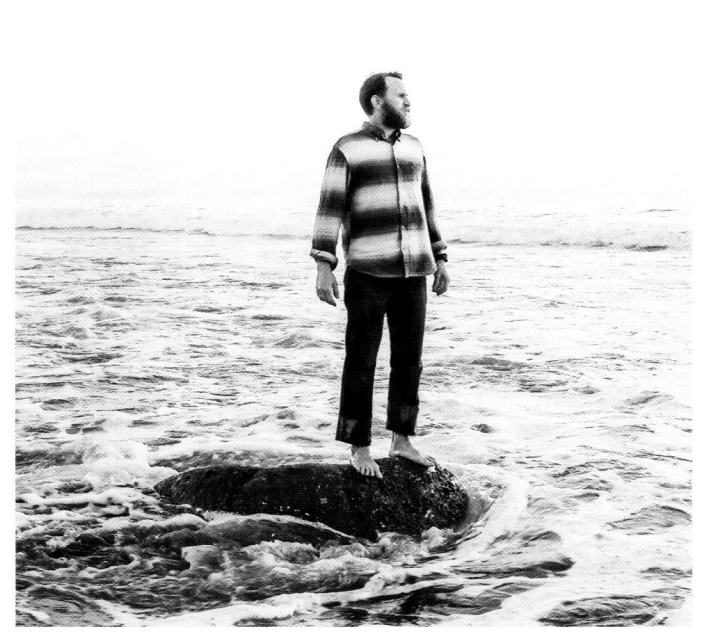

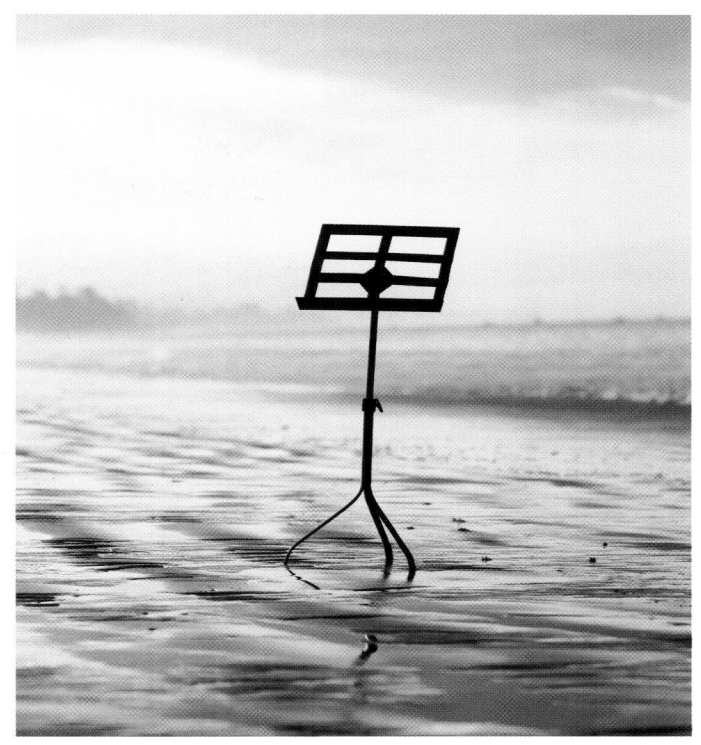

EXERCISE

STEP 1

Life can knock us over. People can be cruel and mean. And so we all have secret vows that we made. Some positive: "I will be smarter next time." And others negative: "I will never try that again." Negative vows siphon and steal our creative juice. Take a moment to think about your own life and vows. If you unearth a negative vow, talk it over with a friend so that it stops holding you back.

STEP 2

Creative risks keep you nimble, flexible, and young. Take a risk this week just for the sake of being alive. Rekindle your creativity by singing a song, writing a poem, painting a picture, or doing something completely off the wall. Be bold and have fun. Embrace the wild that races through your heart. Do something pure and true without posting it on social media or sharing it with friends. Do something without any strings attached.

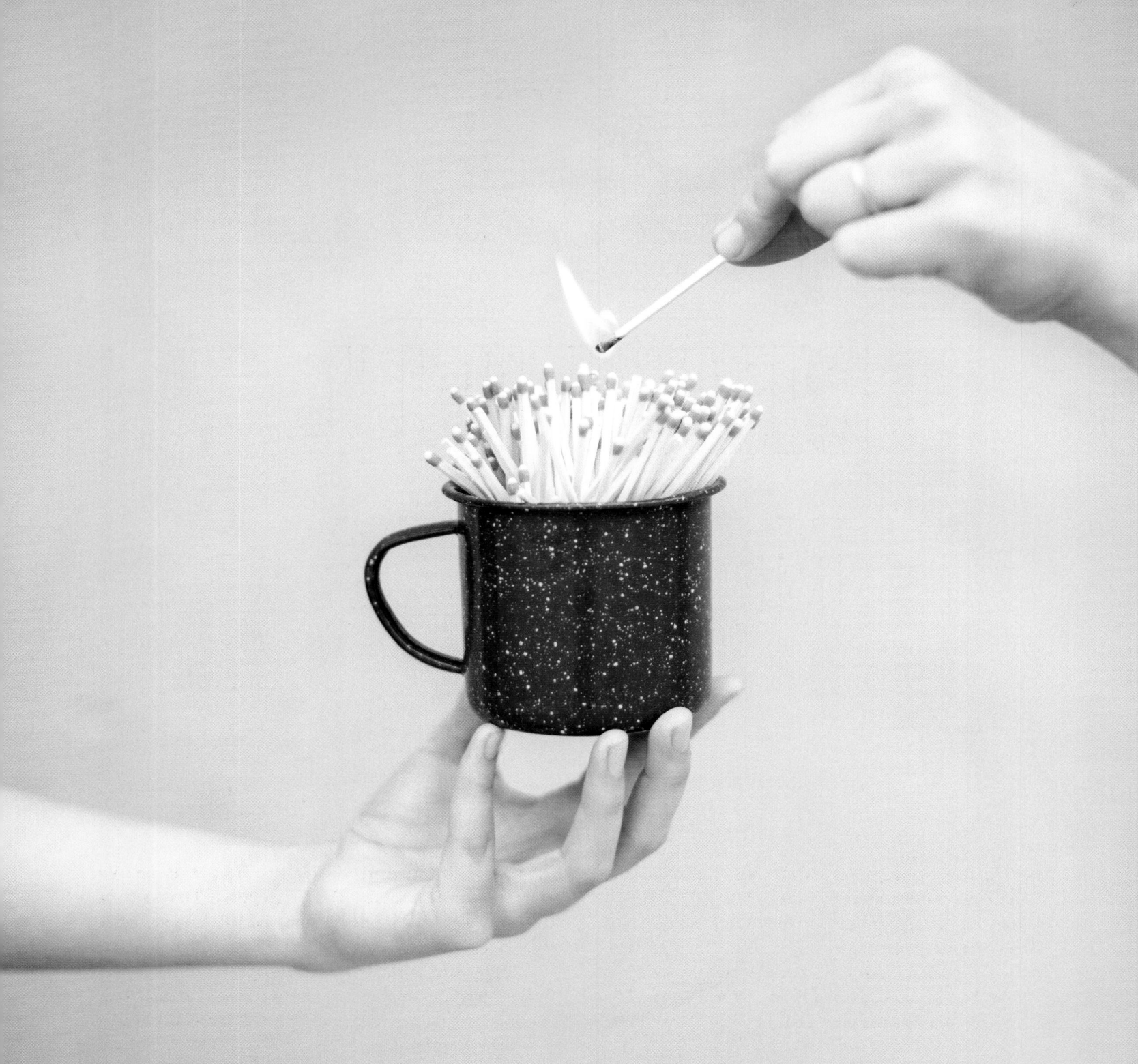

CHAPTER TWELVE

BEAUTIFUL MISTAKES

It was a frigid winter night when Yo-Yo Ma almost dropped his 2.5-million-dollar instrument on the floor.

The sold-out theater was buzzing with excitement. A single wooden chair sat in the center of the stage. The audience hushed and then broke into applause as Yo-Yo Ma appeared. The concert began, and in the middle of a difficult song, Ma's cello suddenly slipped, and then again. On the third slip, it really started to fall. Abruptly, Ma stopped and reached out to catch his 1773 Stradivarius before it hit the floor. The audience gasped. Everyone held their breath. Ma gave a sigh of relief and gracefully pulled the cello back into position. Then he pointed at the cello and wagged his finger as if to scold her mischievous act. The audience erupted into laughter. Ma smiled, straightened himself out, and continued to play.

THE PITFALLS OF PERFECTIONISM The way Yo-Yo Ma handled himself made that blunder become beautiful. He transformed an error into an act of grace. It changed the concert into a community event. After the recovery from the mistake, everyone in the audience was on his side. Yo-Yo Ma was no longer one of the world's top performers, he was a friend. The way he handled his error made us feel safe. To this day, that was one of most powerful and creative musical moments I've experienced in my life.

It was a simple act, embracing the mistake, but it was profound. Who does that? When I make a mistake in front of others, my face becomes flush and I get stressed. Yo-Yo Ma was the epitome of calm. Yet he wasn't just a Zen master who fluidly handled a problem; he was a creative genius who brought out harmony from discord. To do such a thing, it helps to have a deep sense of identity and a vision for a higher goal. Yo-Yo Ma had both. In one interview he said, "You don't play music for perfection. The point of music is to make someone feel." His performance did just that. Embracing that blunder, rather than trying to cover it up, brought warmth into that chilly room.

Perfectionism is made up of two parts: a drive for greatness, and fear. It's the fear and the shame, blame, and judgment that overwhelm. Mix those ingredients together and they become a bitter drink. Perfectionism poisons creativity. Some perfectionists never try to create because they are afraid of being wrong. But being creative requires that we let go of fear, get out of our comfort zone, and make mistakes. As the cliché goes, "Mistakes are proof that you are trying." Yet mistakes can also be proof that you haven't practiced very hard. Making mistakes is never enough.

I walked into one of my client's offices and saw a huge poster that said "Make Mistakes. Make Mistakes. Make Mistakes." At first glance I thought, "that's great." Then I stopped and thought some more. As I stood there I noticed that the poster was hanging in the finance department above the cubicle that belonged to the head of payroll. Instantly, I remembered that a number of my paychecks from this company had been wrong. Suddenly, the message on that poster didn't seem like such a good idea. Making financial mistakes isn't where creative genius is born.

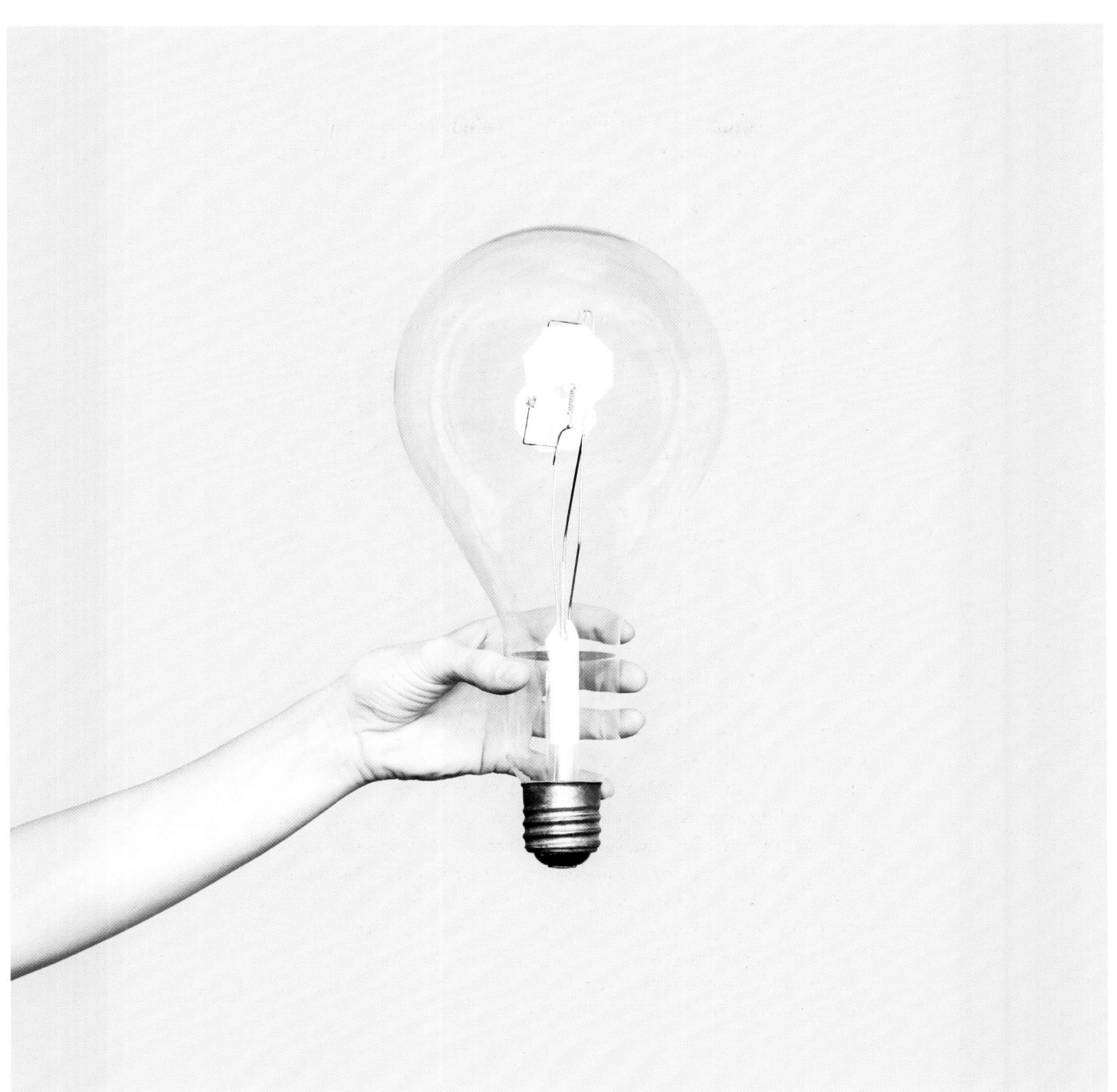

CREATIVE GROWTH Although making mistakes is part of the creative process, it is never the goal. When Edison set out to invent the lightbulb, he desperately wanted to create one that worked. His team made countless mistakes and tested over 6000 types of filaments in trying to find something that would burn bright without going out. In our own drive to succeed, mistakes are inevitable. Yet fewer mistakes are better than more.

If the end game is creative growth, one of the quickest ways to get through mistakes is to have a higher goal. Sustained light is what drove Edison and his team to try so many different types of filament substances—everything from wood shavings to a hair from his employee's beard! It wasn't until after a year of mistakes that carbonized bamboo emerged as the best source.

And Yo-Yo Ma was driven not just to hit the perfect note, but to make people feel. As a result, he was driven to perfection and practiced harder than anyone else. His goal of creating music that resonated in a deep and emotional way gave him drive. When onstage, Yo-Yo Ma considers himself this way: "I'm the host of a wonderful party. You're all my guests." His higher goal changed the whole scene.

So how does this relate to you and me? First, if you have a poster hanging up in your room that says "Make Mistakes. Make Mistakes. Make Mistakes," go ahead and tear it down. Or better yet, just cross out the word *Make* three times. Then replace those crossed-out words with "Accept, Embrace, Transform." When we do that, it opens up the opportunity to learn, to connect with others, and to move ahead. Finally, follow master photographer Ansel Adams's advice: "Strive for perfection. Settle for excellence."

A LIFE SPENT MAKING MISTAKES IS NOT ONLY MORE HONORABLE, BUT MORE USEFUL THAN A LIFE SPENT DOING NOTHING.
—GEORGE BERNARD SHAW

EXERCISE

STEP 1

"Mistakes aren't the problem, it's what we do with them that counts," as Evan Chong once said.
In an effort to handle mistakes with more ease, let's follow Yo-Yo Ma's lead. When Ma
plays a concert, he has a vision for a higher goal. His goal is to connect and to make people feel.

In your own life, think about one area of your personal or professional life that can be compared to a
stage. Think of something that you do when you have to deliver and you have to perform.
Next, write down the task and then try to think up a higher goal. Come up with a few goals and
select the one that fits. In moments of emergency (that is, when you make a mistake), think back to
this goal so that you can handle that mistake with more grace and ease.

STEP 2

Come up with three people you respect who handle mistakes with exemplary ease.
Write down their names followed by a few words that reveal what they do well. Use
these ideas as inspiration for your own growth.

1. ....

....

....

2. ....

....

....

3. ....

....

....

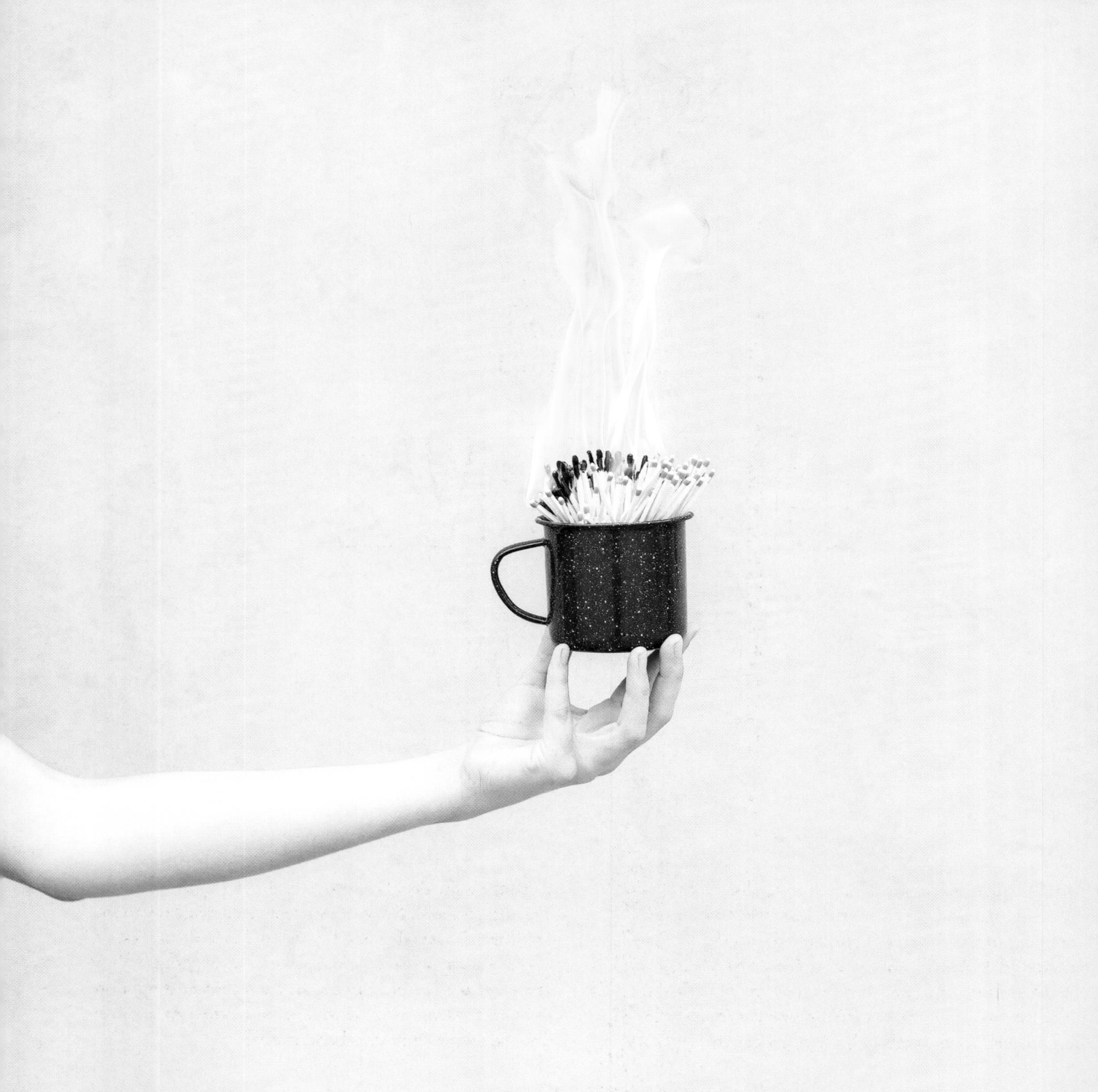

CHAPTER THIRTEEN

THE CREATIVE FLOW

Getting a part-time teaching job at a world-class photography school was a dream come true. I couldn't have imagined a better career shift. So I threw myself into the work and followed W. B. Yeats's advice, "Education isn't filling a pail, but the lighting of a fire." For twelve years my job was to ignite, empower, and help aspiring photographers achieve their dreams. Yet the path to becoming a photographer isn't easy, so the difficulty of my classes and our program reflected the challenge ahead. Not every student graduated; fewer went on to thrive. Those who found success did so in an impressive way—it was the world of sink or swim. Throughout it all, I was always keen to pick up on the clues that shed light on why some students excelled while others failed. After a few years, the telltale indicators became clear.

WHY STUDENTS SUCCEED I quickly discovered that the successful students were a tenacious and driven bunch. They were voraciously creative and surprisingly well composed, even in the face of great challenge. No matter what you threw at them, they wouldn't flinch. When a student stumbled and fell, she picked herself up and tried again.

Two of the most telling signs of a student's potential were how much effort they put in and how they handled critique. After finishing an assignment, the student presented it to the teacher and class for evaluation and review. Regardless of the quality of the work, it is always nerve-racking to have your work evaluated in front of a group. The students who eventually went on to thrive had nerves of steel. This gave them the ability to hear and receive the feedback without being crushed. The best students took it all with a grain of salt but always listened so that they could improve. The worst students were defensive, gave excuses, or just ignored the advice. I came to learn a lot about my students and myself during those times of critique. The most important lesson I learned came as a complete surprise.

CRITIQUE AND THE BOOMERANG EFFECT The value in critiquing someone else's work is that it makes you think about your own. One day as I evaluated some stellar upper-division student work, it struck me that their photographs were better than my own. Yet how could this be? After all, I was a successful commercial photographer and I had written two best-selling photography books. But truth be told, my current work wasn't up to par, and in photography you can't rest on the success of your past. Somewhere along the way I had stopped practicing what I preached, and it was as if I had become like the proverbial cobbler whose kids didn't have any shoes. I had become a cliché. It was time to make a change. I had been thinking about leaving my teaching post for a few years, and this particular realization gave me the final nudge.

The ivory tower is a comfortable place, but it is isolating as well. So I traded in my professorial robes for street clothes. I left the benefits and comforts of the job in order to refine my craft and strengthen my core. Rather than critiquing others, I needed to get some critique myself. So I signed up for a workshop in New York and showed up like an eager new student on the first day of school. The workshop was a wealth of learning opportunities—lectures, conversations, capturing photographs, and portfolio reviews. Eventually, it was my turn to present a portfolio of my work. I was on the chopping block and I was scared.

CONFRONTING FEAR Neurologists tell us that when we are afraid, the area of our brain called the amygdala lights up. The amygdala is known as the primitive or prehistoric part of the brain. It controls our fight or flight response and is often referred to as the "lizard brain," because it's the part of the brain that is reactive and focused on core survival needs. Thought leader Seth Godin describes the lizard brain as horny, hungry, and scared. As Godin explains, it's this part of the brain that's responsible for fear, anger, and sex, and it cares what everyone else thinks. The lizard brain regulates fear and is often to blame for our resistance to risk-taking. For us photographers, it's the lizard brain that prevents us from having courage to show and to create our best work.

As I opened up my box of portfolio prints, my amygdala was flashing red. I felt like a lizard who wanted to run and hide. The workshop instructor started to review and critique my work. I braced myself. He said, "When I look at these photographs I think, 'This photographer is good,' but then at second glance, maybe not. You have a great connection with your subjects in these portraits. I can tell you are committed to the subject... but you aren't committed to the frame. By neglecting the frame, you are letting your subject down." These words burned, but at the same time brought relief.

The workshop instructor was a friend and mentor who I know had my best interests in mind. And he had pinpointed my Achilles heel. It took him just a moment to find the flaw that I knew was there but didn't know how to describe. In essence, his critique pointed out a need to refine my composition skills. And he was right, I wasn't using the frame very

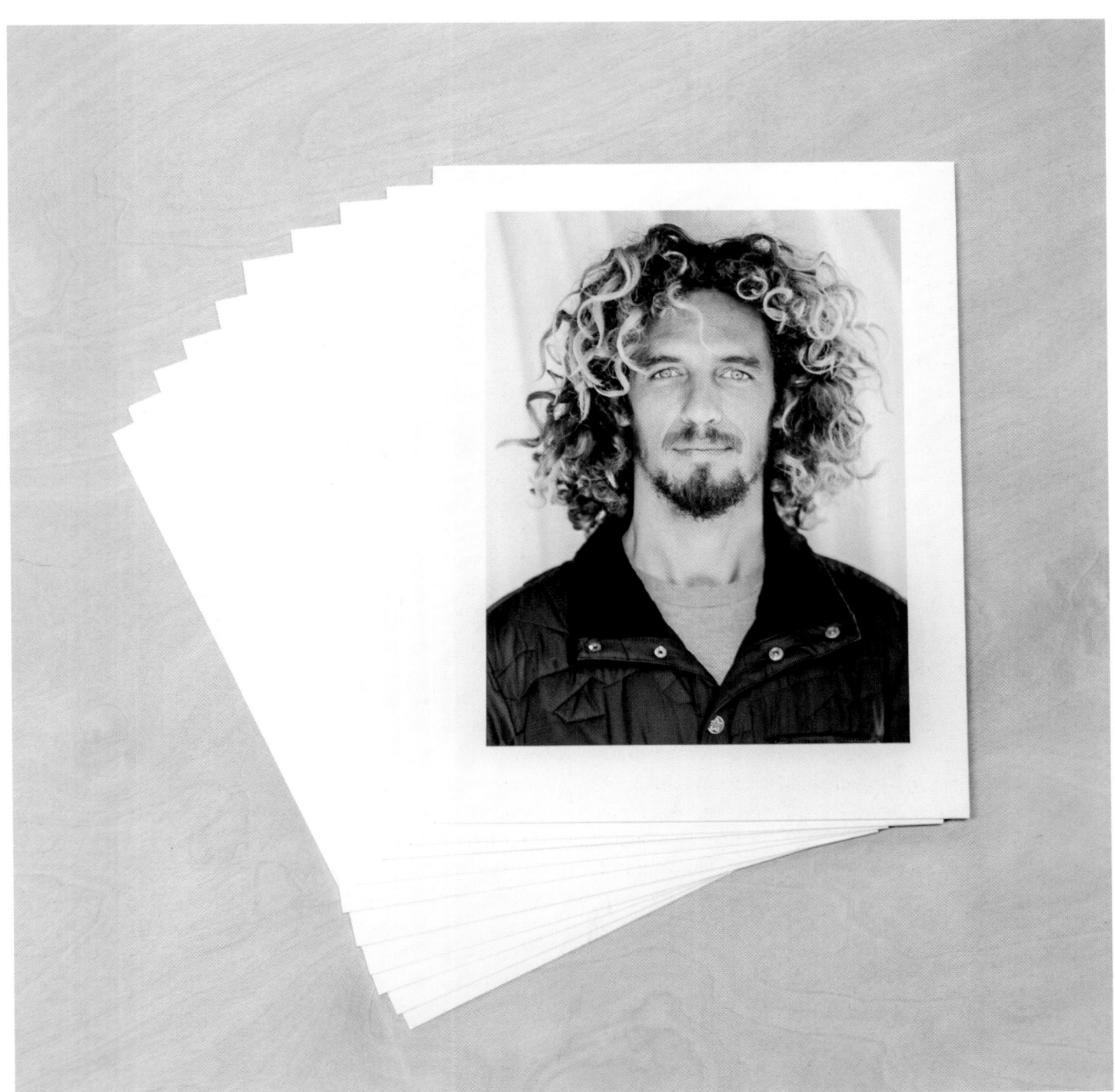

> # TO BE YOURSELF IN A WORLD THAT IS CONSTANTLY TRYING TO MAKE YOU SOMETHING ELSE IS THE GREATEST ACCOMPLISHMENT.
>
> **—RALPH WALDO EMERSON**

well. Yet in the moment, I felt small, like a small lizard sitting on a rock as a predator soared above. I wasn't sure if I should bask in the sun or run and hide. Then as the critique progressed, the predator attacked and grabbed ahold of my tail.

When caught by its tail, a lizard has the ability to detach so it can escape. The scientific name for this defensive skill is "autonomy." Autonomy is what got me into this mess and I needed to find a new strategy to get me out. After all, I was a self-taught photographer who had come a long way. I was a self-made man and a teacher who stood apart from the crowd. Yet there was my flaw, as greatness rarely shines without the help of someone else.

I thought back to my top-performing students and their unwillingness to give up. These students were open to criticism and constantly sought outside help. It was my turn to follow their lead. The workshop was a good first step, but still I was desperate to find a new paradigm for understanding my identity, work, and life.

IDENTITY AND CREATIVE FLOW A few months later, I found some wisdom from an unlikely source while talking with surf legend Kelly Slater. Over dinner we chatted about photography, identity, and life. While Slater may be the quintessential example of cool, in person he is truly a humble and down-to-earth guy. At one point he said, "Chris, I'm embarrassed to admit that for much of my life I didn't realize the difference between the idea of Kelly Slater and the person of Kelly Slater. And because of that I made a lot of mistakes."

Hearing Slater talk about his struggles shed some light on my own. I realized that I had confused the idea of Chris Orwig with a more authentic version of myself. It hit me that the effort of trying to maintain this act was keeping me from contributing in the greatest way possible. It was like discovering that I had been driving around in my car with the emergency brake on. Once released, I was free to be true to myself, and my creativity began to flow in a powerful and unprecedented way.

Creativity always flows the fastest when we are the honest and authentic versions of ourselves. Trying to be someone else will only restrict and impede. Letting go of that begins with a realization that you are 100% unique, and that the more uniqueness in your work, the better it will be.

To begin the process of becoming true to ourselves, it helps to answer a few questions about your life: What makes you unique? What makes you come alive? What dreams and ideas course through your veins?

When asked if writing was hard, Ernest Hemingway replied, "There is nothing to writing. All you do is sit down at a typewriter and bleed." When you read one of his books you can feel the lifeblood in his words. We need more of this in whatever work it is that we do. There is a creative spark hidden deep within the cellular level of your true self. Your job is to find that source and let it flow.

EXERCISE

STEP 1

Get out a journal and take a few minutes to write out answers to the following questions:
What makes you unique? What makes you come alive? What courses through your veins?

STEP 2

Like a fish trying to describe water, sometimes it is difficult to identify our own strengths.
So find a friend, colleague, or mentor and ask them to help. Ask for their insight into what makes
you unique. Ask for their opinion of what strengths set you apart from the crowd.

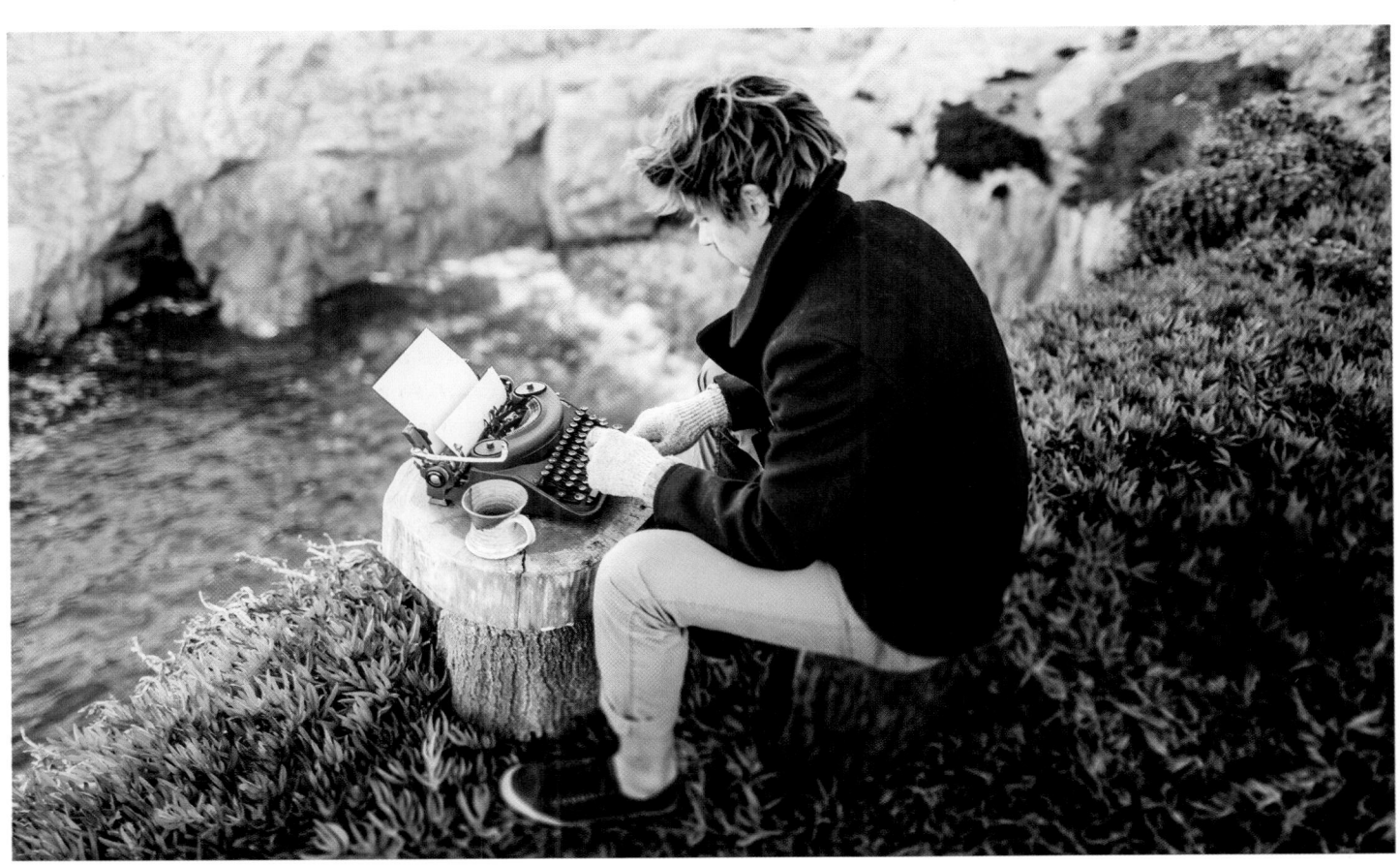

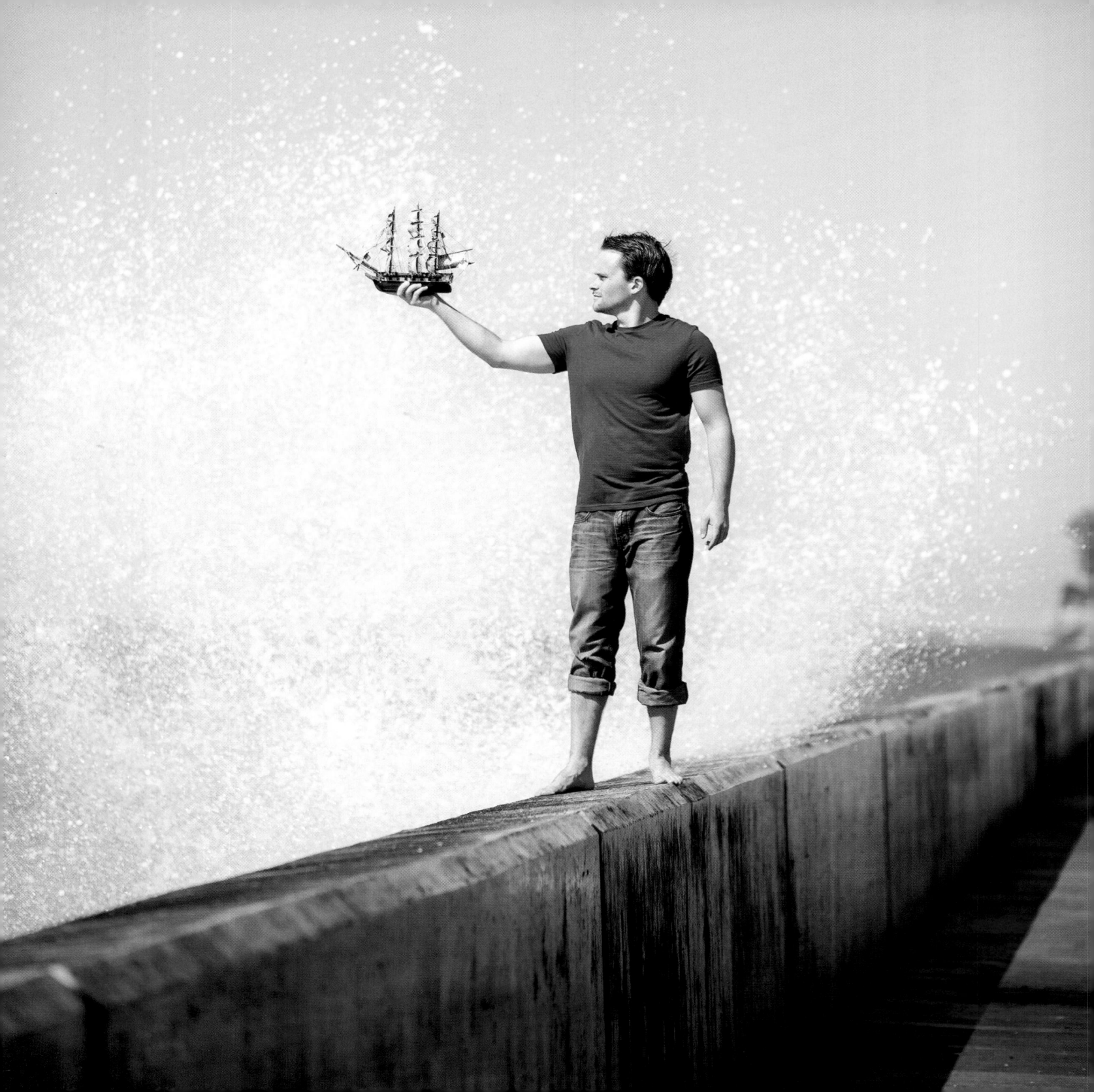

CHAPTER FOURTEEN

SURVIVAL

When it comes to survival, Laurence Gonzales can shed some light. Gonzales is an adventurer and scientist who has been studying the art of survival for over 35 years. In his book *Deep Survival* he seeks to answer the question of why some people survive catastrophe and others die. He writes, "When confronted with a life-threatening situation, 90% of people freeze or panic, while the remaining 10% stay cool, focused, and alive." Recounted in numerous examples, one of the main differences between life and death is the ability to get the amygdala (discussed in the previous chapter) to calm down. Panic is a very uncreative response. When we panic we make mistakes. To survive, we need a more flexible, mindful, and creative approach. And this is true whether we're trying to outsmart a storm or raise kids.

THE UNCREATIVE PARENT When my daughter Annika was little, Fridays were our day to read books, play with puzzles, wrestle, and work on the house. We lived in an 80-year-old home that needed some work. Annika was my helper, and we would putter around the house and fix things. Often I would take her to Home Depot to get supplies. She would sit in the shopping cart as we traveled up and down the aisles. One Friday, I was in a hurry and Annika was in a foul mood. Her fussing and complaining were like the incessant screech of an alarm. Finally, in exhaustion I yelled at her to shut up. As I said those words, a wave of shame and regret flooded my heart. Annika's little lower lip started to quiver as she looked at me with those big blue eyes and began to cry. A passerby who witnessed the exchange looked at me with utter disdain.

Why would I do such a thing? I was tangled up in frustration, so I panicked and acted in a way that isn't congruent with who I am. And my daughter wasn't feeling well, but I was too self-focused to realize her needs. I care more about her than anything in the world, so why did I respond in such an uncreative way? When we are distressed, the amygdala flashes red. Learning how to control your response can be the difference between life and death. Or in my case, the difference between being a loving father and a cruel stooge.

Anyone can act like a lizard and detach their tail and run, but it's a sign of weakness and of being overly self-absorbed. Responding creatively takes self-awareness and strength. Panic is reactive, whereas creativity remains calm. Panic sees limits; creativity sees open doors. Panic shuts the book; creativity flips to the next page. Panic quits; creativity finds a way. Creative parents read books and take classes in order to learn how to respond to their children in loving ways; uncreative parents blow up. Creative parents learn that loving your kids means that you have to adapt.

ADAPTATION According to Gonzales, survivors stay calm and learn to adapt. Even if the glass is half empty, they force themselves to see it as full. Survivors don't belittle their plight but also can't afford to complain. So they modify their view

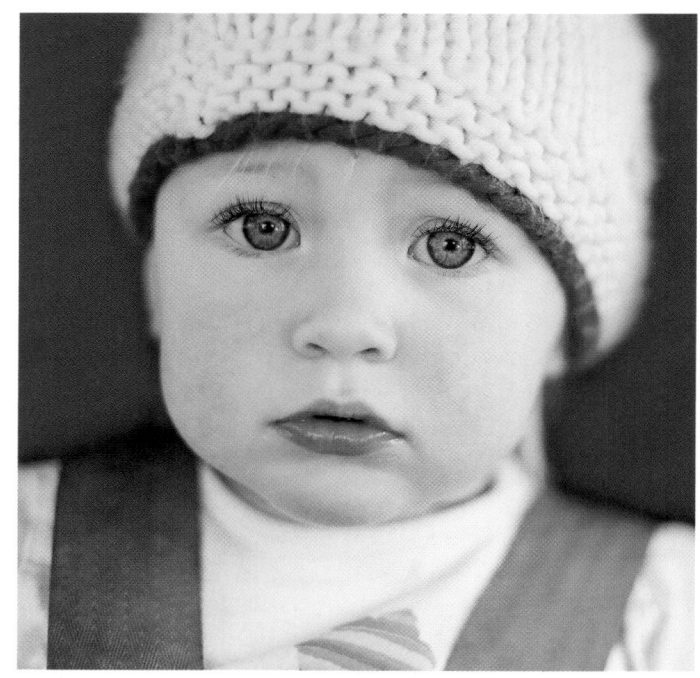

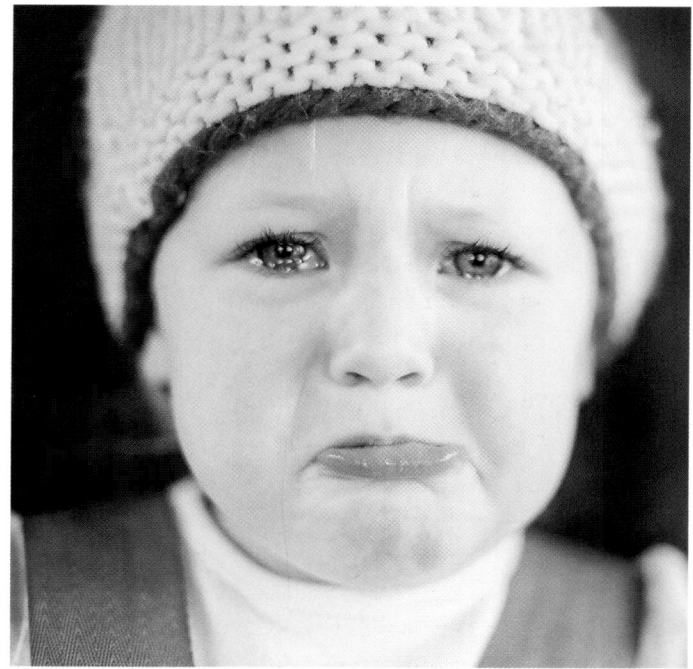

to make the most of what they have. I've always thought of this type of adaptation as one of creativity's close friends. In the parenting class that I signed up for after the "Home Depot event," the instructor gave a lesson on the importance of learning to adapt. In one segment he explained that parenting requires an adaptation to how we understand time. With kids in tow, life takes more time. The stress comes from thinking it won't. According to dictionary.com, the word *adapt* means to "Modify, alter, change, adjust, readjust, convert, redesign, restyle, refashion, remodel, reshape, revamp, rework, rejig, redo, reconstruct, and reorganize." Those are all very creative words. Adaptation is the opposite of being rigid and closed.

Creative adaptation implies change. Sometimes we adapt because of plenty, and others times because of want. Chuck Close's life was dramatically changed when he was 48. After years of acclaim as a painter and photographer, he experienced a catastrophic spinal artery collapse that left him severely paralyzed. After extensive physical therapy, he regained the partial use of his limbs. Now a quadriplegic and confined to a wheelchair, Close still makes art and he thrives. When asked about whether he envies people who can walk, he replied, "Quadriplegics don't envy people who can walk. We envy paraplegics. We think they have a much easier lot." As a quadriplegic, Close has an attitude and approach to life that inspires. As an artist, he made an art out of making art, regardless of the limits he has. After the incident, Close quickly adapted his approach painting by strapping a brush to his arm. And he uses a mechanical device that raises, lowers, and rotates his large-scale canvases so he can access the entire frame.

ROCK-FILLED SHOES Before the paralysis, Close was considered one of the top artists of his time. Now, almost 30 years later, his reputation endures. His work before and after the incident is equally profound. When asked about his paralysis, Close is dismissive and doesn't like to draw attention to himself. He explains, "I don't like to be seen as a hero. I have a few rocks in my shoes, but I paint just as before." When tragedy struck and in the ensuing years, Close remained calm. He

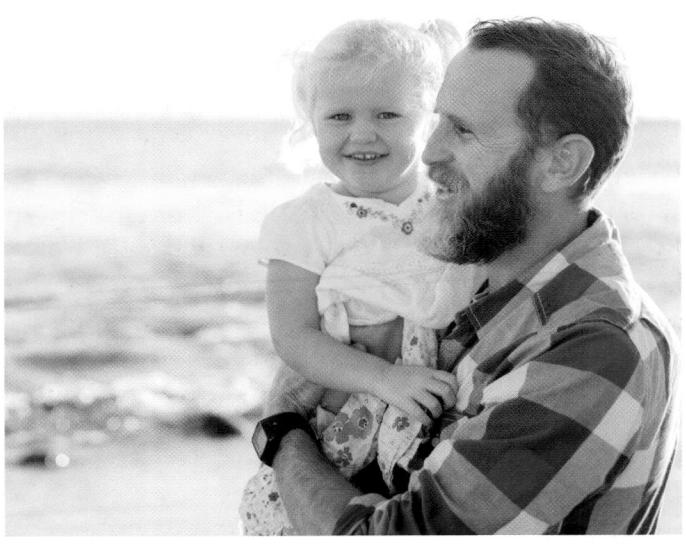

found a way around his limits, and he attributes his success to good luck: "I was just very lucky that I was successful and I had the money to make the changes to get back to work. I've always been very lucky. People say, 'How can you call yourself lucky when you are stuck in a wheelchair and can't use your hands?' You know, the last 18 years have been the best years of my life. I'm back doing what I want to do. I'm able to support my wife and children. I do what I want to do and get paid to do it."

When we see life through a different lens, it changes how we see. Chuck Close sees his life through the lens of good luck and gratitude. This has not only changed what he sees but empowered him to contribute in a more significant way. That's exactly what the most creative people in the world do. Whether artists, parents, or _____ , they don't settle for the kit lens that came with their gear. They realize that how we see is a creative choice. So they search until they find the lens that gives them a view of the world that frees them to create their best work and contribute in the greatest way.

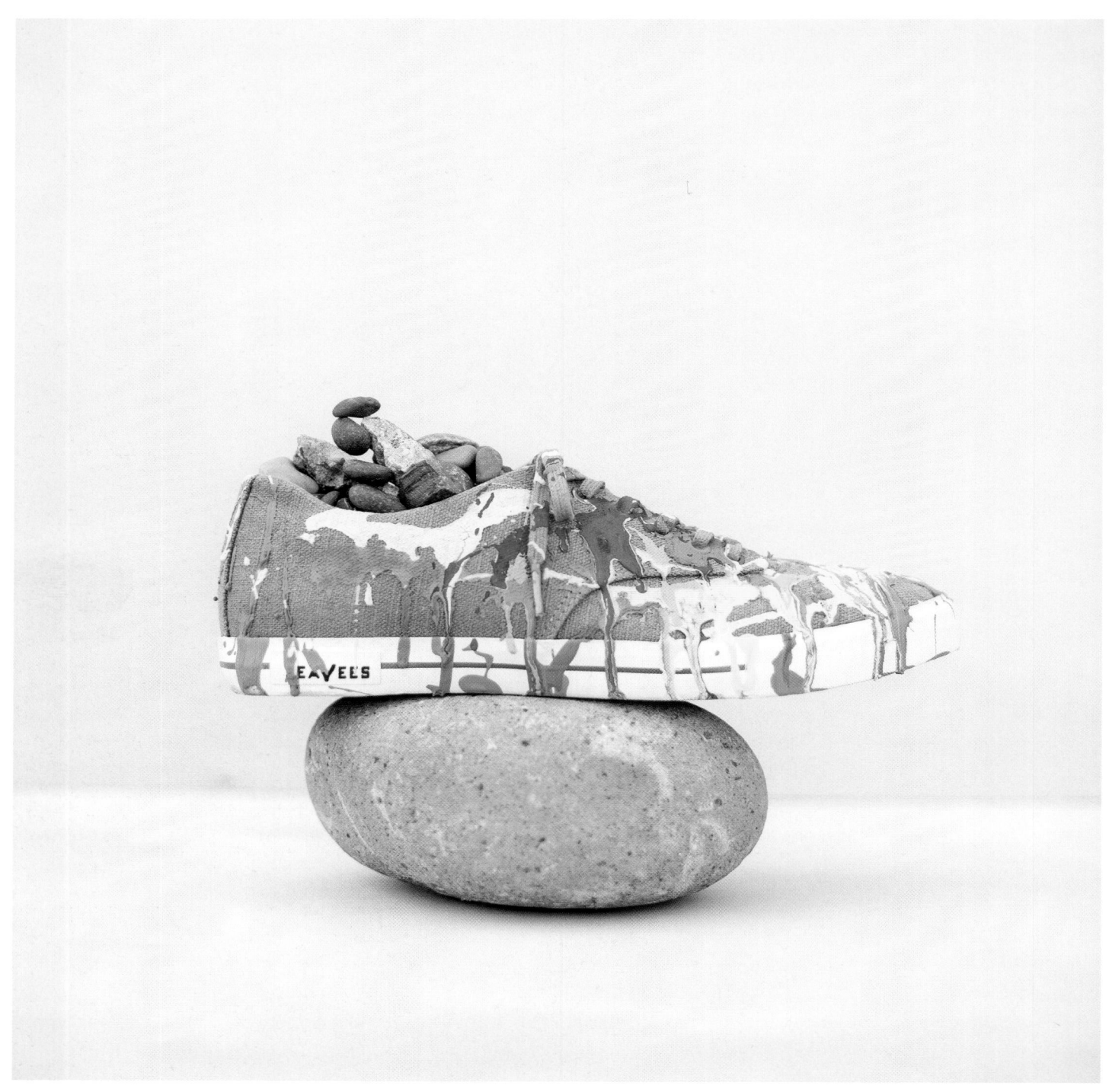

EXERCISE

STEP 1
Identify three problems you are facing right now. List them below.

1. ....

....

2. ....

....

3. ....

....

STEP 2
For each problem, provide new adaptive and alternative ways to view and deal with the situation.
Begin with your mind-set, and finish with a practical step you can take to move ahead.

....

....

....

....

....

....

....

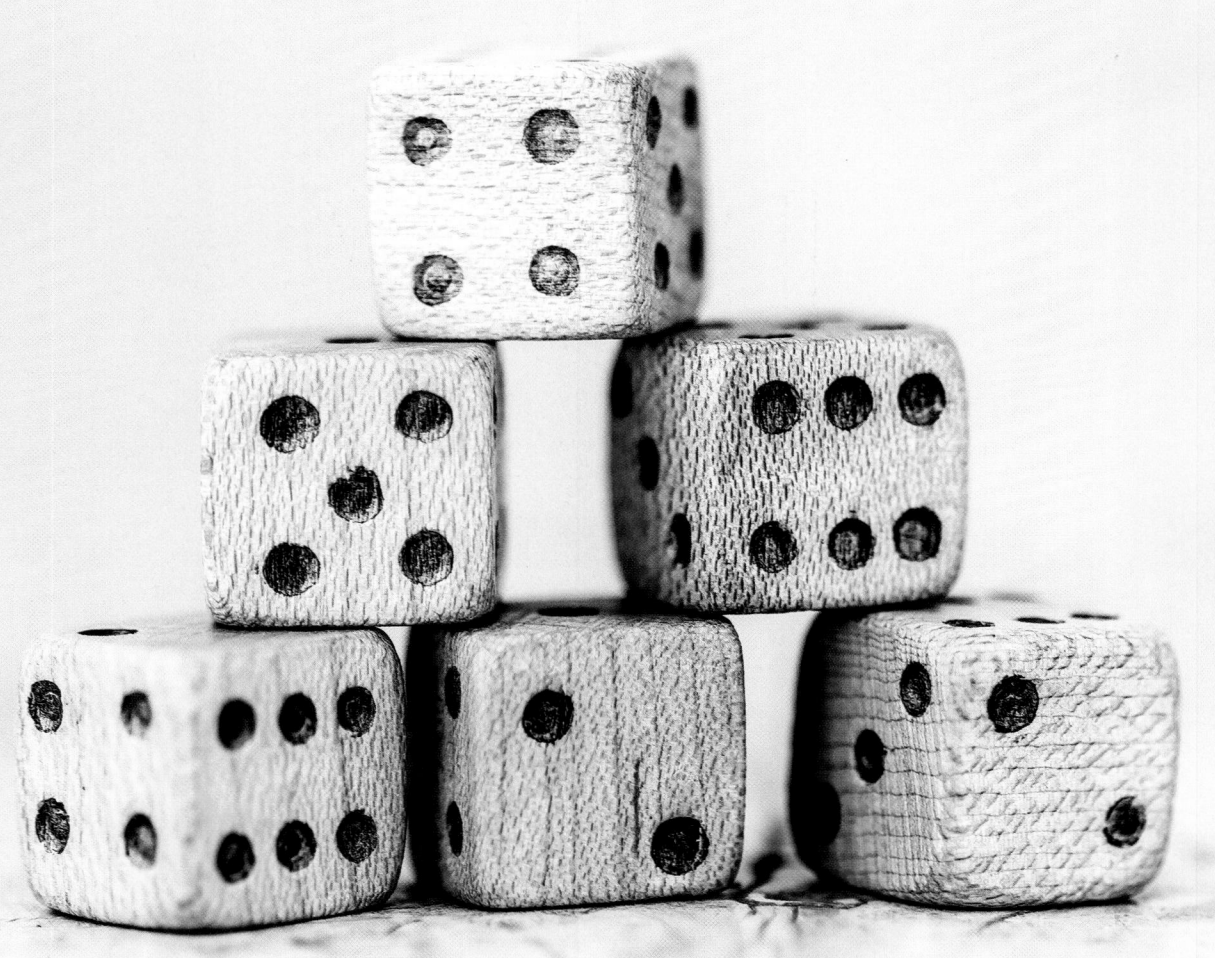

CHAPTER FIFTEEN

LUCKY YOU

What if luck has less to do with chance and more to do with how you live? In his international best-selling book *The Alchemist*, Paulo Coelho crafts an allegorical narrative around this idea. The main character in the story, a young man named Santiago, works as a shepherd until he has a dream that awakens him to a deeper calling for his life. Fear holds him back from responding to the call, but the dream persists.

Eventually, Santiago musters up the courage to follow the path for which he was meant (called his "personal legend" in the book). Leaving his comfortable life behind, he journeys into the unknown and is invigorated with the possibility of this new path. Following his path, or personal legend, seems to have some generative power, almost like a gift that fills him with strength, enthusiasm, and good luck.

WHAT IS YOUR LEGEND? In an interview about the book, Coelho explains that one's personal legend is the path you were designed to take. Following this path invigorates life. According to Coelho, those who ignore their personal legend suffer regret and experience unnecessary pain. The ones who pay attention and respond discover that when you are on the right path, "The universe conspires to help." With the advantages of the universe's help, Santiago accomplishes his journey, and in a metaphorical sense he becomes lucky, as metal turns to gold.

The Alchemist is a beautifully written story that is beloved by many (over 65 million copies have been sold). It is one of those allegorical tales that you want to believe. And within the context of a novel, the themes, ideals, and logic work. But what about in real life? Does following your life's call have some hidden alchemical properties that transform?

Finding your life's call isn't an easy task, so many quit before they try. Rather than give up so easily, start the search by following Howard Thurman's advice: "Don't ask yourself what the world needs. Ask yourself what makes you come alive, and then go do that. Because what the world needs is people who have come alive." We are all designed to be and do certain things, and when we discover our own personal legend, it ignites our lives. Almost like combustion, this spark gives us strength to accomplish great things. As Ralph Waldo Emerson put it, "Enthusiasm is one of the most powerful engines of success."

NOTHING GREAT WAS EVER ACHIEVED WITHOUT ENTHUSIASM.
—RALPH WALDO EMERSON

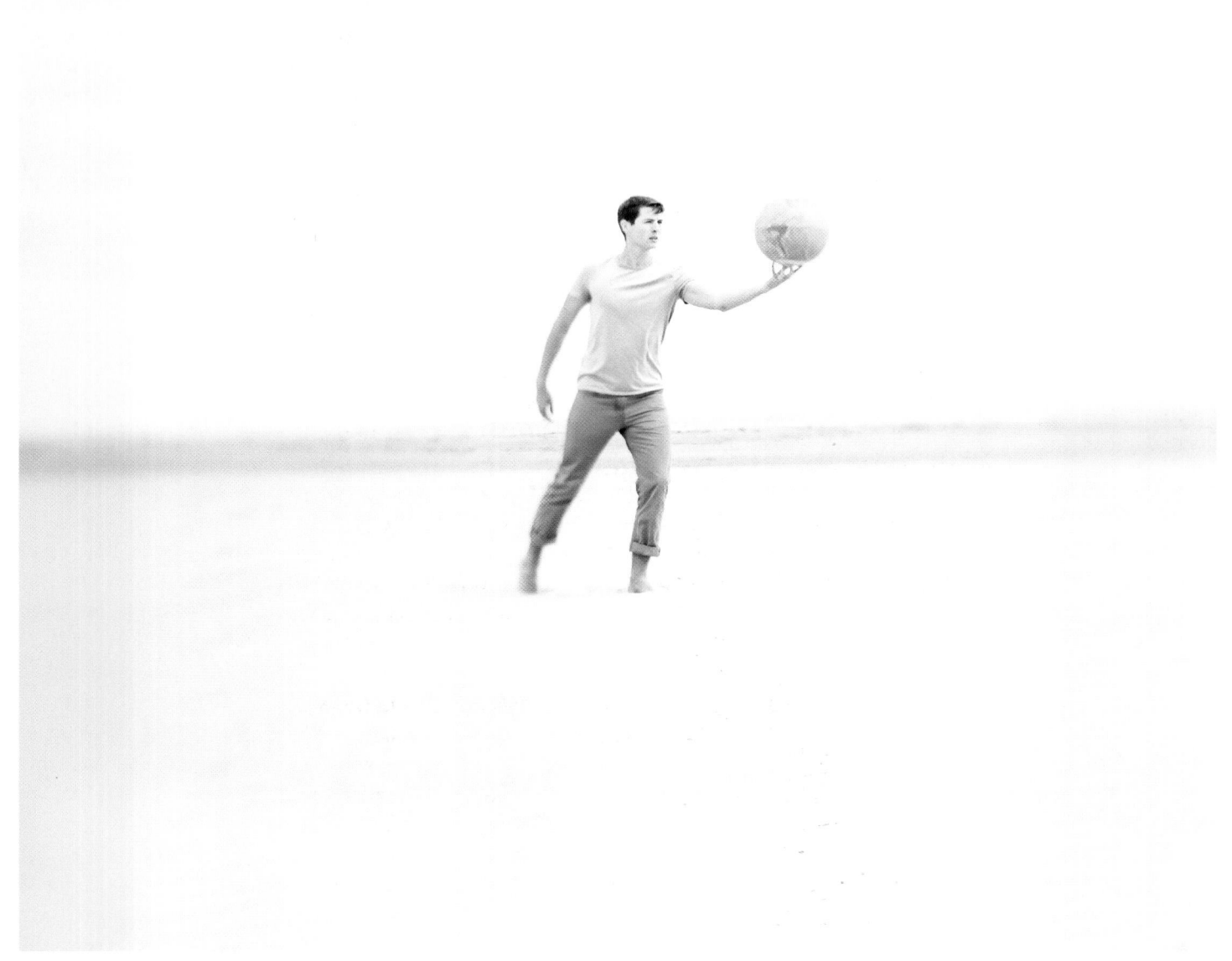

WELLSPRING OF ENERGY Enthusiasm is raw energy for life. The word enthusiasm comes from the Greek *entheos*, meaning "having god within" or "inspired." And this inspiration is a powerful force. When enthusiasm strikes, it renews strength, fortifies resolve, and revives lost dreams. And true enthusiasm isn't something that can be copied or faked. It happens spontaneously when we are on the right path.

Ken Robinson is one of the most enthusiastic and creative people I have ever met. Robinson is an author, TED fellow, and thought leader who is on a crusade to change the way we educate our kids. His passions run deep, and his own story goes back to an early experience in life. When he was just four years old, polio struck and changed the course of his life. Dealing with this difficult experience in his youth fostered in him a lifelong passion to help other kids. Today Robinson still wears leg braces and special shoes that help him stand and walk. Yet all of that disappears when you hear him talk. He champions the idea that "When people are most energized, they are more likely to create their best work." When you watch Robinson in his TED talk or speak to him in person, his energy and enthusiasm are contagious. And as you listen to him speak, you quickly get the sense that in spite of his own difficulties, he feels lucky to be doing what he does.

Discovering your personal legend makes you stand out. Like a lightbulb that is plugged in, you illuminate the world. Ken Robinson shines bright. And people like Robinson, who have discovered their personal legends, are a fortunate lot. They live with less regret. They gain access to a unique source of strength, and they seem to get all the lucky breaks. And such was the case with a young man named Harrison.

Harrison wanted to be an actor, so he left Chicago and moved west. When he arrived in Hollywood he knew he was on the right path, but it was a slow start. After months of bit parts that didn't amount to much, Harrison needed to pay rent, so he picked up work as a stagehand and took on some carpentry jobs. One day a guy named George hired him to install some cabinets in his home. George liked Harrison and invited the aspiring actor to audition for his next film. Talk about good luck; Harrison Ford won the part for George

Lucas's latest film, and his career catapulted to new heights. Anyone who has ever amounted to anything can identify with Harrison Ford's start. Without a bit of good luck, none of us would have made it very far.

ARE YOU LUCKY? Luck is such a random and mysterious thing. Or maybe not? Richard Wiseman, the head of the psychology department at the University of Hertfordshire, decided to see what he could find. Wiseman was curious to see if science could shed some light on how luck worked. So he created an experiment in which he asked volunteers to flip through a newspaper and count the photographs they saw. Certain individuals finished the task in seconds, while others took much more time. The difference had to do with luck. Yet the luck wasn't random or arbitrary but predictable and self-prescribed. Before counting the photographs, Wiseman had asked the subjects to evaluate their own luck. Their responses made all the difference in the world.

Here's how the experiment worked. The volunteers received a newspaper and instruction to count all the photographs on each page. Unknowingly to them, the newspaper was rigged. In addition to the photographs, two messages were planted by the researcher. The first message appeared on page three. It took up half the page and said, "Stop counting. There are 43 photographs in this newspaper." A few pages later, another message appeared in big bold type, this one bigger than the previous, that said, "STOP COUNTING. TELL THE EXPERIMENTER YOU'VE SEEN THIS AND WIN $250." The self-described unlucky volunteers missed both messages and kept counting until they found all 43 photographs. The lucky volunteers found the first message and asked, "Do you want me to bother counting?" The researcher responded, "Yeah, carry on." A few pages later they found the $250 prize. With overwhelming statistical predictability, the unlucky missed both messages, while the lucky finished fast and with a pocket full of cash.

What we see in life has less to do with what's on the page and more to do with what's going on inside our heads. The comedian Jim Carrey put it this way: "Our eyes are not only viewers, but also projectors that are running a second story over the picture we see in front of us all the time." Vision isn't just the domain of the eyes, but it comes from who we are. Who we are shapes the world we see. As the poet Anais Nin said, "I don't see the world as it is: I see it as I am." That's why two photographers can photograph the same subject and capture different results. And that's why some see the glass half-empty while others see it half-full.

The most creative people capitalize on the fact that vision comes from within. And this is true whatever their trade. Take photography as an example. If a photographer is only concerned with what sits in front of their lens, they won't get very far. A great photographer must not only see but project a clear and strong feeling and opinion of what has been seen. As Ansel Adams put it, "A great photograph is a full expression of what one feels about what is being photographed in the deepest sense."

Your unique view of the world is your most valuable asset, regardless of what you do. One way to sharpen and improve this view is by channeling good luck. As Richard Wiseman demonstrated, luck isn't arbitrary after all. And when it comes to luck, it seems we do have the ability to amplify or diminish its effect, as Wiseman later found.

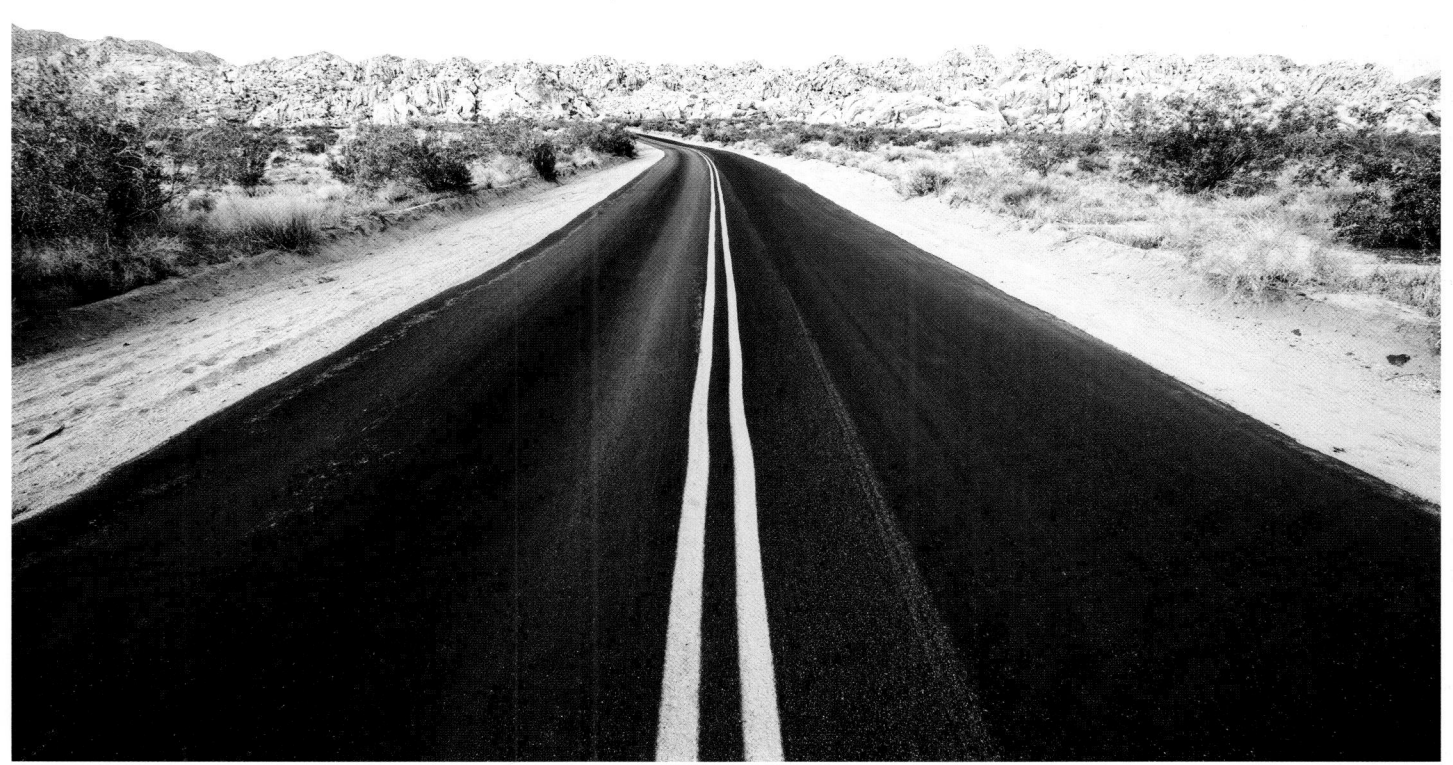

BETTER ODDS AND MORE LUCK After the experiment described above, Wiseman continued to pursue a better understanding of luck. Study after study revealed that lucky people have this almost "magical quality" about how they see the world. They are like metal detectors that are always turned on. According to Wiseman, these people "generate" their own good fortune by following four basic principles: *Create and notice chance opportunities. Make lucky decisions by listening to their intuition. Create self-fulfilling prophecies via positive expectations. Adopt a resilient attitude that transforms bad luck into good.*

Wiseman explains, "Unlucky people miss chance opportunities because they are too focused on looking for something else. They go to parties intent on finding their perfect partner, and so miss opportunities to make good friends. Lucky people are more relaxed and open, and therefore see what is there, rather than just what they are looking for." How does all of this relate to the creative fight? It just so happens that creativity and luck are closely intertwined. Wiseman's description of luck is what makes the creative juices flow. The most creative are able to take off the blinders and make connections between seemingly disparate ideas. These strategies may not help you win the lottery—that requires random luck—but these strategies will boost your creative flow.

I'M A BELIEVER IN LUCK, AND I FIND THE HARDER I WORK THE MORE I HAVE OF IT.
—THOMAS JEFFERSON

EXERCISE

Discovering your personal legend can seem like an overwhelming and impossible task. Yet the best way to begin is to take a few small steps. Here are a few ideas to get you going.

STEP 1

If you want to live a more creative and energized life, begin by reconsidering your path. Are you following your own personal legend or living someone else's dream? Take a few minutes to remember the dream you once had for your life. Start small and write down a few thoughts about what this dream might be.

STEP 2

Trying to find your most singular and significant life's calling can derail and depress. Rather than just thinking in big and broad terms, take a few minutes to get specific and small. Ask yourself, "Why am I here; how can I contribute; what makes me come alive?" But consider answering those questions by using different filters or guides. Get out your journal and write down your thoughts. First, answer considering your roles: employer, parent, photographer, friend, student, musician, and so on. Next, answer considering different slices of time: today, this week, this month, this year, this decade.

STEP 3

Take a few minutes to research books that might help. Try different genres of books, from practical to spiritual. Here are a few ideas to get you started:

- *Finding Your Element*, by Ken Robinson (practical)
- *The Alchemist*, by Paulo Coelho (allegorical)
- *Quiet*, by Susan Cain (temperament)
- *Man's Search for Meaning*, by Victor Frankl (introspective)
- *Essentialism*, by Greg McKowen (productivity)
- *Strength Finder*, by Tom Rath (business)
- *Flow*, by Mihaly Csikszentmihalyi (psychology)
- *The Seven Story Mountain*, by Thomas Merton (spiritual)

STEP 4

On the line below, create a list of books that you would like to read.

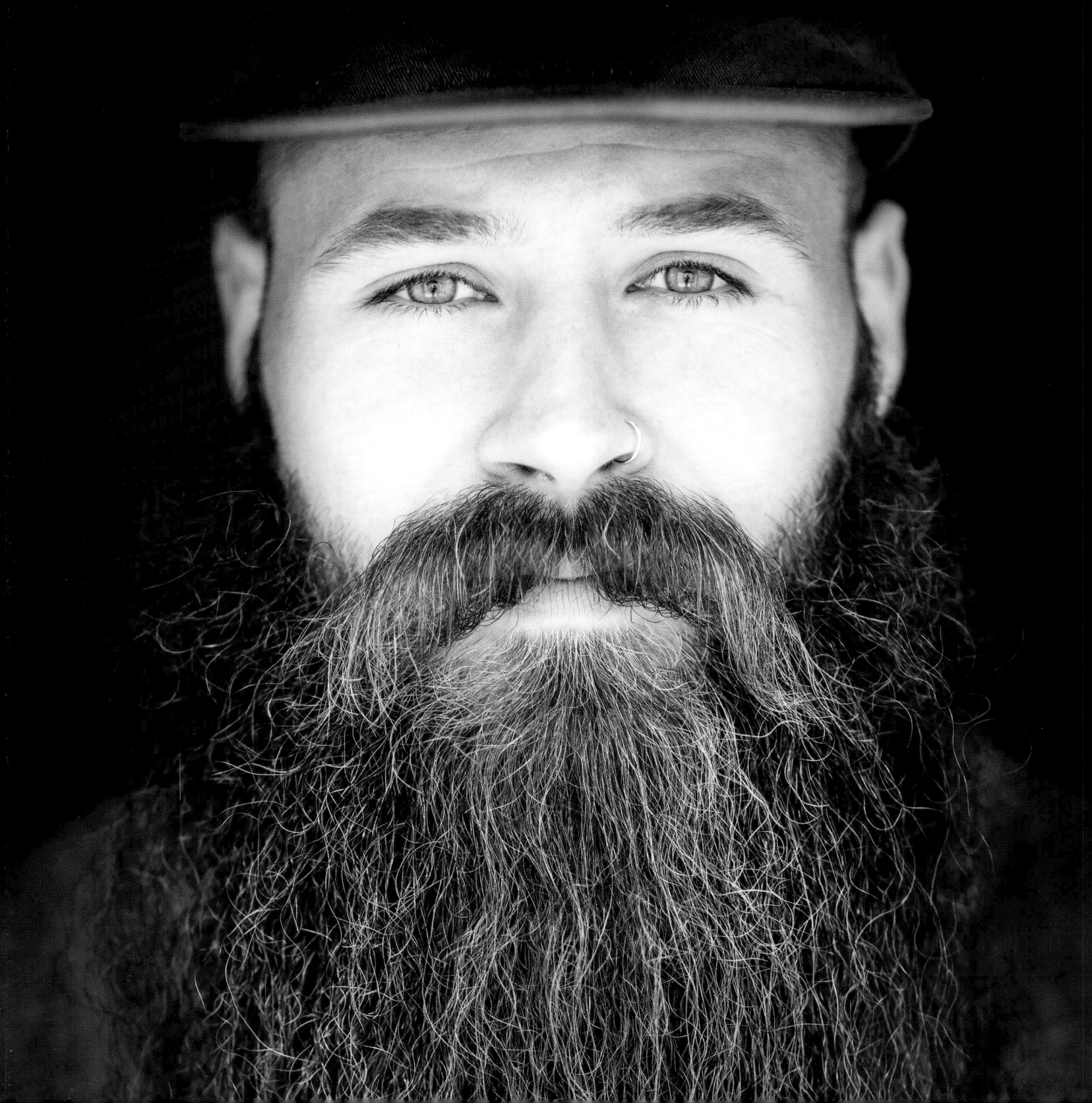

CHAPTER SIXTEEN

TALENT OR TENACITY

A lucky break is one thing, but doing something with it is another. Henry Rollins was working a minimum-wage job at an ice cream shop when his favorite band, Black Flag (a popular punk rock band), called him on the shop phone. During a concert the weekend before, Rollins had jumped onstage and sung with the band like a wild man. Something about his energy left a memorable mark. Now the band was in need of a new lead singer and frontman. They called Rollins to see if he wanted to try out.

He listened in shock as the band invited him to audition. He stared at the ice cream scoop in his hand and then in a flash decided, "Why not?" Henry Rollins went on to front the band to huge success. Decades later, he considers this the best decision of his life.

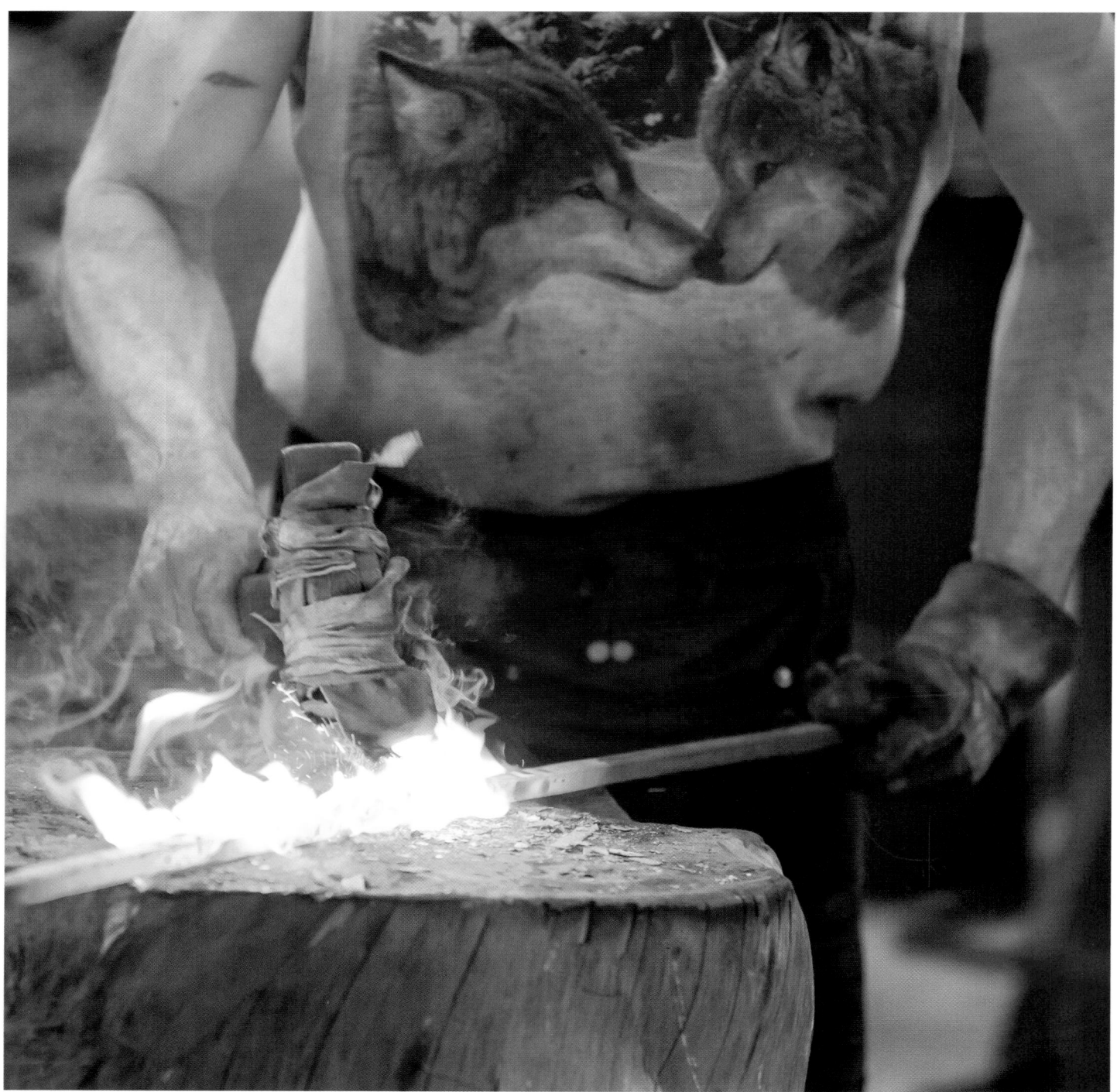

ROCK ON Rollins summarized the journey this way: "My life is a story of a lot of luck and taking advantage of a lot of opportunity and working really damn hard. And that's it. And that's not a unique story. I got a lucky break, but at least I did something with it."

Belief, luck, and positive thinking are mush without the courage to fight. Success always requires less wishbone and more spine. When asked about his talent in an interview, Rollins shot back, "I don't have talent; I have tenacity. I have discipline and I have focus. And I know, without any illusion, where I come from and where I can go back to." When we look at someone standing onstage, we may wrongly attribute their accomplishment to hidden talent that we don't have. But talent is one of the greatest misunderstood concepts of the day. Talent is overrated. To excel you need skill. As Will Smith put it, "Talent you have naturally. Skill is only developed by hours and hours and hours of beating on your craft." And when it comes to living the life for which you were designed, we all start in the same humble spot: square one. Whether a punk rocker, a novelist, or president of the United States, it takes tenacity to rise to the top. There is no shortcut to success.

NEVER GIVE UP The now-famous Jack London wasn't always so. He grew up in a working-class home and was a fighter from the start, getting in schoolyard scuffles even as a young kid. His family couldn't afford school after the age of 13, so he dropped out and went to work earning ten cents an hour in a canning factory. London worked 18-hour days and continued to spar his way through whatever life pitched his way. He picked up a series of odd yet adventurous jobs: illegal oyster thief, deckhand, sailor, and so on. Along the way, he discovered a love of books, and he learned to capture and reframe what he witnessed with written words on a page. Writing became his way to share his adventures, grapple with the complexities of life, and funnel his fervent desire to savor every drop from life's cup.

London's thirst for experience and adventure was vast. At 21 he followed the crowds north to take part in the Klondike Gold Rush madness of the time. The Yukon wilderness was frigid and cold, and after a series of hardships and adventures, London returned home with his pockets nearly empty. Impoverished but not defeated, he desperately needed to find work. Brimming with visceral memories from his trip, he committed himself to a strict regimen of writing based on what he had seen. Hoping his writing would fetch some cash, he submitted his work, only to be rejected again and again.

During that time London wrote to a friend, "I have never been so hard up in my life. If I die, I shall die hard, fighting to the last." In desperation he pawned everything of value he owned, including his watch, bike, and winter coat. He wrote and wrote on a borrowed typewriter, but still the rejection letters came. One publication sent him this rejection note: "Interest in Alaska has subsided in an amazing degree. I do not think it would pay us to buy your story." It seemed his adventures up north wouldn't pay off after all. Little did London know, more rejection was to come. During his first five years as a writer he received an avalanche of over 500 rejection letters, but still he didn't give up.

THE SECRET TO SUCCESS After his books became a huge success, London would say, "You have to go after inspiration with a club." These words weren't catchy ways to motivate others to get off their couch. London was literal. He knew what it meant to fight, and he had witnessed the way a club could be used in the Alaskan frontier. And this wasn't just true for the beginning of London's career. Years later in an interview he explained, "I'm damned if my stories just come to me. I have to work like the devil for the themes." Writing was never easy, so he didn't wait for inspiration to strike but chose habit instead, writing 1000 words every day of the year. London said, "There is no such thing as inspiration. I thought so once and made an ass of myself." For London, inspiration was getting to work, and when he put pen to paper it was like hitting flint with steel.

TIME USED WELL London's rise from 13-year-old dropout to famous writer was not something that fell from the sky. It was the culmination of a huge exertion of force and a philosophical approach to life. London explained, "The proper function of man is to live, not to exist. I shall not waste my days in trying to prolong them. I shall use my time." And use his time is what he did. London only lived to the age of 40, but in those years he wrote almost 50 books. How is it possible that someone could accomplish so much in so little time? Creative fight was the secret of his fame.

A FATHER'S ADVICE Theodore Roosevelt was an energetic but small and sickly young boy. He was plagued with asthma (which was often fatal in that time) and general weakness, so his father decided to step in. Theodore Roosevelt, Sr., went to his twelve-year-old son and said, "You have the mind but you have not the body, and without the help of the body the mind cannot go as far as it should." Theodore's sister, an eyewitness of the event, recalled her brother's response as a half-grin and half-snarl. Clenching his teeth, he committed to change. Without delay, he and his father built a gym in the house, where he would lift weights. And Teddy lived life to the tilt, hiking, exploring, and climbing mountains in all sorts of weather. Nothing seemed to hold him back.

As Roosevelt grew up, iron self-discipline and hard work became his habit, as biographer Edmund Harris wrote. And after a day full of exercise, boxing, voracious reading, rowing, riding, running, and adventure, "He would tumble into bed at midnight where he could luxuriate in healthy tiredness, satisfied that he had not wasted one minute of his waking hours." Even though he started weak, throughout Roosevelt's life his vitality, endurance, and unending energy became a hallmark of this indomitable man. Theodore was never one to give up no matter the cost; whatever obstacle he faced he seemed to tackle it with tenacious resolve.

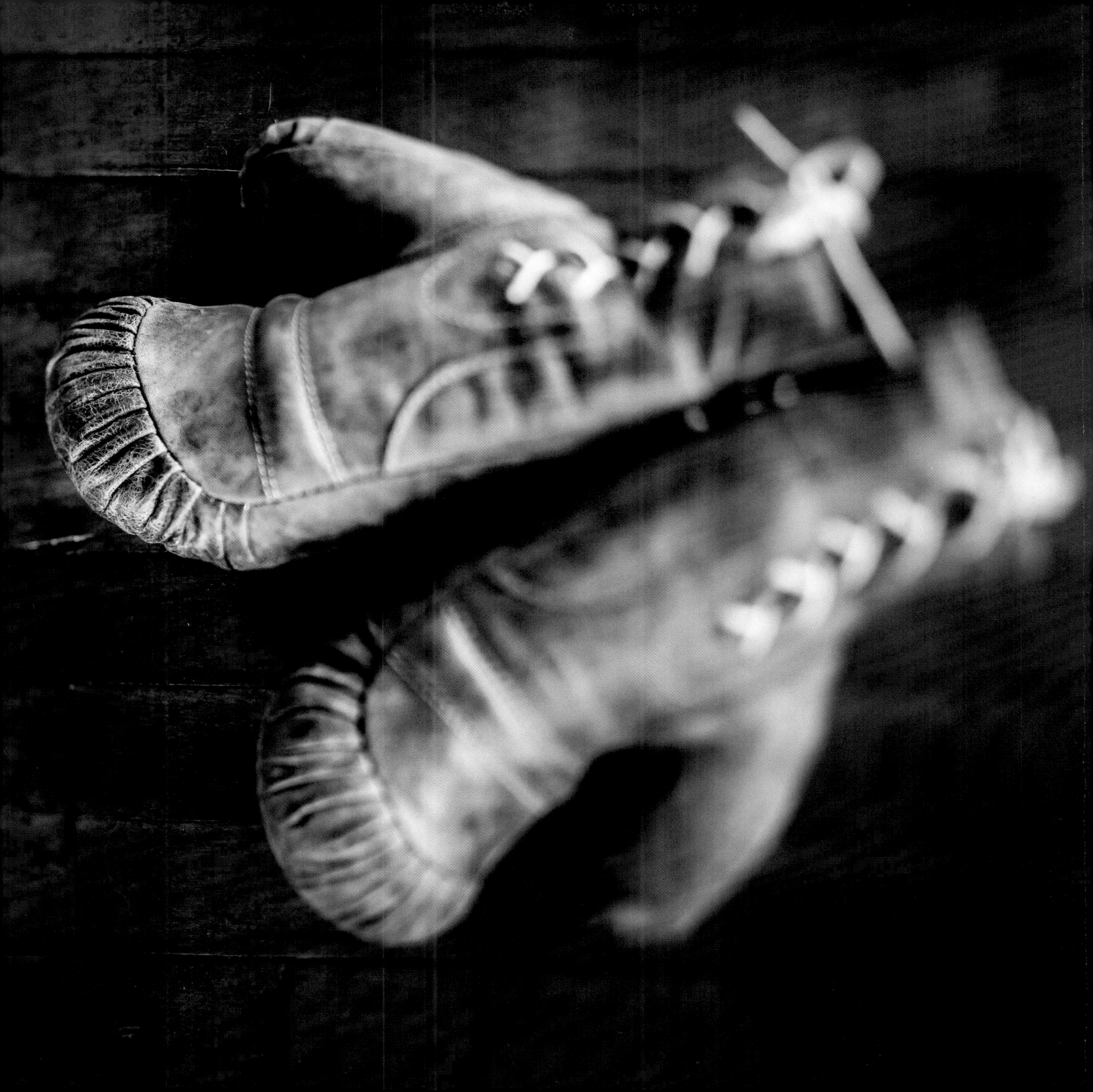

THE CREDIT BELONGS TO THE MAN WHO IS ACTUALLY IN THE ARENA,
WHOSE FACE IS MARRED BY DUST AND SWEAT AND BLOOD;
WHO STRIVES VALIANTLY; WHO ERRS, WHO COMES SHORT
AGAIN AND AGAIN, BECAUSE THERE IS NO EFFORT WITHOUT ERROR
AND SHORTCOMING; BUT WHO DOES ACTUALLY STRIVE TO
DO THE DEEDS; WHO KNOWS GREAT ENTHUSIASMS,
THE GREAT DEVOTIONS; WHO SPENDS HIMSELF IN A WORTHY CAUSE;
WHO AT THE BEST KNOWS IN THE END THE TRIUMPH
OF HIGH ACHIEVEMENT, AND WHO AT THE WORST, IF HE FAILS,
AT LEAST FAILS WHILE DARING GREATLY, SO THAT HIS PLACE
SHALL NEVER BE WITH THOSE COLD AND TIMID SOULS WHO KNOW
NEITHER VICTORY NOR DEFEAT.

—**THEODORE ROOSEVELT**

One family friend described the college-age Theodore this way: "He's not strong, but he's all grit. He'll kill himself before he'll even say he's tired." On his summer breaks from Harvard, Roosevelt spent every spare minute in the great outdoors, rowing, sailing, swimming, and trekking through the countryside. But after he graduated, his asthma and "weak heart" still seemed to be an issue, at least for his doctor. Roosevelt's doctor advised him to take a desk job and to avoid strenuous activity due to a heart condition. Roosevelt decided to climb the Matterhorn instead. But his doctor's warnings were serious: "Your heart is weak and will not hold out for more than a few years unless you quietly settle down." In typical Roosevelt fashion he replied, "I prefer an early death to a sedentary life."

AVERAGE ISN'T BAD As Roosevelt famously put it, "I am only an average man, but by George, I work harder at it than the average man." Roosevelt worked hard at many things throughout his life. He was a naturalist, a boxer, a scholar, the author of 35 books, and president of the United States. One of the threads through it all was his unquenchable tenacity and fight. He overcame countless personal and professional obstacles, including the death of his mother and his wife on the same day. On that day he wrote, "The light has gone out of my life." Yet somehow he pressed on. Roosevelt's advice was simple: "Do what you can, with what you have, where you are." This is perhaps the best credo ever written for the creative fight.

Too often in our own lives, a humble beginning is used as an excuse: "I'm not smart enough, tall enough, artistic enough, strong enough, funny enough…" But as any creative and successful person will tell you, that achievement hinges less on where you start and more on how much you are willing to try. When you peel back the layers, the most successful, creative, and prolific people are just your average individuals who have worked really, really hard.

EXERCISE

STEP 1
Write down 3–5 goals or dreams that you would like to achieve.
Get specific and write down the details in a journal or on a blank page.

STEP 2
Excuses keep us from achieving our goals and dreams.
On a scratch piece of paper, write down the excuses that are holding you back.

STEP 3
Take a moment to reflect on the excuses you have written down.
Then, as a symbolic act of defiance, burn or tear up the piece of paper.

STEP 4
Close your eyes. Take a deep breath and with a Teddy Roosevelt–like snarl,
recommit yourself to achieving your dreams.

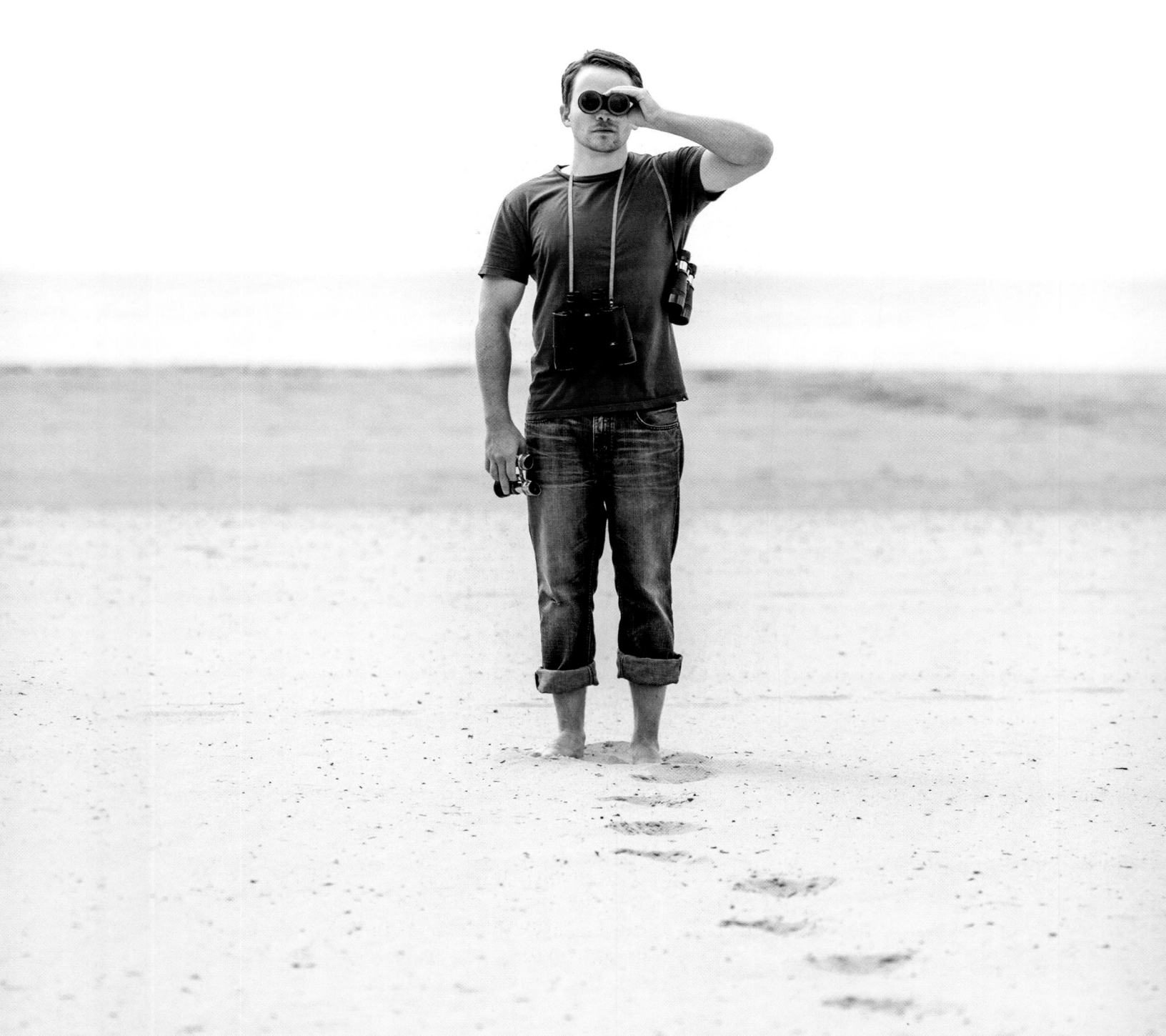

PART THREE: DRIVE

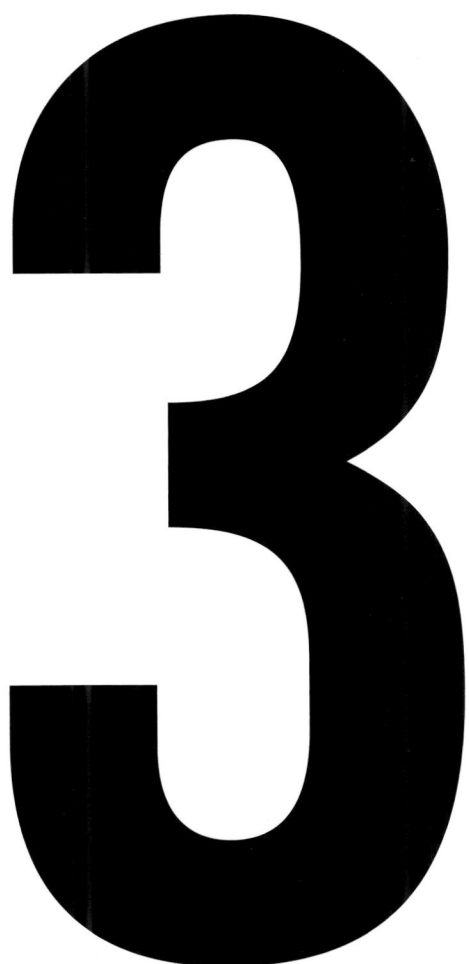

I WISHED TO LIVE DELIBERATELY, TO FRONT ONLY THE ESSENTIAL FACTS OF LIFE,
AND SEE IF I COULD NOT LEARN WHAT IT HAD TO TEACH,
AND NOT, WHEN I CAME TO DIE, DISCOVER THAT I HAD NOT LIVED.
— HENRY DAVID THOREAU

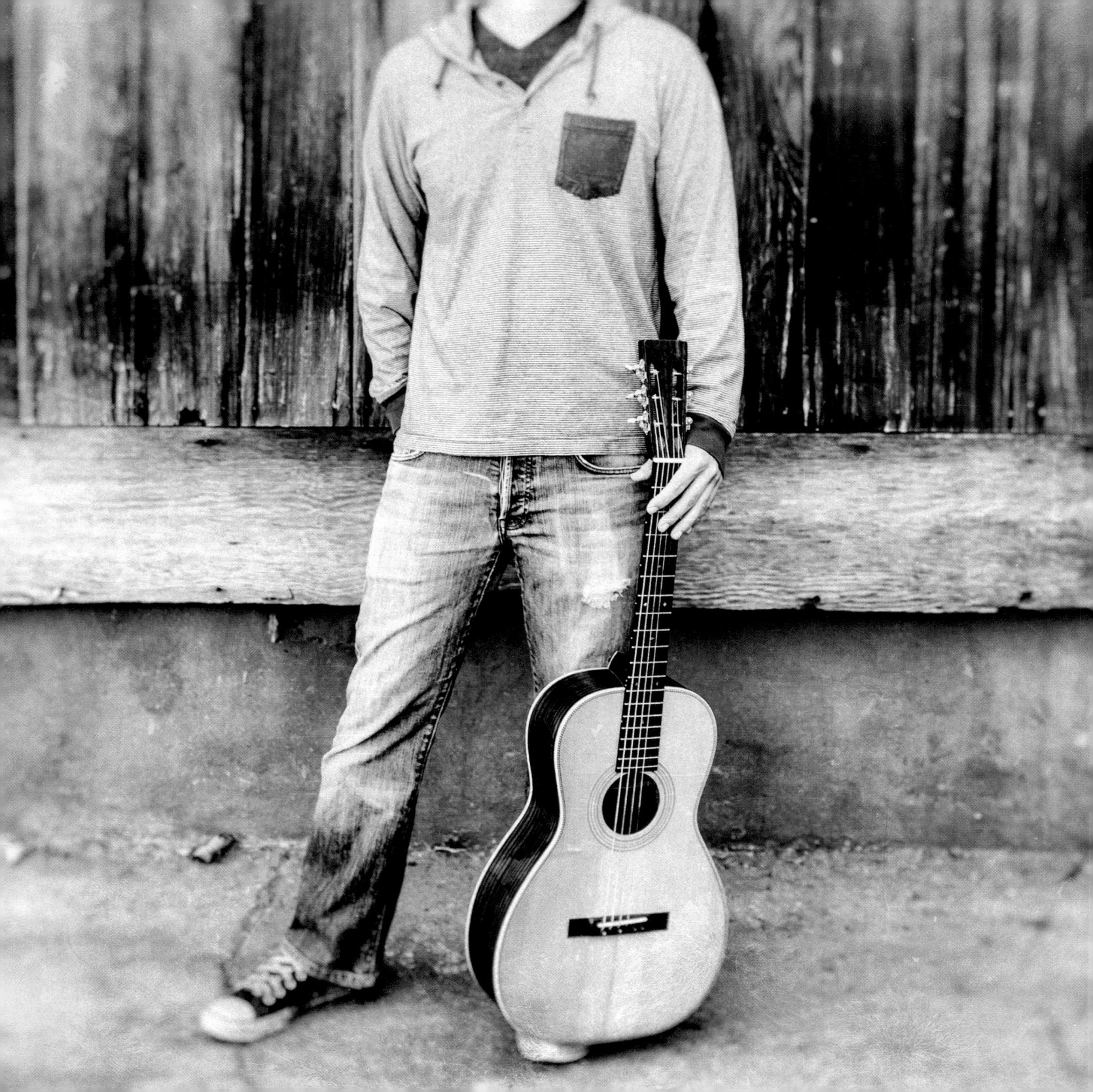

CHAPTER SEVENTEEN

THERE AND BACK AGAIN

Some musicians find luck early, and John was hoping that would be him. He was 22, he loved writing songs, and his band had chemistry. It was time to audition for a record deal. So far his group had performed cover songs in nightclubs in Germany and were tired of the grind. It was time to dream and to go for the big leagues. So they put together 15 of their best songs (only three of them original) and played their hearts out for recording studio executives. The studio recorded the audition in hopes they would find the next big thing. What they heard was disappointing. The response was clear: "We don't like their sound... They have no future in show business." The group was disappointed, but they pressed on. Rejection wasn't anything new, and playing all-night shows in second-rate clubs had built tenacity into the fabric of the group.

DRIVING THE CURVES The road to success isn't paved with gold—99 percent of the time it isn't paved at all. The path to success is made of dirt, and it requires four-wheel drive. When I was in high school, my brother and I bought a vintage 4x4 Jeep. We installed a roll bar, put on off-road tires, and then permanently removed the top and took off the doors. It was a dream machine for two guys in their teens. It stirs my heart to think back on how much fun we had driving that vehicle wherever we pleased. When you drive off-road you learn quickly that you can't relax. If you aren't alert and holding on tight you can get tossed. And just because you made it through one mud bog or over a big rock doesn't mean you're a champ. The time to celebrate is not the middle of the journey but after you have made it back home.

So it is with success. It's easy to get carried away with the roar of the engine and the feeling of invincibility. That's what happened to my brother the time he raced out into the wilderness unaware that a rock had broken something loose. Underneath the Jeep, sparks flew and hillside caught on fire. He had to outrun the fire and go get help. The faster he drove the more fire he spread. Fortunately, the park services were close by, and the fire was contained without causing too much harm. Still, my brother had to pay a significant fine. He was just glad it didn't turn out worse.

Anyone who has experienced success can relate. The journey always includes fires, flat tires, broken axles, and stupid mistakes. These mistakes are what build strength so that the complexity of success can be handled with grace. If success comes too quickly it can be a curse. That's what happened to one kid in our town in 1988. Matt's dad was the president of Atari and then went on to start a toy company that invented things like Teddy Ruxpin and Laser Tag. (If you're old-school like me, you may remember how big these products were.) It was well known that Matt's family was super rich. Plus, it was the era of neon clothes, big hair, and living to the excess. So when Matt turned 16, his dad bought him a brand-new bright red Porsche—imagine that! It took only a few months before he crashed. Fortunately, Matt was OK, but the car was a complete wreck. It was too much car for someone who had just passed his driver's license test. A Porsche is something that needs to be earned.

The fastest I have ever gone in a car was last fall when my friend Bryan took me for a spin in his new Porsche Cayman S. We raced around empty back roads at unbelievable speeds. Bryan wasn't reckless. His driving was like poetry in motion, even when he took a corner at over 100mph. Driving fast was nothing new to Bryan. He had grown up around cars. His father-in-law designed the Laguna Seca racetrack in Monterey, California. He'd been on that track hundreds, maybe thousands, of times. Bryan taught racing classes, and the guy knew how to drive. After decades of driving inferior cars, he was finally able to afford a Porsche of his own. After driving for a while, we hopped out and he tossed me the keys. I gulped. As I stepped on the gas I didn't know what was louder, the growl of the engine or the pounding of my heart. It was thrilling, but I knew I had to keep my ego in check and drive within the limits of my skill.

TAKING CHARGE John and his band experienced a similar thrill when their hit song played on the radio for the first time. They too had to keep their egos from spinning out of control. After having played all-night gigs to a bunch of drunks in a bar, it was nice to have exposure to a larger crowd. The year was 1962, and radio airplay was a big deal. The song peaked at number 17 on the charts. But the group didn't become self-absorbed. They held on tight and continued to refine their songs and even the way they dressed. No more eating, swearing, and smoking onstage, and they adopted a more professional look. The efforts paid off, and within a few more months their band was at the top of the charts.

Much has been said and written about this band's success. The Beatles were an extraordinary group. Yet their journey to success was not atypical at all. The path to success usually follows a familiar bumpy road. It starts off with interests, passions, and ideas. Next come the hard work and the fight to succeed. Then some mild successes, and next some failures as well. Finally, the big break appears. From the outside looking

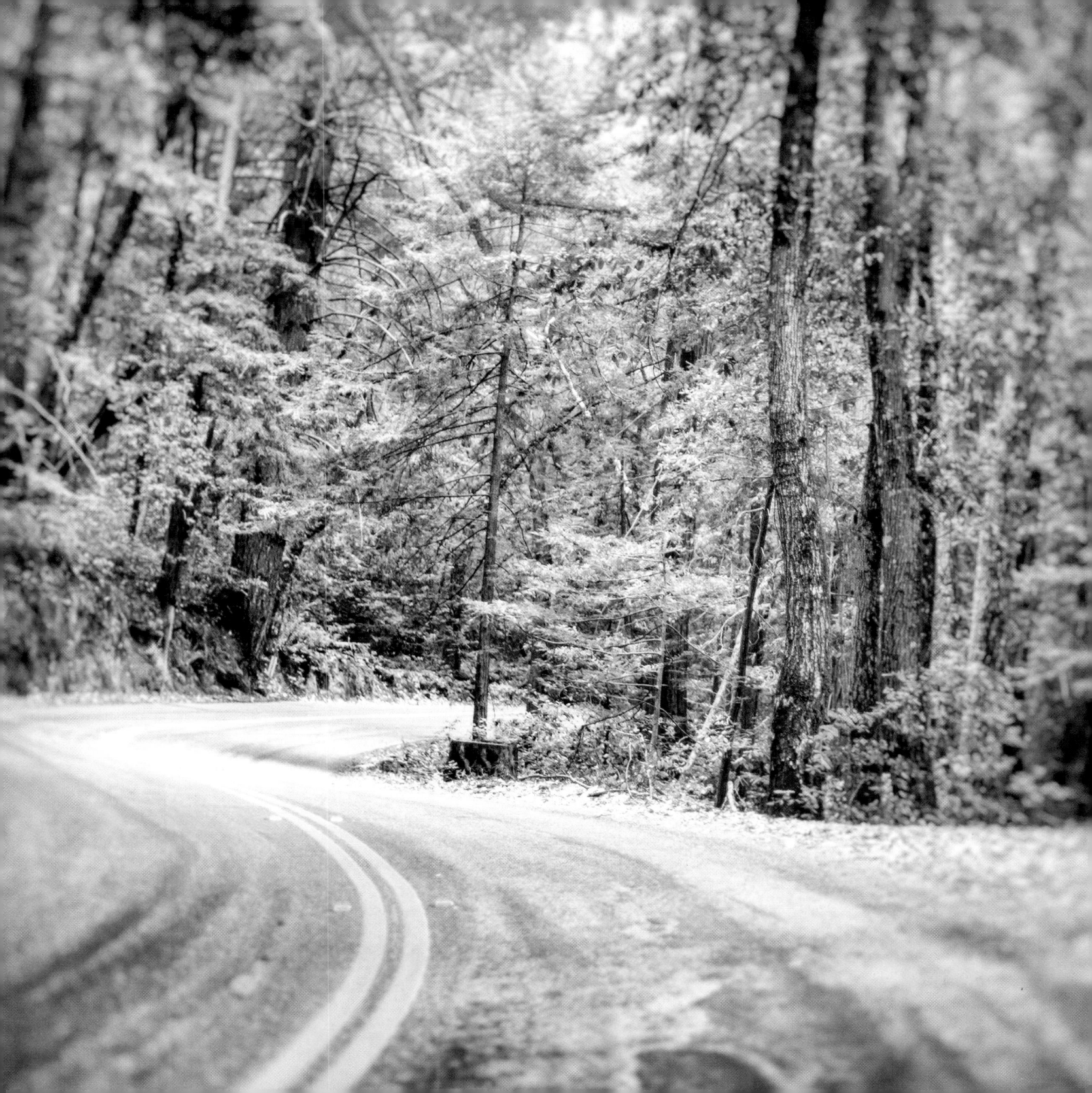

in, this is the moment of arrival. Yet for the individual, the journey is only halfway done.

Creating your life's best work and living the life you imagined requires having a deep drive to reach the top, but also a strategy for making it back home. It isn't very creative to succeed in reaching the summit only to descend to your doom. True creativity requires a more holistic view that includes both the up and the down.

For me, this means many different things. Like figuring out how I can thrive in my career and be the world's best husband and dad. I'm sick to my stomach from hearing about how someone ditched their family or missed out on their kid's childhood because of their job. Family comes first and then work. And it means that sometimes, like today, I have to get up at 4am to work on this book so that I can get a few hours in before I walk my three young kids to school. My family gives me an edge to work smarter and to focus on what matters most. It also means that in the evenings I put away my laptop and phone so that I can be present and engaged.

We all combine work and life in different ways. There isn't a formula for the best way to balance your time. Yet what I do know is that creating your best work requires you to take charge. If the way someone lives their life bothers you, make sure you don't follow their path. You can't let the world decide how you should spend your time.

So climb your way up that mountain, but don't stay at the top so long that you jeopardize it all. The most meaningful success is less of an arrival and more of a round trip.

COUNT YOUR LIFE BY SMILES, NOT TEARS.
COUNT YOUR AGE BY FRIENDS, NOT YEARS.
—JOHN LENNON

EXERCISE

PART 1. DOODLE

The path to success is never a straight line, and it never happens overnight.
Take a few minutes to look back over your own life and sketch out your own path. Becoming
aware of your own journey so far can help you embrace the adventure that lies ahead.

PART 2. ROLE MODELS

Too often for the sake of success we sacrifice what matters most, like family, friends,
and health. Write down three people you know personally or know about who have values
you respect and who have attained the type of life you would like to live.

Their example could be simple—for example, a teacher who finishes all her grading before she
leaves school; a colleague who doesn't work nights and weekends and goes camping a lot;
a professional athlete who has used her influence to help young kids; a famous musician who hasn't
lost his head. Don't try to find a perfect archetype, but rather, a mix of character qualities
that you want to add to your own life. Use your creative powers to let these role models help you
realign your values and shape the way you spend your time.

1.

2.

3.

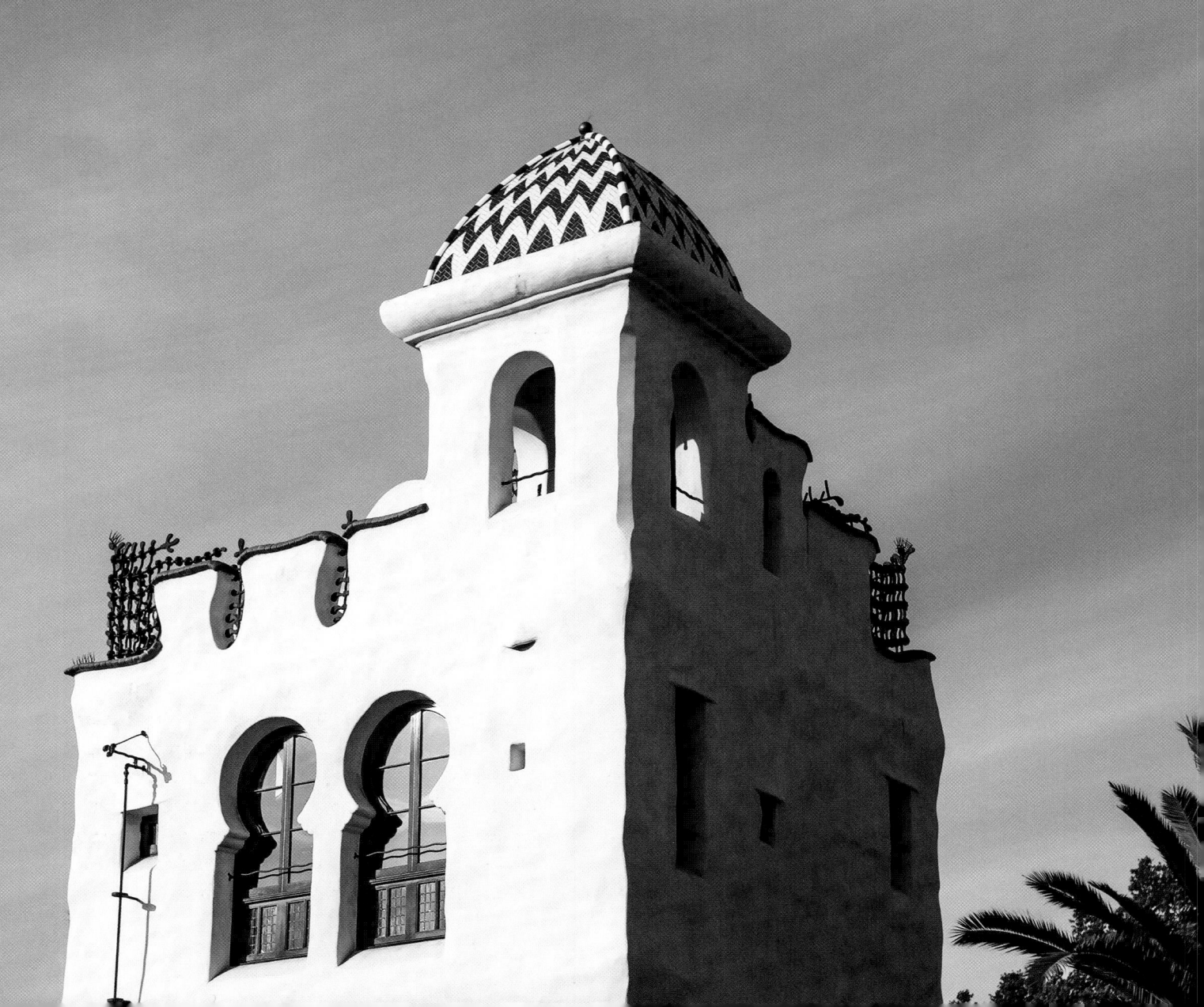

CHAPTER EIGHTEEN

WHY VERSUS WHAT

Jeff Shelton doesn't like computers, right angles, corners, or straight lines. He hand-draws everything he designs from scratch. The best way to describe Jeff's architectural style is one part Dr. Seuss and one part Spanish-style white stucco with tile roofs. The results have brought him worldwide acclaim. Jeff has designed buildings, apartment complexes, and homes of all shapes, sizes, and forms—some large and some impossibly small. Yet they all share the same charm. When clients come to see Jeff about a new project, they want to jump right in and start talking about square footage and the number of rooms. But Jeff knows that's not the way a great house is made. He wants to uncover the story beneath his projects first. The *why* behind the concept becomes the foundation that ensures success. The *why* gives shape to the what.

BEFORE THE WHAT, THE WHY As Jeff explains, "I want to know why someone wants to build a house. Is their marriage falling apart and they're looking for distraction? Is the new house a creative expression or a monument to oneself? Is the home designed to be looked at and admired or to be filled with family and friends?"

While some of Jeff's homes look serene (like the opening image in this chapter) and others seem like a cartoon (see his sketch shown next), each home begins with the clarity of strong reason and a well-articulated "why." And having a well-defined why is what increases the odds of success.

This idea of understanding the reasoning behind a project can also be seen from a marketing point of view. Have you ever noticed that the brands we like most tell us more than dry facts? Take Apple, which goes way beyond selling machines. Apple's marketing message is more like a manifesto full of ideals.

As Simon Sinek articulates in his widely viewed TED talk, "Apple says, 'Everything we do, we believe in challenging the status quo. We believe in thinking differently. The way we challenge the status quo is by making our products beautifully designed, simple to use, and user friendly. We just happen to make great computers. Want to buy one?'"

Whether you want to or not isn't the point. The point is that they realize that a well-articulated "why" is a strong force. Think about how some Apple customers put Apple logo stickers on the back of their cars, while others buy logo shirts. Can you think of another computer manufacturer that has come close to that?

When Giorgio Armani started his business in 1975, it began with a clear idea. He wanted to design clothes, but he did so with a strong "why." Armani was distraught and run down by all the chaos and clutter in the world. So he set out to provide an experience of simple elegance that would counteract the jumbled mess of life. The "what" was his clothes, but it was the "why" that has led the brand to be such a global success. Armani doesn't just provide clothes but also offers aspiration to an ideal—and this is why his brand has such wide appeal.

THE WHAT IS THE SURFACE The what is facts, figures, and nonfiction verse. The why is narrative, the story, and the undercurrent of belief. Why is the domain of the creative arts. And this isn't about designing homes or selling more stuff. The aim of why is not the outward expression but the inward ideal. This is true with the creative fight—we don't become more creative to improve the bottom line.

The best results flow when we pursue creativity for the sake of being a human being. Just as Tom Schulman said in *Dead Poets Society*, "We don't read and write poetry because it's cute. We read and write poetry because we are members of the human race. And the human race is filled with passion." We create because "the powerful play goes on and you may contribute a verse."

Creativity gives us the means of contributing a verse in a more meaningful way. And we become more creative for the sake of honoring our own unique DNA. When we create, the sparks of identity fly and we have a chance at discovering who we are and what we were intended to become. Pursuing the why makes us become more alive whether we design homes, sell iPhones, or assemble words in a poetic and beautiful way.

Mary Oliver has spent her life stitching together small groups of words. She is a Pulitzer Prize–winning poet with a knack for finding beauty in ordinary life. And she also happens to be one of my favorite poets of our time.

In her poem "Messenger," Mary gives us a glimpse into her life's calling. She explains, "My work is loving the world… and standing still and learning to be astonished." Why? Her self-defined job is to notice, collect, and share what she has found. This anchors her work. She has important messages that others need to hear. Her poems are like handwritten and sealed letters passed out to strangers on a busy street. Often her poems ask questions. Sometimes the questions are subtle, and other times they go straight for the heart. In one poem she asks, "Tell me, what is it that you plan to do with your one wild and precious life?"

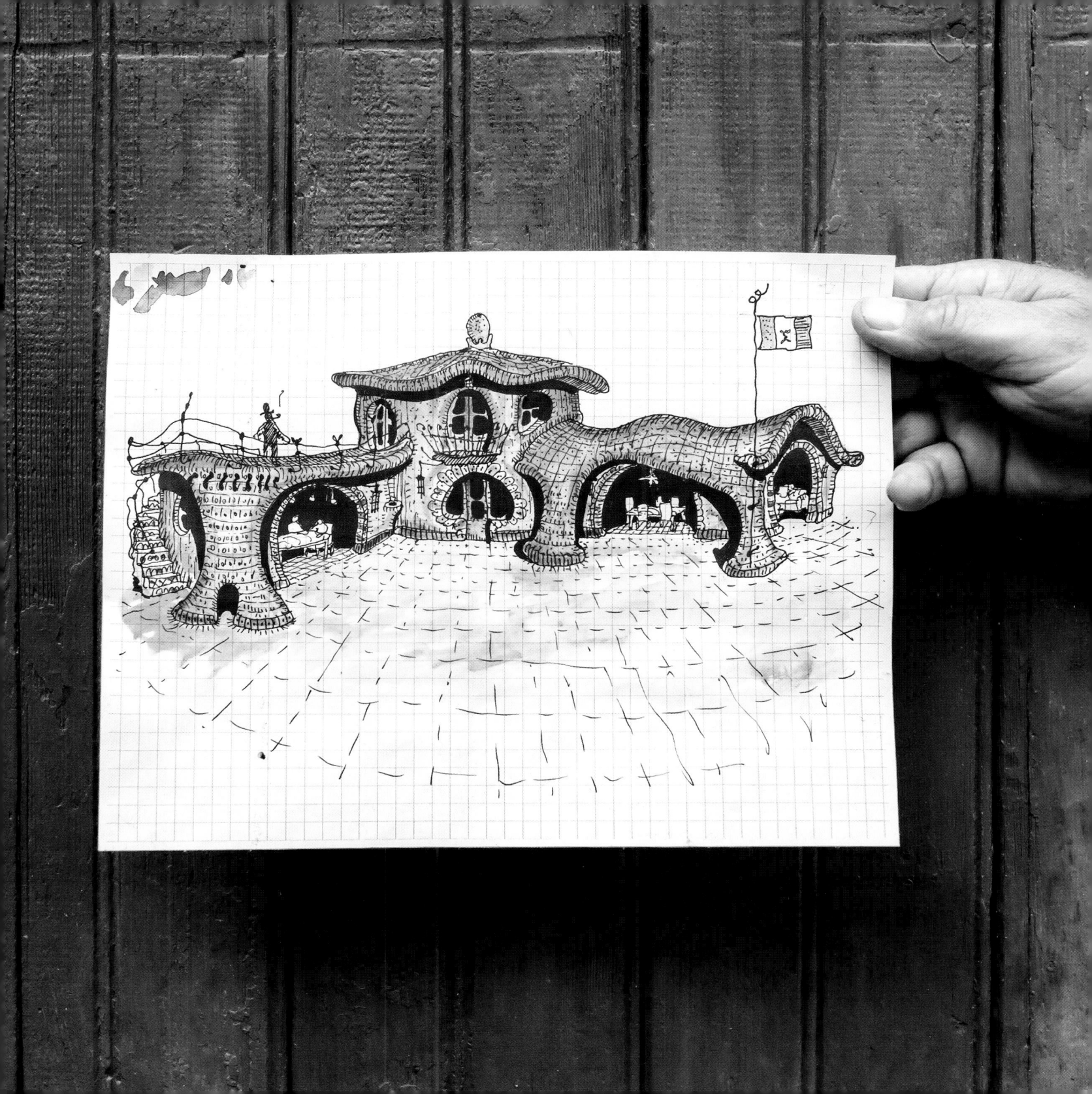

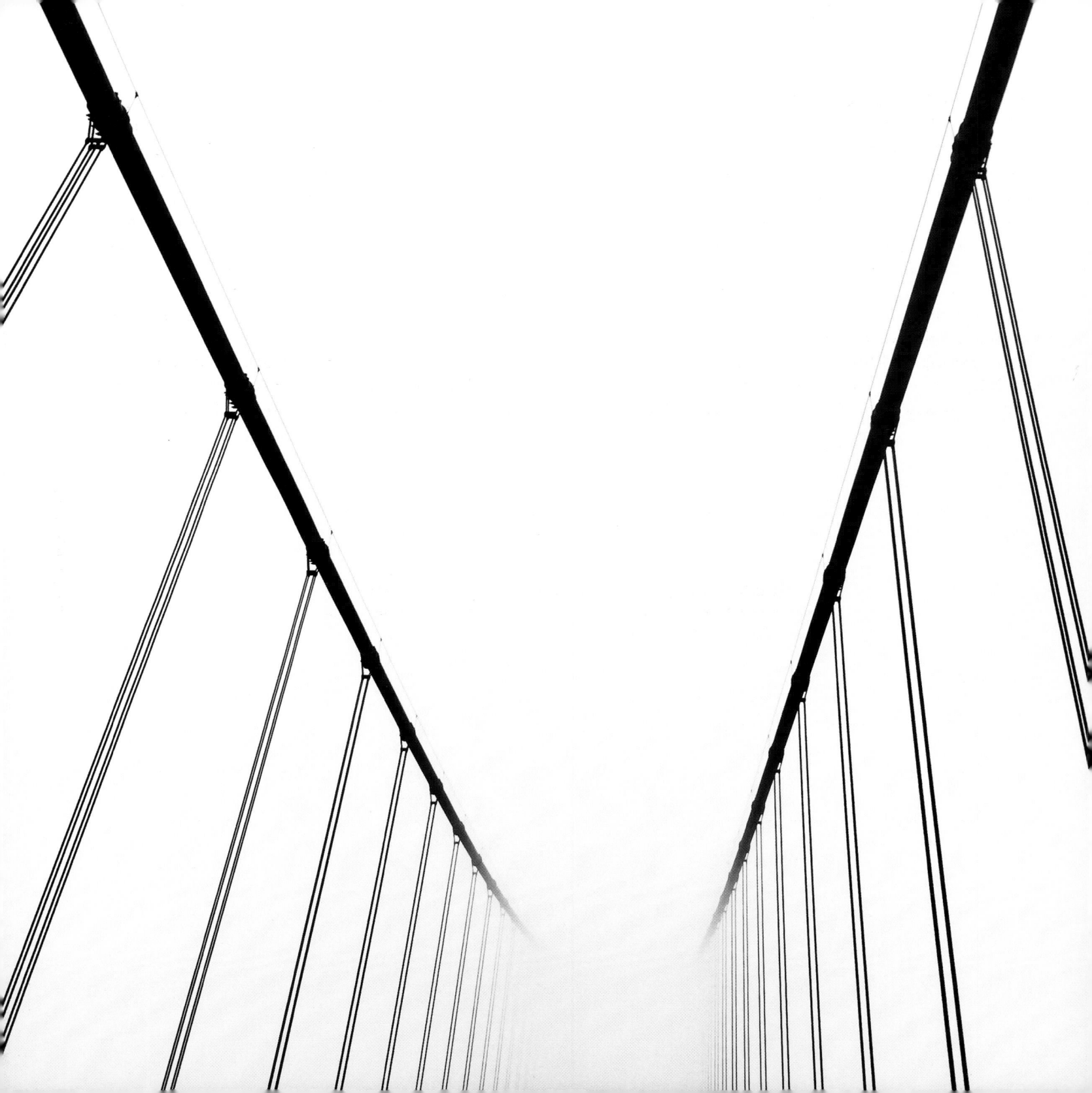

ONE WILD AND PRECIOUS LIFE When meeting a new neighbor a while back I was asked, "What do you do with your life?" I told her I was a photographer and she said, "Wow, that must be a tough job. Hasn't everything already been done? I mean, why take a photograph of the Golden Gate Bridge when you could just buy one instead?" I replied, "Sure it's tough but it's good. Making photographs isn't so much about creating something novel as it is about being changed." She shrugged her shoulders, said "Interesting," and then walked off.

I was left standing there with my own thoughts. In an over-photographed world, why do I persist? I began to think about a photograph I had recently captured of the Golden Gate Bridge (shown on the previous page). As I thought, Herb Caen's words came to mind: "The Golden Gate Bridge. This mystical structure, with its perfect amalgam of delicacy and power, exerts an uncanny effect. Its efficiency cannot conceal the artistry. There is heart there, and soul. It is an object to be contemplated for hours." Ah, here was a reason why. And then I began to make a mental list of other reasons I do photography: because the camera helps me to slow down, discover truth, notice details, meet new people, and learn new things. I use a camera because of the way it instructs and helps me to change. I make photographs because life is brief and the camera helps me to find the magnificent in the mundane and to live life in a more meaningful way.

So what about you? What are you going to do with your life, and why? Develop an answer to that question and it can help you live in a more vibrant and meaningful way.

EXERCISE

Clearly defining your "why" can anchor and fuel your success.
In the space below, write down five things that you do and articulate why.

WHAT	WHY
1.	
2.	
3.	
4.	
5.	

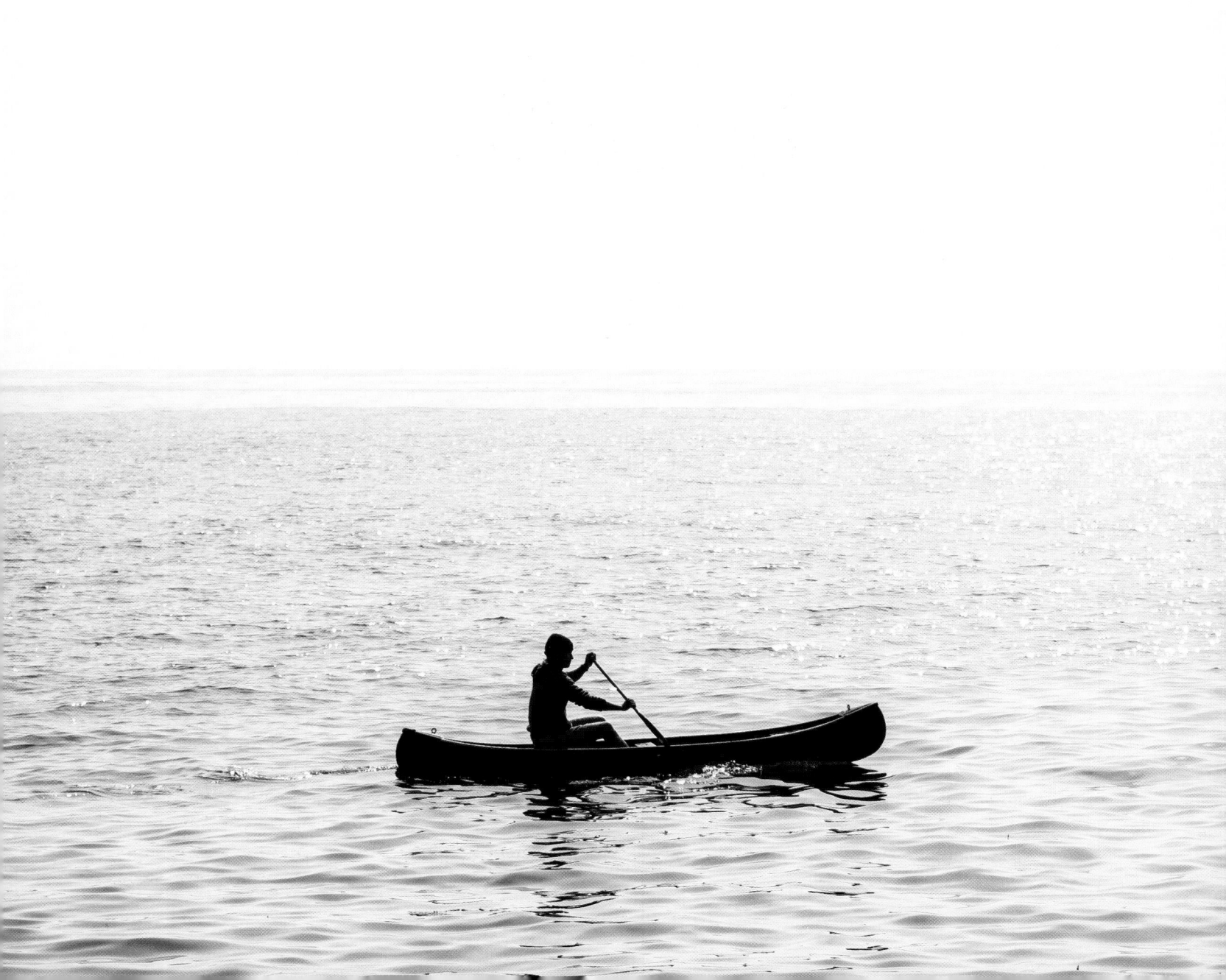

CHAPTER NINETEEN

SLOW IS FAST

Over the last decade, I taught at a leading photography school. The school was expensive and rigorous, so by the time the students arrived, they weren't trying to figure out what to do with their lives. Still, dozens of students dropped out in the first year. Why? These students had mistakenly fallen in love with the idea of being a photographer, without realizing that the journey was so tough. Pushing a button is easy, but crafting good photographs is hard. Like paddling across the sea, it takes consistent work. The students who quit wanted the result without the effort involved. The students who didn't quit found that the journey was the reward. And my job was to help these students succeed. I had to teach them how to create photographs that would last. Because in the era of the instant, it's the permanent that stands out from the crowd.

SLOW DOWN TO ACCOMPLISH MORE Creating photographs that stand the test of time isn't an easy thing to do. And most people can't make photographs that last, because they are moving too fast. Worried about missing the moment, they take pictures at a furious pace. In photo circles we call this "spray and pray." In other words, hold down the shutter and hope. It's easy to do because digital is cheap and because photography is fun. Yet back in the days of film, it cost a quarter (25 cents) per click. That cost motivated aspiring photographers to learn their craft and to focus, concentrate, and compose in a more mindful way. Back then, success in photography wasn't cheap.

In digital photography, you pay the price up front when you buy the gear. Mistakenly, some think that this entitles them to success. Whether your camera costs $1000 or $10,000, it doesn't mean your pictures will be good. Making good pictures requires effort from us. So we shoot a lot of photographs to make up for our lack of skill. But just because you can shoot a lot doesn't mean you should. But still we do. Why? Because less takes more time. Just like with writing letters, as Mark Twain described: "I didn't have time to write a short letter, so I wrote a long one instead." We don't have (or we don't take) the time to take better photographs, so we settle for good. We work quickly and hope for the best. The upside is that with digital we can work quickly and see instantly what we've done. The challenge is to maintain mindfulness so that we don't get carried away with the speed. As with driving a race car, the more power the more mindfulness you need.

**IN THE NAME OF GOD, STOP A MOMENT,
CEASE YOUR WORK, LOOK AROUND YOU.**

—LEO TOLSTOY

The downside of digital is that we shoot too much. The result is too many photographs, too much processing, and too much time searching for a good frame. That's the problem for you, but there's also an expense to everyone else. When you share too many photographs, it becomes dull. Even if the photographs are good, viewing too many makes us numb.

Creating photographs that last means we need to change our pace. Even Ansel Adams used to say, "Twelve significant photographs in a year is a good crop." When you slow down and lower your expected output, you can become an artisan in your craft. The new constraint beckons you to compose in a more thoughtful way. So it is with generating creative work.

Whether or not you care about photography, the lesson stands true: slowing down can help you accomplish more. Creativity isn't just about coming up with more ideas than everyone else; it's about coming up with ideas that are good. In photography, the surest way to do that is to photograph something that matters to you. If you love nature, stop shooting in the studio and go for a hike. Search for that landscape that speaks to your soul. If you can create a photograph that means something to you there is a greater chance it will mean something to me. Good photography comes from within. This is true with every type of work, and it starts with you.

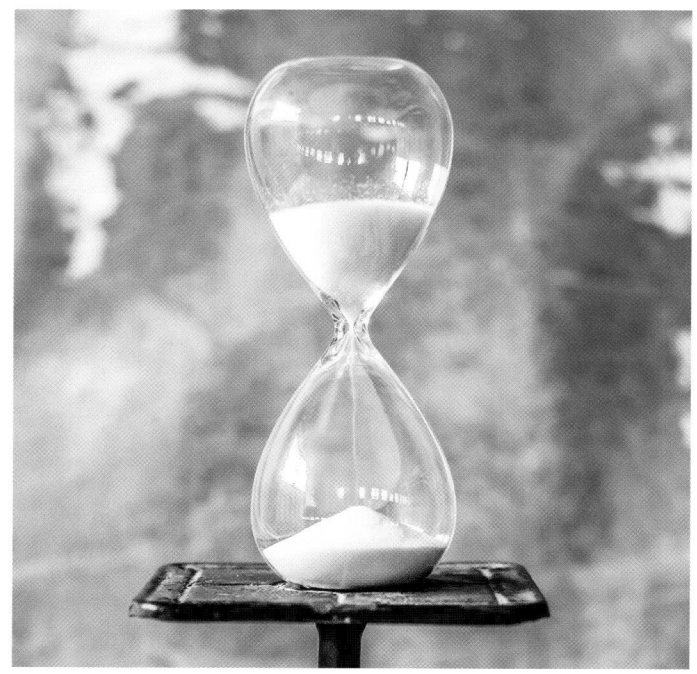

BURN We all have a fire that burns inside. It's that fire that "moves us forward, gives us momentum to our projects, and authenticity to your voice," as David duChemin puts it. He should know—he's been making the pursuit of this fire his full-time gig for years. duChemin is a photographer, best-selling author, and world traveler. When my own passion wanes, he is one of the people I call. Each time we talk, his message has been the same: "The authentic you is better than anything else. Stop trying to please everyone else. Trust your gut and be real." It's amazing how easy it is to forget such a simple truth. We all need people like David who can set us straight. Regardless of your work, you have to find out what makes you tick and pursue that work. The more you do, the better it is for yourself and for everyone else.

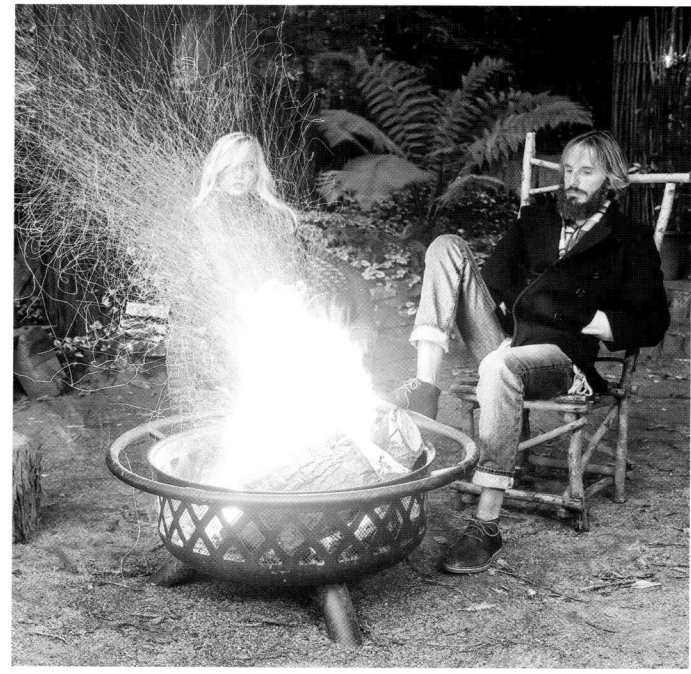

SLOW DOWN EVERYONE
YOU'RE MOVING TOO FAST.
FRAMES CAN'T CATCH YOU WHEN
YOU'RE MOVING LIKE THAT.

—JACK JOHNSON

EXERCISE

STEP 1

Set out to capture some photographs, but do so in a mindful and thoughtful way.
Tread lightly, and only lift the camera to your eye when you are ready to compose.
Aim to capture just 12 photographs of a scene.

STEP 2

Take a few minutes to reflect on the following questions:

Who am I and what matters most?
How can I pursue those things in my work and life?

STEP 3

If your work seems empty, it might be your own fault. Purpose doesn't come from
someone else. The more "you" that you bring to your life, the more creative and alive you will
become. So take a few moments to slow down and ask yourself how you can invest more
of your authentic self into your work.

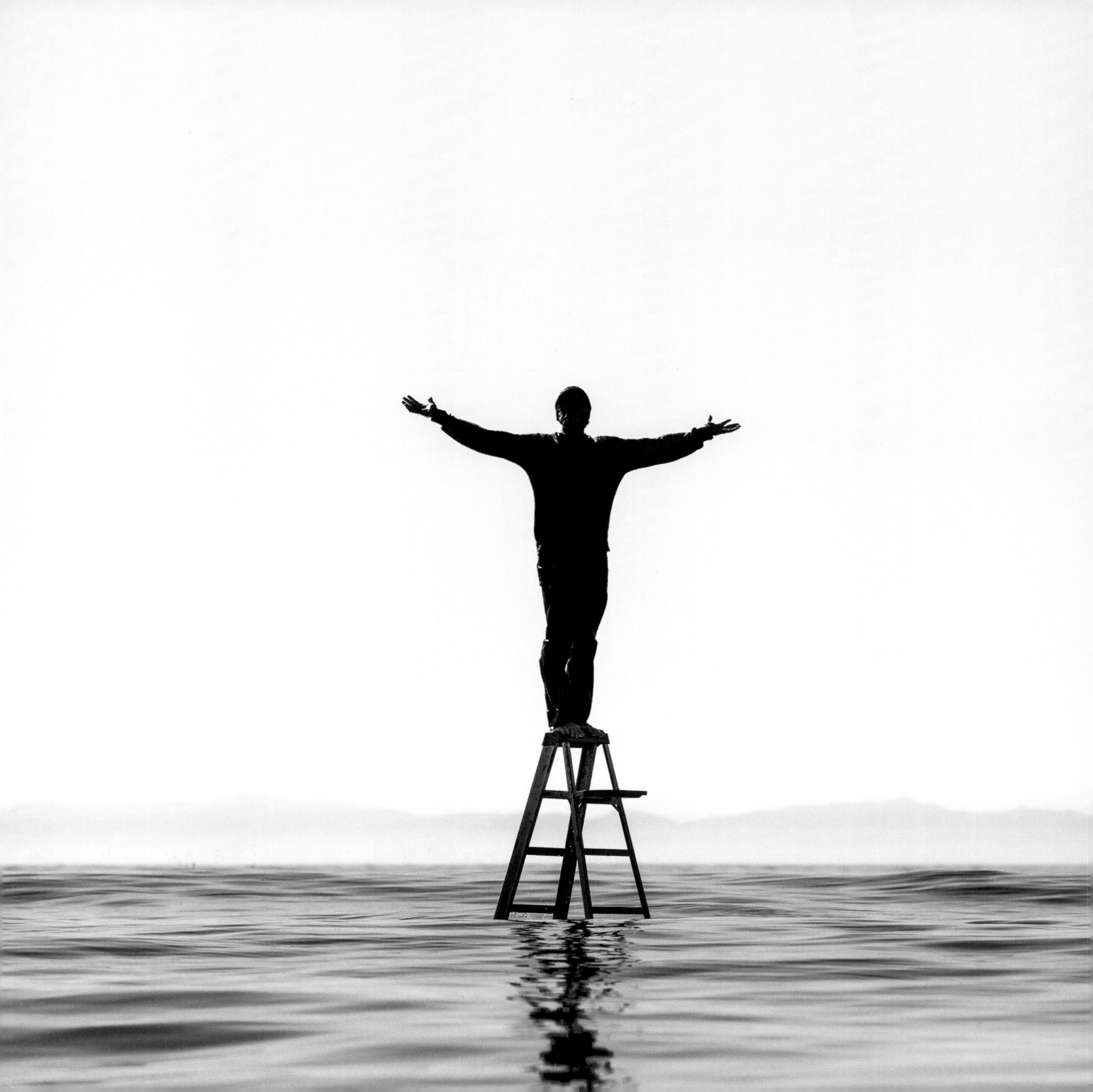

CHAPTER TWENTY

GOOD TO GREAT

No more bulky equipment. No more time spent in the dark. Trade secrets are shared generously online. Getting good at photography is easier than ever before. Even my mom can make good photographs with her phone. Technology has helped us improve our creative output dramatically. The incoming tide raised each and every boat. As a result, there are a lot more good photographers in the world. Good isn't that big a deal. Simply point and click. Yet few of the good photographers become truly great. Why?

Good is easy, but greatness is always hard. Mediocre to good doesn't take much work, whereas good to great is a completely different game. When I started taking photographs, I was horrible. After a few years of failing to create but a few decent photographs, I stopped doing photography altogether.

HIDDEN TRUTHS I stepped away from capturing photographs to try to figure out what was wrong. I talked with a few friends and read a couple of books but still wasn't sure. When it came to me, my focus was off. Not the focus on the lens, but the one within. When it comes to making good photographs, this is the most important lesson you can learn. And I soon discovered that great photography is not about the way an image looks.

The pursuit to make great photographs is a quest for hidden things. That's why the best photographers are such a quirky bunch—like oddly equipped treasure hunters who go out into the world looking for the magnificent. Leaving no rock unturned, they search high and low for the perfect shot.

From the perspective of someone who doesn't know what they are doing, their efforts must look insane. These wide-eyed image-makers stop in busy intersections to capture a shot, crawl through the mud to photograph a frog, and spend more money on their cameras than on shelter, transportation, and food. They pull off the freeway to photograph an old abandoned shack. They look for beauty hidden within a wrinkled face. They search for the truth that everyone else overlooked. With wide and sharp eyes, they believe in magic and look for it every day. The results of such efforts are photographs that go beyond the surface and connect with us in a deep way. They awaken our senses and make us aware that there is more to life than it seems.

At times, viewing such images can make photography seem deceptively simple. We see a picture and it instantly strikes a chord. We think, "What a lucky shot; that can't be that difficult to do!" The obvious catch is that effortless and deep photographs take decades of commitment to the craft.

**A PICTURE IS A SECRET ABOUT A SECRET.
THE MORE IT TELLS YOU THE LESS YOU KNOW.**
—DIANE ARBUS

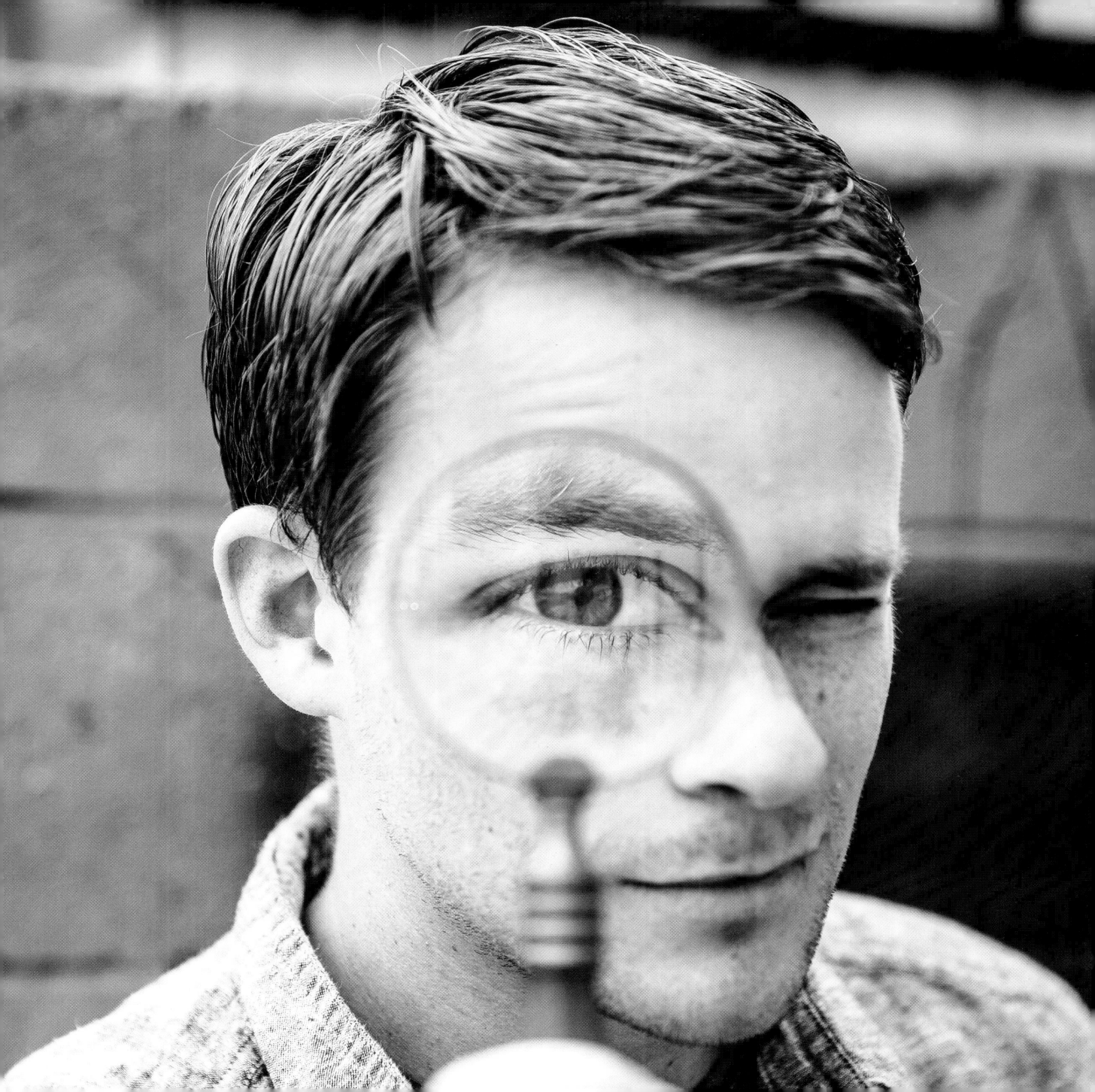

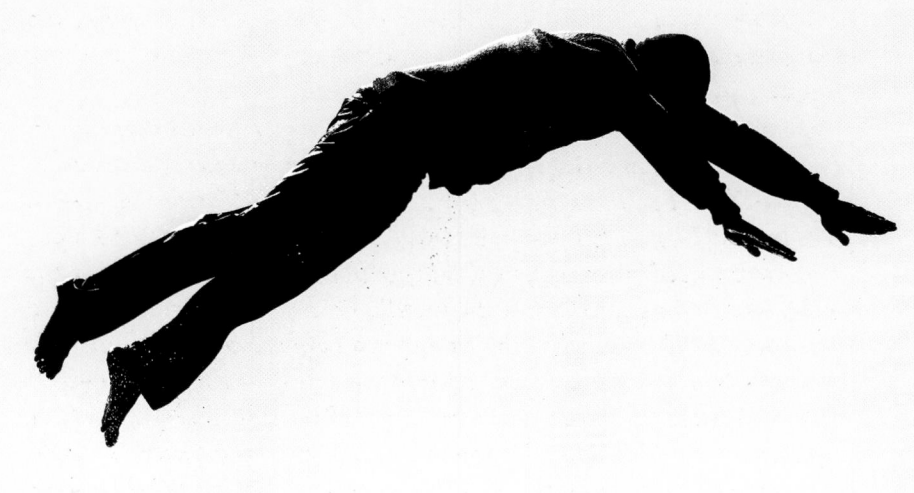

THE CURSE OF GOOD ENOUGH When I taught at a photography school, the students wanted to get good as quickly as they could. Yet getting good too quickly can be a curse, like inheriting money before you've learned the value of hard work. This is something we all tend to forget, or at least think it applies only to everybody else.

But too much good too fast can distract us from a higher goal. When life is good, we stop trying so hard. Jim Collins distilled the concept in this way: "Good is the enemy of great." He explained, "Few people attain great lives, in large part because it is just so easy to settle for a good life."

Becoming good gives us a new vantage point from which to view the world, like finding a ladder in the middle of the sea. We climb up and take a seat. Suddenly, we see the world with new eyes and the world sees us propped up high. We think to ourselves, "How can this be a curse?" Good feels nice. But it isn't a very stable spot. Plus, someone or something might try to climb up and take over our spot. Needing to defend our post, we become stuck in the beating sun. The uncreative person sits still, priding himself on his patience and resolve. The creative person gets tired of sitting around. "This perch is good, but it's dull," he says to himself. The creative person begins to think, "I wonder what's on the bottom of the sea?" Looking down in the water, he sees the glint of gold and makes a leap.

When good is good enough, it stops the creative flow. Not good enough is what drives growth. Imagination is almost always the first step. Next comes the guts and resolve to get something done.

EXERCISE

We all climb ladders that we need to jump off. Without overthinking, answer the question, "What's your ladder and what's your leap?" Write your response and tack it up next to your desk.

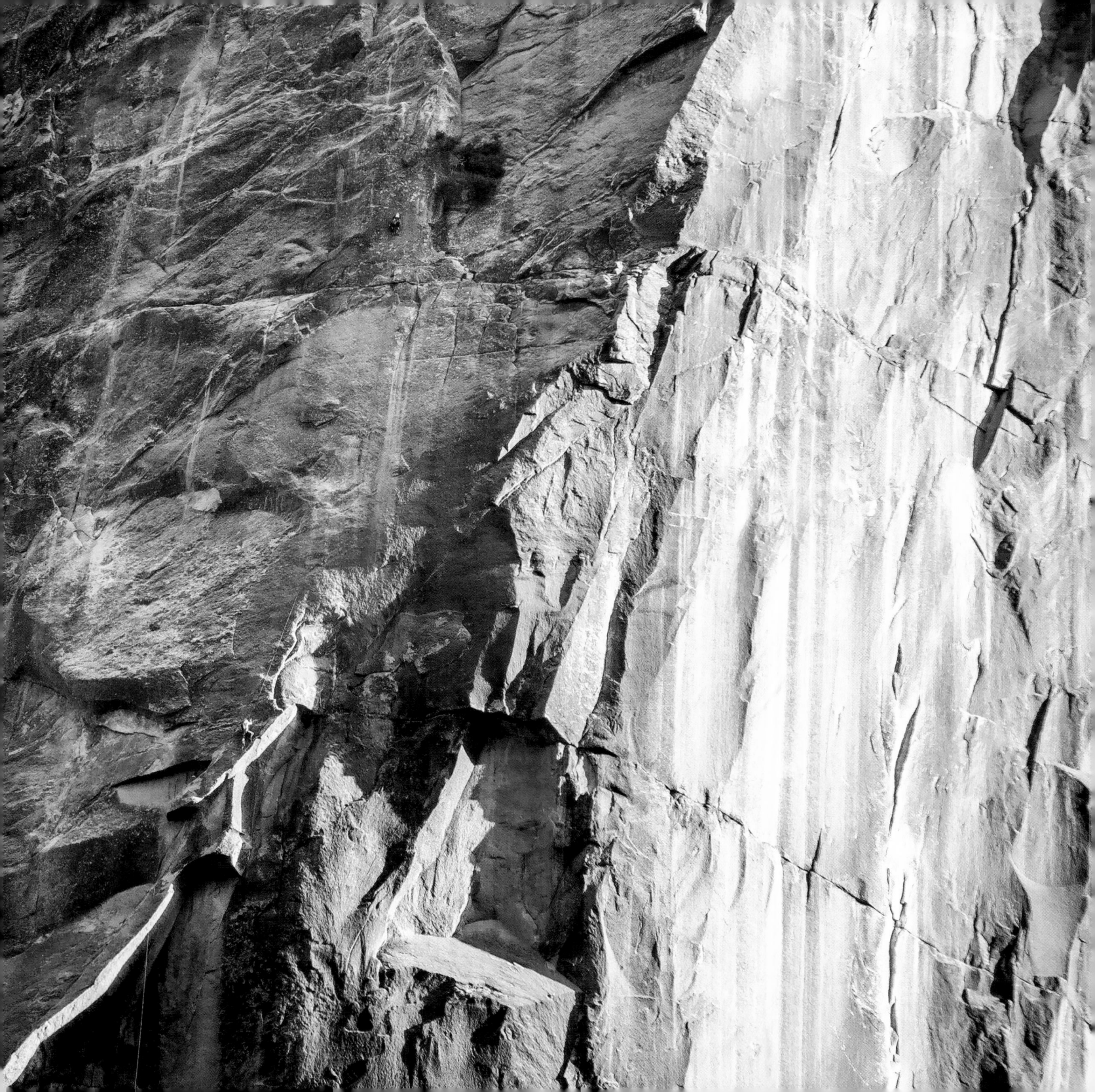

CHAPTER TWENTY-ONE

GRIT AND GLORY

The creative fight is less *Monday Night Football* and more climbing up the sheer face of a rock. Playing in the NFL requires bulk, might, and strength. It's hyped up, and it's loud. Rock climbing is discreet. Climbers use ingenuity, agility, and guts to accomplish their goals. Last year's Super Bowl was watched by 111.5 million fans. Most great rock climbs are witnessed by only a few, just like creative pursuits, which often take place in isolation rather than in front of adoring fans. And football is a fight against another team, but rock climbing is a fight within. The climber must dig deep into his reservoirs of tenacity, technical skill, and creativity to overcome the odds. Football is played to win. Mountain climbers ascend tall peaks "for the spirit of adventure to keep alive the soul of man," as George Mallory said.

AN UPHILL CLIMB

At its most basic level, I think we create with a similar drive in mind. At least for me, I create for the sheer joy of making something myself. As with the climber who looks down the face of the cliff he just climbed, there is great gratification to be had when you enjoy a mountaintop view that you have earned.

After nineteen days and 3000 feet of climbing, Tommy Caldwell and Kevin Jorgeson stood on top of El Capitan peak in Yosemite with joy and tears in their eyes. These two guys had earned their victory. They had just finished a free-ascent climb that took seven years to plan and complete. After years of training and attempts, the impossible had been done—a new route was established as one of the most difficult climbs in the world. Midway up the climb, Kevin posted on Twitter, "This is not an effort to conquer. It's about realizing a dream."

Tommy and Kevin are the champions of their game. Yet if you were to walk by them on the street you wouldn't know you had just passed two of the greatest climbers of all time. It's not uncommon for climbers to be slight in build yet immensely strong. Their strength is often hidden under a layer of fleece and a waterproof shell. The only way you might have recognized Tommy Caldwell is if you noticed that the top half of his index finger is gone.

Tommy lost his finger to a table saw accident more than ten years ago. The doctors were able to reattach the severed finger but told him he'd never climb again. After some trial and error, Tommy had it removed because it held him back. A few months after it was removed, Tommy free-climbed Salathe Wall, another route on El Capitan, in less than 24 hours. He has since climbed some of the most difficult mountains with only four fingers on one hand. Tommy is as tough as they get—not that he'd ever say that about himself. You'd never catch him flexing his muscles for someone to admire. He is humble, mindful, and aware. And so is the creative fight. It doesn't gloat and it doesn't crush. Yet creativity isn't some pushover that's afraid of a difficult task.

Like rock climbing, creativity is a subtle sport that's easy to miss. Just like the first image in this chapter—look closer and you'll see two climbers you might have overlooked.

COURAGE, RESOLVE, AND STRENGTH

Tommy is a role model of the creative fight because of who he is and how he approaches his craft. Most climbers excel in one type of climbing. Tommy is world-class in multiple ways: bouldering, sport climbing, and mountaineering—all demand different skills. As Andrew Bisharat wrote in a *National Geographic* article, "To understand the breadth of Caldwell's athleticism, picture an Olympic runner who is as talented in the marathon as he is in the hundred-meter dash."

Those who join the creative fight know that creativity feeds off hardship just like climbers who are constantly in search of more difficult routes. Difficulty clarifies the creative fight. Tommy put it this way: "Through hardship in my own life, I learned that it is what changes us the most. It puts us in an intensely meditative state where we figure out what we really want." Tommy has been through a lot, including being kidnapped at gunpoint and held hostage by rebels in Kyrgyzstan over a decade ago, but the hardship is what gives him his edge. In his own words, "It motivates me to go for things that I have always dreamed of." Guys like Tommy embody the ideal that the more difficult the challenge the better the reward.

THE GREATNESS OF GRIT

One characteristic that makes someone good at big-wall climbing is grit. Grit can be defined different ways. It can be thought of as tiny particles of crushed rock. The oyster reminds us that without grit, there is no pearl. Grit is a characteristic that is a mixture of courage, resolve, and strength. Like small granite rocks, grit is strength that won't give up. Those who are gritty have a passion to pursue a goal over an extended amount of time. No one is born with grit. It's grown into us through the difficulties of life. Look up the word grit in a thesaurus, and it says it all: "Courage, bravery, pluck, mettle, backbone, spirit, strength of character, strength of will, moral fiber, steel, nerve, fortitude, toughness, hardiness, resolve, resolution, determination, tenacity, perseverance, and endurance."

The grittiest rock climber I ever met is a man named Mark Wellman. I was 18 when I asked him for his autograph and

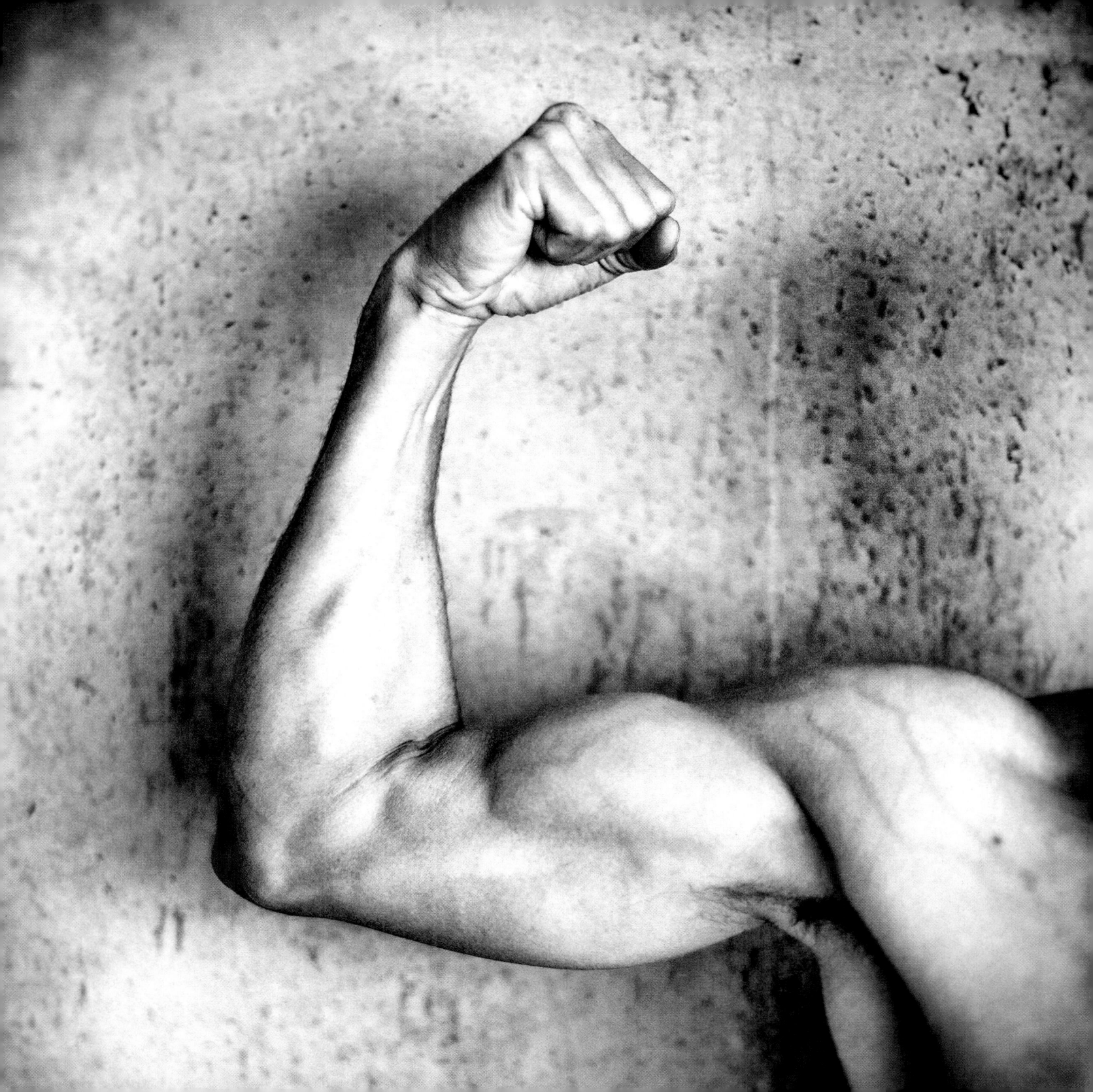

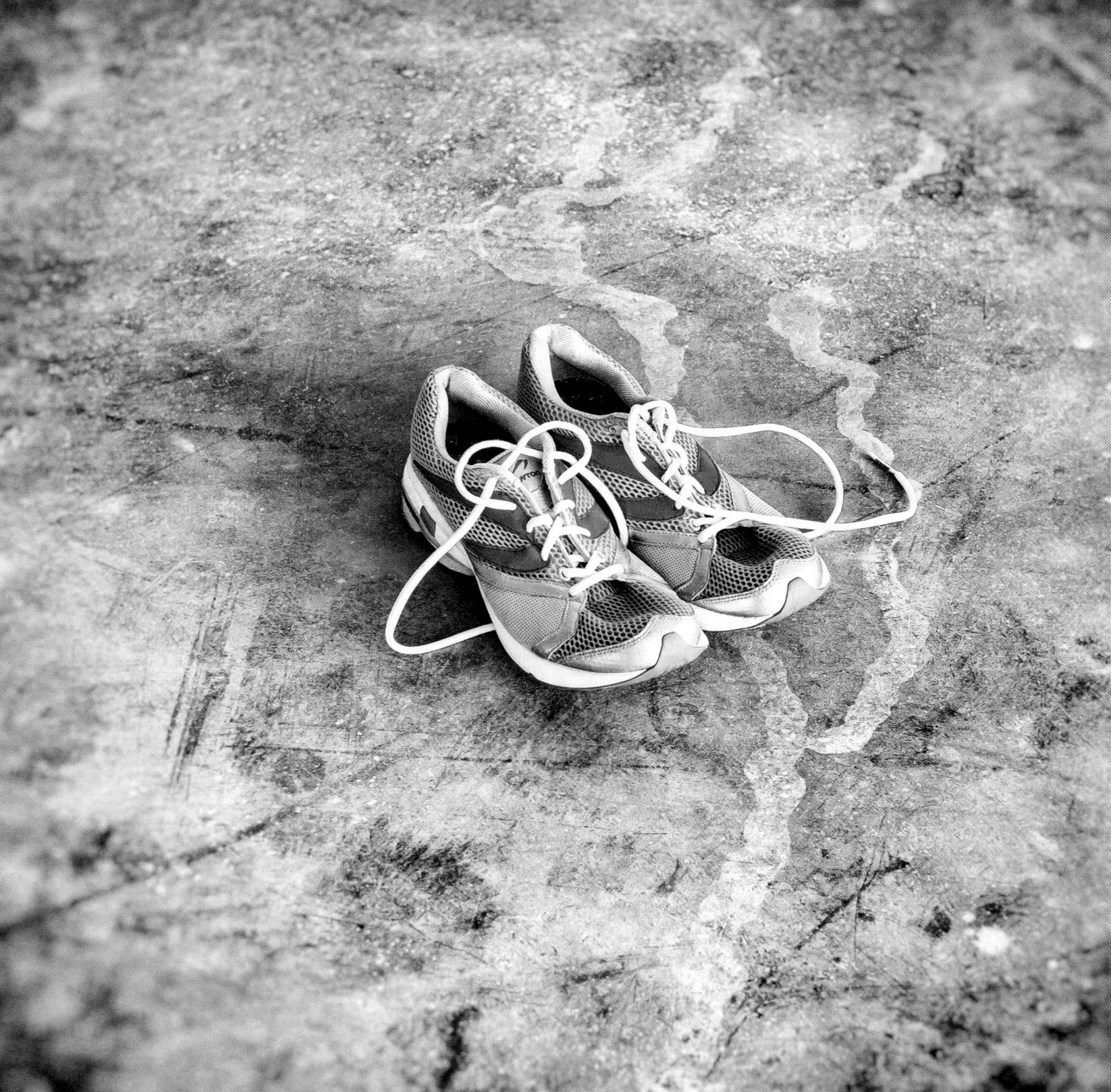

shook his hand. I had recently hiked the well-established trail to the top of Half Dome in Yosemite. At the top there is a rock called the diving board. I inched myself to the edge and peered almost 5000 feet to the valley below. As I shook Mark's hand I was in awe of the strength of his grasp. He had recently climbed up the face of Half Dome without the use of his legs. After 13 days and over 7000 pull-ups, Mark became the first paraplegic to make the climb.

We tend to think our own problems are large. But that's just because we're comparing them to things that are too small. Like me writing this book: "Oh, writing is so hard," I complain. If Mark Wellman can pull himself up Half Dome, I can sit down with my shiny laptop in a comfortable coffee shop and hack out a few words. The obstacle is never a valid excuse. Rock climbers look for obstacles, and that's what lights their fire.

When I looked into Mark's eyes, I saw a kind of strength that I hadn't seen before. When I saw Mark's determination and shook his hand, it changed my life. It was like a transfer of energy had taken place. I had no idea that Mark's resilience would help me develop my own.

TWO SHOES When we are exposed to greatness, it has the potential to awaken our own. I think that's why pilgrims in the Middle Ages collected relics and religious artifacts. They were in search of something that would inspire their own faith, hope, and strength. While I can't relate to wanting a saint's tooth, I do understand their search. Just like what I was searching for when I asked my friend Chris for his shoes. Chris is a world-class triathlete and Ironman champion and is of my closest friends. He trains like a mad man and goes through shoes faster than I finish a pack of gum. One day we were hanging out in his garage and he was cleaning up. Chris was about to throw away a stinky old pair of shoes when I asked if I could have them to hang on my wall. He looked at me like I was a crazy, but he obliged and even signed the soles. Every time I see those shoes I'm reminded of his tenacity and grit.

When he was younger, Chris wasn't much of an athlete but got inspired to do a triathlon after seeing the event on television. After a number of years of insanely difficult work, Chris became a pro—it was a dream come true. Just as his career was starting to take off, his dreams were shattered when some doofus ran over his foot. That culprit was not a stranger but a close personal friend. It was me.

ACCIDENTS AND HOPE That accident was something I will always regret. Chris and I were meeting for breakfast with some friends. He arrived first, when I pulled up in my car and waited for a parking spot to open up. Chris walked up to the car and we began to chat. We kept talking as I started to back up to park. Suddenly, Chris tripped and then fell from my view. He yelled for me to drive forward. I pulled forward and felt the car roll off his foot. He lay on the ground in immense pain. Jumping out, I came to his side. He winced in pain, grabbed my hand, and said, "Bro, it's not your fault. I'll be OK." The X-ray revealed 50 fractures, and the doctor told him he would never run and would have problems when he walked.

Chris fought his way back and went on to set course records and become one of the best in the world. He picked up amazing sponsors, spoke at charity events, and encouraged others to accomplish their dreams. Chris was often featured on the cover of magazines. My favorite cover was the one that his sponsors asked me to shoot.

It's difficult to describe how horrible it feels to injure one of your closest friends. Not to mention that I thought I had ruined his career. The accident was clearly my fault, but there was nothing that could be done. Chris never held a grudge and never gave up. He even used his position to give a boost to my photography career. Chris embodies the creative fight ideals.

When I feel defeated or overwhelmed, I look at Chris's shoe and it restores my hope and drive. That shoe helps me to stop slouching and stand up straight. So does that picture of Mark Wellman and the thought of Tommy Caldwell making his climb. If we allow them to, people who do great things can become like mentors who teach us resolve.

GRIT LESSONS Grit isn't easy to learn—there aren't any grit classes offered in schools. So I asked one friend who climbs El Capitan if grit can be taught. He said, "The only way to learn grit is to get out there and get your ass kicked. You have to suffer and you have to fail." Grit isn't something that you'll find in an online course. It's gained while in pursuit of something big. Grit requires belief that it can be done. That's why having someone to look up to can help. It also helps to be reminded that grit is in the secret sauce for success.

EXERCISE

Grit isn't gained without a challenge; and courage, backbone, and tenacity are born in difficult times. Such adversity scares most people away. Don't let that be you. Surround yourself with stories, images, and artifacts that will inspire you to dig deep and embolden you to press on. Use this exercise to find what will help.

STEP 1. PEOPLE

Write down five people you admire and a few words or a quote that describes why. Consider historical people, colleagues, or friends. Don't worry about getting your list right. This isn't an exhaustive list or a "top 5." Think of it like sketching out a few ideas. Keep this exercise simple and trust your gut. Here are a few examples to get you thinking about your own:

Nelson Mandela. Courage, kindness, and resolve. Imprisoned for 27 years without giving up.
Jeff Orwig (my Dad). Work ethic, deep faith, tough as nails.
Mother Teresa. Responded to human suffering with warmth, humility, and love.
Chris Lieto. Overcame obstacles and inspires others to do the same.
Frederick Douglass. Escaped the shackles of slavery and went on to thrive.
Theodore Roosevelt. Legendary vigor and grit.

PERSON YOU ADMIRE AND WHY

1. ....

2. ....

3. ....

4. ....

5. ....

STEP 2. ARTIFACTS, OBJECTS, THINGS

Select a couple of the names on your list and consider what objects you could display that would trigger and remind you of that person's grit. This could be a biography you display on a shelf or a quote that you print out. Consider these artifacts as more than decoration or fluff. In your mind, treat them like totems or icons that represent a deeper reality. Print out a photograph of Nelson Mandela and let his countenance fortify your resolve to fight the good fight.

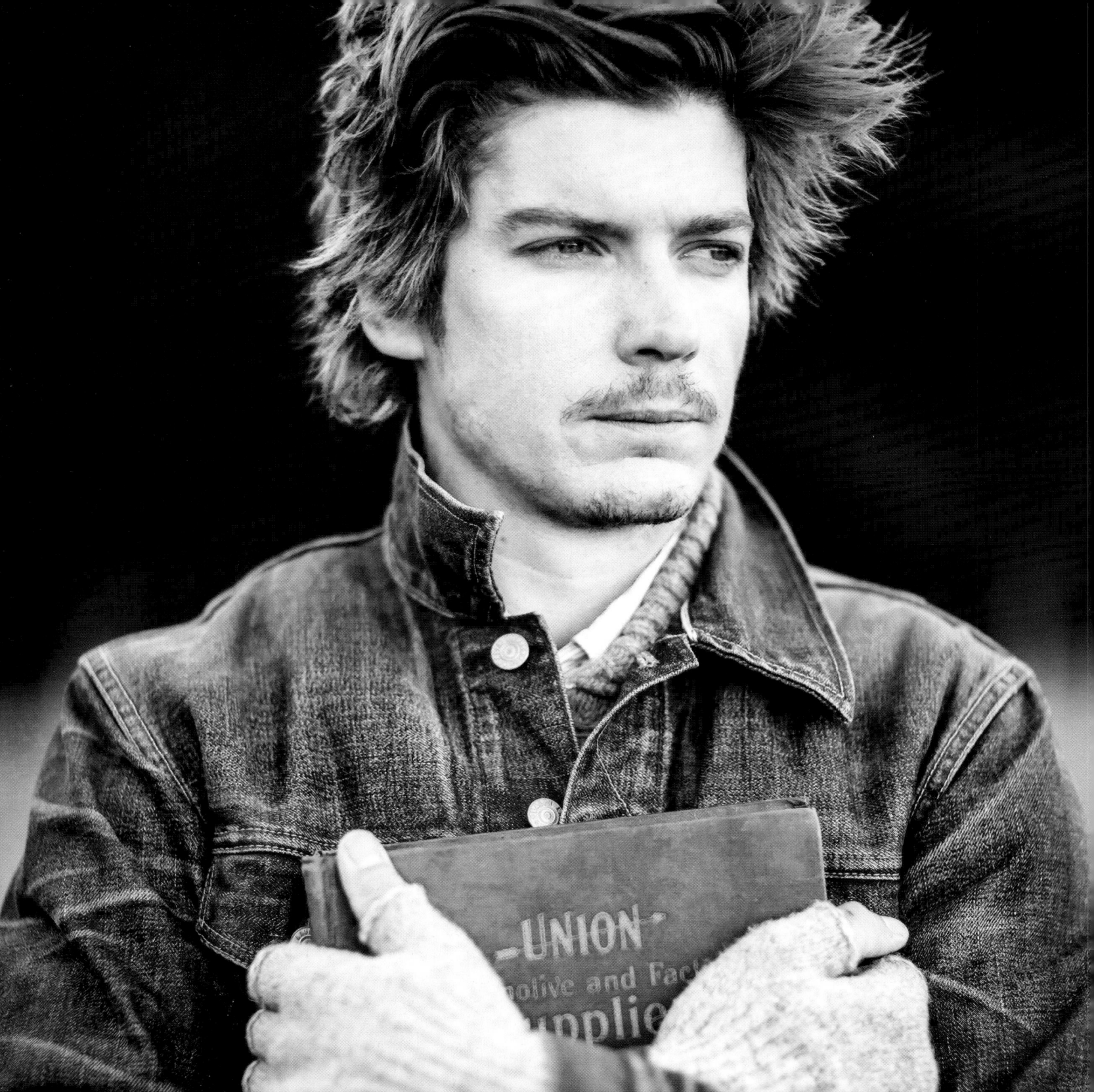

CHAPTER TWENTY-TWO

THE

BURNT

BOOK

The burning of a book is tragically sad, especially when it's been written and illustrated by your own hand. But that's what Ted wanted to do. He was on his way home to burn his book in the incinerator in the basement of his apartment building in New York. The book had been his pride and hope, but it was now a source of disappointment and shame. Maybe his dad had been right after all. Creating the book had been an attempt at a new career path for Ted. But the book was rejected by every publisher who read it. After its 27th rejection, he decided it was time for that book to go up in flames. Rather than bustle hurriedly like everyone else, he walked slowly through the busy city streets. And the melancholy he felt tuned his senses to notice things he might have otherwise overlooked, like the people who passed by.

A TWISTING, SWERVING PATH On the long walk home, Ted caught sight of and then talked with an old friend who had just gotten a new job at a publishing company. After catching up, his friend took him directly to meet the president of the company, and twenty minutes later he was signing a contract for the book he almost burned. As Ted put it, "If I'd been going down the other side of Madison Avenue, I would be in the dry-cleaning business today." That book was the start of a new career that would blossom into great success.

The path to success isn't smooth, and it always involves setbacks, disappointment, and an unexpected twist of fate. And the path is never a straight line. The path veers, swerves, loops back, and winds around. The path looks like it was designed less by Frank Lloyd Wright and more by M. C. Escher or Dr. Seuss. One person's path to success doesn't create the perfect trajectory for someone else. Other people's paths are like treasure maps. They are insightful and fun to look at, but nearly impossible to re-create. Success always consists of taking your own uncharted course.

As Ted later wrote in his best-selling book about the journey to success, "You will come to a place where the streets are not marked." He was not making this up but reflecting on his own journey and life. Success is a funny thing, and it's difficult to describe; it changes shape, and its relevance can quickly disappear. What I mean is that the success that got you where you are today is never quite enough to get you where you need to go next. Yet we are all driven to succeed and hardwired to thrive. That's why we love hearing stories about how someone rose to the top, like with the author Ted. How did he begin?

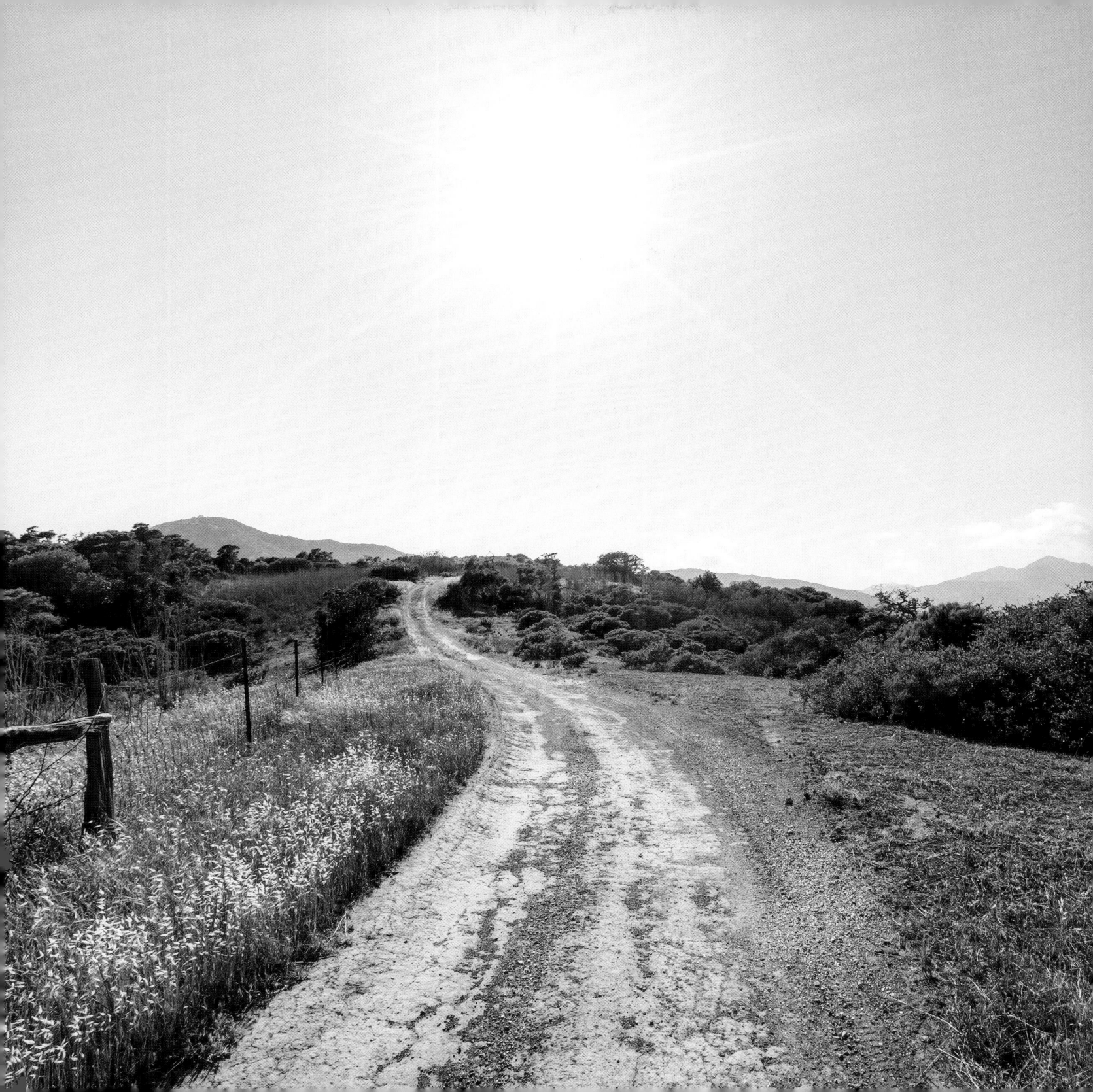

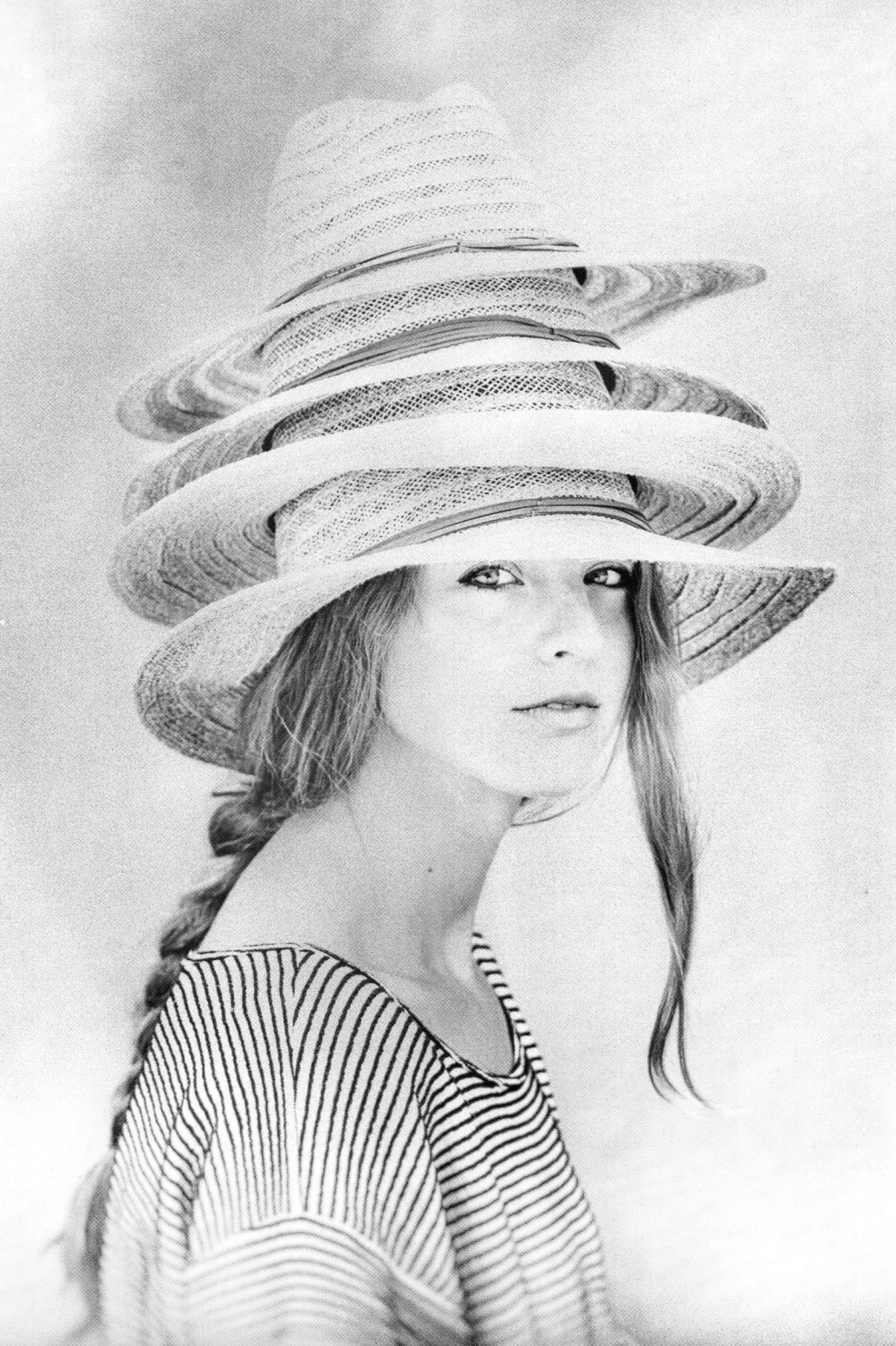

As a young kid, Ted was given a definition of success that he didn't like. His father wanted him to become a doctor when all he wanted to do was draw. After graduating from college, he went to Oxford to please his dad, but he eventually dropped out. Ted tore up the definition of success given to him and decided to write his own. He wanted to draw and write. So he took on a pen name, or *nom de guerre* (fighting name) as the French call it. Ted's new name would be a tribute to his mom and a hat-tip to his dad. His fighting name was made up of his mom's maiden name and an honorary doctorate title even though he didn't earn the degree.

Under his new name, Ted began to draw and write with a drive that was fierce. For the first 15 years of his career he paid his dues by creating advertisements for major companies and magazines. Eventually, he had had enough and he wrote his first book for kids. It was a story about the wild and wonderful imagination of a young boy who later becomes too embarrassed to share his true thoughts. Shopping the book around wasn't easy. Children's books weren't exactly blockbusters back in that time. Eventually it was picked up because of the chance meeting with an old friend, and that's how Ted Geisel—or as we know him, Dr. Seuss—began.

YOUER THAN YOU

In many ways, Dr. Seuss embodies the core values of *The Creative Fight*, and he is an exemplar for all those who are interested in developing their own unique voice, creating their best work, and contributing to the greatest degree. In his writing, Dr. Seuss was a champion for the individual, and his books are a constant reminder to only wear the hats that reflect who you are. As he said, "There is no one alive that is youer than you." When we stop trying to be someone else, we become more alive. Some may dismiss Dr. Seuss's work as a cute collection of books for kids. Yet embedded within the whimsical characters and rhyming verse are profound truths and questions about life. In one book he asks, "Why fit in when you were born to stand out?"

Dr. Seuss was on a mission to make change. He wasn't just writing to distract or entertain. Frederick Douglass once said,

"It is easier to build strong children than to repair broken men." Dr. Seuss wrote books that did both. And his success as an author hinges upon his risk to be himself. His writing wasn't an attempt to imitate someone else.

As a character in a Dr. Seuss book might say, there are at least 457,653 major misconceptions that we have concerning success. Let me highlight two. First, our definition of success is too easily influenced by someone else. We show up in life and are handed a definition of what it means to succeed, when in reality success is something that we should define ourselves. It hinges upon asking the question posed by Mark Twain: "The two most important days of your life are the day you were born and the day you figure out why." Ted discovered his why early on and fought to make it a reality.

Imagine if Dr. Seuss's first book, *And to Think That I Saw It on Mulberry Street*, went up in flames. The world would be a much less meaningful place. Or what if he hadn't ever written *The Grinch*? The commercialism of Christmas might even be worse. When Ted thought of Christmas, he felt like a scrooge. He was sick and tired of how commercialized it had become. So he wrote a story about the Grinch and modeled the main character after himself. Ted was not the hero of his own book but the character that needed to be saved. That's why we all like the grumbly green character so much.

BE REAL AND FIND HOPE

Becoming more creative doesn't mean slapping a fake smile on your face, nor does it mean indulging in negative critique. The creative fight is more having the guts to be real and to find hope even when all is lost. Just like Dr. Seuss, you have something inside of you that is meant to better the world. This is the reason you are here. This is your life's call.

Most of us ignore the passion that pounds in our chest because we think ourselves too small. "How could I make a difference? I'm not as smart, skilled, talented, tall, or connected as someone else." When we tell ourselves these myths, we keep our mouths shut. We compare the number of social media fans and followers we have and think that we can make a dent. We forget that greatness isn't about many but one. As Dr. Seuss reminds us, "To the world you may be one person; but to one person you may be the world."

You have been given certain gifts, talents, and skills. Your life experience has shaped you into a one-of-a-kind, unique human. You can contribute to the world in a way that no one else can. For Ted Geisel, his something was writing and illustrating books. You have to find out what it is for yourself. The only way to begin to do that is to try. It won't happen if you keep your something hidden in a box. Ted had to fight to find his life's call, and it almost didn't come to be. The universe conspired and Ted ran into a friend who kick-started his career. This fortunate event happened only because Ted was out on the street. You need to get out there too and give it a worthwhile fight to make your something be seen.

Second, we tend to mistakenly think that the path to accomplishment is a straight line. That's at least what it looks like when we see someone else succeed. The reality is that the path is always a circuitous route. When I taught college students I was often asked, "How did you get to where you are?" I consistently responded that my story is a long and winding tale. My story wasn't A - B - C. It was more C - A - R - P - E - D - I - E - M. I was the career planner's nightmare at the school where I taught. The students were supposed to study photography and then become photographers—that's it. Yet I had discovered a hidden secret—that the best photographers were those who didn't follow the cookie-cutter path. To make more interesting photographs you have to live a more interesting life. Wild, free, and abundant life has a way of shaping success that is impossible to predict. Yet the more we embrace the adventurous road, the better the odds.

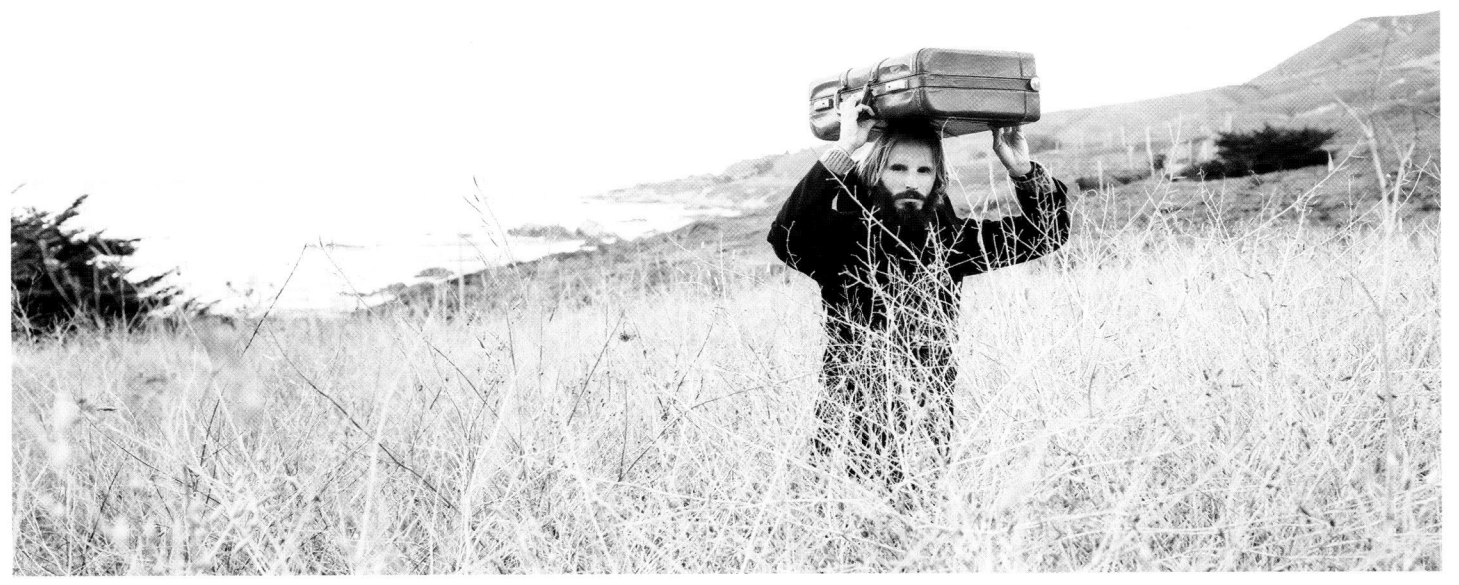

EXERCISE

STEP 1

Selecting a new name can free you from the fetters of the past. Just as actors choose stage names
and soldiers select a *nom de guerre*, choose a name that emboldens you to become
more creative and alive. And use the name whenever you can, like when you subscribe to a magazine
related to your craft. Or use it when you need to muster up the courage to tackle a tough project.
Ask yourself, "What would _____ do?" and then step into those shoes.

STEP 2

Take a few moments of quiet to consider how you might include yourself in your work.
Consider a project that you are working on, and "write yourself into the script"
(like how Dr. Seuss modeled the Grinch after himself). You don't literally need to be part of the
project—just imagine, What if? What if you were a central component of the project at hand?
What if the task weren't so abstract and theoretical but included more of you?

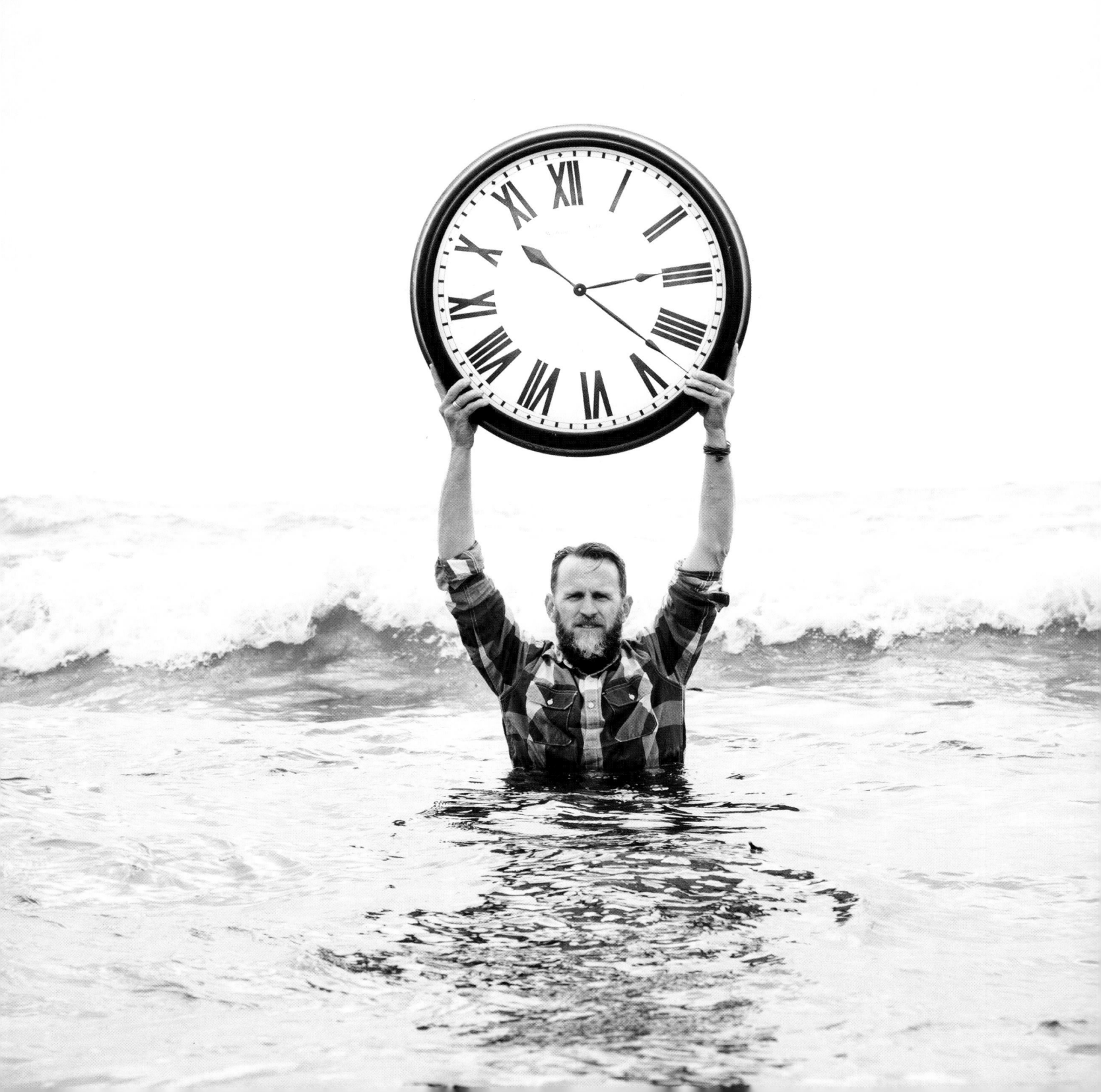

CHAPTER TWENTY-THREE

UNSTUCK AND FREE

In the vast ocean of time, the older we get the more prominent the clock becomes. In our youth, time was simple and slow. Time was unlimited and free. Then as we grew up, it became more of a blur as days, weeks, months, and years become less defined. Time compresses the more we age. Consider the 6-year-old who can't fathom life past the age of 8, versus the 40-year-old who can easily imagine life at 30, 20, and 10.

Looking forward, time looks like a string of yarn stretched out before our path. Time extends to the horizon and we approach it one step at a time. Looking backward, time is like a pile of yarn—sometimes stretched out and other times clumped up into a ball. When gathered up, it's always surprising to see how so much time can fit into the palm of your hand. Time isn't as linear as we like to think.

THE TRAM RIDE Time is both simple and complex, like water rushing around your feet. The current is a refreshing flow, but watch your step or you might be swept out to sea or, worse, transported by a tramline upstream. That's what the British Empire did in the 1800s with injured soldiers during a time of war. The injured were sent up Haslar Creek in Portsmouth. These soldiers were sent by way of a tram, hence the phrase (or so the story goes) "up the creek without a paddle." There they were held prisoner until they recovered or died. The only escape, as some tried, was through the sewers to the creek. Hence the related phrase "up shit creek."

While we haven't literally been transported up Haslar Creek, we all know what it's like to be stuck. When we're stuck, time seems to slow and drag. A minute can feel like an hour, and a month can feel like a year. That's how I felt in my mid-twenties when life hadn't turned out as I had planned. Instead of health and happiness, I was overwhelmed by constant and chronic pain from a car accident years before. Regardless of how I tried, I couldn't see a way out. I was stuck and was coming undone. Time seemed to crawl.

After a number of years, my situation turned for the worse. I saw some of the best physicians around, at institutions like Stanford, UCLA, UCSF, and the Mayo Clinic, but nothing seemed to help. In the big picture of things, my situation wasn't that bad, but when you're stuck it always seems worse than it is. It was a dark night for my soul. I was frustrated, angry, and depressed. On the good days, I had hope, yet the pain kept dragging me down. Chronic pain is a cycle that is hard to beat. Anyone who has been through this (or is going through this now) knows what I mean.

A LIFE RING SHAPED LIKE A SMALL BOX During this time I was living in sunny Los Angeles, but the world didn't seem very warm. Engulfed by my own circumstances, I had a very myopic and bleak view of the world. That was until my dad, out of the blue, gave me a gift. Nudged by an inner voice, he bought me a DSLR camera of my own. This was a significant gift, considering this was before the digital revolution and

during a time when having a "real camera" was a big deal. I was excited to have something that I could do even with the limits that I faced. I had very little experience with photography, but I started to play.

Soon I discovered that the camera is a magical device. When I held it up to my eye the world became quiet and it blocked out my pain. I looked through the lens and the darkness turned to light. No longer focusing on myself, I saw the world with fresh eyes. What was once dismal became divine. The camera changed the way I experienced the world and shifted how I understood time.

Rather than feeling burdened by time, the camera helped me appreciate it one small slice at a time. I discovered within these slices new worlds and hidden truths that previously went unseen. One of my first findings came as I was walking down a busy urban street. Loud traffic rushed by, and hazy smog filled the air. Let's just say it wasn't the most picturesque scene. But when I looked down I saw one of the most beautiful things I have ever seen.

GUTTER PALM There, in the middle of this urban jungle, I noticed a tiny palm tree growing out of a gutter nearby. I stopped and stared as if I were on holy ground. I began to wonder how it got there. I imagined a small and proud palm seed high up in the top of the tree—then, falling from its great height until it settled in a subterranean concrete ditch below. A light rain was enough to help this seed grow. For days and months it stretched for the light above, until one day it pushed past the metal bars and there it was. I was suddenly filled with hope. If this small tree could fight, so could I. And in this strange way, my camera and this gutter palm freed me from my rusty cage.

With experiences like this, the camera quickly became a close mentor and friend. It gave the ability to "savor life intensely at 1/100th of a second," as the photographer Marc Riboud said. The camera became a passport to explore new land. It taught me how to slow down and how to be grateful for the small moments in life. It helped me discover secrets

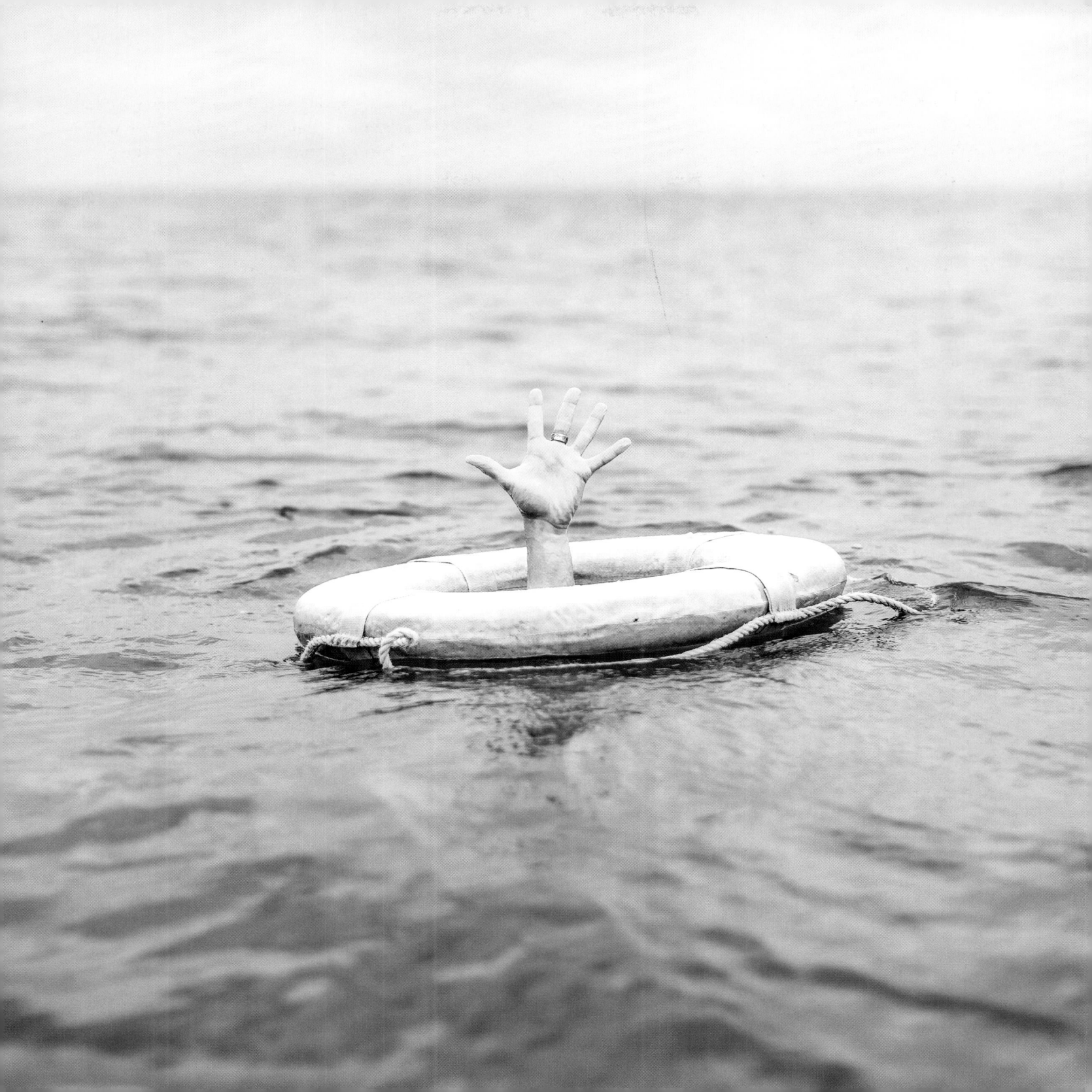

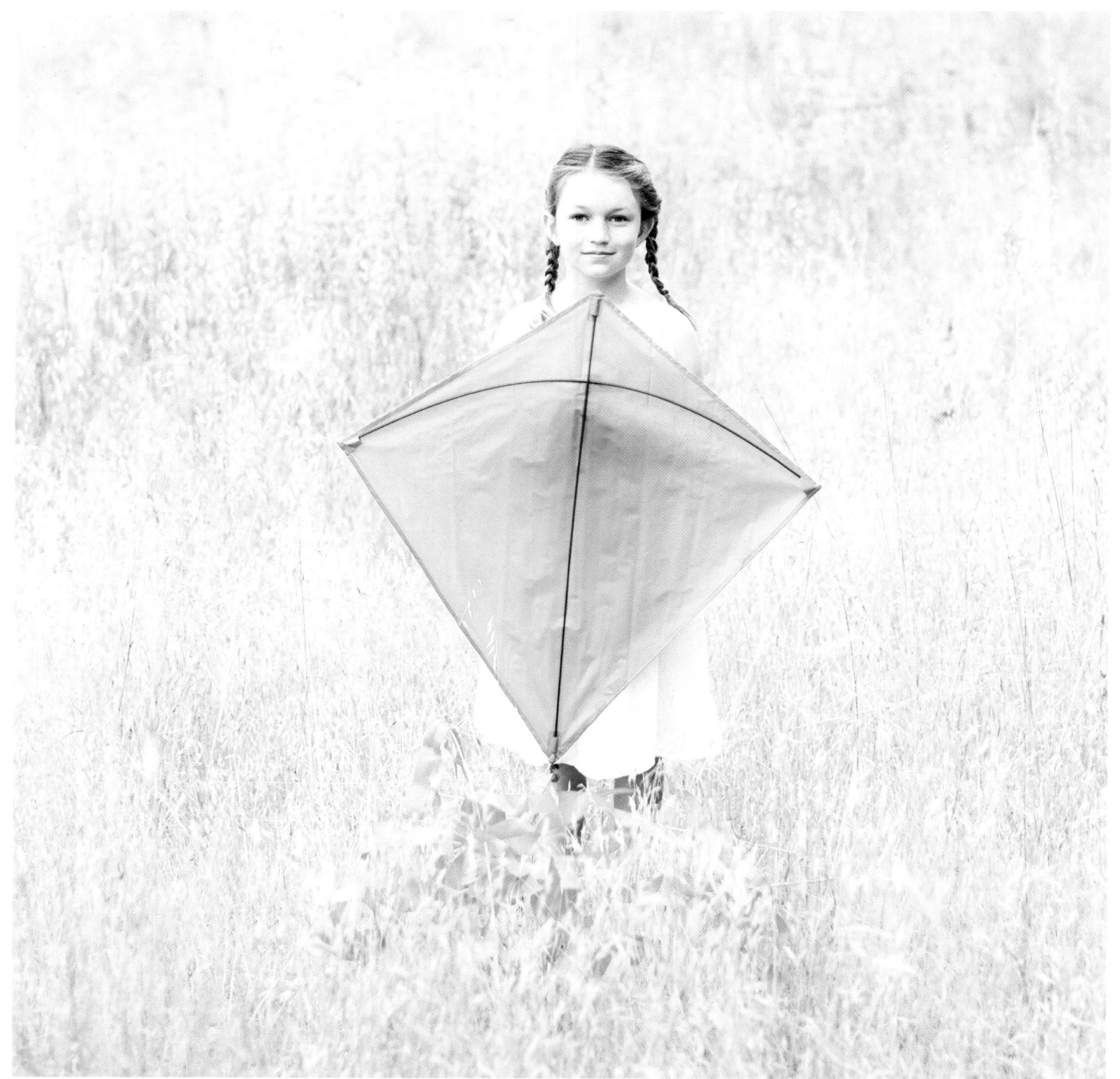

hidden beneath the surface of things. Yet still I found myself getting stuck. So I would turn to my camera and use it like a crowbar to pry my way out. Eventually, my camera turned into a paddle and canoe that helped me navigate downstream. No longer "up a creek," I was free.

STRATEGIES FOR BREAKING FREE There isn't a formula to getting unstuck, but changing your perspective can help. When you are stuck, problems appear bigger than they are. It isn't very creative to treat a big problem like it's small. But it also isn't very creative to treat small problems like they are huge. To be creative we must size up the problem for what it is—which is nearly impossible to do by yourself. When you are stuck, you have to admit the need for outside help. Seek assistance from someone you trust. Don't give up, because you never know when someone will throw you a line.

Next, it takes patience to get unstuck. Yet patience doesn't mean you have to sit still. Like trying to fly a kite on a windless day, it helps to run. Movement builds momentum, gets the creative fibers to stretch, and oxygenates the mind. Clarity comes quickly to those who don't sit around.

Before my dad gave me a camera, my perspective was skewed. Life seemed worse than it really was. I couldn't see past my own condition—the pain constantly calling attention to itself. Without knowing it, I became self-absorbed. When I was given the gift of a camera, it was like a lens cap fell off my eyes and I was finally able to see. Even more liberating, I was suddenly able to focus on something other than myself.

This shift in focus set me free. No longer limited by a dull vision of the world, I began to pay attention to other things. And the more you pay attention, the more beautiful something becomes. I lost myself to the beauty of the world and had never felt more alive.

I was in the zone, or what the author Mihaly Csikszentmihalyi calls "flow." Flow is that experience of being fully immersed and energized by a task. In the flow state we forget ourselves. And herein lies one of the most powerful antidotes to being stuck: self-forgetfulness. Whether achieved by doing an activity or by extending kindness to someone else, when we think of ourselves less, our lives expand. It's one of the great paradoxes of the creative life—a less self-centered view of the world will set you free to become more of who it is that you were designed to be.

EXERCISE

Most of the exercises in this book are about you; this one is about doing something for someone else. Think of someone you know who is going through a rough patch, and consider doing something that will give that person a boost.

Without a hidden agenda, follow my dad's lead and give a gift, write a note, or share an encouraging word. You don't have to be extravagant and give away a camera—sometimes it's a simple act that helps the most. When you're stuck, even the smallest amount of kindness can go a long way. And a bit of generosity and kindness will revive your own creativity as well. While this isn't the goal—it's more of a side effect—pay attention to how being kind affects you as well. Most importantly, do something for someone this week.

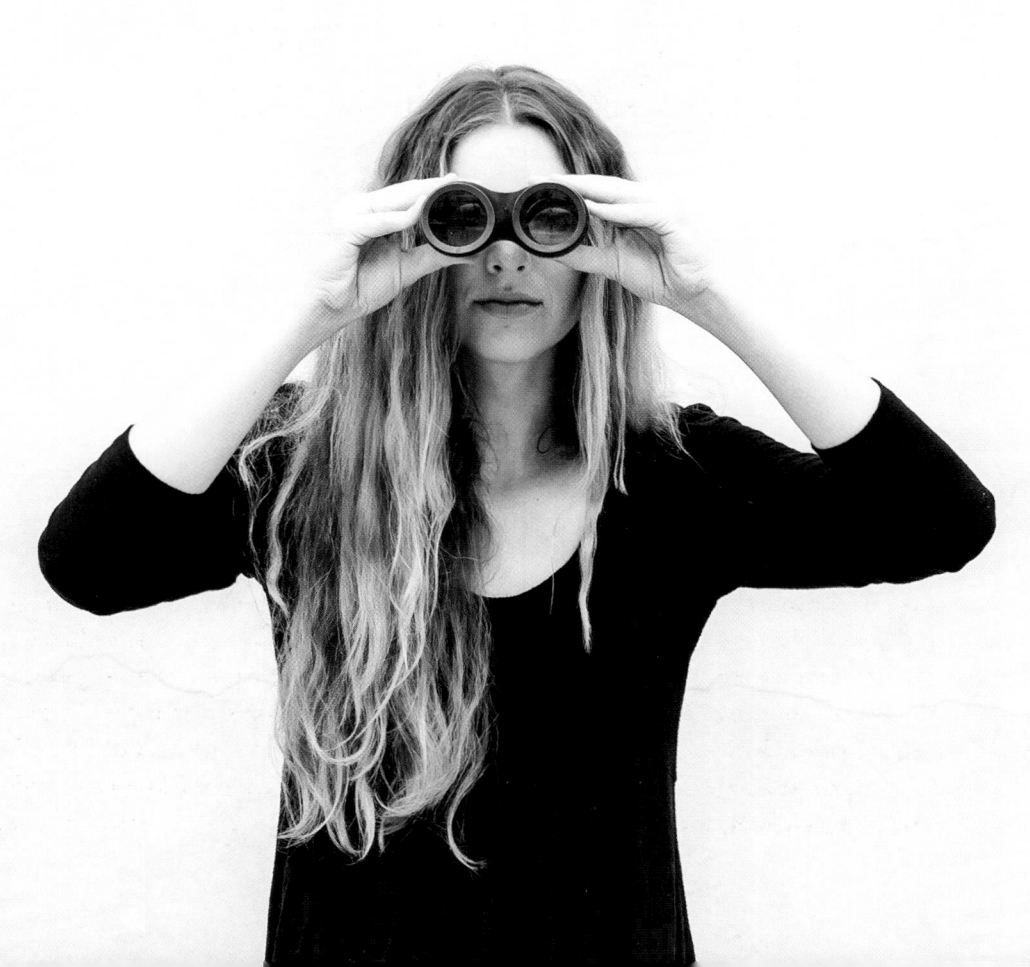

CHAPTER TWENTY-FOUR

THE MISSING MUSE

There is no way to know for certain when the creative spark will strike. Yet as with carrying a lightning rod in a storm, there are ways to increase the odds. As we've seen throughout this book, showing up and working hard can make a huge difference. As Coleman Cox said, "The harder I work the luckier I get." And I say that the harder you work, the more creative you become. Effort and creativity are closely intertwined.

The celebrated American painter and photographer Chuck Close put it this way: "The advice I like to give young artists, or really anybody who'll listen to me, is not to wait around for inspiration. Inspiration is for amateurs; the rest of us just show up and get to work." And this isn't just a flippant, off-the-cuff remark. Chuck Close was tragically paralyzed over twenty years ago, yet as an artist he continues to thrive.

151

HARD WORK ISN'T ENOUGH The idea that creative inspiration strikes when we put in the time and effort is a strong theme throughout this book. Yet that isn't the only way. Creative inspiration is complex, and it doesn't always come like a lightning bolt from the sky; sometimes it arrives like a quiet voice that comes to you while floating in the middle of the sea. Inspiration is as unpredictable as the waves. Regardless, inspiration does ignite most often when we begin the work, yet sometimes all the tenacity, grit, and self-discipline in the world aren't enough to pave the way for inspiration to appear.

A few years ago, I began to think more and more about what it means to live the creative life. I filled countless pages in my journals with ideas, sketches, and quotes. The creative juices flowed in an effortless and exciting way. Then a small light bulb went off in my head: What if these ideas could turn into a book? My enthusiasm swelled. I began to imagine how the project might evolve. I put together a proposal and after a few revisions sent it off with high hopes.

IDEALS ARE EASY My excitement was off the charts when I received the good news—my book proposal was approved. I took a deep breath and triumphantly raised my fist into the air. I was proud and it was time to begin. Without any hesitation, I began by journaling a few thoughts. I quickly wrote about the type of book that I wanted to write. I began with an ideal. Here's what I wrote: "I want to write about the adventure and reward of the creative life. I want to write something that stands the test of time. Simple, uncluttered and true. A guiding force. A magnetic north. A reference book. A survival guide. I want to write a book that is authentic and alive. I want to write something that is without veneer. I want to write something that will help people live more creative and meaningful lives. I want to write a book that will bring change. I want to write with steel strong words with carbon fiber ink. I want to write a book that I can be proud of, one that I can display and evangelize without a second thought." I wrote and wrote, the words gushing forth in an uninhibited flow. With the vision cast, now it was time for the real writing to begin. I cleared my schedule for the following day, left for home, and my confidence soared.

The next day I walked into my studio with a victorious stride, saying aloud, "This book is going to write itself." Little did I know that I was going to have to eat my words. With a book title like *The Creative Fight*, how could I have been so naive? I sat down to write and suddenly all of my momentum disappeared. The gush turned into a slog. The once bright creative spark became dull. Instead of enthusiasm, I was full of dread. I tried to write, but the words came out like chatter and noise. The sentences read like empty platitudes and worn-out clichés. I felt like an imposter—no, I was an imposter. Self-doubt stiffened my joints. Days turned into weeks and weeks, and I still hadn't written a single usable word.

Picasso said, "Inspiration exists, but it has to find you working." Picasso must have lied, because I was working but inspiration never found my door. Or maybe it was my fault? Maybe I was working in the wrong way, like showing up for a boat trip but arriving at the wrong dock. Maybe inspiration was waiting for me somewhere else. I felt adrift, unequipped, and in over my head, like a tourist who stood in a sailboat for a photograph but was suddenly blown out to sea. I was out of my element and ill prepared. The immensity of the situation made me feel like a small speck on the endless sea.

THE VISITATION Floating alone in the vast ocean, I was lost, inspiration nowhere in sight. But then, as if I had been visited by a muse, Steve Callahan's plight came to mind. During a solo transatlantic race, Callahan's sailboat struck an unidentified object and sank off the coast of Africa. In the darkness of night he escaped with a small life raft and a duffel bag of supplies. Stranded and alone, he drifted across the Atlantic Ocean for 76 days. It was a miracle he survived. Yet it was on this voyage that he came to know himself and become the most alive. Callahan later reflected, "To my mind, voyaging through wildernesses, be they full of woods or waves, is essential to the growth and maturity of the human spirit. It is in the wilderness that you really learn who you are."

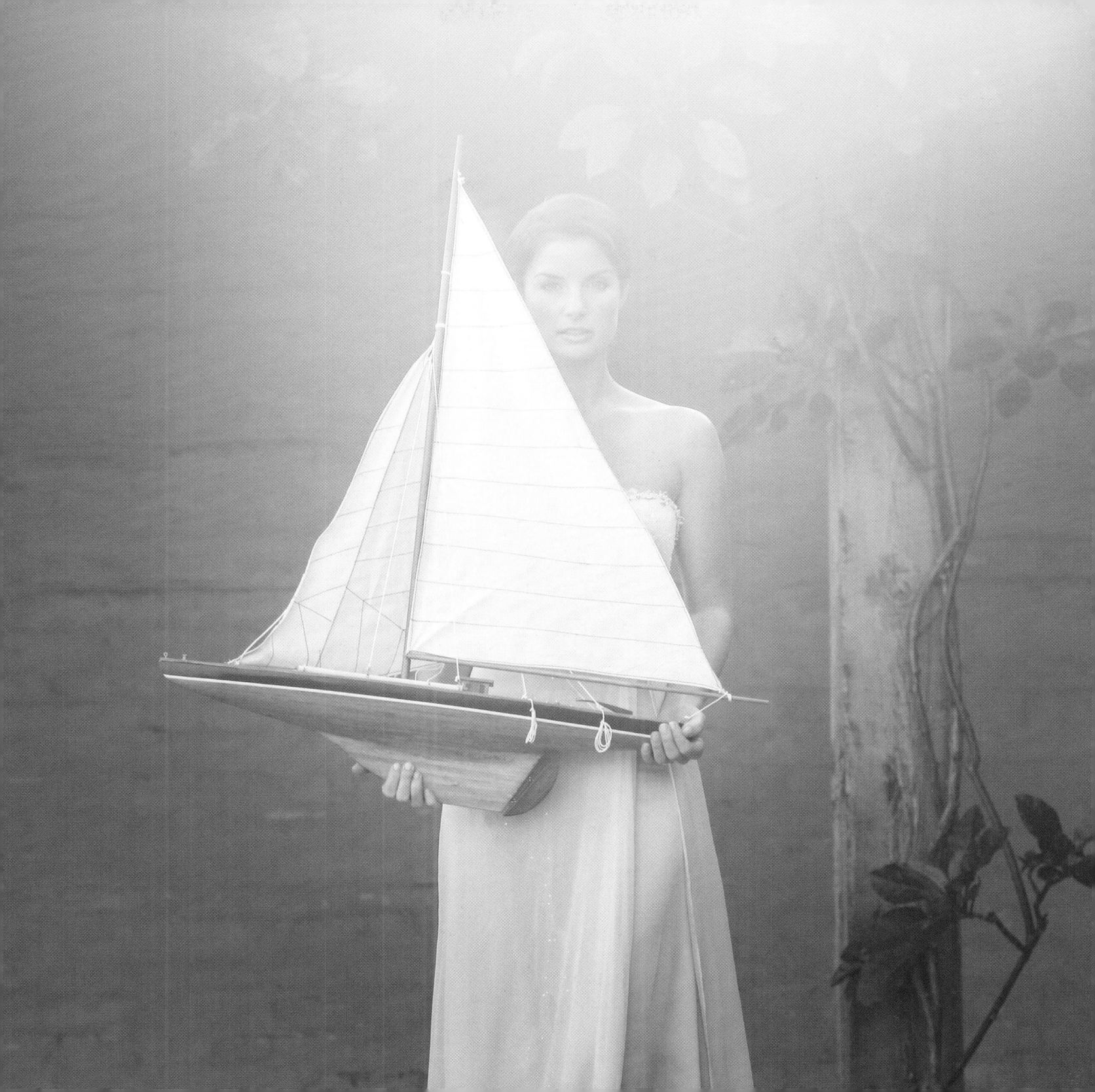

It was as if a muse wanted me to revisit Callahan's story to give me insight into my own. It became clear that my problem was not about talent or skill but about identity and control. I had been trying to subdue and wrestle the ideas of the book, when what I needed most was to get lost in the wilderness in order to grow. Rather than work on the book, I needed the book to work on me.

Before I could make progress, I needed to abandon the extra baggage I had unknowingly brought along. After doing this, I then realized I was out of fuel. I was depleted and couldn't figure out why. The muse spoke and reminded me that the energy needed to prepare for a voyage is different from the energy needed to set sail. And a voice whispered, *When your ship sinks (as it inevitably will), you have to stay calm.*

ADRIFT Alone in my life raft, I had been nervous and scared. Worse, I didn't want my weakness to show. So I acted like I had it all together, stood up, and pounded on my chest, but the ocean didn't seem to care. Defeated, I crumpled up at the base of the raft. I felt so small. The muse brought more of Callahan's words to mind: "The heartfelt realization of one's insignificance yields a calming sense of being completely connected to a greater whole." Like a key that opened a lock, smallness and isolation gave way to connection and grace. I realized my mistake. After my book project was approved, the creative spark vanished because I was trying to write from a posture of conquest and strength. This type of book could only be written as one who was adrift on the sea—for it is from a position of weakness that you find strength.

WHY DO WE LOVE THE SEA? IT IS BECAUSE IT HAS SOME POTENT POWER TO MAKE US THINK THE THINGS WE LIKE TO THINK.
—ROBERT HENRI

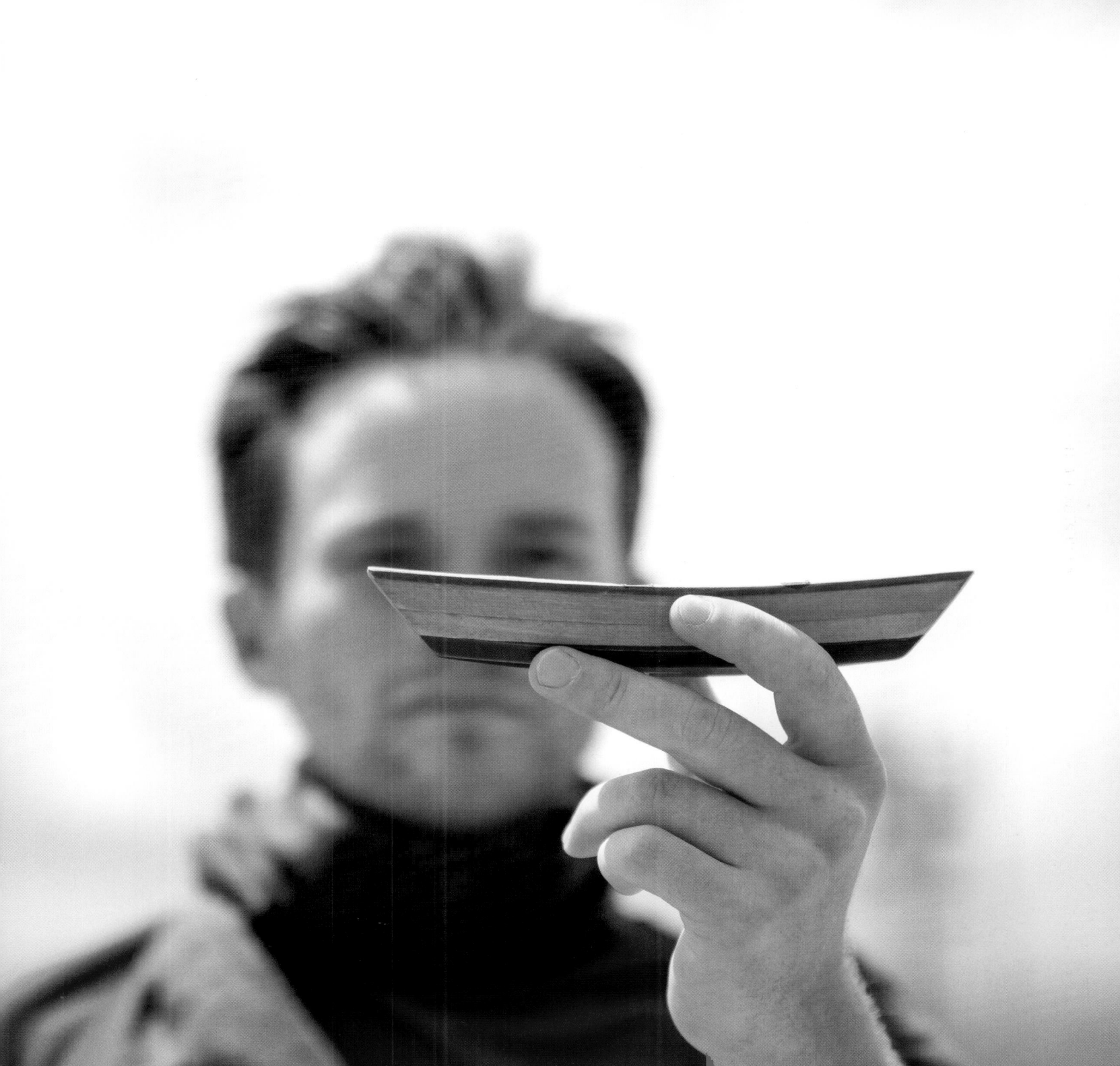

Creativity flourishes most when we stop pretending. And creativity always prefers honesty over show. It became clear that this project couldn't be about making myself look talented or smart. And it couldn't be written with the ending in mind; this book was a journey into the unknown. Like most worthwhile creative endeavors, it was a risk and the possibility of failure was real.

When we are stuck, working harder can help, but it can also make the problem worse. At first glance, this may sound contradictory to the basic premise of this book. Yet the creative fight isn't just about climbing the ladder, but making sure that you have found the right one. Letting go of ego and admitting that creative inspiration isn't always something that we can generate ourselves is a surefire way to speed up the search for the ladder you were destined to climb.

MANY MUSES The ancient Greeks were a culture inspired. Collectively, their creative output wasn't just a spark; it was a blaze. Yet the Greeks believed that inspiration came not from within, but from an outside source. For the Greeks, the epicenter of inspiration was not the individual but a muse. The ancient myths told of nine muse goddesses who provided inspiration for literature, science, and the arts. These nine daughters of Zeus fueled the fire.

Thousands of years later, the ideas and myths surrounding the muse have evolved. In modern times, we have traded in the limited and ethereal archetype muse for a more ubiquitous form. Today, a muse might be a musician who inspires us to sing, a mountain that motivates us to paint, or the flight of a bird that inspires us to get out of our locked cage. Muses take on countless shapes and forms. Some are predictable, like the calm ocean at dusk, whereas others go unseen, like the feeling you get when you climb up a tree.

I once climbed to the top of an ancient redwood. Out of breath and tired from climbing, I clung to the now-small tree trunk that fit inside my two hands. Hundreds of feet below, the fifteen-foot-wide trunk was anchored to the ground. Swaying in that treetop, I felt that I was in a sacred space. I took a deep breath and drank in the pine scent, clouds, and light. Up in the tree, I felt on top of the world, as if I could almost touch the heavens above. My soul took flight. It was a surreal and spiritually refreshing experience to be perched so far off the ground.

THIN PLACES AND MYTH The ancient Celts might say my experience was divine. Celtic mythology considers some places—including trees—thresholds or doorways to the divine. Such places are called "thin" because they occur when the visible and the invisible worlds practically touch.

As one traditional Celtic saying explains, "Heaven and earth are only three feet apart, but in the thin places that distance is even smaller." Thin places are often associated with wild landscapes, mountaintops, rivers, and oceans. What makes a place thin isn't so much the geography as the experience there. As poet Sharlande Sledge wrote, "Thin places are where the door between this world and the next is cracked open for a moment, and the light is not all on the other side."

The concept of "thin places" is an old and beautiful one. When I get stuck or just feeling dull, I visit places that make me feel refreshed and clear my head. This experience doesn't always include a spiritual glow, but sometimes it does. My favorite place to go is an ancient redwood grove. And I love to walk to the water's edge, whether on the sand or at the end of a pier. Or I like to get lost on the mountain biking trails behind my house. The refreshment of nature restores my hope and belief, belief that my situation can improve. This faith acts like kindling that keeps the creative fire aglow.

Thin places aren't limited to epic landscapes and mountaintops. You can create a thin space in various ways. When I'm stuck somewhere that isn't ideal, I find that closing my eyes and taking a few deep breaths can help. Other ideas include lighting a candle or using a Tibetan meditation singing bowl. Rather than do something different every time, be consistent so that the peace and refreshment can more readily flow. Try it for yourself, even now. Pause reading. Close your eyes and take a breath with the idea of seeing your space as thin.

EXERCISE

STEP 1. CREATE AN ENERGY MAP
Creative progress isn't easy; it requires different types of energy at each stage:

Stage 1. Energy to plan
Stage 2. Energy to execute
Stage 3. Energy to recover when you fall
Stage 4. Energy to finish strong

For an upcoming project, goal, or dream, create a map that clarifies the three types of energy that you will need. Mapping this out can serve as a reminder to shift gears as you transition, and it can act as a guide to help you maintain the right type of energy for the task at hand. In your journal, write out a few characteristics of the type of energy. For example:

1. Plan = excitement, imagination, inhibition
2. Execute = grit, tenacity, steadfast strength
3. Recover = calm, patient

STEP 2. CREATE YOUR OWN MUSE
Myths spark the imagination. The Greek myths told of nine muses for different domains (poetry, dance, comedy, song, and so on). The muses had names, personalities, and skills. The ancient poets, dancers, and other creatives turned to a muse for help.

As a way to modernize this concept, write a myth of your own. The simplest definition of a myth is a story with meaning attached to it. Write a myth that describes five muses of your own—consider selecting muses that are people who inspire you to live in a better way. This might be an author, a musician, a pastor, a poet, a friend, or a comedian of international fame.

STEP 3. DEFINE THIN PLACES
Thin places are sacred and special places that open you up to the divine. Select a few thin places that inspire you. Consider finding thin places in your town, city, state, country, and world. In your journal, write out a list of five, and then visit one of these in search of the divine.

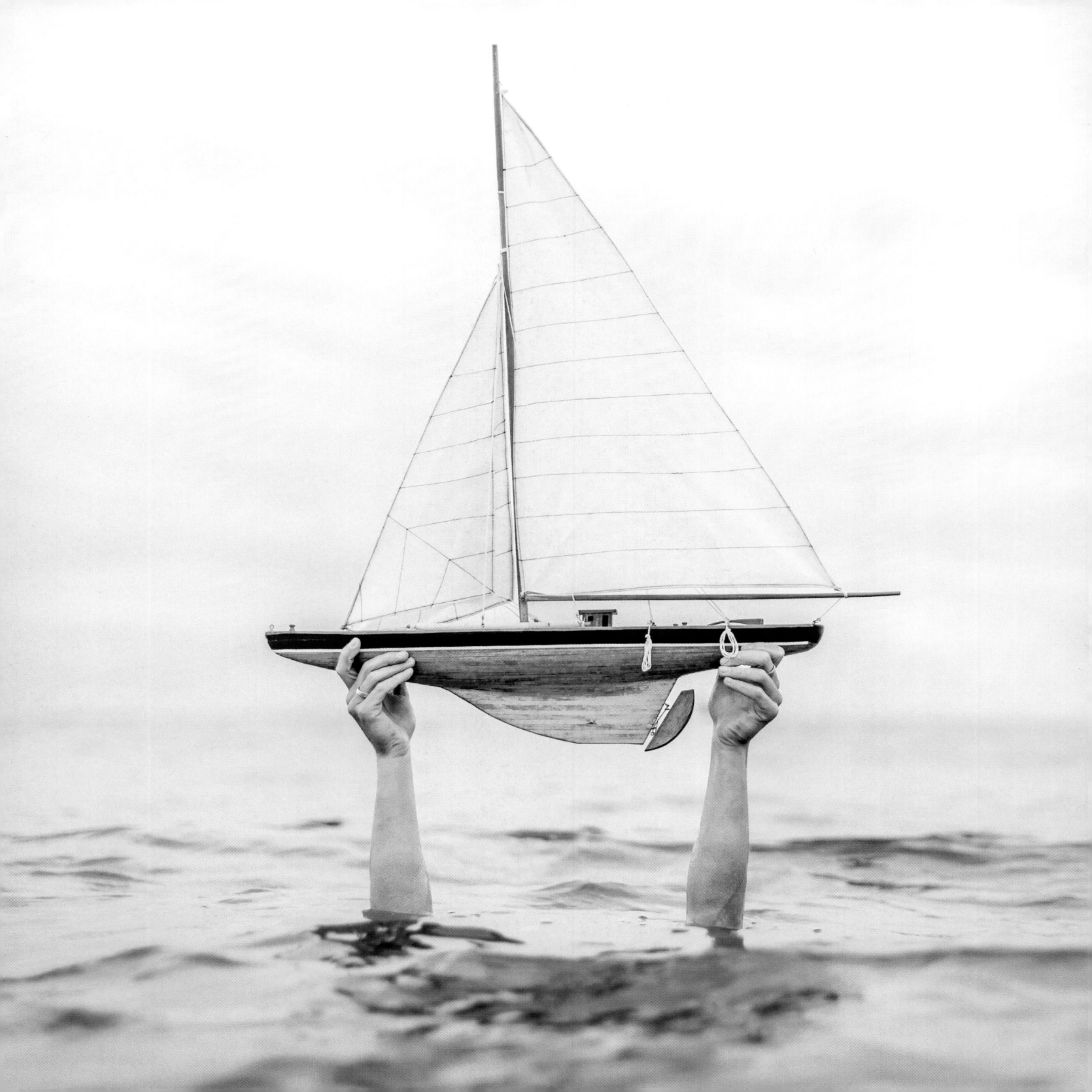

PART FOUR: THRIVE

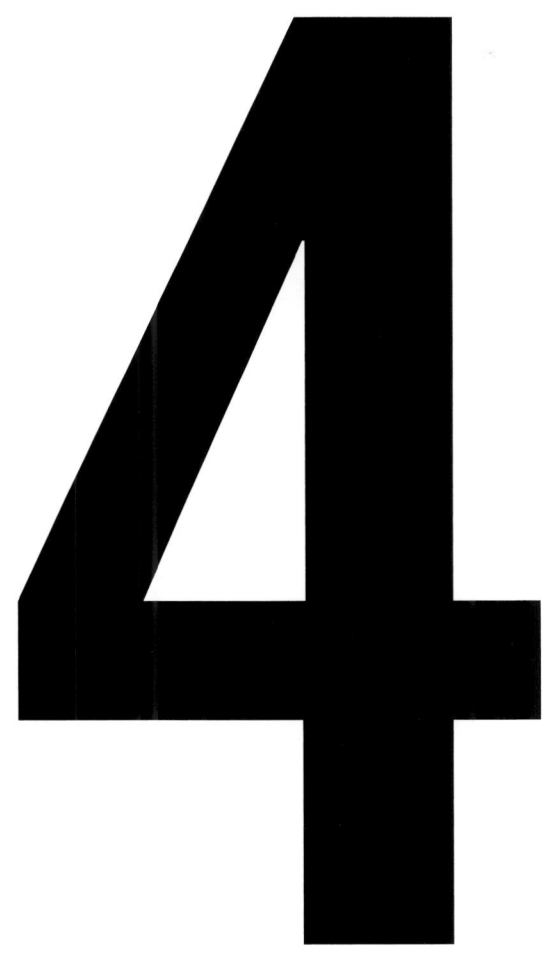

NOT LIFE, BUT GOOD LIFE, IS TO BE CHIEFLY VALUED.
— SOCRATES

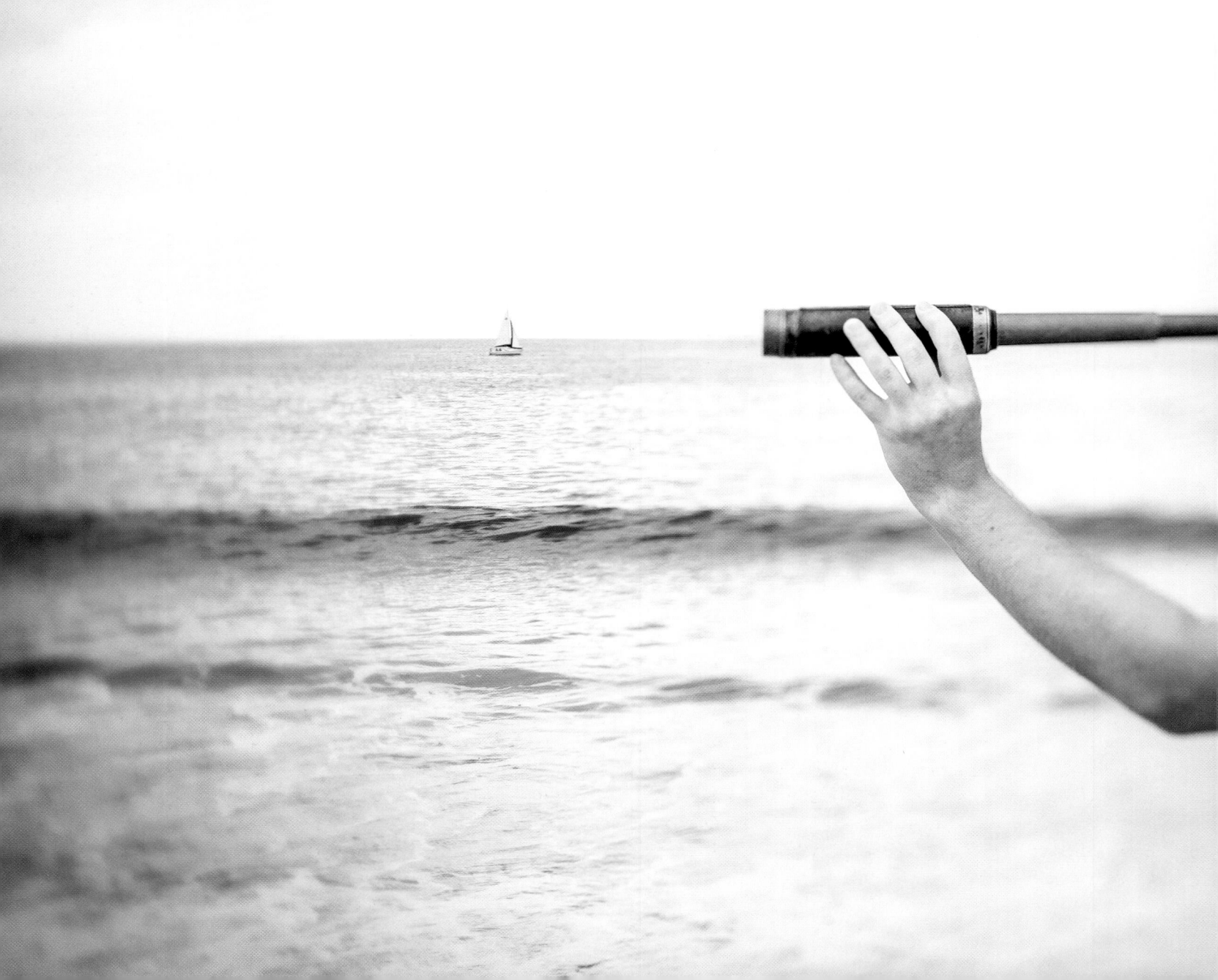

CHAPTER TWENTY-FIVE

PICTURE PERFECT

Picture-perfect creativity doesn't exist. That's why perfectionists have a tough time getting their creative juices to flow. Perfectionists like to control, but creativity likes to be free. Creativity is inherently uncertain and unknown. It's like the experience of driving at night—you have to trust that the lights will illuminate enough of your path, knowing that the whole road will never be clear. You have to trust that you'll see just enough in order to make it home. And so creativity requires a mixture of faith, confidence, conviction, and hope. It's not a religious faith but a faith that looks at the world with optimistic eyes. The uncreative person doubts that anything meaningful can be done. The creative soul is convinced that a solution can be found, that beauty exists, and that we can make the most of what we have.

CREATIVE OPTIMISM Some think of my friend Steve as a creative genius for what he makes and how he works. I once asked him his secret to his success and he said, "My passion is fueled by creativity. And my creativity is fed by optimism." It's that mix that keeps Steve afloat. Most people think of optimism as shallow or naive, but that's the opposite of Steve. His optimism is grounded in reality, and this helps him see what others overlook. Rather than thinking of the glass as half full or half empty, he notices the pitcher and the fresh water stream. Steve is a creative optimist. Such people believe that more exists, and they don't see the world through a scarcity lens.

As the old story goes, there are two types of people. One type says, "Life is like an apple pie. There are a limited number of slices. Get your slice before it's gone." The other type says, "Life is like an apple pie. There are a limited number of slices. Get your slice before it's gone. And when all the slices are gone, let's bake another pie." The second type is a maker, baker, and creative genius who not only improves his own life but the lives of others as well. This person isn't naive, but rather is stubborn in the belief that the goodness doesn't run out or expire.

Believing that more is possible is a mind-set that helps when facing problems that resemble a tangled mess. Pulling harder against such problems only makes them worse. Like the tangle in your iPod earbuds cord, pulling more forcefully only makes the knot worse. The only way to undo such a problem is to slow down, relax, and lightly untangle the snarled mass. That's exactly what Einstein did when he was tangled up in complex thoughts.

MY OPTIMISM WEARS HEAVY BOOTS AND IS LOUD.
—HENRY ROLLINS

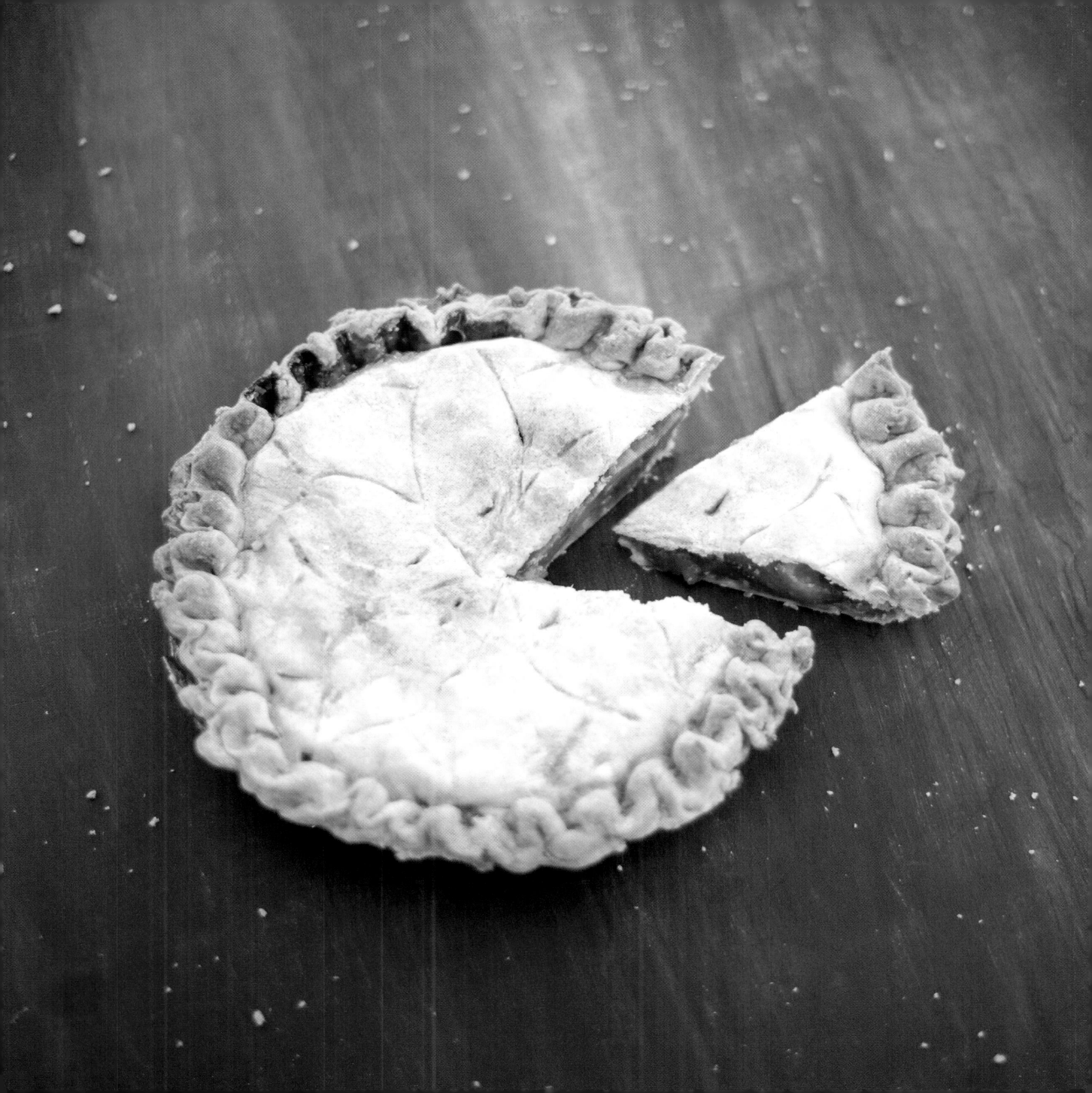

UNTANGLED When Einstein was just 26, he was working 40 hours a week as a patent examiner. After hours, he worked on theories of his own. It was during this time that he came up with his most groundbreaking work. With so little time to devote to his own work, how did he manage to untangle so many knots? Einstein explained, "The theory of relativity occurred to me by intuition, and music is the driving force behind this intuition. My parents had me study the violin from the time I was six. My new discovery is the result of musical perception." Throughout his life, music was a refuge and a source that helped him think.

Einstein once said, "If I were not a physicist, I would probably be a musician." It was known that Einstein loved to play music and that he used it to unwind. As musician Jack Liebeck reflected, "He used music to clear his mind while it was twisted up with all these tortuous concepts. The violin helped him to stand back from the problem and crystallize his thoughts." Einstein's own kids said that their dad often used music as a way to figure things out. Einstein even attributed some of his greatest breakthroughs to taking violin breaks. He believed that these breaks connected different parts of his brain in new and unlikely ways. Later in life Einstein bought a sailboat that he named *Tinef*, which is Yiddish for "worthless" or "junk." Einstein loved to take breaks from his academic life to sail so that his thoughts could drift freely as he was pushed along by the wind.

Taking a break from a difficult problem can seem like a counterintuitive thing to do, but that is exactly what creative geniuses do. They give the problem some space rather than wrestle it to the ground. Just like the knotted earbud cords, some problems need to be handled with a lighter touch.

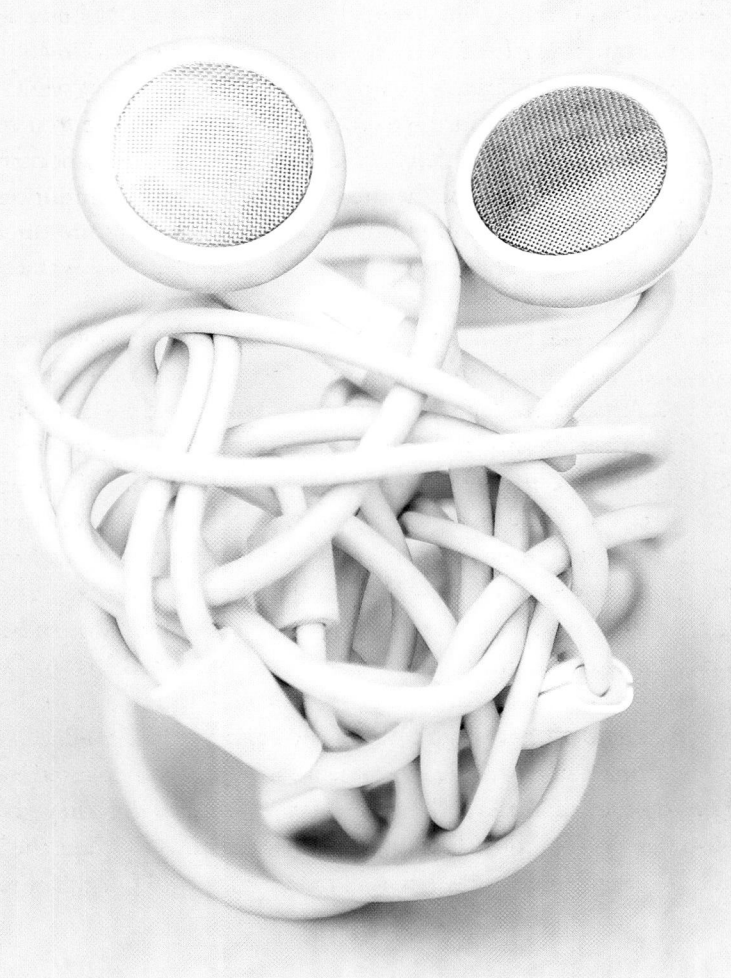

One of the reasons Einstein's violin breaks were so effective is that he had been playing the violin since he was a kid. He was a good musician who loved the process of playing and the resulting sound. His muscle memory was deeply embedded, and playing the violin became a way to relax. For you or me, playing the violin might be the absolute worst thing to do. The screeching sounds and ensuing frustration probably wouldn't help our creativity to flow. But what might help is to go for a walk.

UNLEASHED Sometimes we have to unleash our minds from the shackles of deep thought—just like with our family dog Daisy. She has the most fun when I unhook the leash and she runs free and wild. I let her run off leash as often as I can. Perfectionists have a hard time believing that unhooking the leash is worth the risk. What if the dog runs away and never comes back? What if it's just a waste of time? But letting go is exactly what needs to happen if we want our creative capabilities to grow.

I went to college at the University of California Santa Barbara (UCSB), and my first-year dorm room was just steps from the ocean. UCSB is situated in one of the most beautiful places in the world. Upon hearing that I attended a school in such an idyllic place, many friends would say, "I could never go there. I wouldn't get anything done!" I found the opposite to be true. Being surrounded by beauty was a motivation to work hard and then to take refreshing breaks. The breaks consisted of running on the beach, surfing, or mountain biking up in the hills. And it was during those sessions that my most creative ideas flowed. This experience wasn't mine alone. It was shared by my peers, and it was even scientifically supported by research done by one of the school's faculty.

Jonathan Schooler, a PhD and a professor of psychological and brain sciences at USCB, has devoted his career to studying how we arrive at more creative thoughts. Schooler is a world leader in cognition and creativity. One of Schooler's findings explains that "disciplined mind wandering" leads to better ideas. As a result, he goes for a daily walk along the ocean's

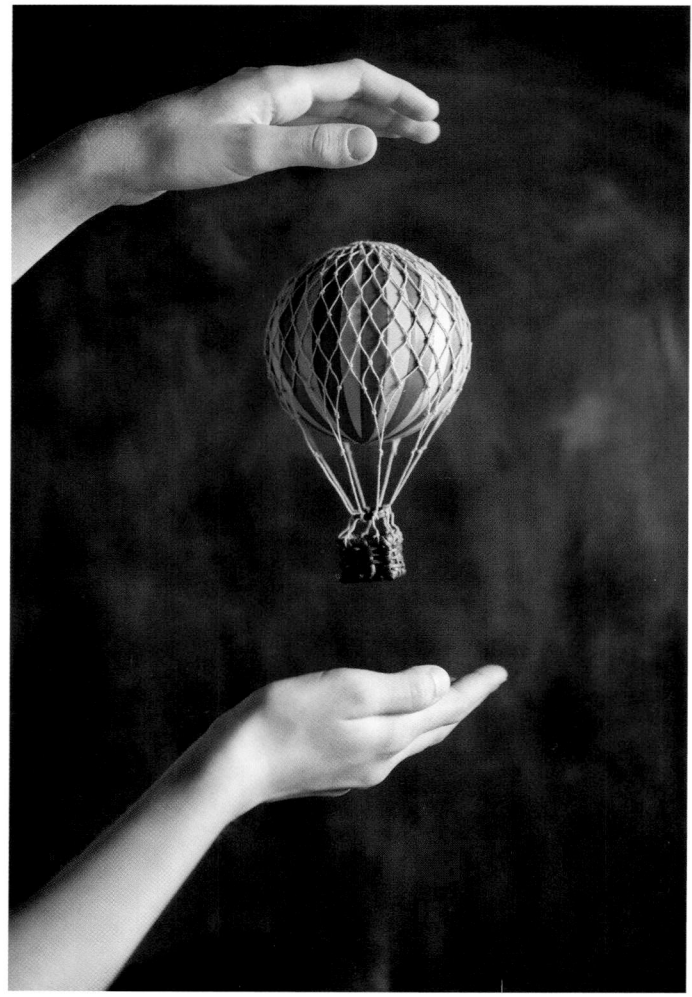

edge in order to clarify his ideas. Schooler's research suggests that when we let our mind "run off leash" we are able to make and connect new ideas. Schooler's discoveries are based on something artists have known for years: creativity cannot be forced. And these ideas aren't just relevant for California dreamers who want to get their creative juices to flow.

David Berkus is an economist and venture capitalist who agrees with Schooler's approach. The way he sees it, "When you work on a problem continuously, you can become fixated on previous solutions." This makes the problem worse because

WHAT WE NEED IS MORE PEOPLE WHO SPECIALIZE IN THE IMPOSSIBLE.

—THOMAS ROETHKE

the fixation limits our ideas. But when you take a break it allows the mind to relax and for the old solutions to fade. As Berkus puts it, "This frees the mind up for eureka moments to occur." Regardless of your line of work, whether you're an academic, an architect, or a financier, breaks can lead to substantial breakthroughs.

Yet arriving at eureka moments isn't as simple as stepping away. According to Schooler's research, what you do on your break matters. He found that mind wandering is most productive when we do something that isn't too difficult or too dull. That's why going for a walk or hike can provide just the right context for creative ideas to grow. For Einstein it was playing the violin or going for a sail; for me it is getting out on my bike. The key is to identify what activities help your creativity to thrive and then to consider these activities as part of your job.

EXERCISE

STEP 1

Identify three activities that allow your mind to rest without completely drifting away:

1. _____

2. _____

3. _____

STEP 2

Follow Einstein's footsteps and take a few minutes this week to use one of those activities as a way to untangle your ideas.

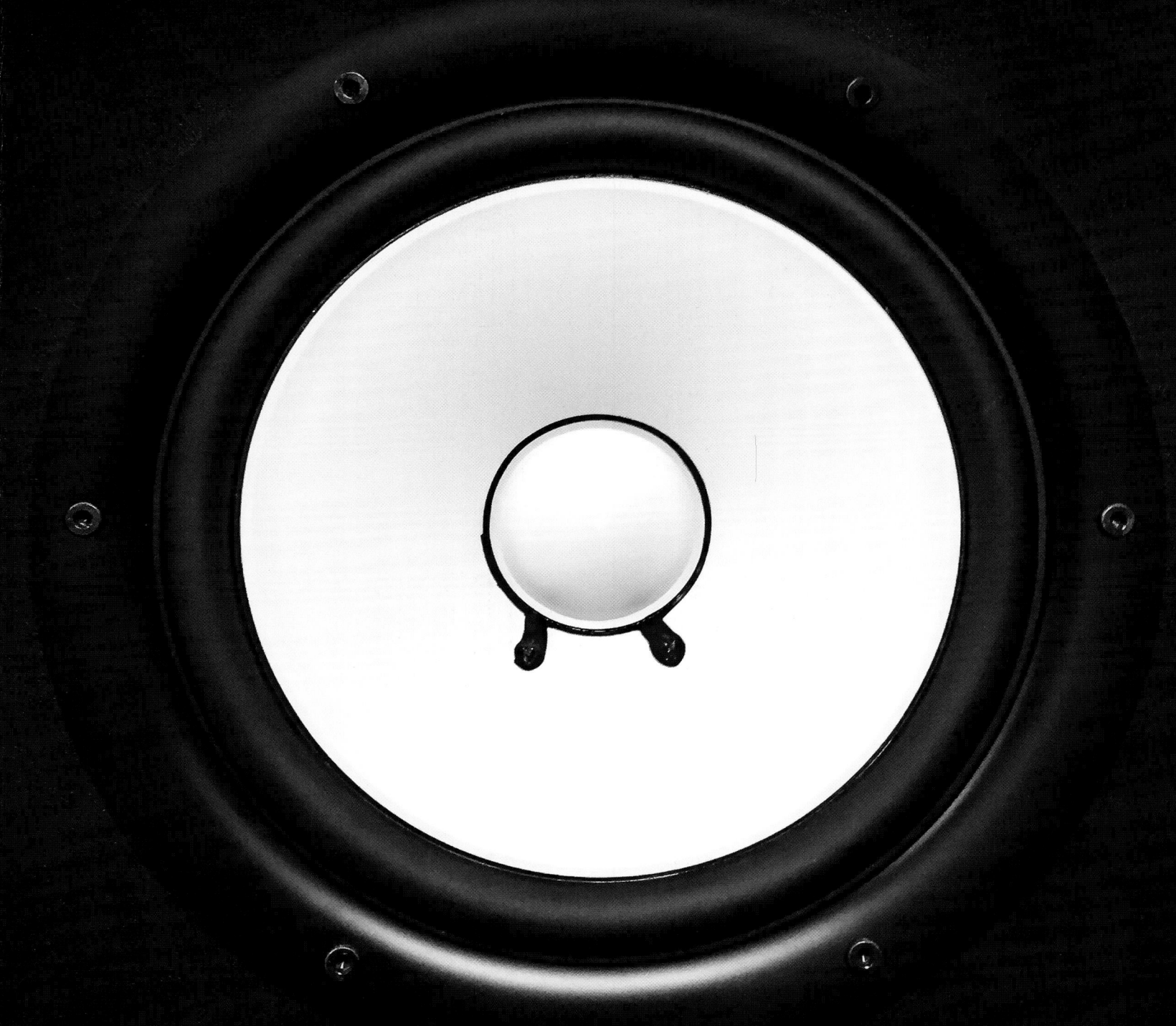

CHAPTER TWENTY-SIX

SILENCE AND SOLITUDE

The jackhammers started early today and I can barely hear myself think. My studio is in a converted warehouse and they are making some improvements next door. So I crank up my music in a feeble attempt to drown out the noise. It doesn't work. I have to get out of here. As I pack up my laptop, I think of Swiss philosopher Max Picard's words: "Nothing has changed the nature of man so much as the loss of silence."

Now, I am in a quiet place and I take a deep breath. I find a comfortable seat in an almost empty coffee shop, sip some tea, and reflect on Picard's words. In the five decades since he said those words, silence has become increasingly rare. As a result, I've become the reluctant student who has learned what happens when silence is lost; namely, I become uncentered, and I lose mindfulness and maybe even a bit of soul.

169

PROFOUND SILENCE Noise diminishes our best self; silence brings it back. You know that best version of you who values patience and compassion, and who doesn't snap at the kids or get frustrated when someone on the freeway cuts you off. When we take time to quiet our mind, we see more clearly and our best ideas emerge. That's why I'm drawn into photography. All photographs are quiet. All photographs are silent and still.

Photography gives me what T. S. Eliot called "the still point of the turning world." It requires that I focus and become fully engaged. And this focus has become the thread that keeps life from splitting at the seams. You can't make great photographs without slowing down to look, listen, and see. A distracted photographer rarely makes good frames. And the best photographs speak to us without making a sound.

Getting good at photography requires that we mentally turn down the noise so that we can look at the world with quiet eyes. And with less noise, we are more likely to notice the profound. Having an internal silence can help us to see.

The art of photography has less to do with what's in front of our lens and more to do with the internal state inside our minds. Too much noise drowns out what lies within. This is a problem because our pictures are made from what we carry in our souls. Here Ralph Waldo Emerson's words come to mind: "Though we travel the world over to find the beautiful, we must carry it with us or we find it not." And so it is with silence. Unless we nurture it within us, it's nearly impossible to see.

Photographers have long known that what we carry with us affects the type of images we make. That's why we are obsessed with what gear fills our bags. Yet it isn't just gear that shapes the type of photographs we make.

LET US BE SILENT SO WE CAN HEAR THE WHISPERS OF THE GODS.
—RALPH WALDO EMERSON

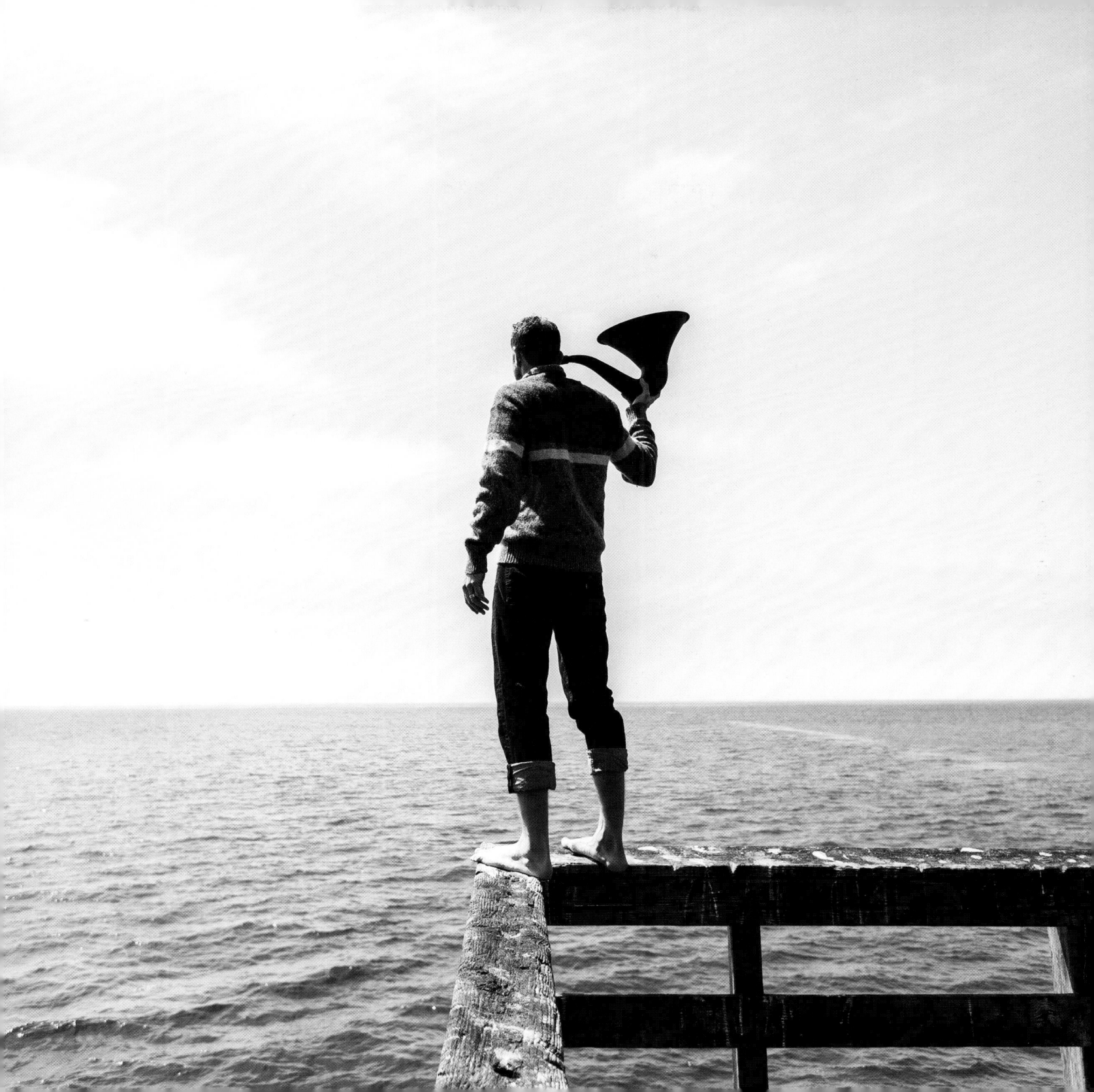

SOLITUDE Picasso once said, "Without great solitude, no serious work is possible." If you want to create better work, consider embracing the stillness and quiet that is so essential to craft. Craftsmen rarely achieve greatness while they are gabbing away. Rather, they retreat into their own world, and it is there that the divine muse appears. As Mother Teresa put it, "God is a friend of silence." God shows up when we quiet down. That's why the great religions of the world consider quiet to be such a sacred thing. Why not visit a cathedral or monastery to gain your own solitude, or just begin by shucking off the loud distractions of life and carve out time to silence your soul. In doing this, you will discover that solitude can replenish and refresh your creative flow.

Sometimes I find solitude in my studio, and other times it occurs outdoors. Being surrounded by nature is a great way to cleanse away the worries of daily life. John Muir put it eloquently: "Climb the mountains and get their good tidings. Nature's peace will flow into you as sunshine flows into trees. The winds will blow their own freshness into you, and the storms their energy, while cares will drop away from you like the leaves of autumn." Solitude never comes easy, but it's always good. You have to fight to carve out the time to get into the right state of mind. And you have to practice soaking it up. At first, it can feel awkward, but solitude gets better with age and the passage of time. Solitude can be painful in youth but restorative as we advance in years. William Penn said it like this: "True silence is the rest of the mind, and is to the spirit what sleep is to the body, nourishment and refreshment."

The more time you spend in silence, the more you will discover that solitude is a strength that quiets your soul. It leads to being open to look and to listen in new ways. The most creative people I know have learned its secrets, like how to quietly listen rather than speak. While out making photographs in Yosemite Valley, the renowned black and white photographer John Sexton explained his secret to making profound frames: "I listen to the trees." The listening frame of mind is a state of openness. It requires quiet and calm. You can listen with your ears, your eyes, your posture, and your heart. You see lovers do this all the time.

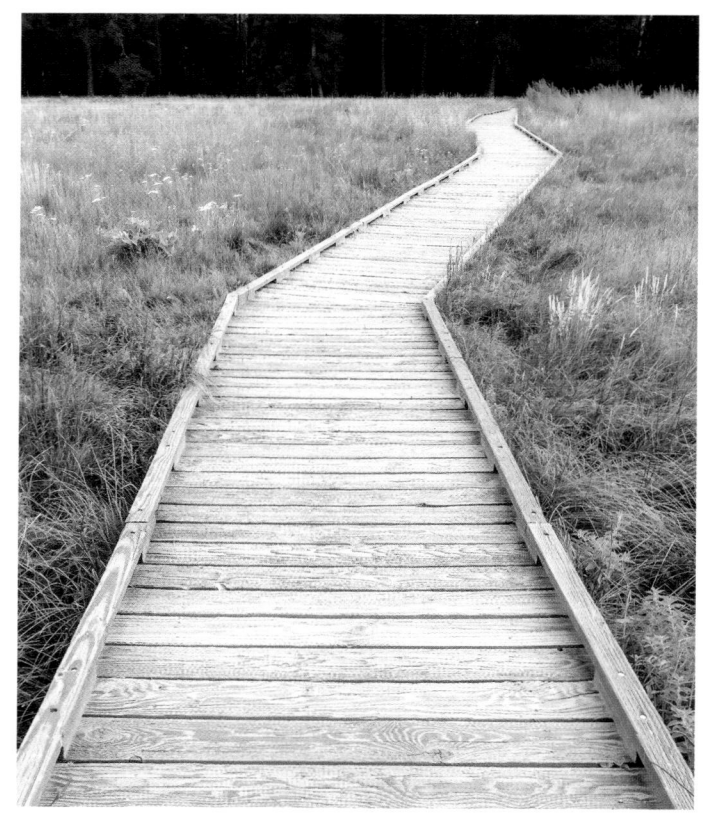

IN SOLITUDE ONE'S INNER VOICES
BECOME AUDIBLE [AND],
IN CONSEQUENCE,
ONE RESPONDS MORE CLEARLY
TO OTHER LIVES.

—WENDELL BERRY

Solitude is a doorway to discovering a hidden side of yourself. It uncovers creativity and imagination that has been buried by noise. It helps you strengthen and define who you are. As Jeanne Marie Laskas said, "Solitude helps you to differentiate, define the borders of the self. Solitude helps you to figure out where everybody else stops and you begin." And solitude is a compass that will show you the way. Unfortunately, for many of us, the solitude and sense of self we had as children has eroded away. We once dreamed of becoming artists, firefighters, and teachers, and somewhere along the way traded in our dreams for mediocre jobs. Solitude revives and begets courage that has been lost. e e cummings wrote, "It takes courage to grow up and become who you really are." Solitude can foster the courage that is needed for you to become the best version of yourself. Without silence and solitude you'll never be able to hear the voice that is leading you on.

It goes without saying that the world is restless and full of repetitive noise. And there are plenty of people who create work that tries to drown out the noise. Too often such messages get lost in the fray. What we really need is an army of creatives who are willing to embrace solitude and share the whispered the truths they have found. And in the sharing of wisdom, all of our lives will become more profound.

EXERCISE

**Nurture silence and you will become more free and
your work will become more profound.**

STEP 1
Embrace solitude by going for a walk outside. Leave your phone behind and walk without saying a word. Walk in silence and soak up the world. Walk as a way to let the noise calm down. Walk and let the wind blow its freshness into you.

STEP 2
After walking for a while, find a place to sit. Sit down and take a deep breath. Quiet your mind and look at the world with listening eyes.

STEP 3
After the walk, return to your work and let the silence direct and guide your craft.

STEP 4
This week, when you normally listen to something, whether running or commuting to work, turn off the noise and welcome the quiet. At first it may seem dull, but after a few days the silence will deepen your senses and cleanse your mind.

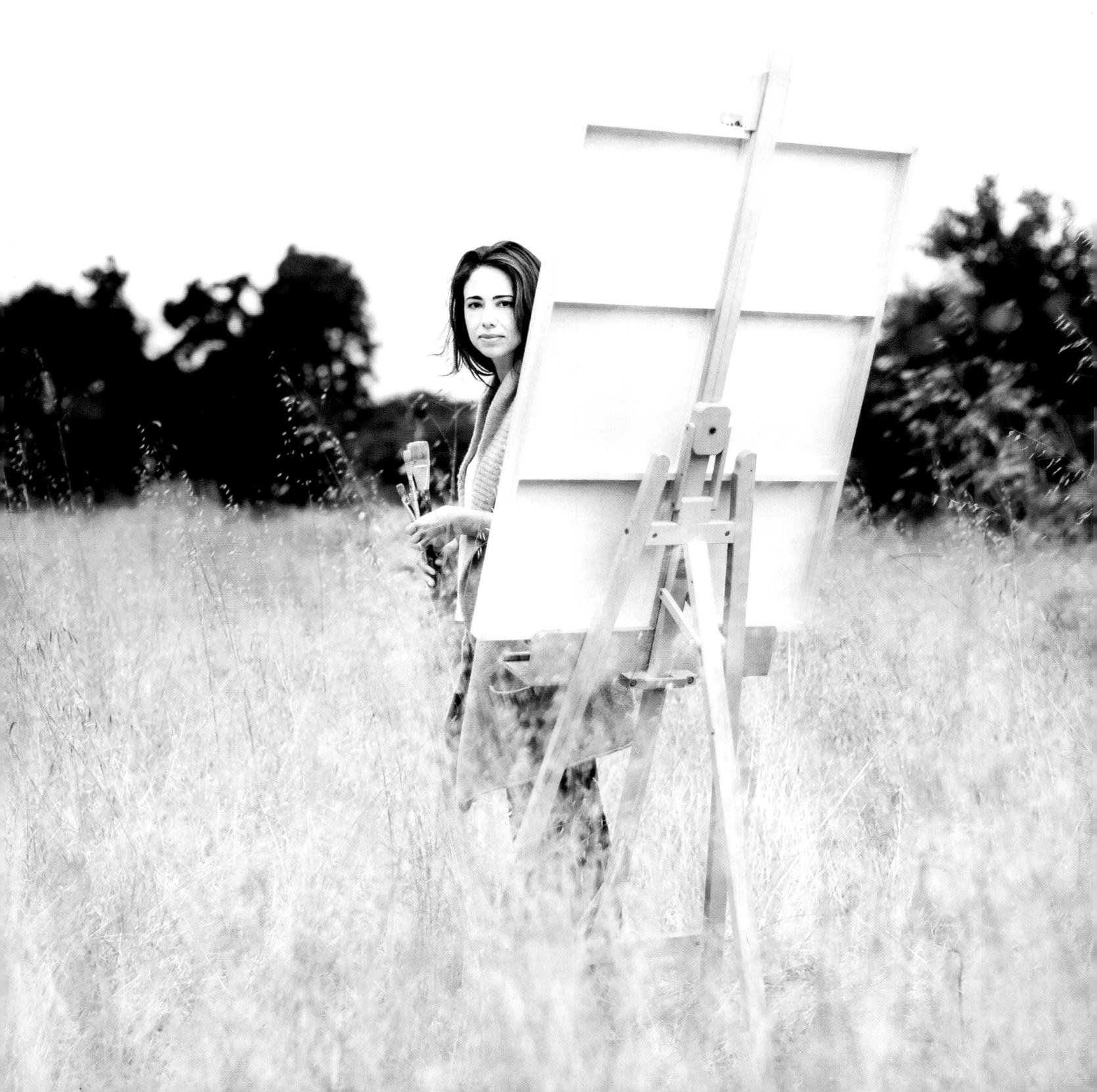

CHAPTER TWENTY-SEVEN

DISTRACTED BY DISTRACTIONS

The blank page. The empty canvas. The vacant screen. Some people find the moment before creativity so unbearable that they quit. Rather than endure the uncertainty of making something new, they look at their phones. And that's just one of many things vying for our attention. Unable to take it all in, we split our attention into small fragments to handle everything that is coming our way.

Worried what we might miss, we continually search, scour, and scan. We check our devices nonstop, never turning them off. Linda Stone calls this "continuous partial attention," and it leads to worry and an artificial sense of constant crisis that permeates our lives. So we feel overwhelmed. And with so much to process, we are forced to become experts in not going very deep.

THE PAUSE BETWEEN THE NOTES The constant influx doesn't leave any time, focus, or energy to create. Like aging athletes who stop practicing their sport or turn to unhealthy eating habits, we become out of shape. Not wanting to admit defeat, we try to do it all, which depletes us even more. This half-baked and partially attentive approach doesn't lead to living life as if it matters. Climbing the ladder and living life to the fullest degree is an art that doesn't include being distracted all the time.

Almost every form of art requires focus and thought. I like to think of art as occupying the space between the noise. I love how the renowned musician Artur Schnabel reflected on his craft: "The notes I handle no better than many pianists. But the pauses between the notes—ah, that is where the art resides."

To create art, or to make life a work of art, is to get beyond the surface and to connect in a deep and meaningful way. As Aristotle argued, "Art isn't about the outward appearance but the inner significance of things." The best art connects, resonates, and makes us feel. It stirs up our senses and provokes change. And I'm not just talking about art in the traditional sense. Art isn't only painting, photography, or dance. Art can be anything that's done with the right intent. You can restore a car or make a sandwich as if it were art. And sure, there are "capital *A*" and "lowercase *a*" art. But that isn't the point. The point is that most of us have abandoned art because we have wrongly believed that it was the domain of someone else.

Art isn't just for them; it's also for you. Regardless of your age, gender, or skill, you have artistic potential. Artists aren't only those with cameras, pens, or brushes in their hands. There is an art to relationships, commerce, war, telling jokes, and grilling in your backyard. The author Seth Godin nailed it when he said, "An artist is anyone who uses bravery, insight, creativity, and boldness to challenge the status quo. An artist takes it personally." Creating art is not about materials but about your aim. And the greatest work of art you should pursue is making your life more than it is.

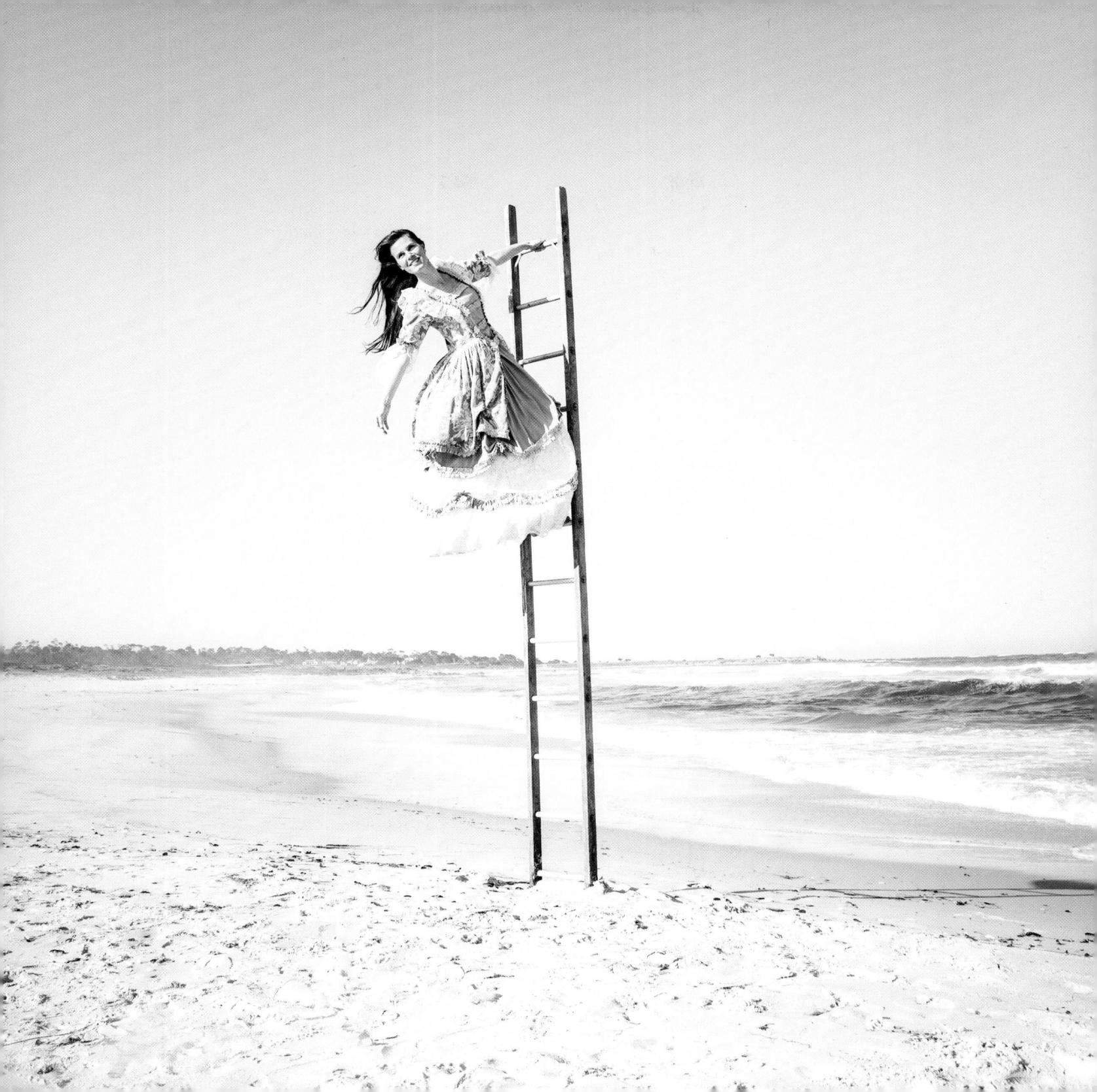

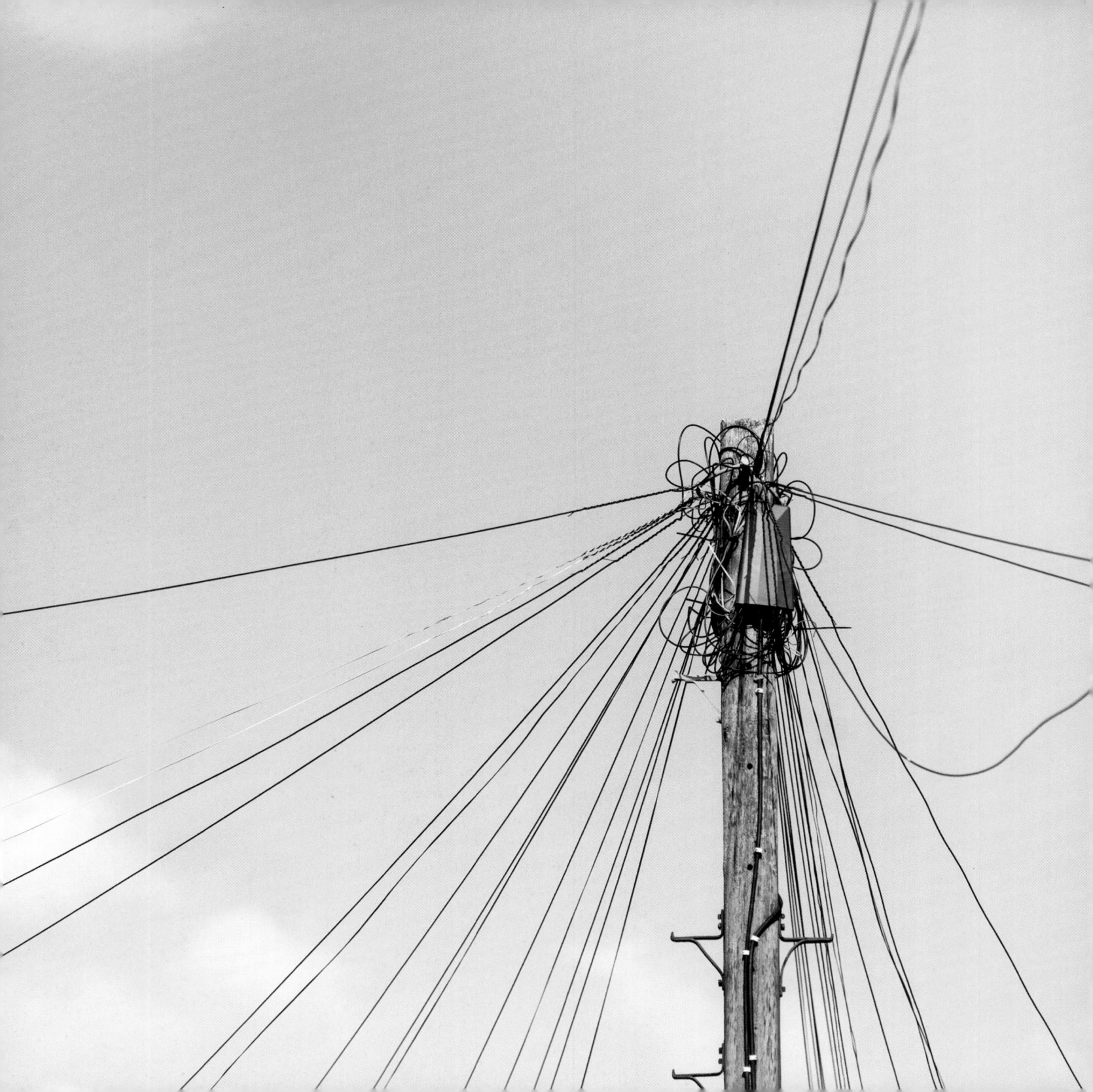

HABITUALLY DISTRACTED Unfortunately, the art of living isn't easy to master. And constantly distracted by anything shiny and new, our attention spans have all but disappeared. As T. S. Eliot said over fifty years ago, "We've become distracted from distraction by distraction." Flash-forward to today and it's more complex. We have become habitually distracted. We walk around in public checking our phones. We answer a text while someone else speaks. Distractions have become the norm. We are all guilty to a greater or lesser degree, and we all have some room for growth.

If Aristotle was right and "we are what we repeatedly do," then we are in trouble. Deep trouble. All these distractions are killing our creativity. As the Buddhist teacher Judy Lief suggests, "Distraction is the very foundation of ego, the way we protect ourselves against both the pain of life and the open space of awakened mind." When we are bored, frustrated, angry, or sad we reach for our phones. This cuts us off from key emotional states that could potentially help us create. And it might be that all this distraction is holding us back from creating our best work and leading better lives.

It doesn't really matter to me how many times a consumer checks her favorite social media site. But it does matter to me if you are a creator. If you are a student of the creative life—and if you want to be a creator—you should care as well. For creators, the more distractions there are, the less significant the work is. If you want to create something worthwhile, you have to step out of the fray and practice your craft—the cook to the kitchen, the scientist to the lab, and the writer to the page. Otherwise, the habit of distraction can even change the way you think. Neuroscientists tell us that repetitive actions form habits and that habits mold the very structure of the brain. The more we practice a habit the stronger it becomes. As the scientists like to say, "Neurons that fire together, wire together." After multiple years of giving in to distraction, imagine how strong the nerve wires have become. The neural pathways are hard to resist.

SWITCH-TASKING In our always-connected world, multi-tasking seems like the only way to survive. But our multi-tasking has gotten out of hand. A better word to describe what we do is "multi-switch-tasking" because of how quickly we change what we do. And this behavior is praised as the new way to thrive. It's not uncommon to hear the self-congratulatory cliché "I'm killing two birds with one stone." But stop to think about that phrase. Killing birds is cruel and unkind. When I was a young boy, I accidentally killed a bird with a BB gun. As I watched its life pour out onto the dirt, I felt so horrible and ashamed. I think of that bird every time I hear someone use that cliché. Yes, productivity is good, but not if it takes away life.

When we are distracted we stare at the world with vacant eyes. And it used to be that a vacant stare meant that you were ill. Now it just means that the phone in your pocket buzzed. Socially, being partially present has become OK. We all switch-task, so we don't mind it so much when others do as well. When families sit down to eat, some do so without looking each other in the eyes. When one person pulls out a phone, others can do the same. And who's to blame? It's hard to resist all the distractions in our frenetic and fast-paced lives. Life is more complicated than it used to be, at least that's what we tell ourselves. But it isn't true.

DOUBLE DOORS AND TORTOISE SHELLS Distractions have always vied for the attention of our hearts and minds. The sirens in the Greek epic poem the *Odyssey* tried to lure sailors, of course. So Odysseus made his men put wax in their ears. And throughout history, distractions have come in many forms. In the mid-1800s, distraction came to one man by way of noise.

Charles Dickens was a struggling author who couldn't "hear himself think," so he hired a carpenter to help. On the entrance to his upstairs study, he had the carpenter install two thick doors. Dickens knew that nothing

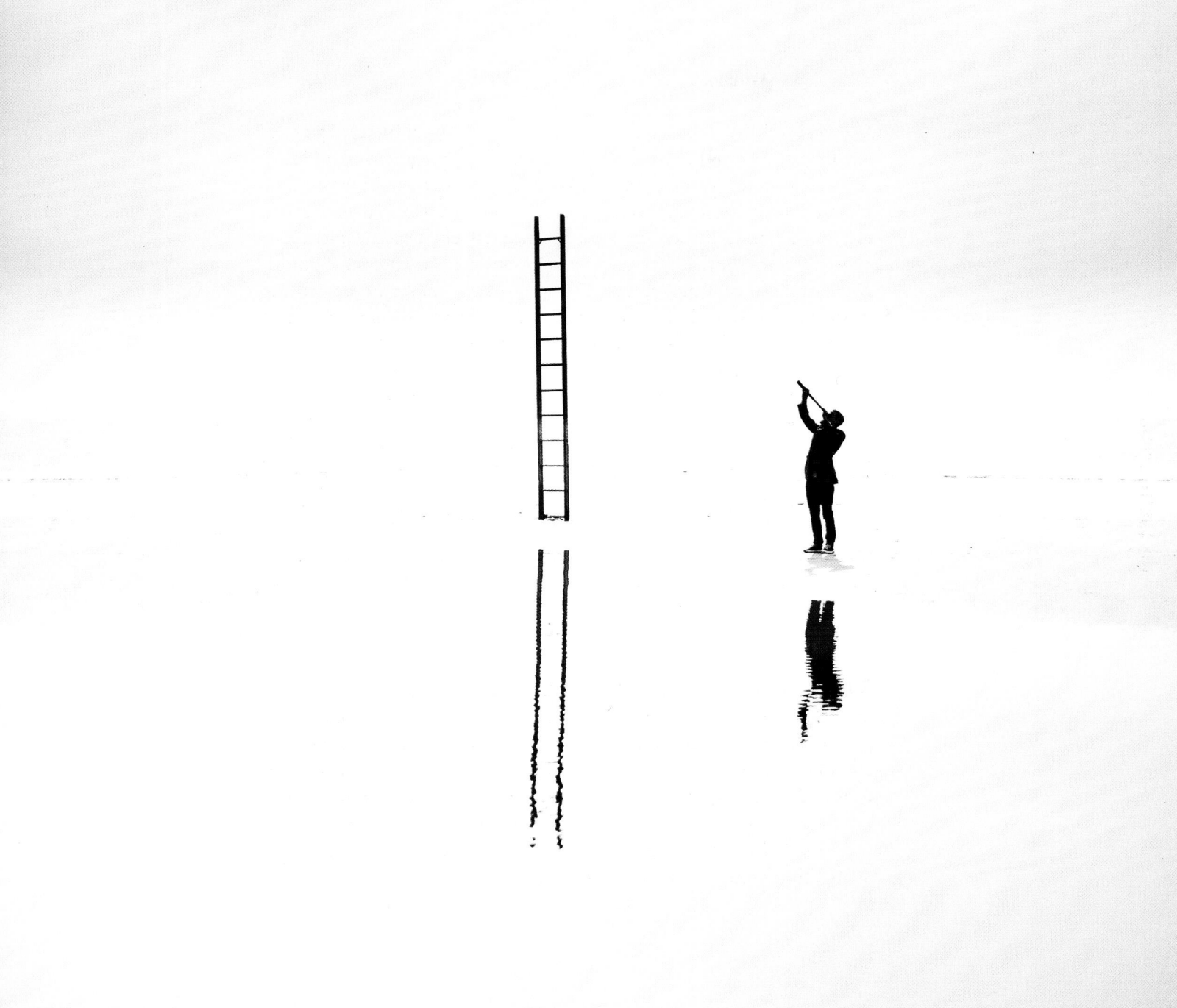

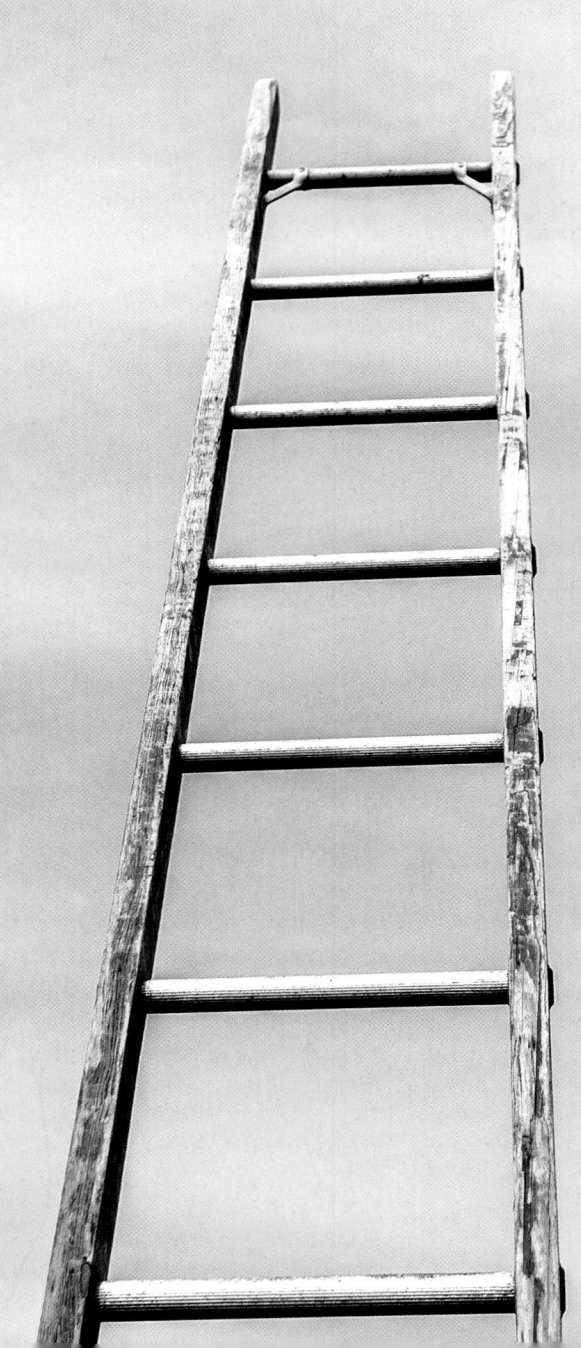

is more dangerous to the creative spark than distraction and distress. So he blocked out the noise by creating a barrier that was twice the size of most.

A few thousand years earlier, Buddha was worried about his followers and their fragmented minds. So he taught them ways to cultivate mindfulness that comes from within. Whether we go back a few hundred or a few thousand years, distractions have always been present.

The humorist John Cleese (of Monty Python fame) said, "We don't know where ideas come from, but we do know that they don't come from a laptop." For Cleese, the key to creativity is to get into a "creative state of mind." The best way to do this is to create space and time that is free of interruptions. He calls this the "tortoise enclosure" of the creative mind. Cleese explains, "If you're racing around all day ticking things off lists, looking at your watch, making phone calls, and generally just keeping all the balls in the air, you are not going to have any creative ideas."

In order to generate more creative thoughts, we need to climb up a simple ladder and retreat. Away from the responsibilities of day-to-day life, the creative mind flourishes. We need to take time to relearn how to concentrate and think. That's one reason that meditation has become such a widespread practice in the western world. Alain de Botton sizes the problem up this way: "Relearning how to concentrate is one of the great challenges of our time. To sit still and think, without succumbing to an anxious reach for a machine, has become almost impossible." And it's not just concentration that we need—we need focus, clarity, mindfulness, and empathy if we want to become more creatively alive.

EXERCISE

**Here are three ideas to regain some clarity and get the creative juices to flow.
Modify these suggestions to suit your own needs.**

IDEA 1. DIGITAL SABBATH
Select one day a month to live without the help of an electronic machine. Turn off and tuck away your phone, computer, iPad, and TV. Commit to a complete day without devices and plan to do something else—ride your bike, hike, hide, draw, or build something out of wood.

IDEA 2. 30-MINUTE BREAK
Schedule a regular break from your devices, computer, or phone for 30 minutes once a day for a week. Consider this your "lunch break" from the constantly connected world.

IDEA 3. MEDITATE
Science strongly supports the idea that meditation benefits the brain and body. The simple act of meditation can help you become more mindful, reduce anxiety, improve relationships, and give you a creative edge. Try it out for one week. The app I use and recommend is called Headspace. Download it and your first 10 sessions are free. Learn more at headspace.com/science.

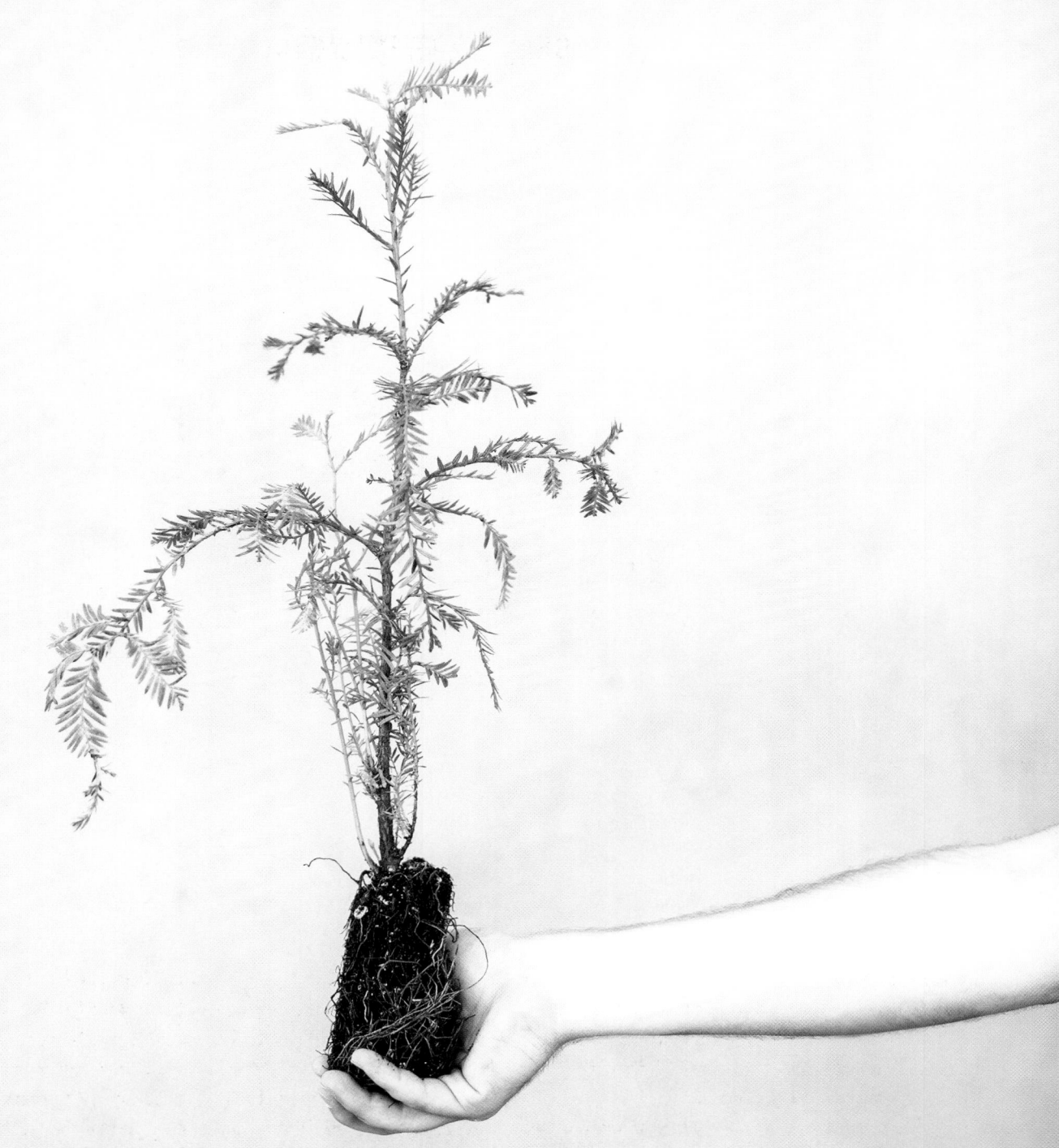

CHAPTER TWENTY-EIGHT

HABITAT

The tallest trees in the world can be found only along a narrow strip of the California coast. And the coast redwood isn't just the tallest tree on planet earth; it's one of the most majestic as well. These trees tower up to 379 feet tall, and they create their own ecosystems that sustain life in many forms. Redwoods are thirsty trees, absorbing water from rivers and creeks when they can, or soaking up 40 percent of their water from the fog in the dry summer months. California isn't just the perfect habitat for these trees—it's the only natural habitat where they can thrive. Plant a redwood somewhere else and it might grow, but not well. The stressed appearance of the tree will betray its desire to return home. There is only one place on the planet where these trees reach their full height.

TALL TREES AND SHALLOW ROOTS With such enormous heights, you would assume that the redwood tree's roots go deep. But rather than deep, their power comes from the spread. The roots go down only five to six feet, but they extend to over 100 feet from the trunk. And these roots intertwine and connect with the roots of other redwood trees. This interlocking system creates strength and sustenance for the trees. Here's how it works. Redwoods that live in a valley near a stream will have plenty of water but not much sun. Trees on top of the ridge will have sunshine but little water. So the trees trade resources. Using the intricate root system, the trees near the stream send water up to other trees, which might be a mile away. And the trees that bask in the sunshine above send back the much-needed nutrients to the redwoods deep in the shade.

If we look at redwood trees through an anthropomorphic lens, we might say that they like to be surrounded by good friends. The network is the secret to their success. And these trees need the obvious inspiration of water and sun, but they can also absorb inspiration in unlikely ways. Redwood trees are like those artists who soak up and breathe in sustenance from the air—like Ernest Hemingway wandering the streets of Paris; it's not just the obvious sights but the mood and atmosphere that most directly fill the pages of his books. At first glance, redwoods may seem simple, but the more you look the more you realize that they are complex and wonderful trees that flourish in only one place due to their specific habitat needs.

The perfect redwood habitat is not a single tree by itself but a forest. Height and health cannot be achieved in any other way. The habitat determines how well the trees will do. So it is with our creative soul—there are habitats that help us thrive and others that just won't work. Just as with the redwood tree, there is an ideal habitat for your own creative growth. Especially if you want to create your best work and live a more meaningful life, you need to deepen your awareness of how a habitat can help or hinder your growth. This may mean constructing greenhouses to nourish your budding ideas, building watering systems for your full-grown thoughts, or changing your environment altogether to better suit your needs.

A SHACK, A HUT, AND A GLASS ROOM Jeff Shelton (mentioned in Part 2 of this book) is a prolific and celebrated architect whose colorful and whimsical homes and buildings remind me of Dr. Seuss. Shelton has two separate office habitats that help him accomplish his work. The office his clients visit is in the heart of downtown; his other office is just a small shack in his backyard. The shack is a beautiful little handmade structure built out of reclaimed goods (shown here). Jeff loves his little abode. I once heard him say, "The shack is where the magic happens. The downtown office is where I go to make it legal." For Jeff, this two-step approach really works. In his shack he can doodle, dream, and draw. In his office, he makes those drawings architecturally sound. Each habitat brings something different to his work.

When the children's author Roald Dahl moved to the country he took a similar approach. Dahl wanted a place where he could be free from the world. So he had a friend build a small hut in the garden. This hut was his home away from home. Nearly every day he would walk out to the hut and begin by sharpening six Number 2 pencils, and he wouldn't take a break until they were all dull. When asked about his writing process he once replied, "It's really quite easy. I go down to my little hut, where it's tight and dark and warm, and within minutes I can go back to being six or seven or eight again." For Dahl, the hut was his sanctuary and the space where his books came to life. It was almost like a fort for a grown-up kid. Dahl explained that in the hut, "You become a different person… and go into a completely different world and time disappears."

After being exiled from France, Victor Hugo found shelter on the British island of Guernsey. It was there that he lived and wrote for over 15 years. Hugo set to work right away and turned the glassed-in conservatory on the roof of his home into his writing den. It was a sparse room with walls made of glass, a small bed, and a fireproof chest where he kept his manuscripts. A wooden pulpit served as a desk, and he wrote standing up looking out across the sea to France. From this perch, which he called "the lookout," Hugo wrote extensively and created some of his most original and celebrated works,

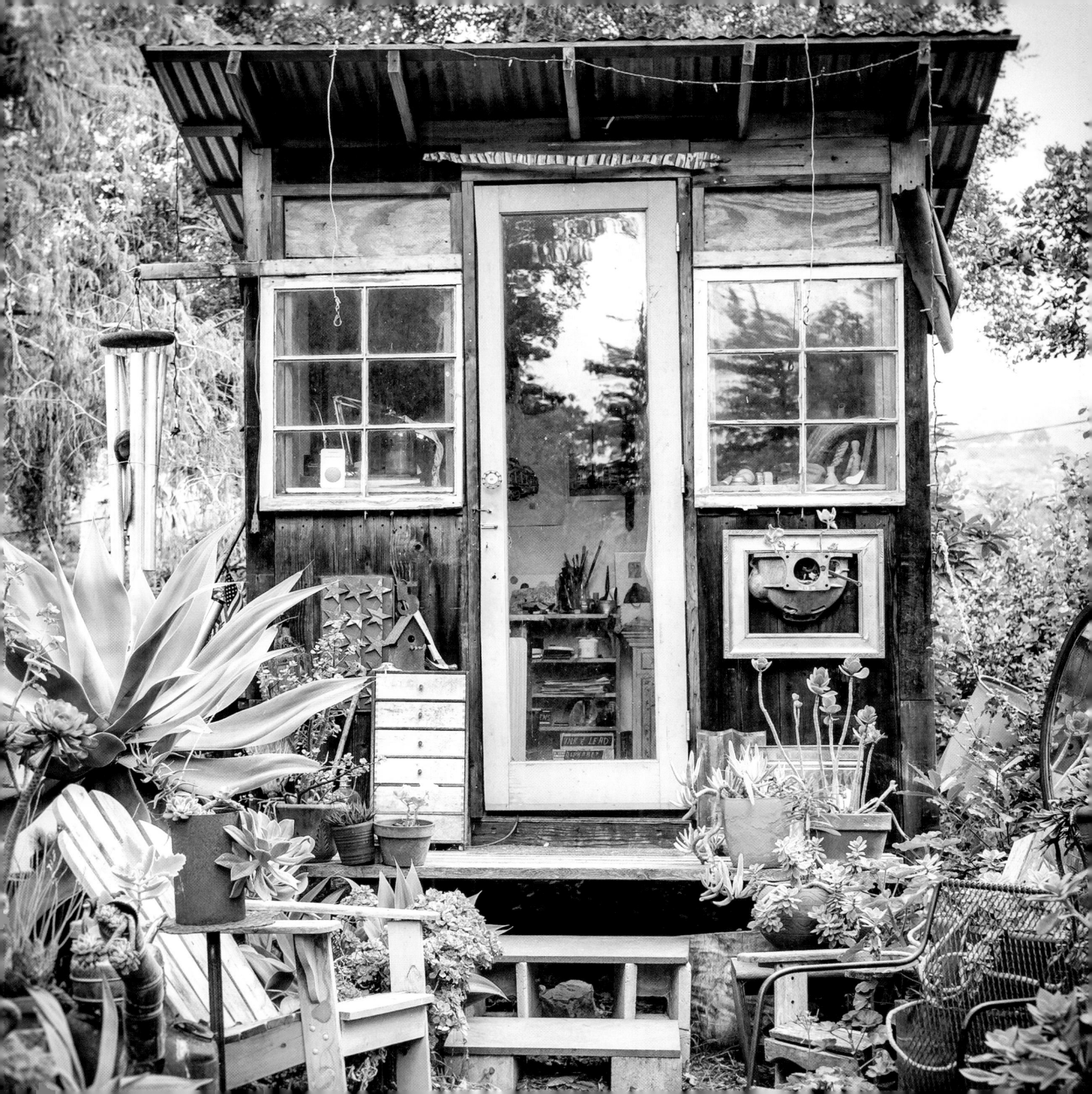

including *Les Misérables*. Living in exile and looking out over the sea filled his work with an undeniable depth. And the pulpit was fitting, almost as if it helped him preach the truths about which he so much cared.

The point isn't to go out and build a shack or write on your roof—this isn't about copying somebody else's space. Like different varieties of trees, we all have unique habitat needs. The point is to start thinking about your space and about how it can help your creativity flourish and grow. As a photographer, author, and teacher, I need a space that is conducive to creative ideas. So when I moved into my studio, I took time to think about the design. I slowly brought in artifacts, photographs, and objects that remind me of who I am and who I want to become. So now when I step into my studio, I feel like I'm stepping into the life that I want to lead.

OASIS Each day when I bike home from the studio, I pass a small altar that has been built into the corner of a busy street. There, amidst the traffic, is a statue surrounded by candles and flowers. Patrons stop to kneel, pray, and pay their respects. It is a beautiful little oasis in an otherwise industrial part of town. I like the idea of creating an oasis so that your creativity can grow. That's what you need to do. Your oasis doesn't have to be elaborate, and it doesn't have to cost a fortune to make. More important is your intent.

Keith Carter is a celebrated fine art photographer, a mentor, and a friend. His home is an intricate work of art. It's filled with curiosities, travel mementos, sculptures, and art. When you visit his home you instantly understand how Keith sees the world—he finds beauty even in broken and discarded things. It's no wonder his photographs are filled with the same. When his wife Patricia was diagnosed with cancer it was devastating news. The doctors told them that Patricia would be hospitalized in a nearby city for a few months. So Keith packed up the car with carpets, paintings, photographs, books, and art objects. He was intent on transforming her small, bleak hospital room into a work of art. Like a little oasis, her room became a sanctuary during that difficult time. That's

what creative people do. They do not accept the status quo but create something out of nothing so that life isn't so bleak.

If you are feeling like your cubicle is dull or you don't have enough space, let Keith Carter be an inspiration for you, and transform whatever space it is that you have. We all need places where we can feel more alive. Life is too busy, difficult, and overwhelming not to try.

GREENHOUSE One of the ways I have attempted to make my office more creative is by bringing in four different desks. This may sound like overkill, but you can't imagine how much it has helped. One desk is devoted to writing, another desk to computer work (Photoshop, email, and so on), and a third to photography gear, and the fourth is an old wooden desk used only for journaling, thinking, and reading books. On the fourth desk, computers, tablets, and phones are not allowed. That desk has become my most sacred space. It's where I go when I need to concentrate or just clear my head. The other desks are where I get work done, but the wood desk is where I tend to my creative soul. As for the rest of the space, it is filled with inspiring photographs, books, and other objects and artifacts that make my creative juices come alive. Stepping into my workspace makes all of my senses come alive. It's the whole habitat that helps me thrive.

If you don't have a dedicated studio or workshop, that's OK. There are other ways to define and create your own personal greenhouse for growth. This might be as simple as selecting a coffee shop that inspires you to open your mind. Or maybe you could rope off a corner of your garage and dedicate it to making art. Designing a creative habitat takes effort, but creativity rarely shows up when it is forced. The trick is to find a space that blends the idea of work and play. You have to build the habitat with that in mind. As L. P. Jacks once said, "A master in the art of living draws no sharp distinction between his work and his play; his labor and his leisure; his mind and his body; his education and his recreation." Ideally, you want to create a space that allows you to let go of worry and fear so that you can play and tinker with ideas.

EXERCISE

Take a few minutes to strategize about how to create an ideal habitat for your own creative growth.

STEP 1. CONTEXT

Begin by thinking of your ideal habitat in a comparative way. Is it more like a bungalow, base camp, refuge, retreat, harbor, home, hut, tree fort, tent, outpost, cabin, or cabana? Is the space simple, stark, cozy, or grand? Let your imagination run wild, and come up with a few ideas.

STEP 2. SURROUNDINGS

Like an extrovert, a redwood tree grows best surrounded by others. The forest feeds and spurs the growth. Other trees may grow better separated from the crowd. Just like with trees, everyone's seclusion or social needs are unique. Evaluate your own needs and reflect on how you can change your habitat so that it better serves your goal. Circle the value that reflects the ideal conditions for you:

SECLUDED   5 4 3 2 1 0 1 2 3 4 5   SOCIAL

Based on your self-evaluation above, what is one step you can take to modify or change your environment to better suit your needs?

STEP 3. MATERIALS

List the materials that inspire you (think of things like paper, canvas, wood, metal, paints, pens, pencils, sketchbooks, scissors, and so on). Make your own list. Are these readily available in your creative habitat? If not, create a shopping list. Circle the value that reflects the ideal conditions for you:

SUPPLIES ORGANIZED IN DRAWERS   5 4 3 2 1 0 1 2 3 4 5   SUPPLIES READILY SEEN

STEP 4. KINDLING

If you put too much kindling on a campfire, the fire doesn't have a chance, whereas the right type of tinder can help the fire turn into a blaze. Similarly, the wrong type of clutter can stifle the creative spark. Take a few minutes to evaluate the clutter that surrounds you. Is there anything that is blocking your way? As John Lennon said, "Creativity won't come through if the air is cluttered." I heard of one cancer patient who had a garage sale after finishing chemo and sold half of everything she owned. Afterward she said, "I now have less, but I feel more." Make a list of the stuff in your space that inspires and the stuff that you might want to remove. Circle the value that reflects the ideal conditions for you:

MINIMALISM   5 4 3 2 1 0 1 2 3 4 5   CURIOSITIES AND ART

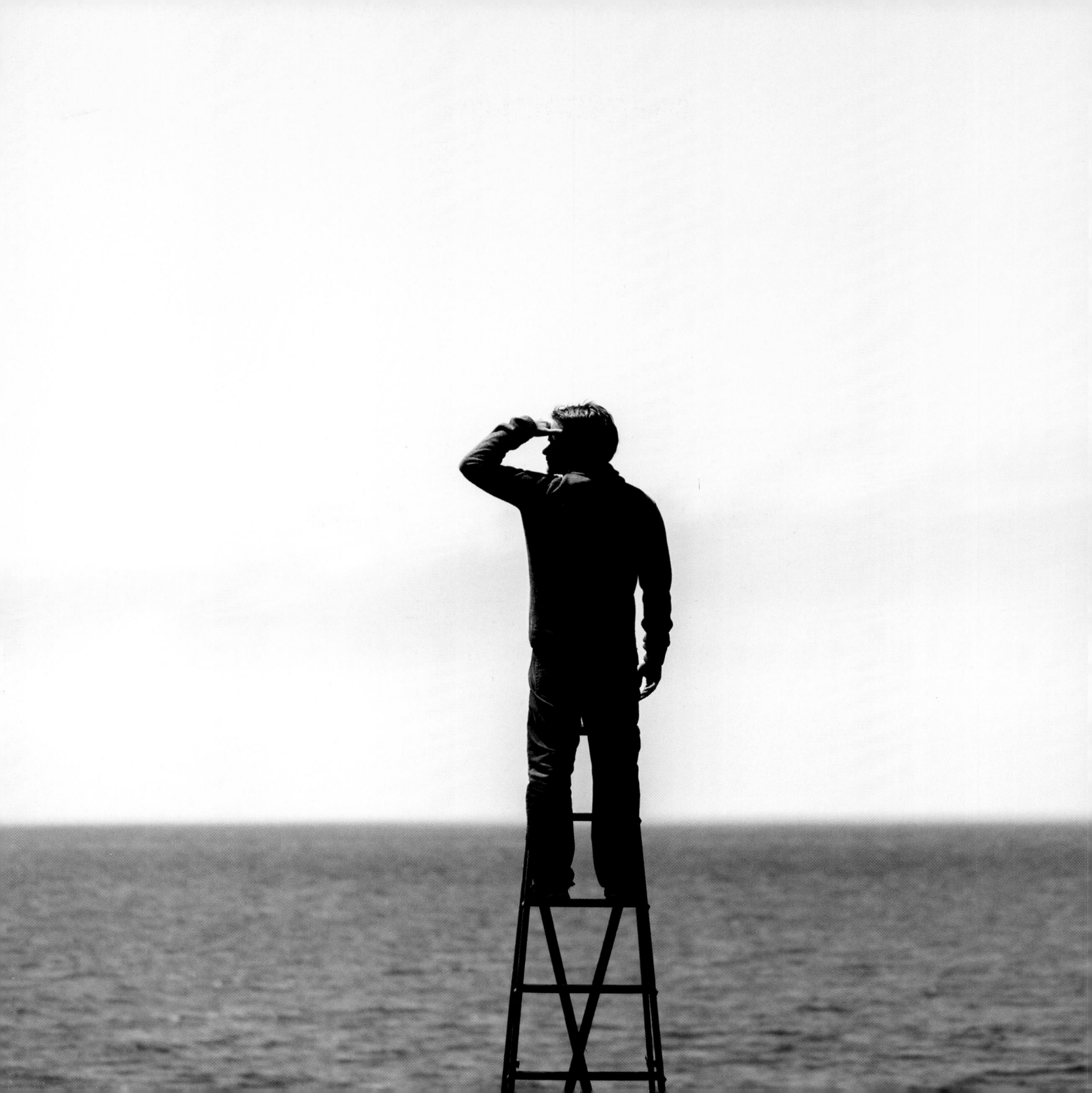

CHAPTER TWENTY-NINE

THE CREATIVE CRAFT

When it comes to improving your craft, shortcuts rarely work. One of the most common—and misguided—photography shortcuts is to buy more expensive gear. But gear does little to improve the quality of one's work. Another misleading tip is this: "To take better photographs, you need to stand in front of more interesting things." Yet it's not what you photograph, but how. Good images come from within. Buying a nice camera and visiting a beautiful place is easy; making meaningful photographs is hard.

After teaching at a photography school for 12 years, I could easily spot the students who would succeed. Those who relied on tips and tricks didn't get far. The ones who avoided the shortcuts were the ones who thrived. This is true for any craft. You can't cut corners if you want to gain skill.

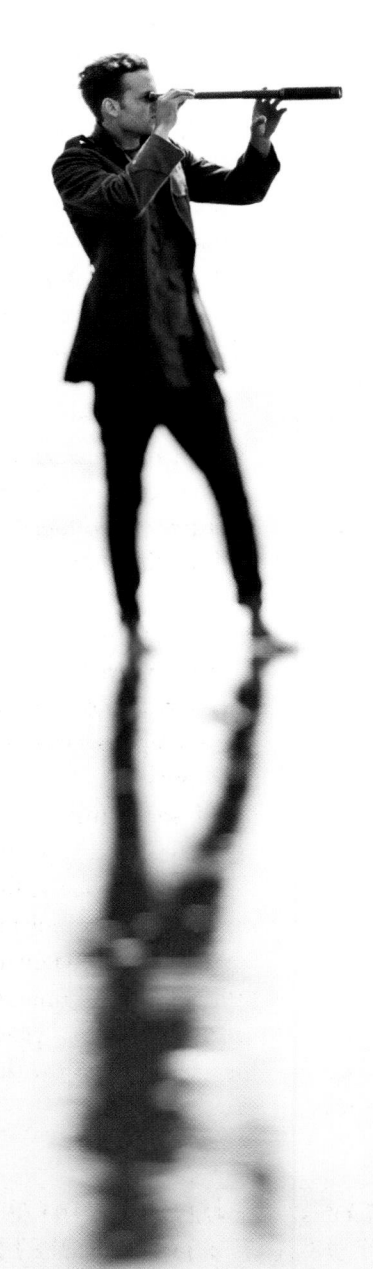

THE SIREN'S CALL The problem with most shortcuts is the way they entice. The time-saving advice initially rings true. That's because most shortcuts are half-truths that have been bent into an odd form. For instance, take the one about creating better photographs by standing in front of more interesting things. Of course it's important to consider what you shoot—subject matter is critical. Of course it's helpful to photograph a beautiful place. Yet more interesting subjects won't necessarily improve your craft. Often the more impressive and beautiful the subject matter is, the worse the frames. And over the last dozen years, I watched as many of my students visited far-off lands or hired expensive models only to return with disappointing and mediocre photographs of fascinating things.

The excitement of photographing an impressive person or a stunning scene can lead to weak photographs. The singer and songwriter Marcus Mumford said it this way: "Don't tell me that I am fine. When I lose my head, I lose my spine." And making photographs without a strong backbone doesn't turn out very well. The photographer who wants to create meaningful photographs must keep her head. She must guard against being overwhelmed and bring her own voice to the scene. Without a strong point of view, the photographs will fail.

Without a clear vision and voice, the best gear and the most stunning subject can't help. As Ansel Adams famously put it, "There is nothing worse than a sharp picture of a fuzzy idea." Good pictures come less from the subject and scene and more from strong ideas.

SEEING THE UNSEEN The surest way to come up with better ideas is to nurture a curious and imaginative approach. Curiosity helps us to look at the typical and to see something that was previously unseen. And imagination is curiosity set ablaze. Imagination is the art of seeing beyond the surface of things.

Those who imagine see what isn't visible to the eyes—sometimes an outlandish idea and other times an undercurrent. The best writers, poets, filmmakers, photographers, architects, artists, and so on constantly look for hidden truths. When you look at the world through the imagination's eye, you begin to see the invisible pulse that was previously ignored.

While studying in Spain, I signed up for a college art history course at the Museo del Prado in Madrid. Each week the class met in front of a painting. With notebooks in hand, we stood in awe as our teacher gave us insight into why these masterpieces hung on these walls.

I liked to arrive early in order to view the paintings before the lecture began. In those moments, I tried to appreciate what I saw, but these world-famous paintings just looked kind of dull. Then when our teacher arrived, she revealed the mysteries that made these paintings so profound. She helped us embrace the secret truth hidden within the frame. By the end of the lecture, the connection we felt with the paintings was deep. After a few months, I realized that our art teacher wasn't just teaching us about a specific piece; she was teaching us how to be curious, how to imagine, and, ultimately, how to see.

This experience taught me the value of looking deep. I came to appreciate the mystery of art. The paintings of Rembrandt, for example, seemed to reveal ideas that could not be conveyed in words.

Mystery ignites the imagination. That's why the best photographs, songs, paintings, and movies are the ones we can't quite figure out at first. They are subtle, less obvious, and sometimes incomplete. They tell us enough but not too much, engaging the imagination and inviting the viewer to complete the idea. Such imagination is like dreaming while you are awake. And this practice isn't just for kids who are bored in school. It's a worthwhile pursuit for all of us who wish to lead better lives.

THOSE WHO DREAM BY DAY ARE COGNIZANT OF THINGS WHICH ESCAPE THOSE WHO ONLY DREAM BY NIGHT.

—EDGAR ALLAN POE

CLOUDS AND RAIN Imagination is often visually represented as a cloud. Bright and white. Ethereal and odd shaped. Imperfect yet ideal. Temporal but real. Yet imagination isn't just floating in the sky. Imagination is learning to find the invisible dots that, when connected, create a discernible line. Buddhist philosophy illuminates this idea in a poetic way. As one traditional saying goes, "We must learn to see the cloud in the tree." At first blush, this sounds like an unintelligible sentence made up of two seemingly unrelated things. But when we look closer, a connection forms. Without the cloud there is no rain. Without rain, the tree cannot grow.

Imagination helps us see hidden connections between clouds and trees and between life and death.

In Jack London's gripping story "To Build a Fire," the protagonist sets out to cross the Yukon wilderness on a frigid and sunless day. The deep snow and subzero conditions are par for the course. But early in the story, London foreshadows doom: "The trouble with [the main character] was that he was without imagination. He was quick and alert in the things of life but only in the things and not their significance." Ultimately, it is his lack of imagination that leads to his demise.

Imagination helps us conjure up a vision of the icy river under the snow or the life force that flows through a tree. Imagination is the art of seeing beyond the shell. The painter Diego Velázquez, whom I studied in Madrid, was a master in this approach.

I AM CERTAIN OF NOTHING BUT THE HOLINESS OF THE HEART'S AFFECTIONS AND THE TRUTH OF THE IMAGINATION.
—JOHN KEATS

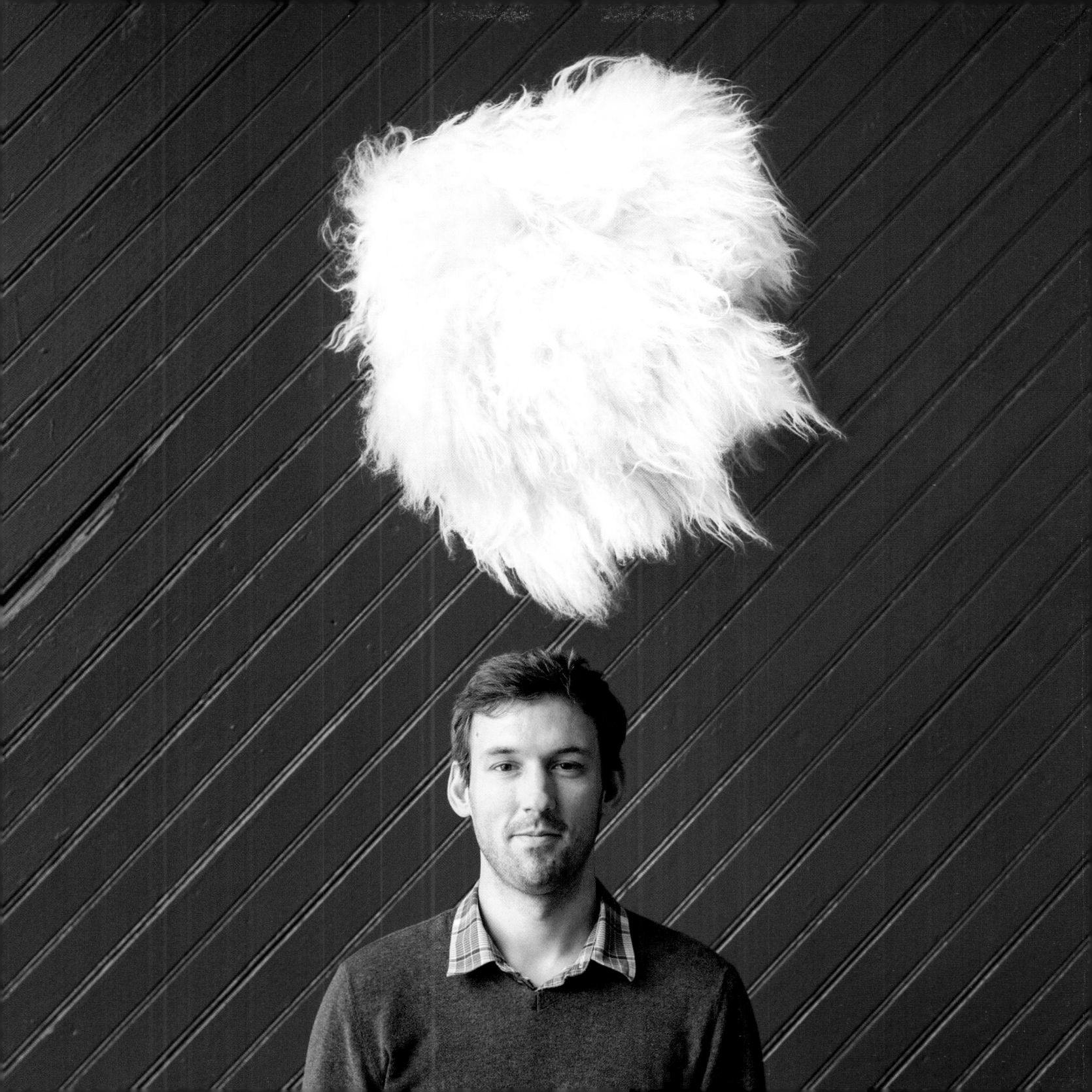

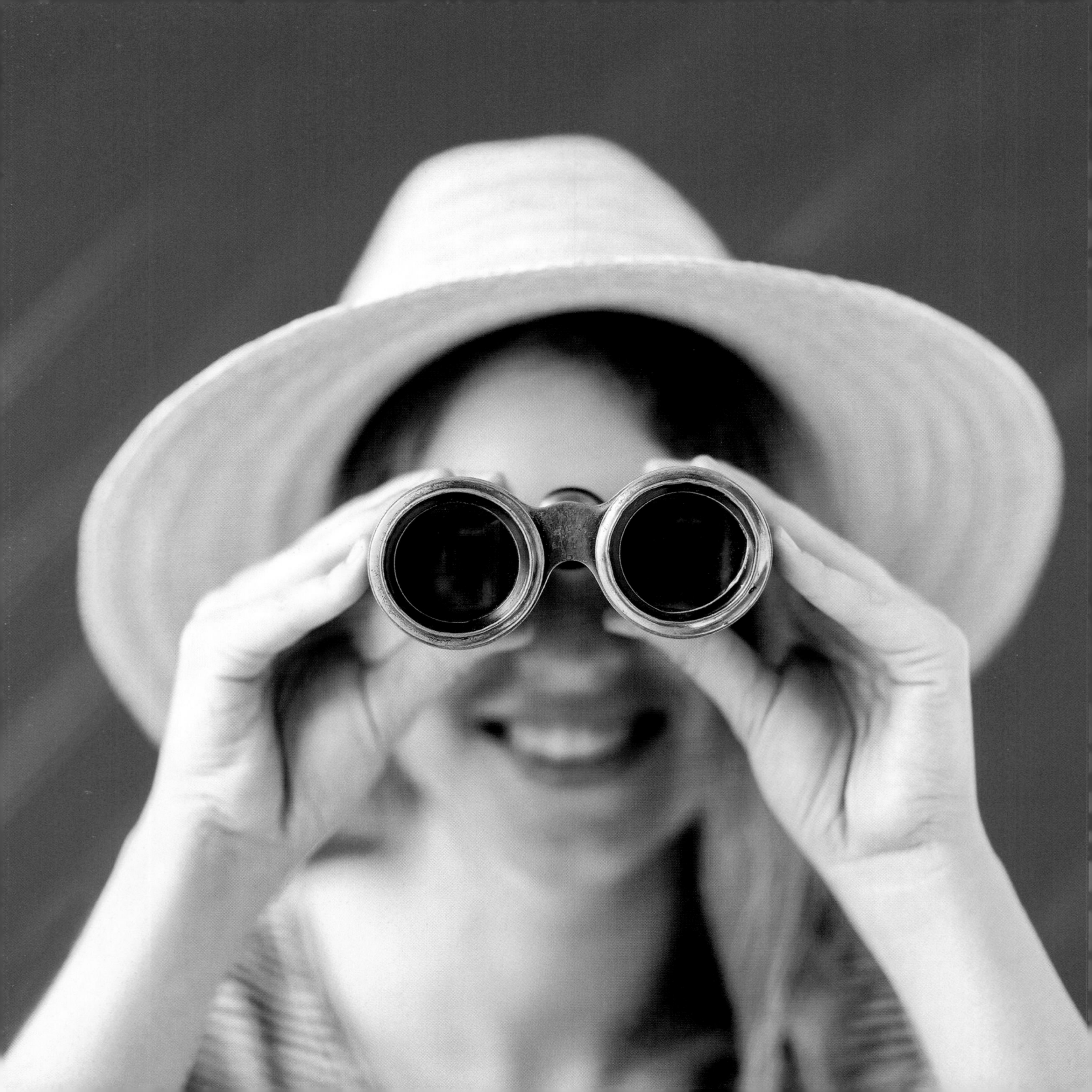

ONE'S DESTINATION IS NEVER A PLACE,
BUT A NEW WAY OF SEEING THINGS.

—HENRY MILLER

HUMANITY During a time when canvas and paint was precious, Velázquez did not let his gear go to his head. Nor did he let his position squelch his inner voice. As the painter for the Spanish royal family, Velázquez's work was not flattery but true. In an era of idealism, Velázquez painted people with authentic respect. Velázquez didn't typecast; he painted the hidden humanity underneath the shell.

Rather than paint an idyllic king, he depicted a real man whose countenance engendered sympathy, pity, and respect. When painting dwarfs (as they were called then), it wasn't to belittle or make fun. In such portraits we see wisdom, caring, and courage. While others saw an arrogant king, ugly daughter, humorous jester, or misshapen body to laugh at, Velázquez saw deep into the humanity that connects us all.

If there is a secret to creating better art, it isn't to buy new gear or to stand in front of better things. If you want to make more interesting photographs, become a more interesting person yourself. Follow Henry Miller's advice: "Develop an interest in life as you see it; the people, things, literature, music—the world is so rich, simply throbbing with rich treasures, beautiful souls, and interesting people." And when working with a subject that may not have an ideal look, it's your job to find the humanity within.

The most ordinary person is the greatest subject of all, not the other way around. The arts are about finding that kernel of beauty or truth that is hidden inside. For such endeavors, you can't rely on your eyes. Imagination is the only way to find invisible things.

EXERCISE

STEP 1

Visit an art museum with the intent of "seeing the cloud in the tree." Look for the invisible dots that connect, and strive to discover the mystery behind a piece. If it isn't readily apparent, talk to a docent or read something online. And let your imagination out of its cage. Enjoy the art for the way it makes you feel and for the thoughts it generates.

STEP 2

Create your own art that speaks in a less direct way. Rather than taking a typical portrait, have someone hold something that blocks part of his or her face. Or compose the image so that we can't see the whole scene. Rather than making literal photographs, make photographs that show us what we have overlooked.

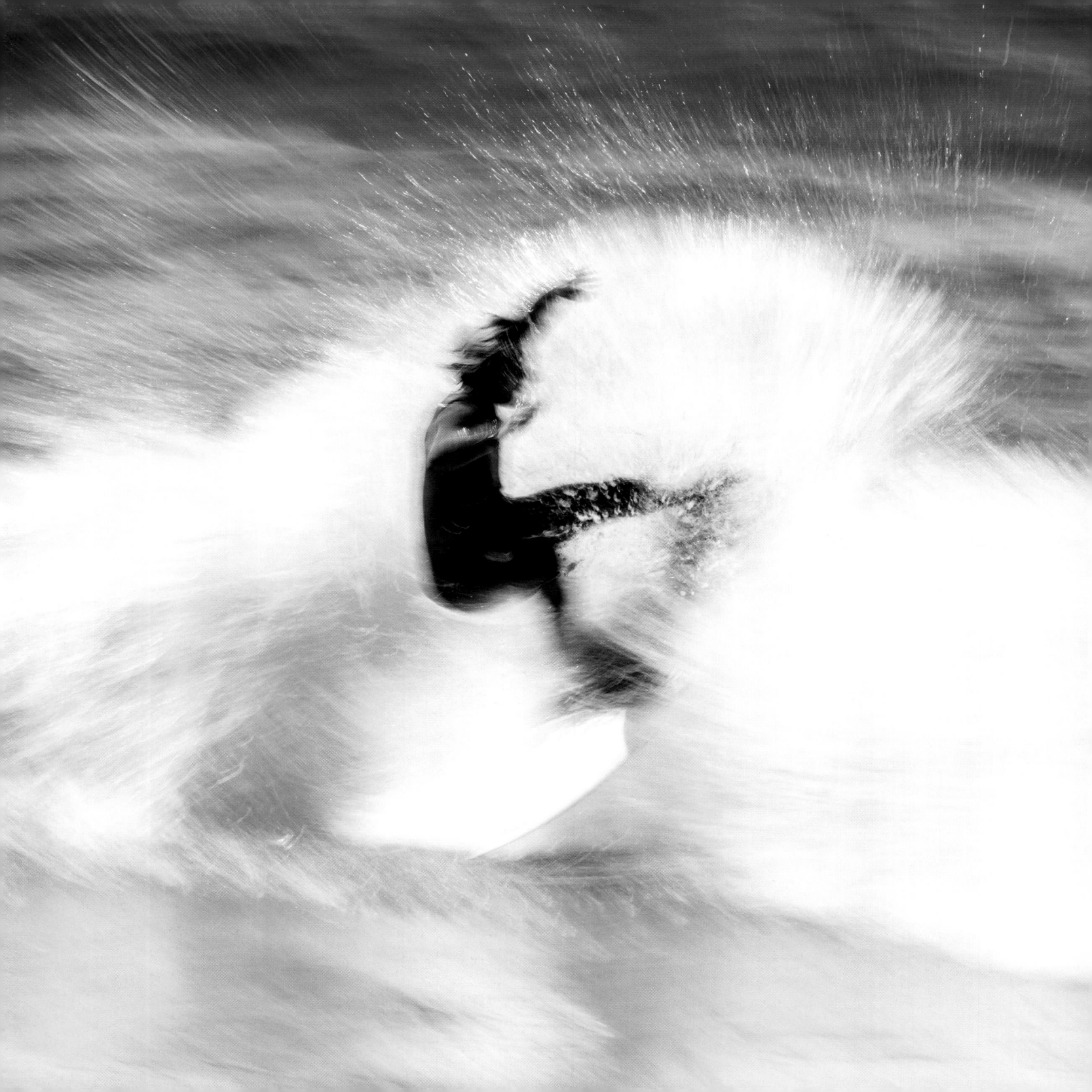

CHAPTER THIRTY

FUEL THE FIRE

Growing up, Neil was one of the craziest friends I had. He skateboarded the fastest, surfed the biggest waves, and jumped off the highest rocks on his skis. Neil played fast and hard, whether pounding on drums, jamming on an electric guitar, or screeching around a corner in his little green car. Plus, his smile was contagious and he could make anyone laugh.

Everyone loved Neil—he made life more worth living. And

Neil lived life to the hilt, whether working out with the track team or studying for a final exam. He always told us that he had big dreams and that he would retire young. We balked at the idea, but Neil just smiled and hopped on his skateboard and launched a 180 boneless of the curb. But what looked like goofing around wasn't so—Neil was smart and he worked hard. He just made work look like play.

LIVING THE DREAM If you asked Neil why he attended one of the top universities in the country, he would respond, with a mischievous grin, "Because it's located near really good surf!" After college, it was no surprise when Neil told us he was moving to Costa Rica to start a surf guide company, or later when he mentioned nonchalantly that he was joining an expedition to circumnavigate the globe. If there is one thing that Neil knows, it is how to live. Whether going to college or pursuing his dreams, the key to Neil's success was to combine ordinary things in unexpected ways, like painting on rocks or strapping a camera to his arm.

When Neil's college buddy Nick decided to start a company, Neil jumped right in. The idea for the company came from surfing sessions with friends. While in the water they wished they had some way to capture and document the fun. So Nick came up with a plastic case for a cheap film camera that you could strap to your wrist. That way, on the way back out after catching a wave you could take photographs of your friends. Neil was employee number one, and he began to drive from surf shop to surf shop to make a few sales. At first the idea wasn't exactly a huge hit. Nick slept in his VW bus, and Neil lived in a converted garage. But they were having a good time and it was that sense of play that kept the dream alive.

When they made the leap to digital, things started to take off. Soon their small startup became the fastest-growing camera company in the world. Nick's invention, the GoPro camera, started to dominate the scene. But they didn't let that go to their head. They kept having fun with it, and the contagion began. Soon everyone seemed to have a GoPro strapped to their helmets, skateboards, or bikes.

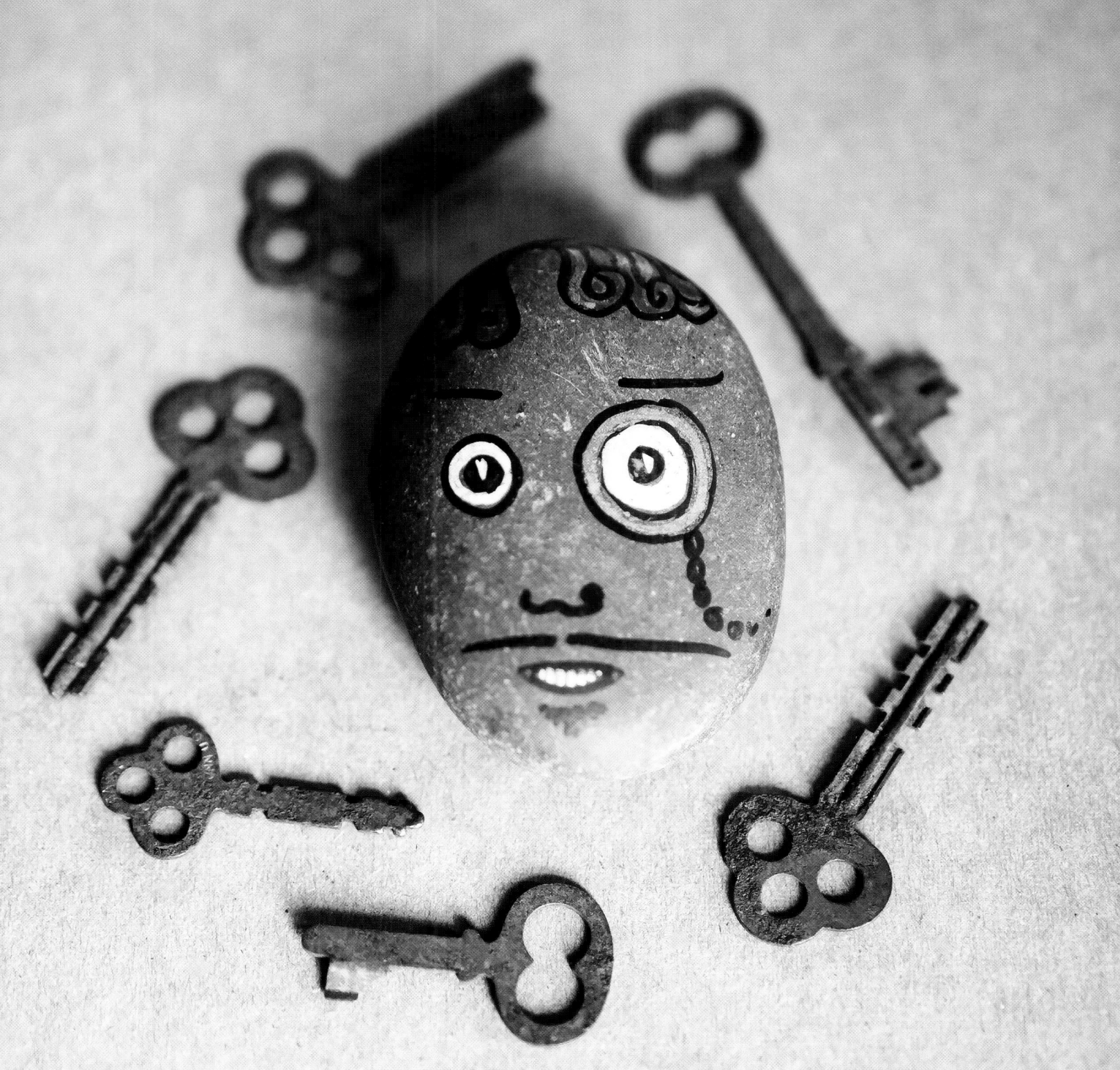

A MATCH MADE IN HEAVEN From their early days, their company took on an adventurous, playful, and imaginative approach. The idea was to create a company that would be a mashup of sorts. They were inventing something new but wanted it to be anchored in what was already around. First, it was a combination of cameras and sports. Second, they imagined Apple computers and Red Bull getting hitched. If those two companies were to have a baby, GoPro would be the result.

Years later, it's a fitting description for the best-selling camera in the world. At first it was a bit more Red Bull than Apple, but they worked on that. Now, it's a legitimate device that has significantly changed the world. And just in case you're wondering, Neil could retire young just like he said, but more important is that his zeal for life and others has in no way changed. He's just more generous, and his adventurous spirit continues to grow.

Like any good idea, the GoPro now seems obvious and inevitable. "Of course!" we think to ourselves. It's the same with any great invention, whether smartphones, amazon.com, or electric cars. Once the invention has gone global, it's proven true. All great ideas start small as a spark in the recesses of someone's brain. As William Blake said, "What is now proved was once imagined." The biggest and most obvious ideas weren't always so. What made the GoPro spark succeed was the willingness of its founders to imagine, play, and dream. They passed this spark on with their cameras, and a global movement began.

Neil's story reminds us that the pursuit of one's passions fuels the fire of unexpected growth. And as even the most amateur GoPro user knows, passion and a sense of adventure mixed with a touch of insanity can be a great recipe for living a more abundant life. Yet living the life you imagine won't happen by itself. Nor will it happen if you just watch someone else. The way to make life come alive is to strap on the camera and jump off the cliff.

THIS IS THE REAL SECRET OF LIFE—TO BE COMPLETELY ENGAGED WITH WHAT YOU ARE DOING IN THE HERE AND NOW. AND INSTEAD OF CALLING IT WORK, REALIZE IT IS PLAY.

—ALAN W. WATTS

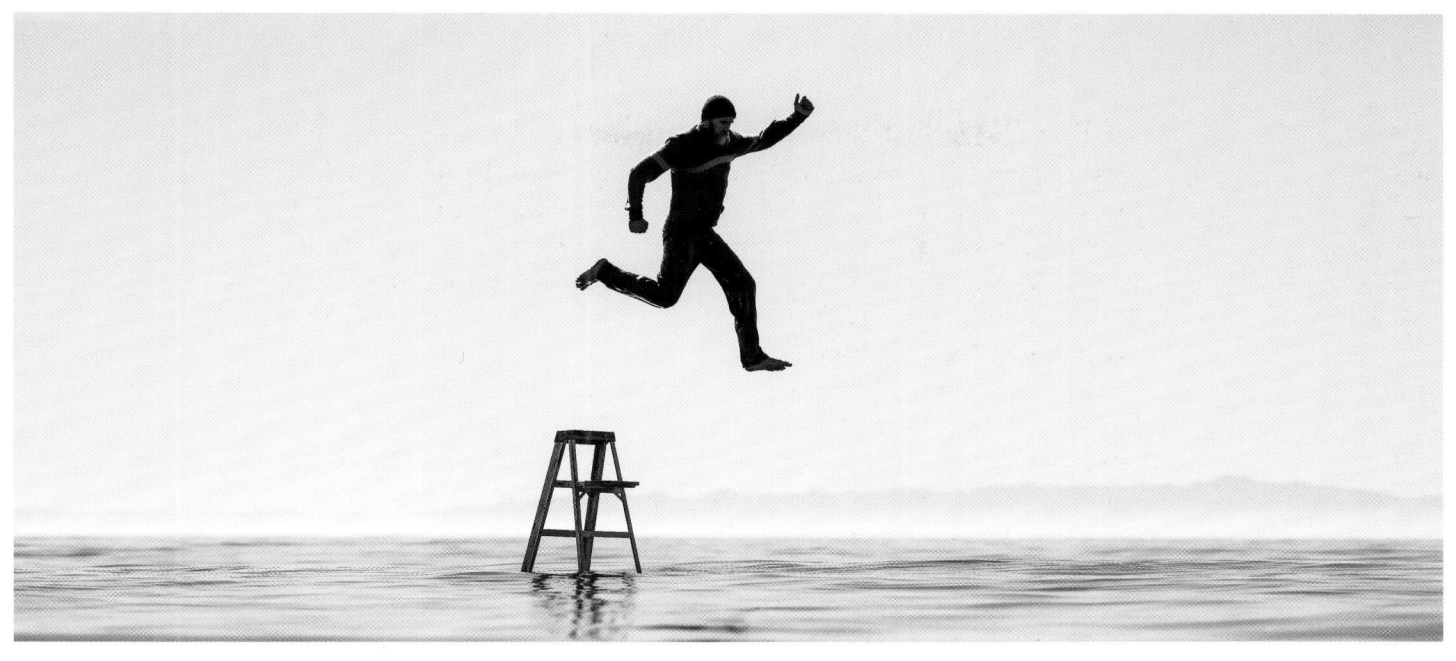

EXERCISE

STEP 1

Owning a GoPro camera isn't enough—after making the purchase you need to get out there
and put it to use. Make a list of your passions and dreams. Think about the mountains you would like
the climb, and do so without criticizing your own ideas. Let your imagination run free.
After making an initial list, circle your top five passions or dreams.

STEP 2

Passion without a plan is like gasoline spilled on the ground. Select one of your passions from the
list above and come up with a plan to pursue it with more focus, fun, and resolve.

STEP 3

Originality comes from mashing up old ideas. In order to come up with some
great ideas, follow GoPro's lead and think about the marriage of two things and what
the offspring might be. And don't just limit your imagination to one category;
consider multiple topics, like music, commerce, and art.

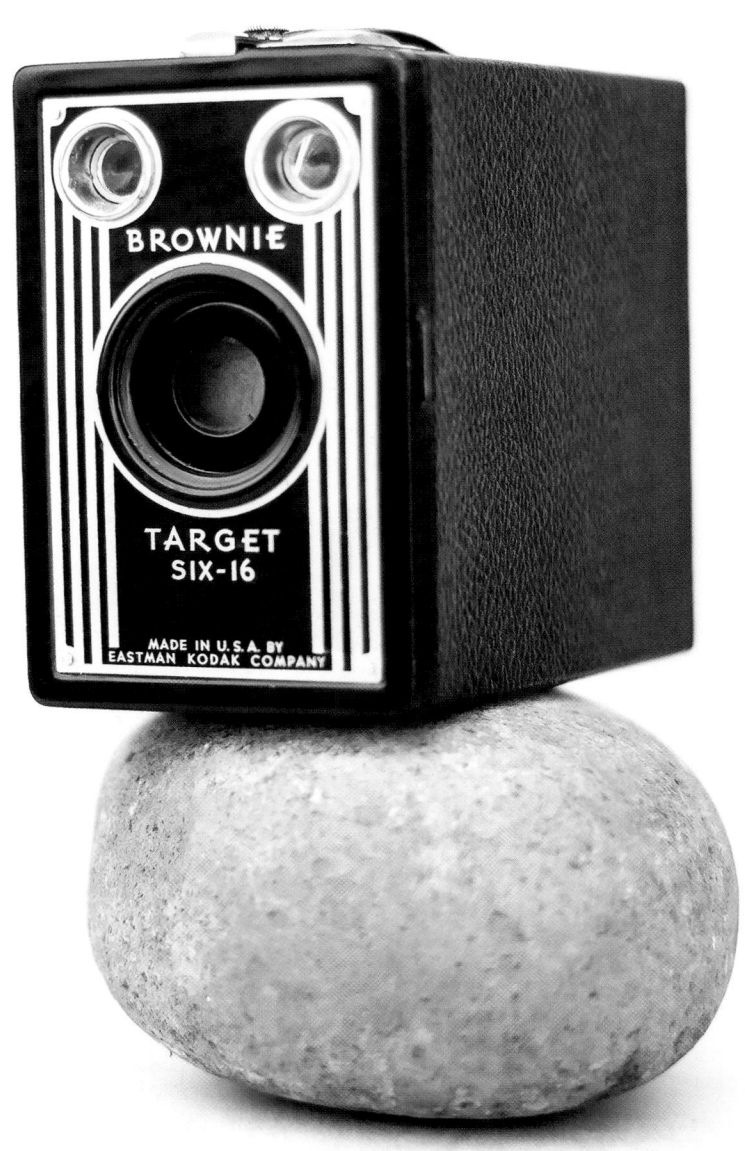

CHAPTER THIRTY-ONE

THE POWER OF PLAY

When George Eastman introduced his camera, the Brownie, all the other cameras were awkward, imposing, and huge. Eastman's camera had a friendly face. It was a curious little box that promised fun. The camera cost only $1 and wasn't hard to use. As the marketing slogan said, "You press the button and we do the rest." The Brownie was a huge success—it was the GoPro of 1901.

The original Brownie and the GoPro gave ordinary people the ability to savor and celebrate life. Life moves so fast; cameras help us slow it down. And making photographs helps us remember and cherish those special moments before they fade. The challenge for most photographers is not conjuring up the desire to make pictures but taking the time and putting in the effort to learn how to use the tool.

LITTLE BOXES CAN BE LOTS OF FUN In comparison to their counterparts, the Brownie and GoPro were laughable little boxes that had hardly any features at all. Without all the serious features that photographers had come to expect, these cameras seemed less like tools and more like toys. The elitists scoffed, but the amateurs picked up these magic boxes and started to have fun. The secret to the wild success of such cameras was the features they didn't have.

Fun and simple cameras have broad appeal. Consider the iPhone, the most popular camera in the world. Even my 3-year-old knows how to take photographs and scroll through the frames. And without the worry of making a costly mistake, the camera becomes an extension of who we are. Without the burden and expectation that comes with heavy and expensive gear, the photographer stops being so concerned. And without the pressure of performing, we become more relaxed. When we let go of our self-critical bent, we take more risks. The self-imposed stress melts away, and creativity ignites like a sparkler on the 4th of July.

Picasso famously said, "The chief enemy of creativity is common sense." Common sense is a con artist that steals growth and joy. Most of us have bought into its lie and become too practical in our old age. We've stopped playing like we used to when we were kids. But nobody hits the bull's-eye on the first try. It takes multiple tries and a quiver of arrows in order to achieve that goal. But we grow up and forget—especially when we get an important job. The more important the job, the more we justify our stress. So we get serious, grit our teeth, and furrow our brow. But with such stress it's nearly impossible to iterate, experiment, and learn.

LEAD VERSUS INK When it comes to creative growth, the pencil is mightier than the pen. The pencil allows us to doodle, sketch, play, iterate, and test out new ideas. Those who practice a creative art know that such iteration and practice is essential for growth. The musician practices a riff. The writer goes through rough drafts. The painter sketches her ideas. The poet jots down a few lines. The most productive practice happens when we can block out the critical voices in our heads. Practice makes perfect only if we feel safe.

When asked about learning to act, the actor Ewan McGregor said, "The best thing about going to acting school was that it was a place that you could make a mistake and it wouldn't affect your next job." We all need schools, studies, sanctuaries, labs, and practice rooms where we can let down our guard in order to try out new ideas.

The neuroscientist Dr. Stuart Brown says, "Nothing lights up the brain like play." When we play we worry less and the creative juices flow without any effort at all. Play diminishes stress and helps us relax. Play and work are similar; it's just that play is more fun. And don't make the mistake that play isn't profound.

According to the American Academy of Pediatrics, "Play develops imagination, dexterity, and physical, cognitive, and emotional strength." But play isn't just for kids, nor is it about playing foosball at work. Play involves/requires a mental shift that changes how we approach our work. And it isn't just for those in overtly creative fields. Whether you are a supervisor or a scientist, play can help you grow. As Einstein once said, "Play is the highest form of research."

CREATIVE PEOPLE ARE CURIOUS, FLEXIBLE, PERSISTENT, AND INDEPENDENT WITH A TREMENDOUS SPIRIT OF ADVENTURE AND A LOVE OF PLAY.

— **HENRI MATISSE**

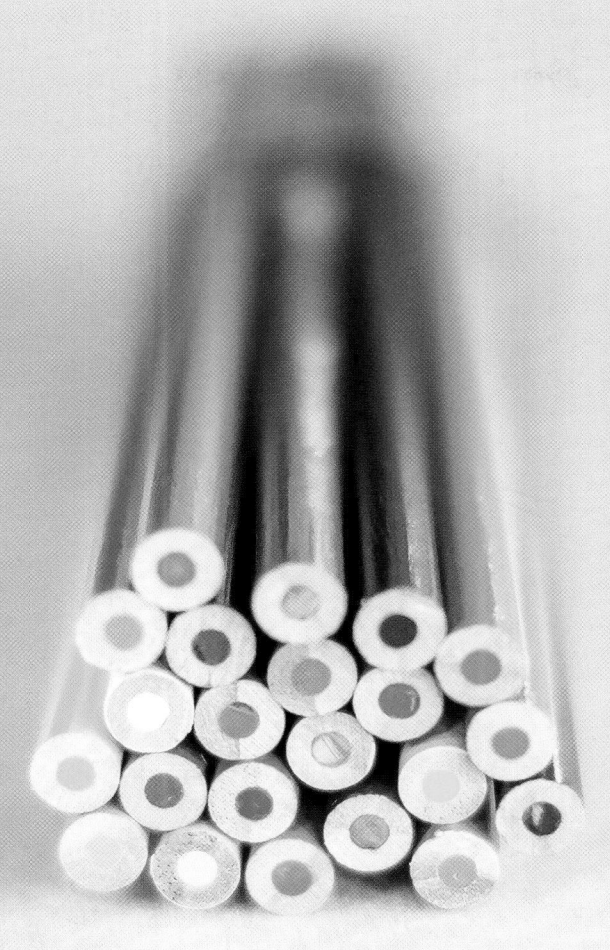

YOU CAN'T PLAY IN YOUR GRAVE The opposite of play isn't work. It's more like apathy or something worse. Some, like Dr. Brown, believe that the opposite of play is depression, whereas others think it's more like death. Whatever we call it, without play life is bleak and dull. The trouble is that we play less and less as we age. George Bernard Shaw put it this way: "We don't stop playing because we grow old; we grow old because we stop playing." In his research, Dr. Brown found this to be more than just a catchy idea. Brown concluded, "When we stop playing, we start dying." Play isn't just a game; it keeps us creative, flexible, and young.

But too often, as we grow up the creative spark falters and the more self-critical and self-conscious we become. When we're comfortable in our own skin, like we were as kids, the spark shines strong. Harvard psychologist Maria Konnikova puts it like this: "Insight may seem to come from nowhere, but really, it comes from somewhere quite specific: from the attic and the processing that has been taking place while you've been busy doing other things." That's why good ideas come to us in a flash when we are taking a shower or sitting on a train. The best, brightest, and biggest ideas cannot be forced. That's why serious and stodgy people rarely create great art.

Of course we need some degree of mental toughness to be an adult, but not at the expense of being able to think like a kid. Kids are creative without knowing what they've done. They make up games with toy cars and without self-awareness or a self-critical voice in their head; they let their creativity freely go where it may. As we grow old, we stop being so free. But freedom is only a few steps away. As the poet Sharon Olds said, "Whenever we give our pen some free will, we may surprise ourselves."

So why not try something that you have never done? Why not take that risk to iterate and test out new ideas? Look deep within and you'll see a creative force bubbling up inside. This force wants to be free. It wants to roam wild. Let it off leash and give it some space. You might just be surprised at how wonderful it will make your life become.

IT IS A HAPPY TALENT TO KNOW HOW TO PLAY.
—RALPH WALDO EMERSON

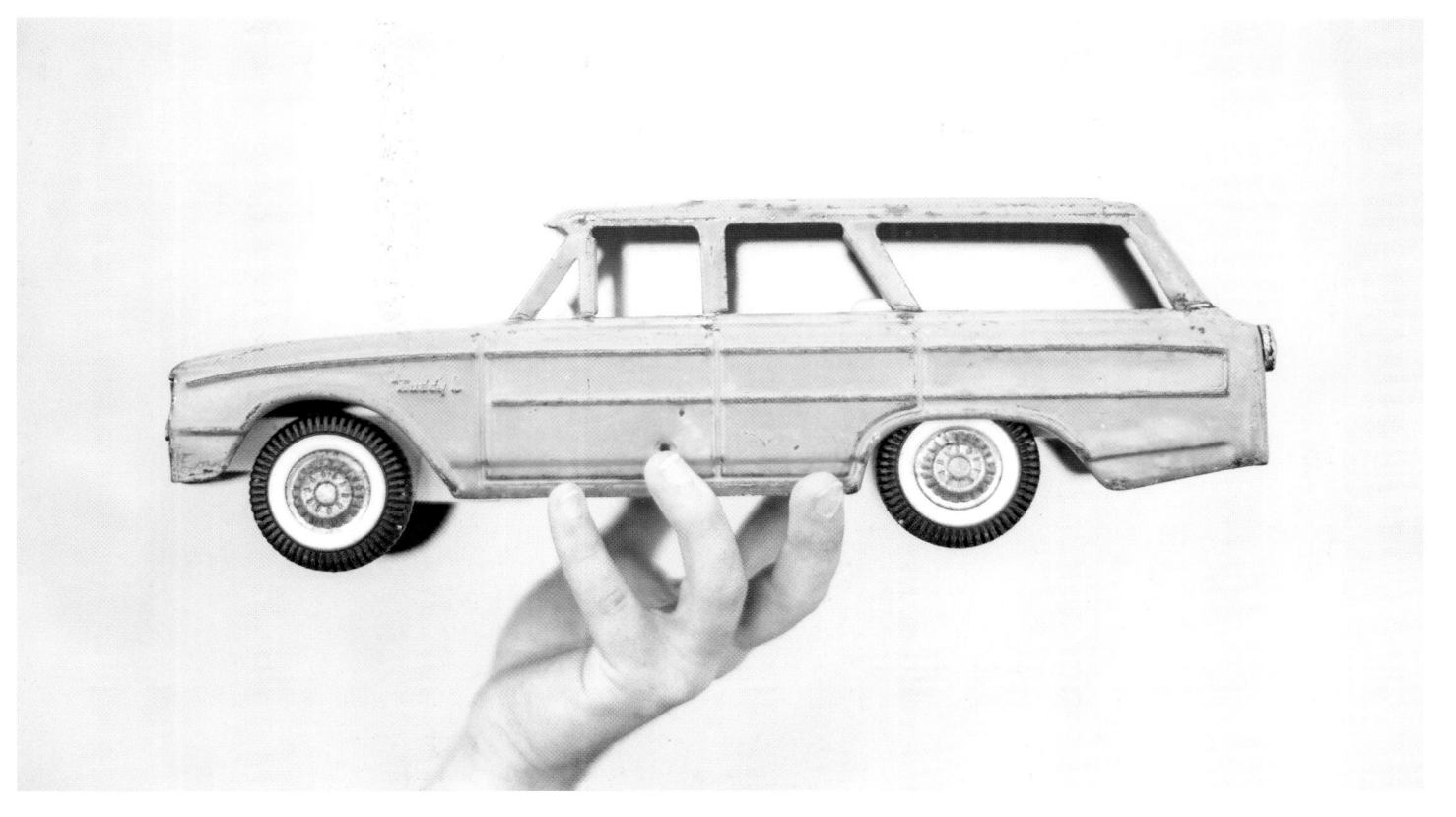

<u>EXERCISE</u>

STEP 1

Without tools and raw materials—whether bikes, building blocks, crayons, cardboard boxes, instruments, motorcycles, chisels, or spools—it's difficult to play. Go out and buy yourself a few tools and toys. Whether a chisel to carve wood or a dartboard to hang on your wall, get something that will help you keep your creativity alive.

STEP 2

Carve out some time this week to play in a way that is natural to you. You don't have to draw with crayons or build a LEGO spaceship. Find something that will help you keep your playful spirit alive. Set aside 15 minutes and mark it on your calendar as an appointment for creative growth.

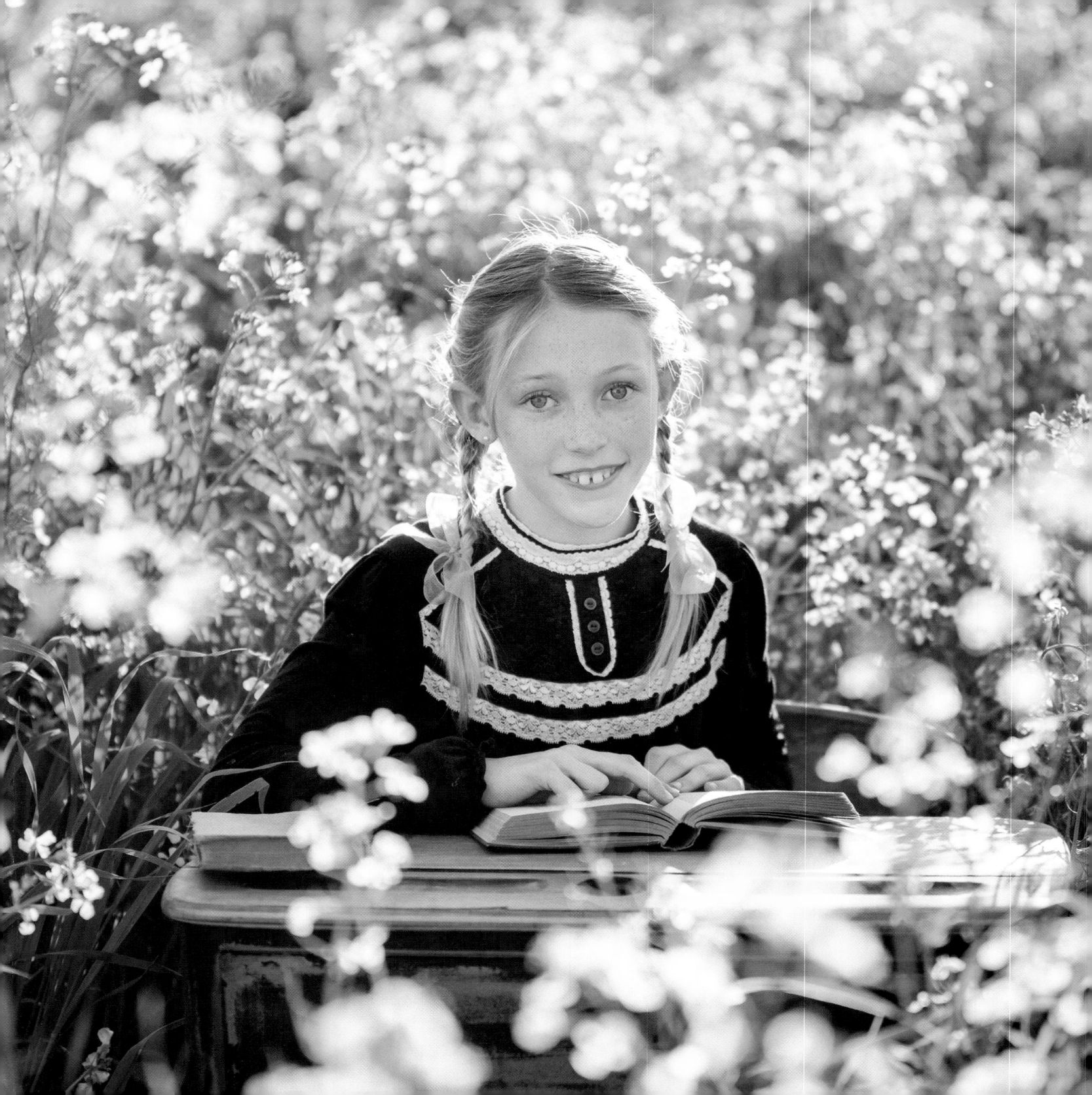

CHAPTER THIRTY-TWO

UNLIKELY EDUCATION

Education doesn't only happen in school, and wisdom is rarely just picked up within the safety of a roof and walls. Many of the most significant lessons of my life happened out in the field or on the journey to somewhere else. Herman, born centuries before our time, could relate. His most significant schooling began at sea.

Herman took his first boat trip when he was 18. The trip didn't last more than a week but the effect was profound. The salt air and open sea stirred his imagination and compelled him to want more. A few years later this drive led him to embark on a journey that would last three years. He was hired to work on a whaling ship, which traveled far and wide. When the boat stopped in Polynesia, he and a crewmate deserted the ship only to be captured by cannibals. After four months as captives, they escaped. Over a decade later, Herman used what he learned at sea to craft one of the greatest novels of all time.

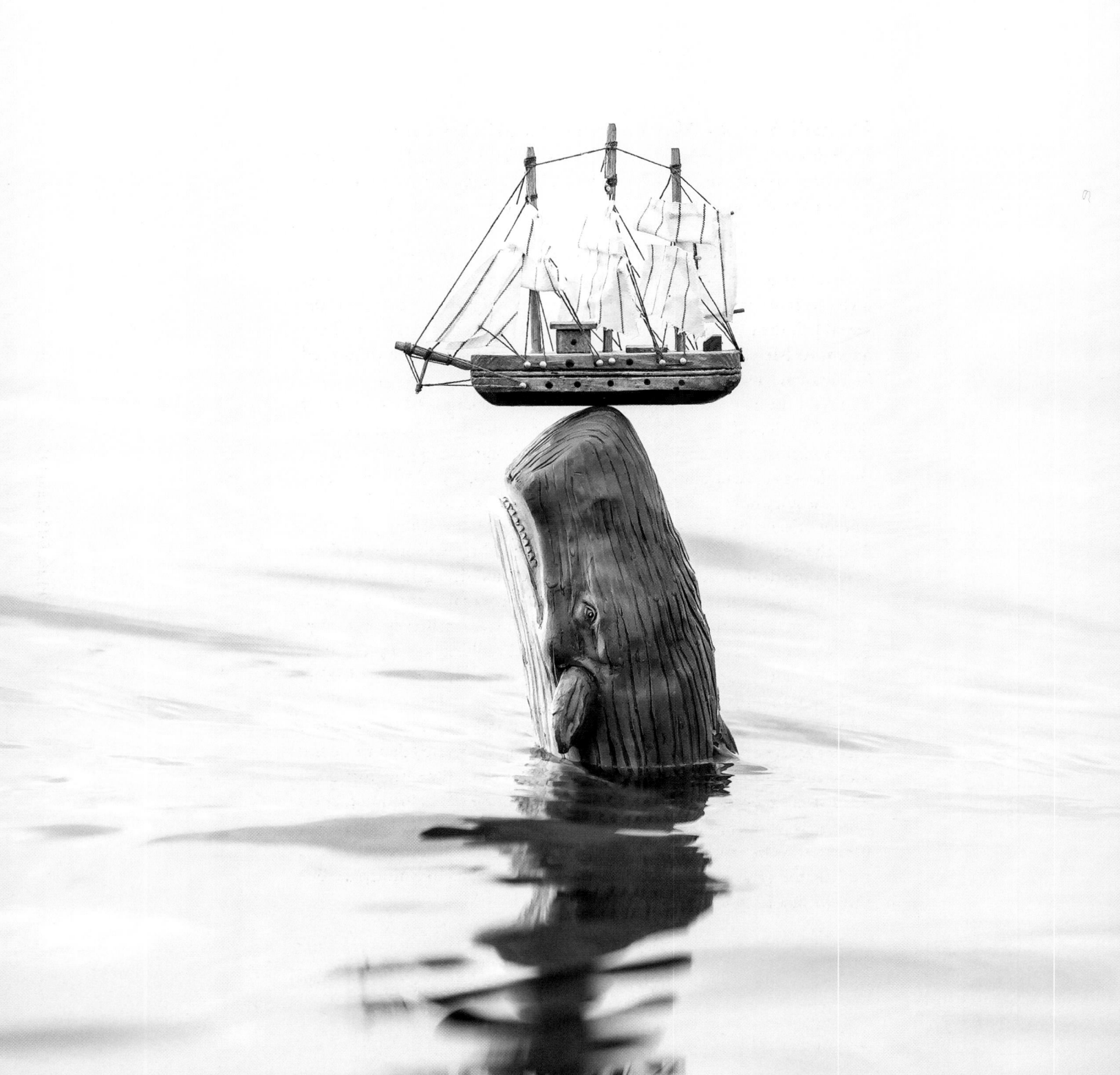

A SCHOOL WITHOUT WALLS "Call me Ishmael" is how the novel begins. With three simple words, the reader is hooked. Yet Herman Melville didn't learn how to craft catchy opening lines while at school. He had to come up with this by himself. He learned as he went. As he once said, "A whaleship was my Harvard." And thank goodness that he went to that school; otherwise, we would never have benefited from his masterpiece, *Moby Dick*.

Melville's book is a complex and tightly woven story that stands on its own—it is original through and through. The originality came from the sea and all the difficulties he experienced there. And this was not without intent. As Melville said, "It is better to fail in originality than to succeed in imitation." He did not set out to tell a story that was simply about those who hunt the behemoths of the sea, but to use that context as a way to say more. Creatives always do this. They take the ordinary and run it through their imagination in order to create and to say something new. What we thought was a whale story is really about defiance, duty, God, and death.

As the story of Melville's "education" illustrates, school isn't a place—it's a point of view. Every experience has the possibility of teaching you truth. And the deepest truths, those tested by time and referred to as wisdom, never come easily. These truths require patience and strength; they come at a cost most of us are unwilling to pay. We may prefer to learn from a book rather than taking the time and risk involved with a treacherous ocean trip. Plus it's more comfortable and convenient to live life at a distance. From there we can observe and pontificate, at one with our own intoxicating superior thoughts.

Out on the sea you are immersed and surrounded with situations you cannot ignore or control. As a ship hand, Melville discovered that we do not stand alone—an interdependence is needed to sustain life away from land. As he later explained, "We cannot live only for ourselves. A thousand fibers connect us with our fellow man." Wisdom like this comes only from living life as a traveler would. And the more life we live and the more difficulties we face, the greater potential for wisdom to be stitched into our souls, like threads that keep it from coming undone.

WE GIVE OUR SUFFERING MEANING BY THE WAY WE RESPOND TO IT.

—VIKTOR FRANKL

FREE ADVICE The trouble is that most of these threads are bound together so tightly that they are difficult to extract. The artist Austin Kleon found a way to shine a light on the threads without pulling them out. Kleon's approach begins with the theory that "all advice is autobiographical." With that premise in mind, he decided to write a book titled *Steal Like an Artist*. It was a collection of wisdom and advice for his younger self. The book went viral. Turns out that giving advice to our younger selves is a great way to access the wisdom that is woven into our lives.

My favorite piece of advice from Kleon is "Write the book you want to read." Sage words for all of us no matter what it is that we want to create. When we stop creating for someone else, we become more original in our thoughts. And the core sentiment of this advice can be applied in so many ways: "Live the life you want to live" or "Climb the ladder you want to climb" or "Fix the problem that annoys you most." The most powerful creative ideas come from deep within. And this isn't just about having a positive outlook on life or taking a cruise ship on sunny seas. Sometimes the only way to break through is to witness the cruel and brutal killing of a whale.

This is true in both a conceptual and personal way. Thomas Edison put it this way: "Discontent is the first necessity of progress." As all entrepreneurs know, the secret to finding good ideas is to pay attention to what bothers you and what you think the solution might be. Most of the best businesses were started this way.

Yvon Chouinard was a pioneer rock climber in Yosemite Valley in the 1960s. Frustrated that he couldn't find reliable and high-quality rock climbing gear, he made his own. Others wanted the product too, so a company was born. Years later his company, Patagonia, was huge.

Chouinard didn't stop innovating after he first forged metal climbing gear for his friends. From the beginning, he traveled and searched the globe for ways to improve the quality and impact of the company he owned. On one trip he revisited a remote South American town he had been to years before. The smiling children's faces he remembered from before were replaced with kids who had gone blind. The town's water source was being polluted by a business upstream. Chouinard was deeply upset. So he began to donate a portion of his company's profits to help with situations like this. He started an organization to get others involved. And he committed his company to high environmental standards before it was a trend.

The idea of transforming discontent into positive change is not just about business; it's about personal life as well. The psychologist and Nazi prison camp survivor Viktor Frankl once said, "What is to give light must endure burning." What we endure is what gives substance to the content that we create. The deeper the suffering, the higher the reach. Viktor Frankl's life work and writing are a testament to that. Yet this isn't just for people who have been through extreme hardships. The principle applies regardless of the degree of suffering or whether we are young or old.

James was six when his older brother died. His mother was devastated. She could barely cope and fell into a deep depression. James was upset but wanted to help. In an effort to comfort his mom, he put on his older brother's clothes and whistled like he used to. During this time of grief it occurred to James that his dead brother would never grow up. He couldn't get this idea out of his head, and it stuck with him for the rest of his life. Even thirty years later when he wrote his most enduring work, the pain was still there. But now it was transformed into characters on the stage. And the play, *Peter Pan, or The Boy Who Wouldn't Grow Up,* still resonates in a timeless way.

SUFFERING AND LIGHT Suffering is dark, and I do not want to belittle the suffering that you have endured. And in no way do I want to call that suffering good. But I do want to suggest that the difficulty you have faced might be fuel for doing something good. When we revisit suffering in this way, sometimes we discover a pure center of light within the dark circle of the difficulties of life. And maybe what you have experienced can bring a unique brightness to the world.

Adopting a creative mind-set can help us find light when all seems dark. You may have suffered, but maybe that suffering has written a hidden story in your soul. It took James M. Barrie over thirty years to uncover his; maybe yours is yet to be. Or the challenges you have faced may be preparing you for a new stage in life. You might have an unlived life hidden inside, waiting to be revealed. Maybe there's an author, photographer, chef, poet, or CEO just beneath the surface, waiting to be born. Maybe all the difficulties are really just soil and sustenance for this unlived life to grow. Like a lotus flower that floats on the surface but is anchored in the mud below.

EXERCISE

STEP 1

What advice would you give your younger self, or what would you have done differently with your life? Record your responses in a journal and then share them with a friend. Write them out in a non-linear and non-hierarchical form. Let go of the critic in your head and write free. Here are a few of my own to give you an idea: I would have slept outside more often. I would have stopped worrying so much about what other people thought. I would have cut my parents more slack. I would have listened more closely to God's quiet voice.

STEP 2

Unattended and ignored, discontent can turn sour. Paid attention to, discontent can bring new life— that's what the architect Jeff Shelton found out. Shelton discovered his life's calling when some ugly cinderblock buildings were built near the idyllic setting of his family home. His disdain for the buildings gave him the resolve to become an architect himself. This was just the nudge he needed. Today his whimsical, colorful, and vibrant buildings have become world renowned.

In light of this idea, take 15 minutes to write a stream-of-consciousness response to the question "What bothers you most?" Think about problems big and small. After venting, don't let the negativity sit cold. On another page, use the discontent as fuel for coming up with strategies or solutions for growth.

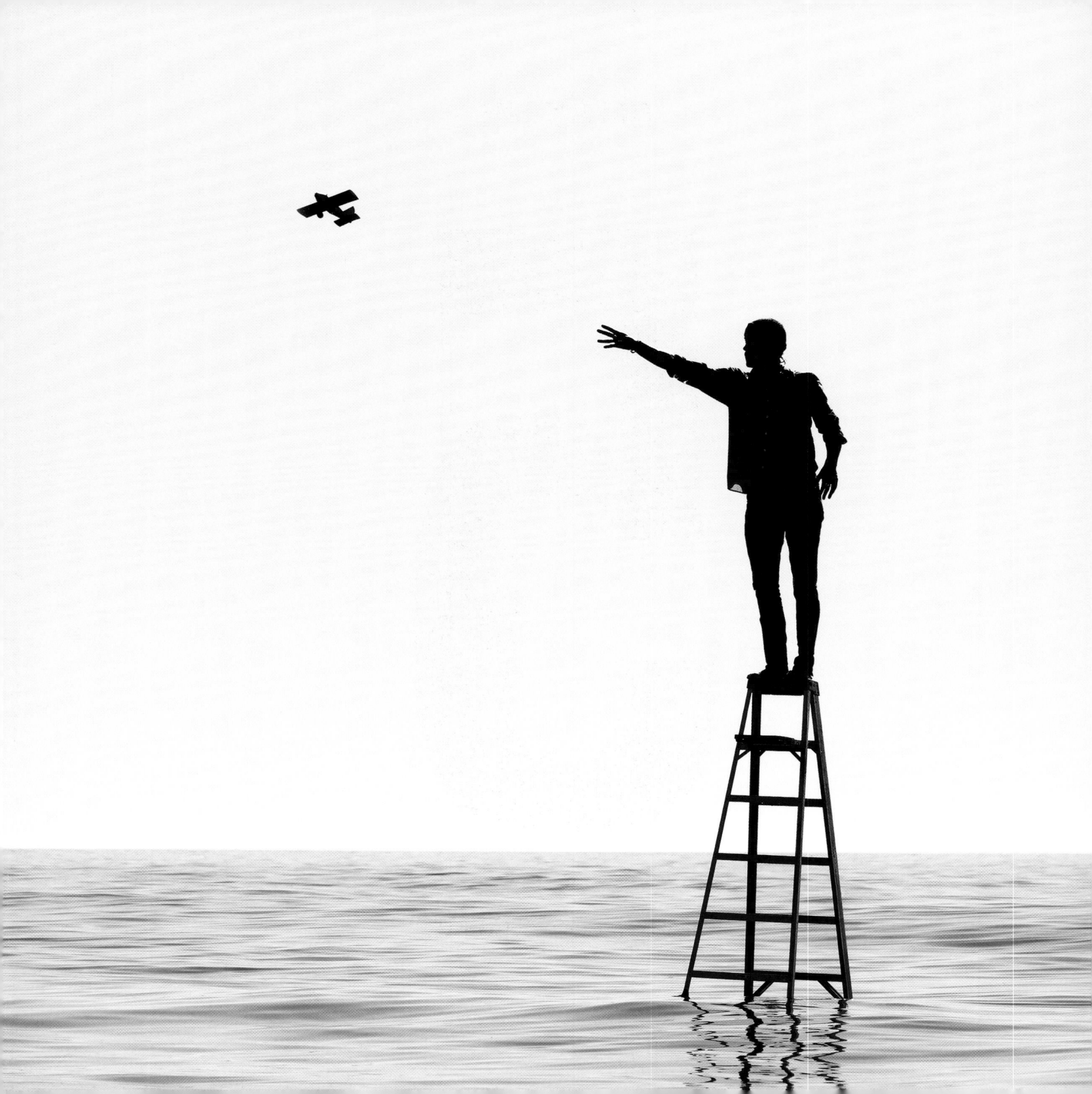

PART FIVE: TIME

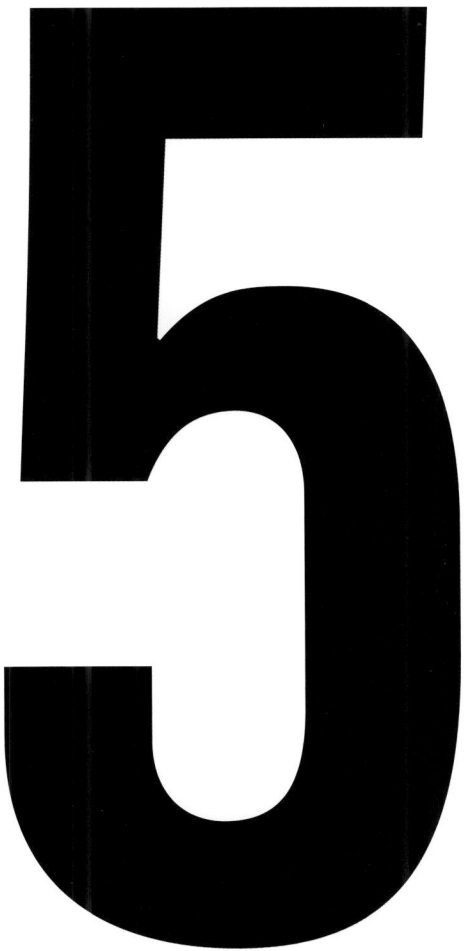

WE ONLY HAVE TODAY. LET US BEGIN.
— MOTHER TERESA

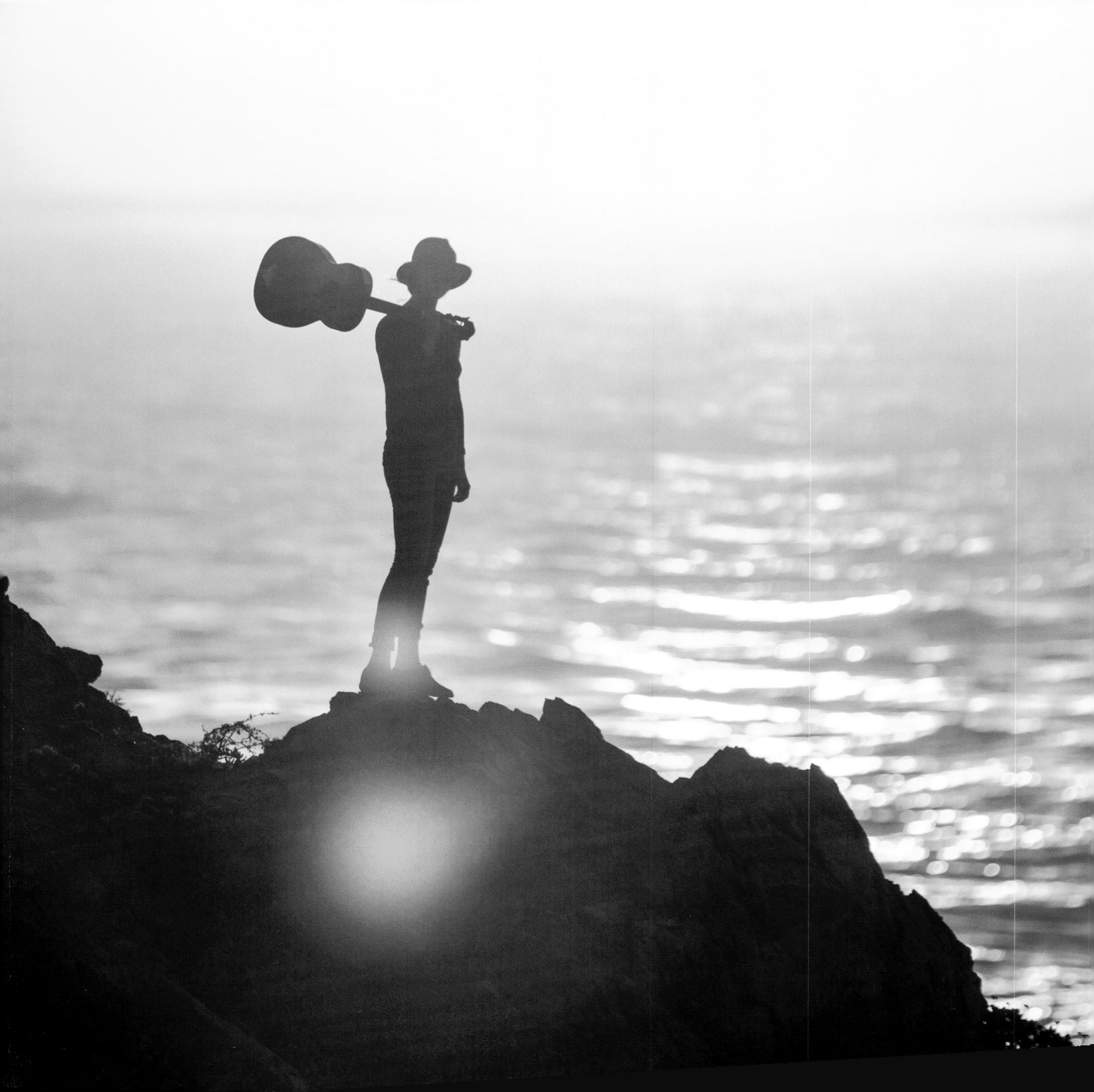

CHAPTER THIRTY-THREE

KEEP THE EDGES WILD

When Linford and his wife Karin moved from the city to a farm, Linford's father gave them some advice: "Leave the edges wild." It was a curious suggestion for someone who was new to a rural land. Linford's dad was a bird watcher, and he knew that if you make a farm too perfect, you won't leave any space for the native birds. He said, "Leave the edges wild and let the birds have their hidden places for their untamed music."

As a singer-songwriter duo, Linford and Karin picked up on that phrase and integrated the spirit of it into their work. The phrase became a metaphor for how they approached music and life. It wasn't just about the birds, but about how to provide space for the cultivated and untamed aspects of life to thrive. If the neat rows of vegetables provided sustenance for the body, then the wild edges would provide it for the soul.

BEAUTIFUL MYSTERY In one interview Linford explained, "Music is one of those unseen, powerful gifts or mysteries that we can't hold in our hands. The ancient Greeks thought of music as the opposite of astronomy. Astronomy was about discovering and mapping the furthest reaches. Music was all about discovering the unknown." My own favorite music isn't perfect or over-produced, but rather leaves space for the mysteries of life to be explored. Music that's too perfect sounds like it came from a machine. Rough and wild edges give music some soul.

Leaving the edges wild is a great mantra for any creative pursuit. Life can become so pasteurized and predictable that there isn't any space left for mystery or surprise. Wild edges create a zone for the unfinished and untamed to thrive. Einstein once said, "The most beautiful thing we can experience is the mysterious," and it's true. Think of your favorite song, book, movie, or romantic love—you can only explain it so far, and there is always an intangible and incomprehensible element that resonates within.

Our deepest experiences cannot be rationally explained like rows of soybeans on a farm. The most beautiful, most wonderful, and most magnificent push past the barriers of our limited minds. Where words fall short, art steps in. Art, music, photography, film, poetry, and painting help us articulate hidden truths. Whether our own creation or the work of someone else, art reminds us that life is more than it seems. And it's the mystery of art that awakens and stirs our soul and helps us stop being so caught up in the chaos of our small lives.

ENORMOUSLY SMALL Rarely does a work of art resonate in a timeless way. When it does, it's difficult to explain why. Take the *Mona Lisa*. Why has this painting kindled the curiosity of so many who have gazed upon her face? Most admirers attribute it to her smile. For a moment, imagine if Lisa's smile were a perfect and toothy grin. The painting would have been lost decades ago. Perfect is predictable and dull. It's the slight mystery of her smile that draws in thousands each year. And Mona Lisa's smile isn't fake but authentic and true.

Leonardo da Vinci worked on *Mona Lisa* for over 16 years. His work wasn't a constant flow, but still he lived and worked with that painting for a long time. One scholar, Pascal Cotte, who has spent more than 3000 hours studying the painting, discovered using X-ray–like technology that da Vinci originally painted Lisa with a wider face and a more expressive smile. He opted for a subtler look and, by doing so, made Mona Lisa more intriguing and serene.

When visitors to the Louvre see the famous painting for the first time, it's common for them to be shocked by how something so significant can be so enormously small. The painting sits in a small frame, and as you take a closer look you can't help but notice the cracks on the surface of the paint. It is a shock to realize that this painting is eroding. Then you stare at Lisa's captivating gaze. The more you look, the less you understand. The mystery of her countenance sets your imagination to work. You start to wonder who she is and why she is looking out of the frame. Quickly you realize that Lisa isn't an idealized archetype that is putting on airs. Rather, she appears to be an ordinary but beautiful soul that seems so real.

BECOMING REAL "Becoming real takes a long time," wrote Margery Williams in her beloved children's book *The Velveteen Rabbit*. Williams explained, "That's why it doesn't happen often to people who break easily, or have sharp edges, or who have to be carefully kept. Generally, by the time you are Real, most of your hair has been loved off, and your eyes drop out and you get loose in the joints and very shabby. But these things don't matter at all, because once you are Real you can't be ugly, except to people who don't understand." When you view the *Mona Lisa* it quickly becomes apparent that she wasn't someone with sharp edges but was warm and kind. As you look even closer, you'll notice that her eyebrows have been worn off. Like the velveteen rabbit, Lisa has been well loved. And she may be hundreds of years old and lacking eyebrows, but that only draws us in. I often wonder if the missing features, vague smile, and crackled paint are flaws that make the painting so interesting to the crowds.

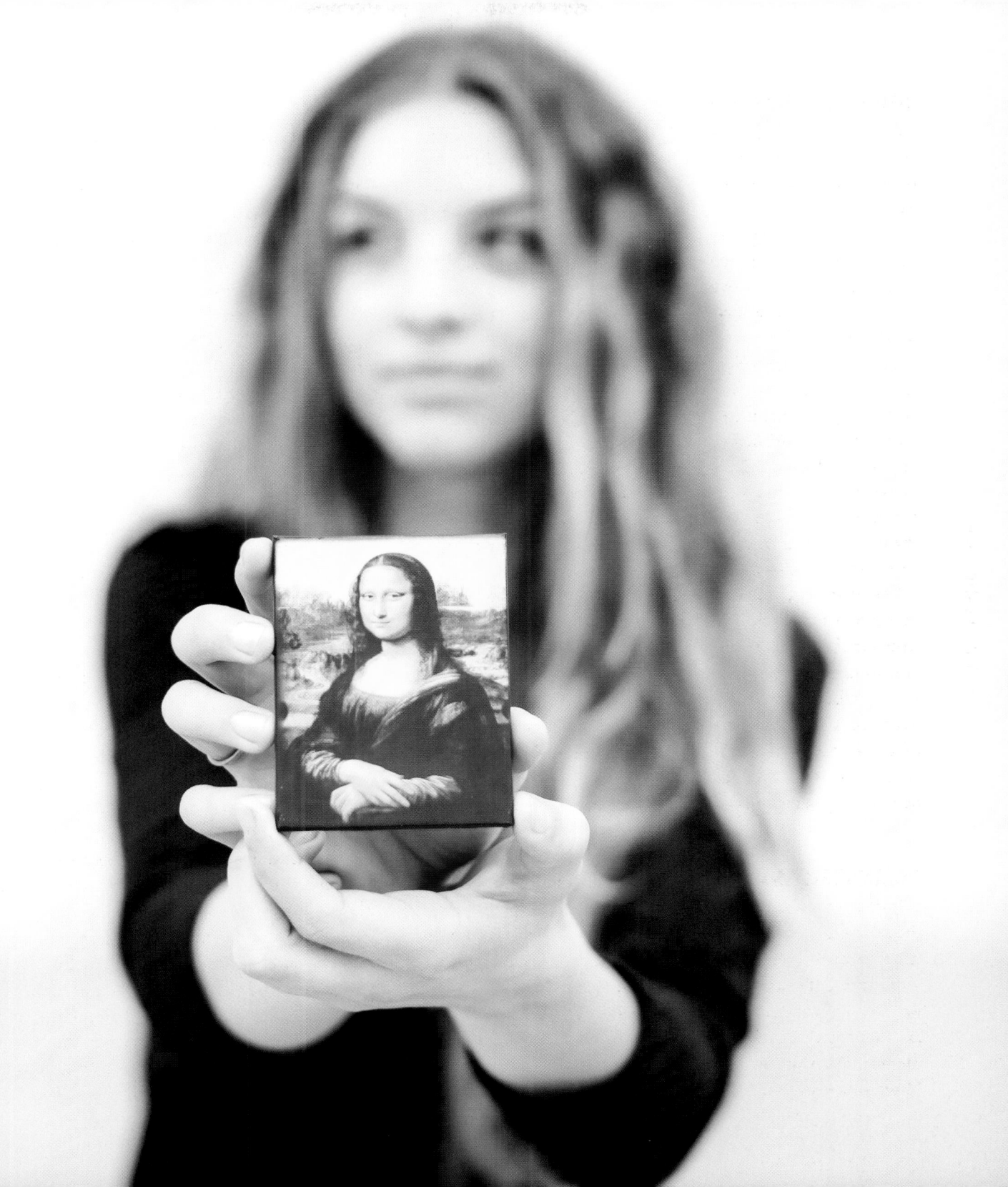

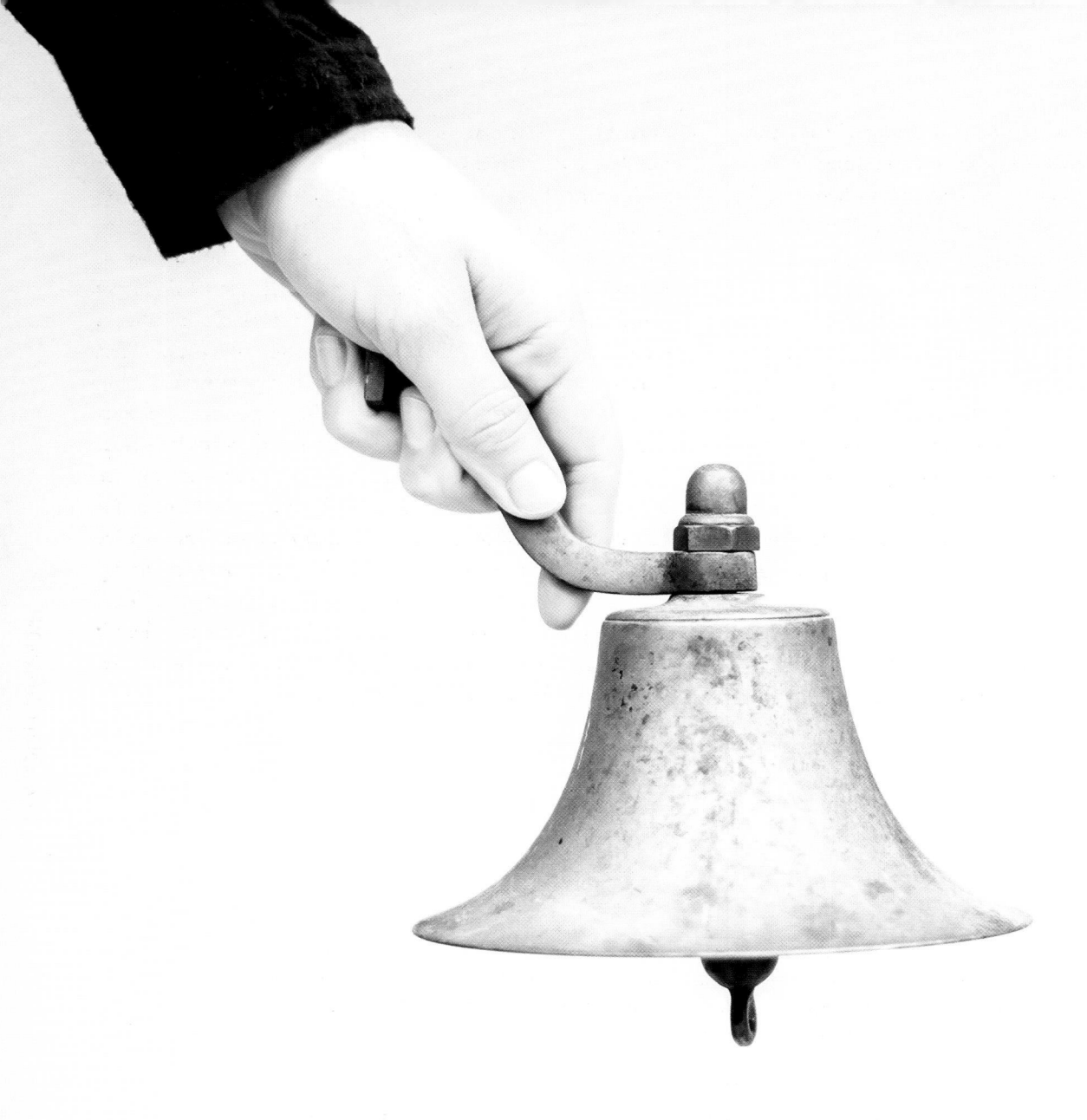

CRACKS AND LIGHT Leonard Cohen once wrote, "Ring the bell that still can ring. There are cracks in everything. That's how the light gets in." Flaws are what make us authentic and real, flaws are what make us shine, and authenticity trumps perfection every time. Those who ring cracked bells are the ones who make the biggest difference in our lives. They are the musicians who write the best songs, the artists who make the most meaningful art, the poets who write the strongest lines, and the people who make the best friends. When all hell breaks loose, their presence provides hope because it's real. Nobody wants to spend time with a perfect person when their world is falling apart. We want to be with people who understand. Rather than make us feel ashamed, they empathize with our pain. Rather than fix our brokenness, they reveal the light even in dark times. Not all cracks are bad; some are just wild edges where the untamed music can be heard.

My good friend Shaun is a woodworker who salvages old barns and turns them into beautiful tables with a rustic and soulful look. We commissioned him to make a piece for our home. He showed me the raw and worn-out planks that he intended to use. After over 100 years of use, the wood was in rough shape. Scratches, stains, nails, and tread marks made it hard to envision this wood being beautiful once again. Shaun asked, "How much do you want me to clean it up?" I responded, "What do you recommend?" He said, "I think we should clean it up just enough but not too much. It's always better to leave some of the character and story of these boards." And so it is with our lives. Without the roughness everything looks the same. It's the rough and wild edges that make us unique. And it's here that our character and creativity shine.

Those who come into our home often comment on the unique beauty of the salvaged wood. Flaws can be beautiful if you can learn to embrace them for what they are. The creative process is not perfect, but is inherently flawed. And creativity flows the fastest when we strive to create great things but leave some openness on the fringe. Creativity grows best when it has plenty of space to breathe. So leave the edges wild and let your untamed and hidden spirit grow.

EXERCISE

STEP 1

Some ideas are worth tattooing on your arm, while others are worth writing out and tacking up on the wall. The phrase "Leave the edges wild" is one that I have above my desk. Try doing the same and live with the phrase for a week. Tack it up, and let it spark ideas and conversations and shape how you approach your work.

STEP 2

Take a few minutes to reflect on the wild edges that you value most. In your journal, write down a list of five to ten wild edges that enrich your life.

STEP 3

As a symbolic gesture, do something today that celebrates the idea of wild and imperfect edges. Set yourself free.

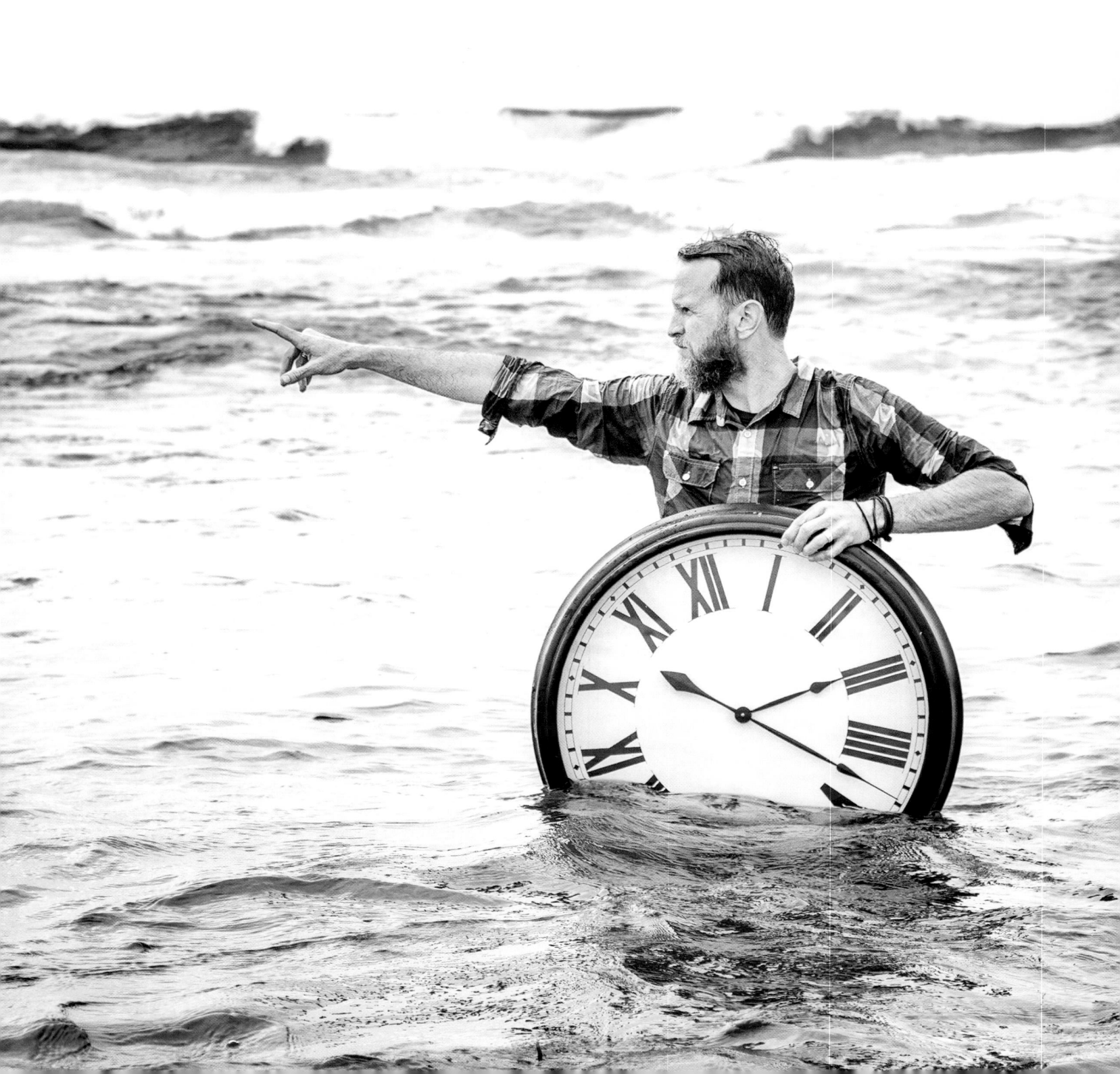

CHAPTER THIRTY-FOUR

NOTHING TO LOSE

It wasn't a surprise when Martin received a C in his first speech class in graduate school. Martin's intellect, depth, and passion burned bright, but he stuttered and his speech impediment was tripping him up. Then one day, as if by miracle, his speech impediment disappeared. Martin's friend Harry once asked him about how he was able to leave his stutter behind. Martin explained, "Once I accepted death, I stopped being bedeviled by these things." Accepting and facing the fact of limited time has a clarifying and cleansing effect. No longer afflicted with a stutter, Dr. Martin Luther King, Jr. went on to become one of the most famous orators of all time. And accepting death didn't just improve the way he spoke, but gave him courage to live the life to which he was called and contribute to a higher cause.

LIFE DISTILLED Finding one's true destiny always involves a deeper awareness of death. Otherwise, the fear of death holds us back from having the courage to accomplish our dreams. Steve Jobs put it this way: "Remembering that I'll be dead soon is the most important tool I've ever encountered to help me make the big choices in life. Almost everything—all external expectations, all pride, all fear of embarrassment or failure—these things just fall away in the face of death, leaving only what is truly important. Remembering that you are going to die is the best way I know to avoid the trap of thinking you have something to lose. You are already naked. There is no reason not to follow your heart." Death distills life into its simplest form. Death can build courage, but it can also take it away.

In the face of death, the grief of loss can overwhelm. When my friend Todd lost his dad he said, "The sun will never shine the same." Death does distill, but it can also diminish and overwhelm. When Candy Chang was processing her grief over the death of a close friend, she began asking questions like, "How do I now find joy in the everyday?" and "How can we live the life we have to its fullest degree?" In the face of darkness, questions like these help us begin to see the light. Chang decided to pursue these questions further by creating a small art project to help her process the pain.

WALK AROUND FEELING LIKE A LEAF. KNOW YOU COULD TUMBLE AT ANY SECOND. THEN DECIDE WHAT TO DO WITH YOUR TIME.
—NAOMI SHIHAB NYE

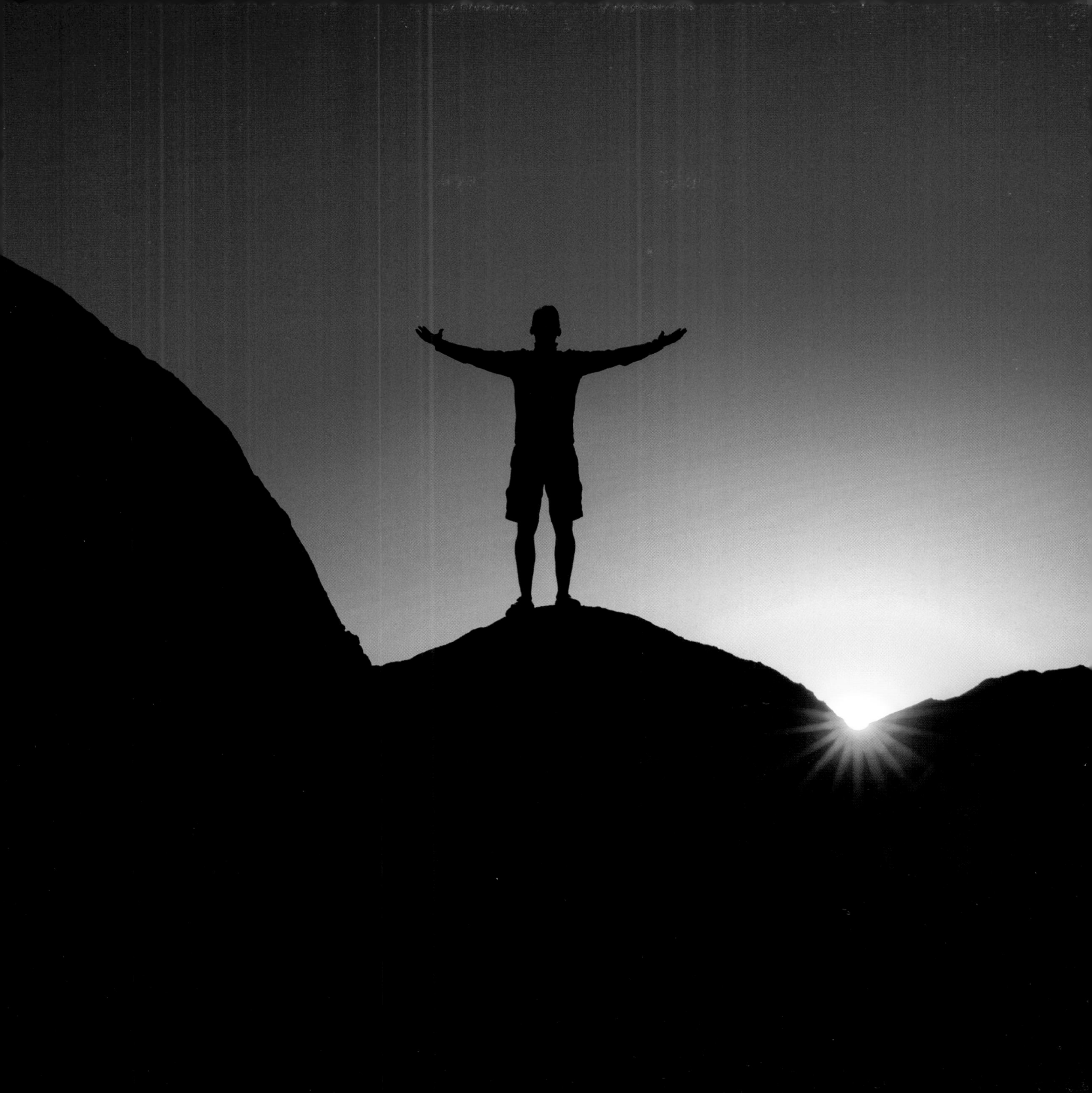

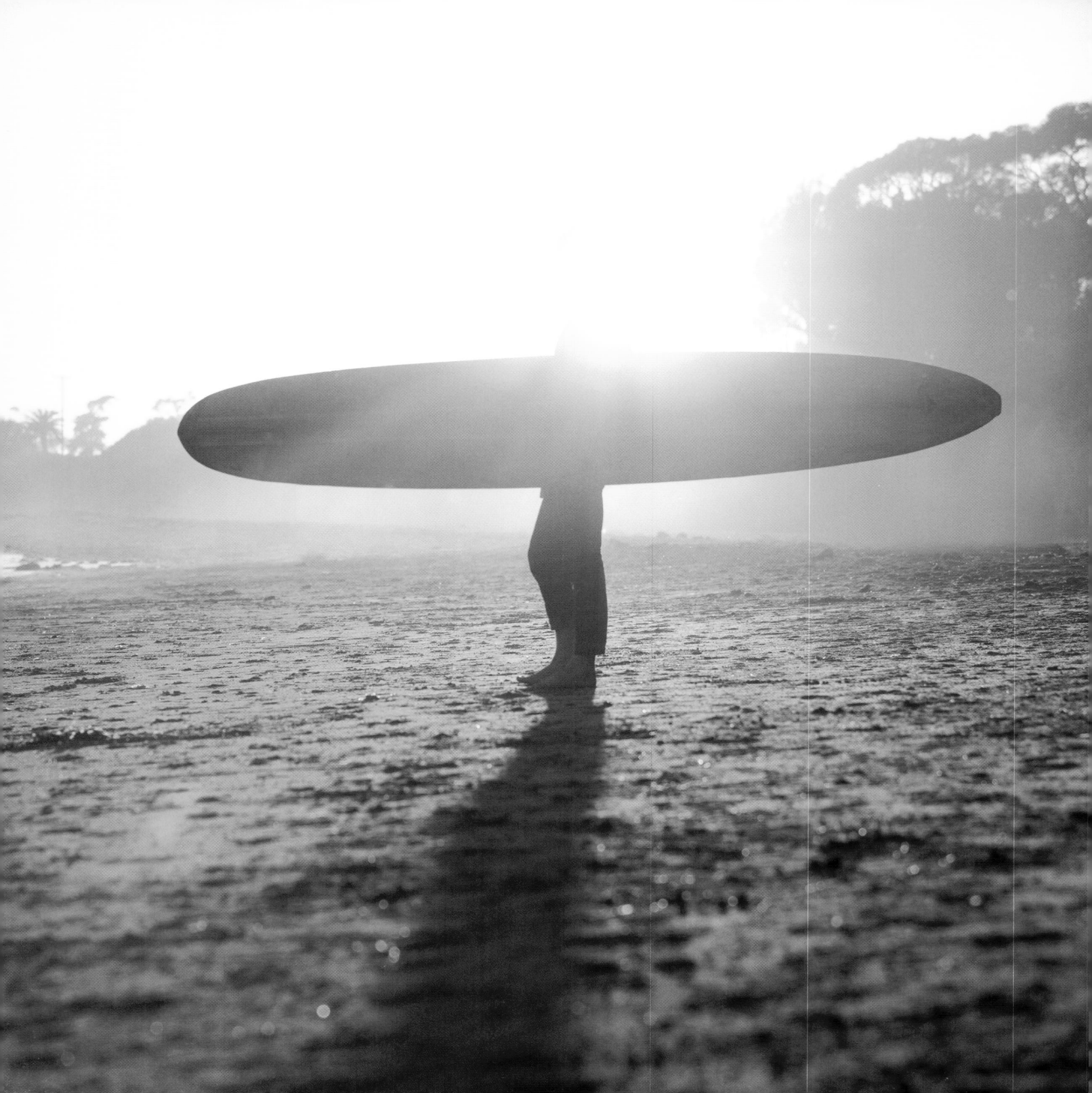

BEFORE I DIE Chang took to the streets and painted the side of an abandoned house in her New Orleans neighborhood with chalkboard paint and then stenciled the sentence "Before I die I want to _____." She left plenty of chalk so that others could fill in the blanks. Within a day the wall was covered with chalk dreams as neighbors stopped and reflected on their lives. This first project ignited others. Currently, over 600 "Before I Die" walls have been created in over 70 countries. Chang has since given a TED talk about the walls, and photographs of many of the walls have been made into a book.

What's interesting to me about the walls is how collaborative and contagious the project is. Reading someone else's response makes you want to write your own. And the responses are profound. Had the wall just said, "I want to_____," the responses would have been shallow and smug. But by adding the reference to death, the tone takes on a more creative and beautiful form, removing the risk of self-consciousness about what you are going to write. Death is the great equalizer and helps us stop worrying about ourselves. Death reminds us that in the grand scheme of things, all of us, great and small, will meet the same fate.

Chang's "Before I die…." question reminds us that death can help us dream. The composer Leonard Bernstein once said, "To achieve great things, two things are needed: a plan, and not quite enough time." Chang's question helps us with both. It reminds us of both the brevity of life and that we have to get to work chasing our dreams. The sun sets soon, and none of us have enough time. You don't have enough time. And your time is running out.

Like all of us, you probably feel busy and overwhelmed, but this slice of time is all that you have. You will never have more time than you do right now. The time to live is now. We tend to forget these truths, thinking that we can defer life until another day. Cyril Parkinson explained, "Work swells to the amount of time we give it." In other words, give a project a week and it will take that long. We give life too much time. Thinking that we have forever, we delay doing what matters most. Squaring off with death reminds us that we do not live by a perpetual clock. And considering your death in the future heightens how you live in the now.

LIFE FROM DEATH Awareness of death can give you the gift of presence and ignite a deeper desire for life. One way to gain these gifts is to practice death before it sweeps us away. It sounds strange, but such a practice can help us thrive. As one of my Jewish friends explained, that's exactly why some Jewish communities celebrate the holiday of Yom Kippur. The most common prayer of that day is called the Unetaneh Tokef. Rabbi David Wolpe explains, "This prayer reminds us that our lives are like the wind that blows and the flower that fades." Other traditions include wearing white to connote purity and to represent the shrouds in which we will be buried. Rabbi Wolpe sums it up: "In Yom Kippur we emulate corpses: not eating, not drinking, freed of the body. This will one day be our fate." Such a celebration really makes sense—facing your own death so that you can live. This idea shows up as a theme in other world religions, in literature, and in one of my favorite films, *Dead Poets Society*.

In one scene, the protagonist, English teacher John Keating, leads his students into the hall. He asks his pupils to look at the photographs of past students who have died. Keating asks his students to stare into their eyes. He raises the point that these students are just like them. They too believed they were destined for great things. Their eyes shone with hope. Keating's students stare in silence. Then he makes his point: "If you listen real close, you can hear them whisper their legacy to you. Go on, lean in. Listen. Do you hear it? (*whispering in a gruff voice*) Carpe. Hear it? (*whispering*) Carpe. Carpe diem. Seize the day, boys. Make your lives extraordinary."

The entire film hinges upon those two words, *carpe diem*. This is not an antiquated and innocuous phrase but a call to fight. Seizing the day isn't a passive phrase. And life is too short to let it slip away. Such inspiration rings true no matter who we are or what our age. We have all been designed to be and to do certain things, but fear holds us back. Let the idea of death help you to overcome. Let it be a fuse that ignites your creative soul. This life is your one wild chance—don't let it drift away. Stop living a half-lived life. Your time is running out. You will die. Make the most of what you have. Live life to the fullest degree by letting death distill what is most important to you.

DEATH IS OUR FRIEND PRECISELY BECAUSE
IT BRINGS US INTO ABSOLUTE AND PASSIONATE PRESENCE
WITH ALL THAT IS HERE, THAT IS NATURAL, THAT IS LOVE.

—RAINER MARIA RILKE

EXERCISE

STEP 1
Follow your gut and fill in the blanks below:

Before I die I will ....

Before I die I will ....

Before I die I will ....

Before I die I will ....

Before I die I will ....

Select one of your entries above and map out a few practical steps
that you can take to achieve that dream/goal/idea:

1. ....

2. ....

3. ....

STEP 2
Locate a vintage photograph of a family member or friend who has passed away. Tack it up next to
your desk, or carry it around in your journal. Then stare into their eyes and listen for
their voice. Follow Keating's lead: "If you listen real close, you can hear them whisper
their legacy to you. Go on, lean in. Listen." What is their message for you?
Write it down and live on its hint.

STEP 3
I believe in the idea of *carpe diem* so much that I've created a website, carpediemsupplyco.com,
as a resource for those who want to live a more creative and inspired life. Visit the site
and you can find helpful videos, audio courses, and more.

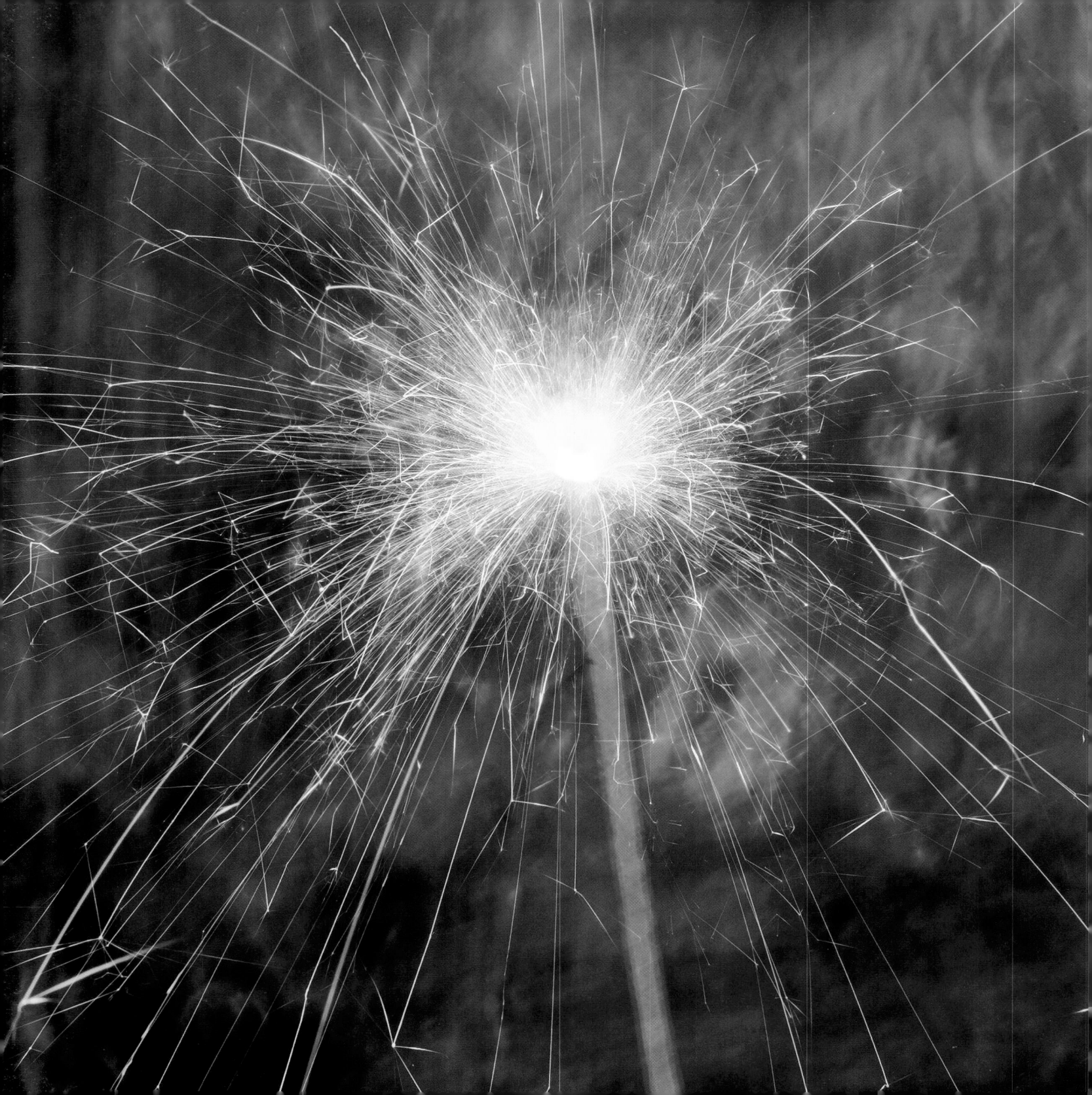

CHAPTER THIRTY-FIVE

IGNITE

The most important words the gospel singer Mahalia Jackson ever uttered weren't in a song. Even though she was known as the "queen of gospel" and was one of the most influential gospel singers in the world, it wasn't just her songs that brought about change. Jackson was a civil rights activist who took part in the march on Washington in 1963. She sang to the 250,000 people who had come to take a stand against the racial inequality, oppression, and violence of the time. It was a dark and difficult time, but her music was the sound of hope. That's why she sang. As she explained, "When you sing the gospel you have a feeling there is a cure for what's wrong." The hope and the truth of her music encouraged the crowd. Yet it wasn't just her singing that made the difference that day; it was her guts to pass on a message to a friend.

THE UNWRITTEN SPEECH Mahalia Jackson performed after two dozen speakers and musicians had already been onstage. After she sang, there were only a couple of speakers left. Joachim Prinz came next, and he spoke out against discrimination, saying, "The most urgent, the most disgraceful, the most shameful, and the most tragic problem is silence." The crowd roared. Next came a speaker who spoke with such conviction and wisdom that his words were like galvanized steel. He was a friend of Jackson's and was just 34 years old. Wise beyond his years, this man was a force to be reckoned with. He was a charismatic leader and preacher whose congregation was anyone who believed in civil rights. Jackson listened intently to his speech and, like a parishioner at a revival church, responded with heartfelt halle-lujahs and amens.

The night before, our young speaker and the other leaders of the event met to talk about the focus of the speeches for the following day. After two years of planning they still had a lot to work out; there were strong opinions about what should and shouldn't be said from the stage. Eventually, the gathering broke up and the 34-year-old went back to his hotel to finish writing the speech he was working on. He wrestled with the speech and wrote until 4 a.m. A few hours later, he handed his aides a manuscript of the speech so it could be typed up and distributed to the press.

Now the event was in full swing, and the preacher was nearing the end of his words. The crowd hung on every thought. Jackson and others shouted "amen" in agreement with what they heard. So far, the speech had followed the script just as planned. But then, as he was nearing the end of his message, he paused. It was then that the gospel singer Mahalia Jackson spoke up and contributed just the right nudge. She shouted, "Tell them about the dream, Martin!"

**WE MUST ACCEPT FINITE DISAPPOINTMENT,
BUT NEVER LOSE INFINITE HOPE.**

—MARTIN LUTHER KING, JR.

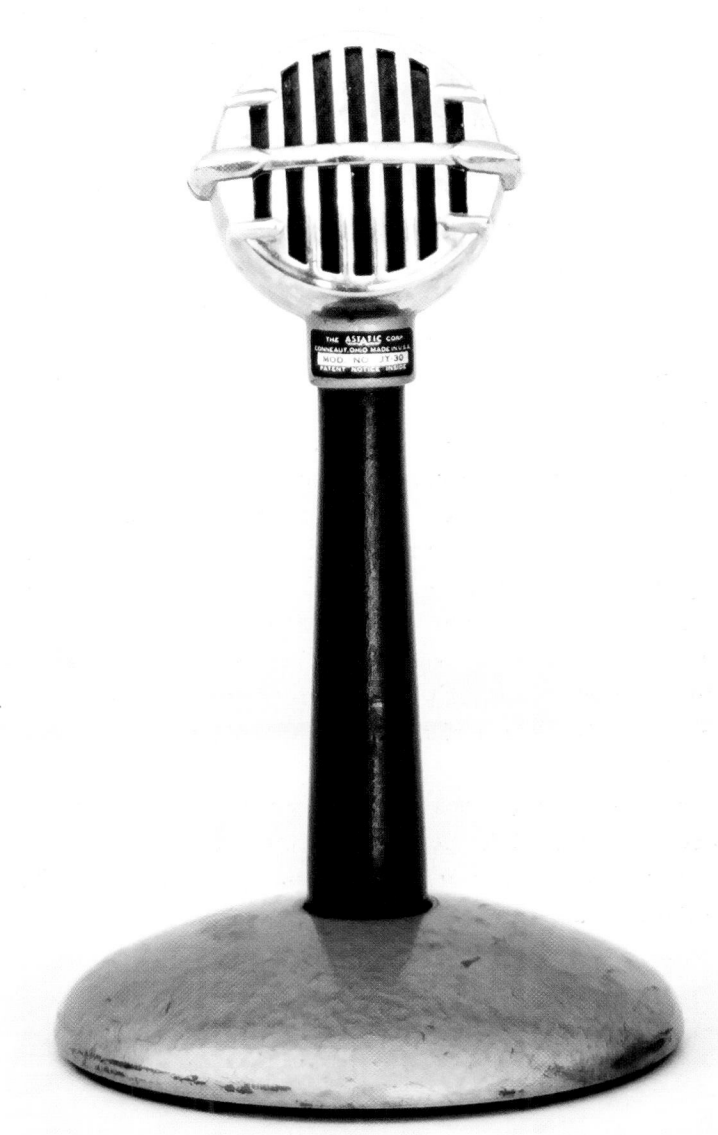

THE WILD AND WONDERFUL DREAM Martin Luther King, Jr. picked up the cue and abandoned his script. He started slow and then with rising momentum began to improvise: "I have a dream… I have a dream that one day this nation will rise up and live out the true meaning of its creed: 'We hold these truths to be self-evident, that all men are created equal.' I have a dream!"

At the end of the speech, the crowd erupted in applause. That speech has become one of the most significant and celebrated messages in the world. I take time to listen to it once a year. When I do, I'm always struck by the conviction and power of King's words. It's odd and amazing to ponder the fact that the phrase "I have a dream" didn't exist in the original manuscript. And what didn't exist came to symbolize and summarize the spirit and leadership that he brought to the world. Throughout his life, Martin Luther King, Jr. contributed in innumerable ways, but it was his dream that was most contagious and is still growing today.

King's speech and the march on Washington were a huge success. Both helped to bring new momentum to the cause. And in a giant collaborative effort, everyone involved contributed in their own unique ways. As for Jackson, she used her gifts of song and of speaking encouraging words. It makes you wonder what would have happened if she hadn't sung or shouted from the edge of the crowd. It's impossible to know, but I'm thankful that she did. It was the right time for Martin Luther King, Jr. to share his dream.

IGNITED IDEAS The story of Jackson prompting King to share his dream is beautiful on so many levels. Perhaps an entire book or film could be made around her words "Tell them about the dream." From the angle of this book, we might consider how such a powerful creative spark came to ignite. As most singers, civil rights activists, and artists will tell you, creativity ignites most frequently once the work begins. For King, it happened near the end of this speech. For Jackson, it happened after she sang and while she listened to a friend.

The challenge for us is to get out of our armchairs and get to work. The most difficult moment in any creative act is the start. We all have great ideas, but very few of us write the speech and then step up to the stage. We are more comfortable mulling our ideas over or talking about our dreams. Meanwhile, nothing gets done. Or maybe we get the courage to start to write but can't get past the first page. The reason we don't get very far is because we are afraid.

OVERCOMING RESISTANCE A deep and primal fear holds us back. In his book *The War of Art*, Steve Pressfield calls this fear "resistance." Pressfield says, "Resistance is the most toxic force on the planet… Its aim is to shove us away, distract us, prevent us from doing our work." If resistance is our enemy, then momentum is a friend. The secret all successful creatives know is to show up and get to work even if that means staying up until 4 a.m. Sparks will never fly if the hammer and anvil sit still. You have to pick up the tool and start to pound away at your dreams.

This pounding isn't a blind fight, but one that channels the momentum and remains alert. You have to swing hard but still have the sensitivity to pick up on creativity's cue. Sometimes this may mean veering from your manuscript or having the guts to shout an encouraging word. The creative process is always a collaborative thing. Rare is the creative genius who accomplishes his or her work alone. Too often we get so caught up in the grandiosity of our own creativity that we ignore the voice on the edge because we think it is too small. But more often than not, it's the small, wild, and untamed idea that comes to us in the middle of our work that can ignite and change the world.

EXERCISE

STEP 1

The creative fight can be a lonely road, so we all need people who encourage us to share our dream. And we need to have the guts to encourage others as well. Creativity is always a combination of multiple things. When it comes to encouragement, it can provide just the right combinatory energy to spur us on. The best way to foster this type of energy is to give some to someone else. Make this a habit and it will not only help others but ignite your life as well. Begin today by writing an encouraging note to a friend or colleague who could use the spark.

STEP 2

Without conflict and a deadline, Martin Luther King, Jr. would never have written his speech. So for yourself, set a deadline for a creative project you want to accomplish. Make the due date close—give the project too much time and it might never get done. Define your project and your deadline and post it in a place you can't ignore.

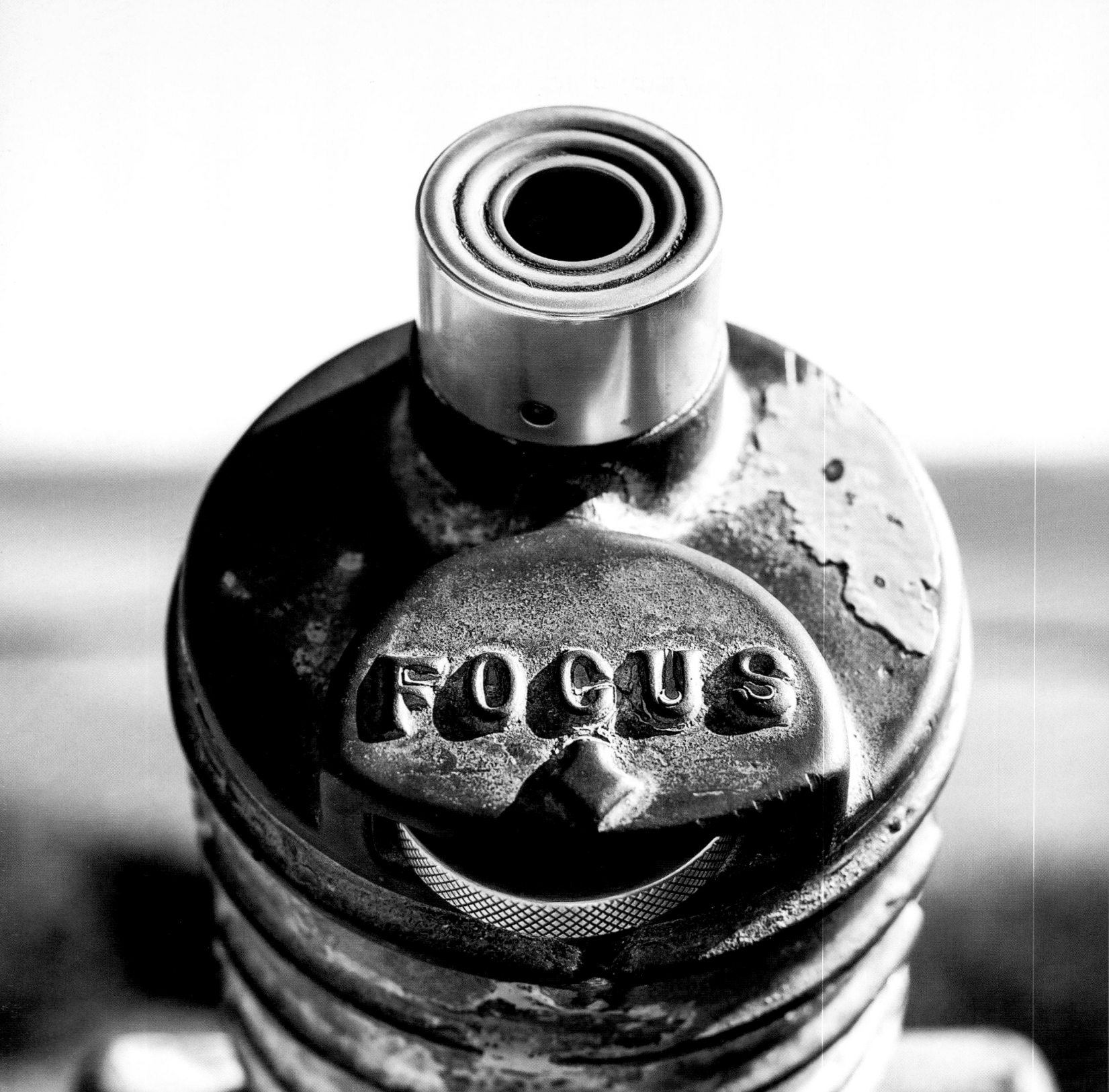

CHAPTER THIRTY-SIX

WAKE UP

It was a bright clear day when I began to fall. Ninety feet was a long way down. Time stood silent and still. Everything was focused and clear. This was the end, my end. Moments before, I couldn't have been more alive. Without the burden of ropes or harnesses, I felt free. Adrenaline raced through my veins. I was invincible and 18. Then suddenly, I lost my grip. I leaned into the sheer rock wall to slow myself down. I slid and began to fall. Suddenly, my wrist burned with pain as my climbing partner grabbed hold. In one motion he swung me to safety on his other side. Death wouldn't win this time. Life rushed through every atom of my being. To breathe was divine. I had never felt more alive. I was reborn. We stood quietly on that rock wall. Everything was still. Deep in my soul, I vowed to never again squander my time.

SUNSETS AND COMFORTABLE CHAIRS Near-death experiences are a wakeup call you can't ignore, like an earthquake, fire alarm, and flashing red light all rolled into one. They awaken deep and primal senses and make you realize that life is real. So far I've had two such calls, and I don't want a third. Who would? We all prefer to be woken up in more gentle ways, like seeing a beautiful sunset, walking through an ancient forest, or looking at an old photograph album from when you were a kid. Sunsets, forests, and photographs do awaken us, but they don't have the same amount of activation energy as death. Death gets us out of our comfortable chairs. And sunsets are predictable, whereas death always uses the element of surprise.

Death loves to catch us unaware. This first happened to me when my pet rabbit, named Strawberry, died. Next, without warning, my cousin Matt, whom I looked up to so much, was killed. The surprise of death just didn't make sense. I couldn't comprehend the finality. It didn't seem real. Yet its message was clear: life is short, too short. This I could comprehend, even though I was young.

LIMITATION AND LOSS Later in life I was in an accident that was a wakeup call of a different kind. The accident led to limited mobility and nagging chronic pain. The pain was persistent and wore me thin. Plus, I was no longer able to do so many things that I loved: run, bike, hike, surf, or walk. With any kind of chronic situation it's easy to get caught in a downward spiral, and this spiral had me spinning. It was a bleak and dark period of my life. As I wrestled with the loss of mobility and the fatigue from the constant ache, I discovered an unexpected gift. The pain, as horrible as it was, awakened my soul. It slowed me down, and I noticed things I hadn't seen before. I became more sensitive and gained empathy for the suffering of others, which I had previously ignored. In so many ways, the pain opened my eyes to truths that I would have otherwise overlooked.

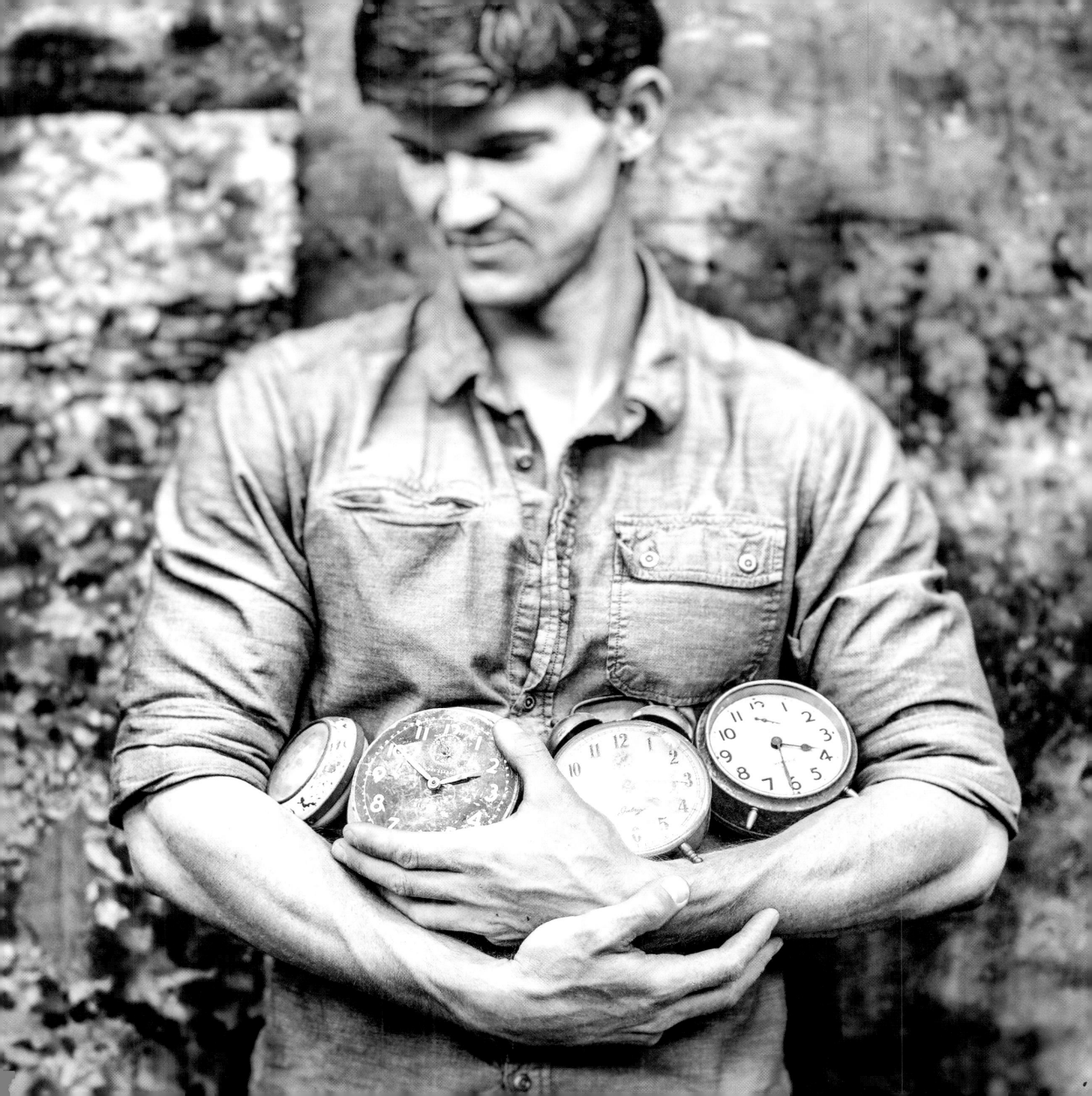

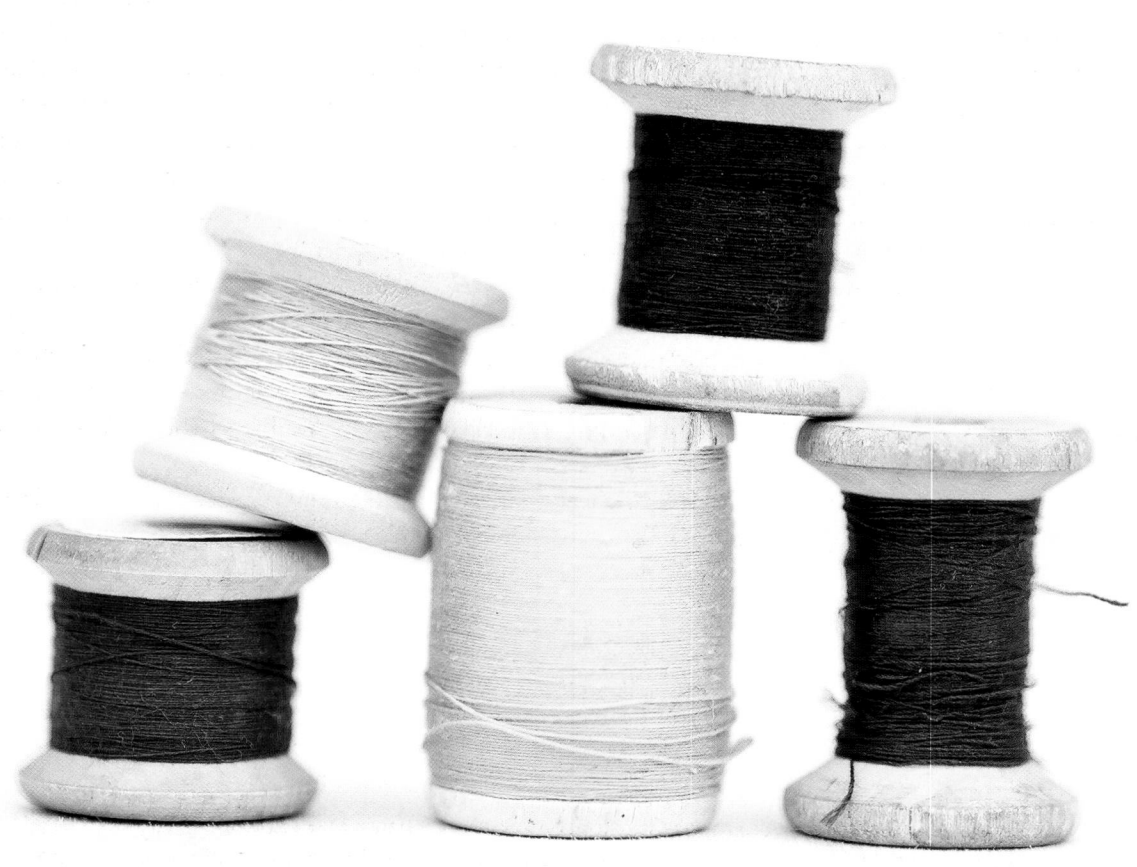

While in graduate school, years after the incident, my health got worse. So I threw myself into my studies to distract myself from the pain. It was comforting to spend time with books. I was getting by, but at the same time I was stuck. That was until my academic advisor informed me that I needed to do some practicum volunteer work. I was assigned to work in a hospital and was given the cancer floor. And so I spent my days, weeks, and months visiting people who were facing the most difficult challenges of their lives. In doing this, I was changed.

My job throughout was to visit and offer kindness and a listening ear. Because I was a neutral (non-family, non-friend) party, many of the patients opened up and many talked without constraint. I was honored and deeply moved. Without knowing it, these patients shared wisdom I had never heard. And their struggles with life and pain helped me understand my own.

When you spend time with someone who is dying, you cannot help but learn about life. Those patients became my teachers in the art of life, or the art in learning how to live even when all is bleak. And they gave me some of the most important lectures of all time. Their wisdom changed the course of my life, and they helped me thrive in new ways. They gave me the courage to fight to live the life for which I was designed. They gave me focus and drive. And in many ways, they taught me the core skills I use in my life and career every day. It was like a boot camp for getting on with living in a meaningful way. And they taught me that life is too short and that it will slip away unless you take the time to hold it tight and cherish it in your arms.

STITCH BY STITCH To this day, I pursue my craft (be it parenting, photography, or teaching) with those patients in mind. I often think about how many of them fought hard but didn't win. Their loss of life runs through me and all of my work. "Everything I do is stitched with its color," as the American poet W. S. Merwin once said. Sometimes the thread is red and urgent, or peaceful and green, or maybe even blue like the wide-open sky.

We all want life to go on forever. But the amount of time we have is out of our control. We can either ignore or embrace this idea. Ignoring it makes life cheap. Embracing it sweetens the deal. As Emily Dickinson said, "That it will never come again is what makes life so sweet." This life is your one and only chance. You will never have more time than you have now. Make the most of what you have by first accepting that it will end.

EXERCISE

STEP 1

When we encounter death, it poses a question: how will we now live?
Take a few moments to sit in silence and ponder your response. Let the idea of death be a muse that clarifies who you are and what you want to do. Let death add delight to the life that you have.

STEP 2

Take a few moments to remember somebody you know who has passed away. Close your eyes, take a deep breath, and remember the way they smiled, the way they walked. And then commit to honoring their life by living yours in a more complete and honest way.

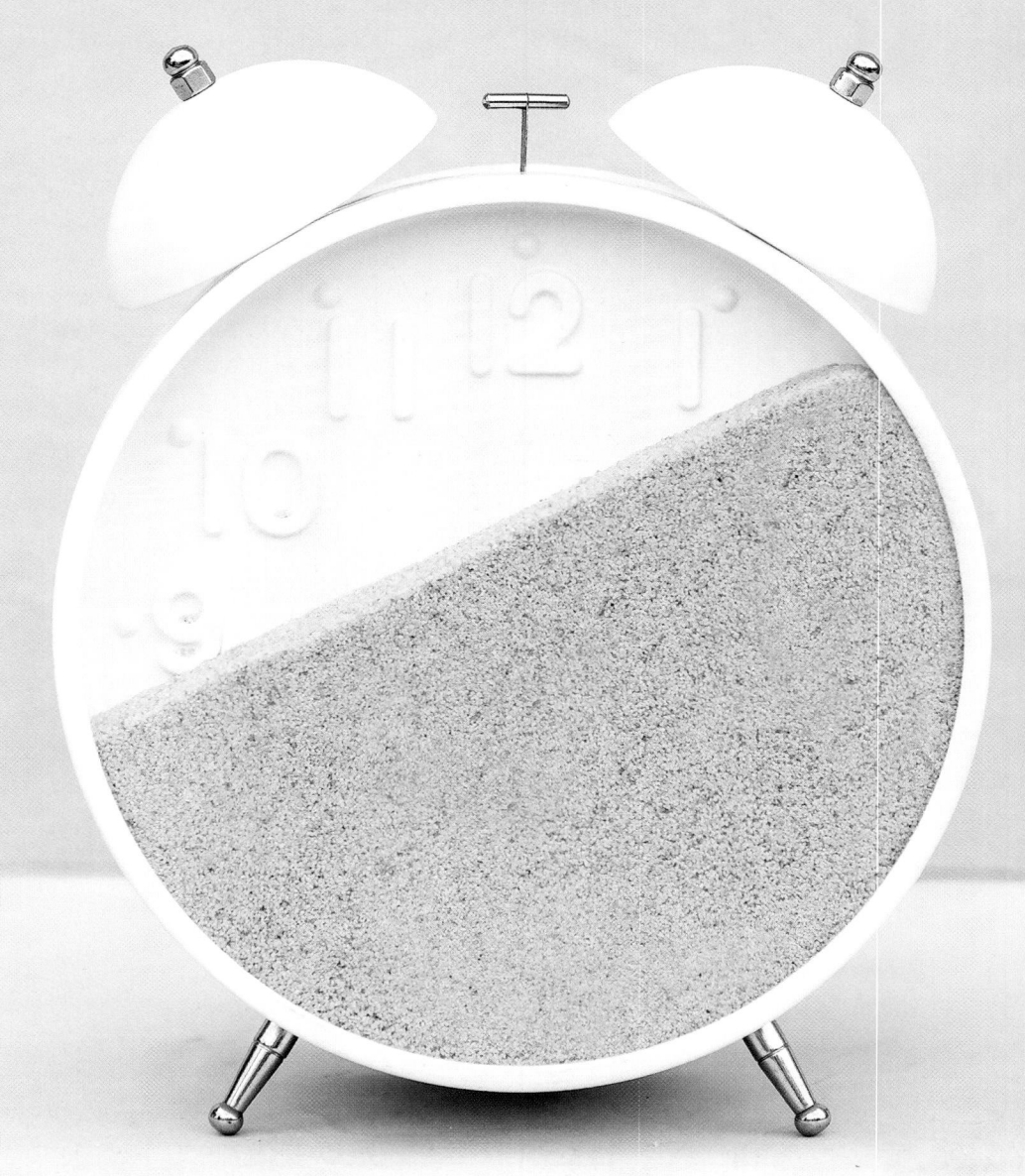

CHAPTER THIRTY-SEVEN

THE BREVITY OF LIFE

In the ancient Indian epic poem the *Mahabharata* (sometimes described as the longest poem ever written), the wise king is asked, "What is the most wondrous thing in the universe?" His reply is unexpected, especially to our western ears. The king says, "The most wondrous thing in the universe is that all around us people are dying and we don't believe it will happen to us." We disbelieve death because we are afraid. So we find ways to tune out the reality of limited time. Mostly, we get on with the task of living our day-to-day lives. And the distraction works, until the cracks appear. Like when James told me that he was going to die. I didn't know what to say. He appeared so healthy. With a weary voice he said, "I'm not worried about myself; I've lived a good life. I just can't stop thinking about my wife and three girls."

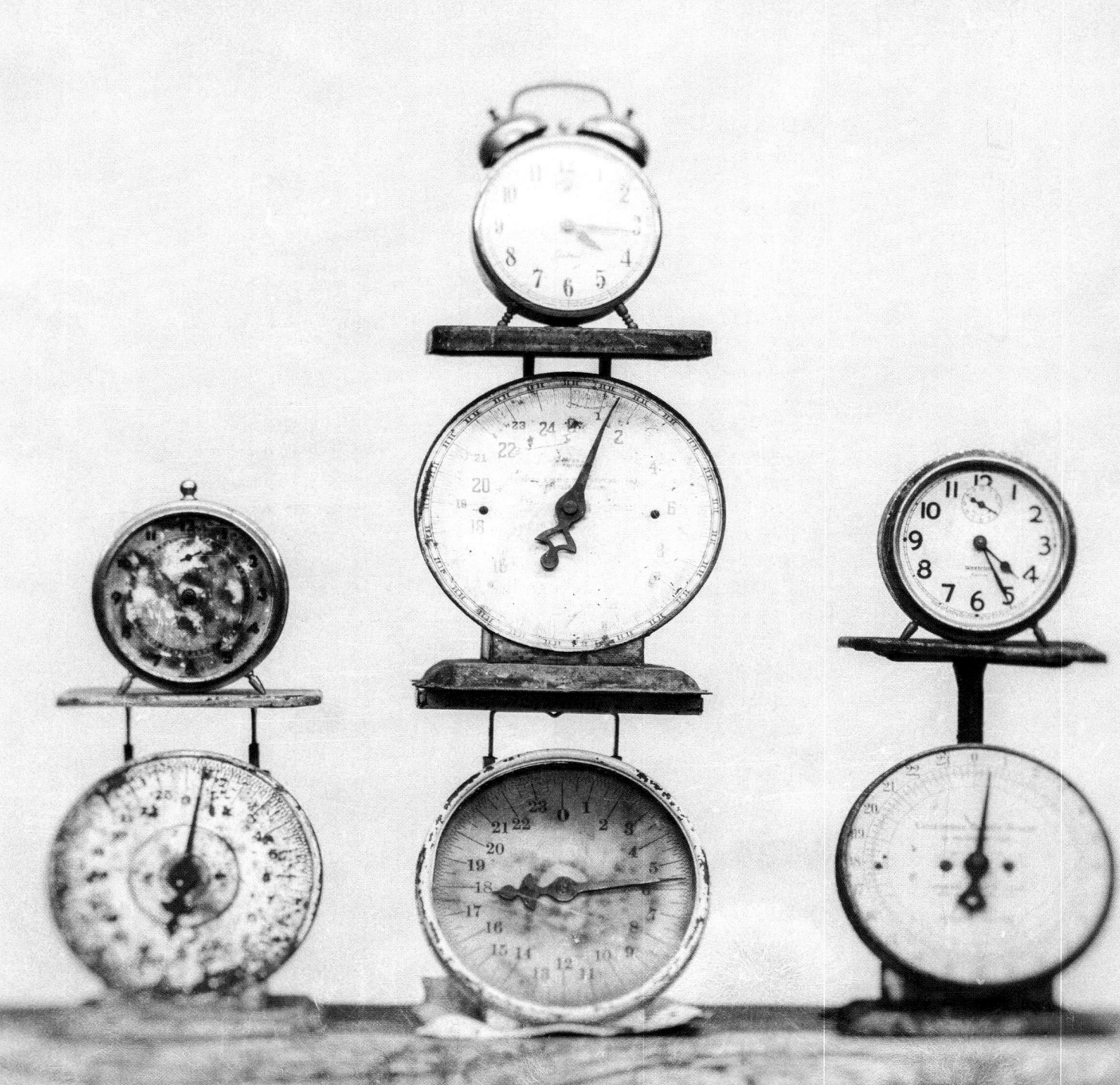

THE WEIGHT OF TIME Over the following days and weeks, I was flooded with sadness as I thought about James and his family. In the deluge, I began to consider how much I take for granted. I realized how ungrateful I am for simple things like good health and the gift of time. James's condition made me reflect on my own. He and I lead parallel lives. We are the same age, do the same type of work, and both have three young daughters. Like looking into a mirror, James's situation forced me to face the frailty and brevity of life in an uncomfortable way. Each time he said, "Time is short; use it well," the message went deep.

The fissures start small, like little crow's-feet around the eyes or like the hairline fractures you see on a Renaissance painting when you look up close. The cracks and crow's-feet reveal something that we didn't first realize was there. Suddenly we see it, and the thin veneer that separates life from death becomes clear. The veneer's patina quietly reminds us that the passage of time is real. I think that's what makes old paintings, antique photographs, and old age such beautiful things. They help us settle our differences with death. When we behold the blemishes and cracks, we begin to reconcile with the reality that one day we will follow the same path. The wrinkles of time will increase. But seeing and studying such things helps us be authentic and true. And truth is always more beautiful than a lie.

Still, it's hard to believe that we are all going to die. At the same time, it's impossible to ignore. Facing the fact of death is something that we desperately need to do. It's good for the soul. And settling our differences with death can give us new eyes. Facing death clarifies life. At least that is the premise of my favorite ghost story of all time. Like most ghost stories, this one begins on a cold night in a bleak and decrepit house.

THE YEARS TEACH MUCH WHICH THE DAYS NEVER KNOW.
—RALPH WALDO EMERSON

THE VISITATION The house creaks as a bitter old man settles in for the night. Suddenly, he is awakened by a familiar face. He squints and realizes that it's a ghost! This apparition moans and bellows, warning of three more otherworldly visitors to come. As the ghost vanishes the old man disregards it as his imagination gone awry, the result of an undigested piece of meat. But then, as foretold, another ghost appears. There is no doubt that this one is real. The ghost is well dressed and seems kind, and he takes the old man on a journey into the past. The old man views scenes from his childhood as if they were happening again. He reminisces in a warm yet sad way. His heart softens. He doesn't want to leave these memories, but they vanish and the ghost disappears. Unsettled, the old man falls back asleep.

Suddenly, another apparition appears. He is jovial but unsparing with the truth. The ghost shows the old man the present-day lives of people that he knows. Like looking at his life from the top of a ladder, this bird's eye view is difficult to digest. The old man winces to hear how he is belittled and scorned. The mockery and laughter at his expense hurts. Before he can make sense of the pain, the ghost takes him to see the suffering of those he previously ignored. Anguish and regret fill his heart. But the ghost disappears before anything can be done. The man collapses back into bed.

A BROKEN HEART Moments later he is awakened by the sight of a foreboding figure wearing a black hood. The old man shivers in fright. This spirit is dark and silent. The ghost shows the old man the future, beginning with the death of his employee's son and concluding with the old man's grave. The old man trembles and breaks down, and the ghost vanishes into the night. In utter exhaustion, the old man falls asleep on his floor.

The next morning, the sun shines bright and the old man awakens to a new life. His face glows with the gratitude of having been given a second chance. As if reborn, the man is changed. He proclaims, "I will live in the Past, the Present, and the Future. The Spirits of all Three shall strive within me. I will not shut out the lessons that they teach!" And he is true to his word. The once selfish, cold, and cruel Ebenezer Scrooge becomes the epitome of generosity, love, and warmth. The first and second ghosts opened his mind and thawed his heart. The last one broke it in two. That's what death does. It illuminates life like nothing else can.

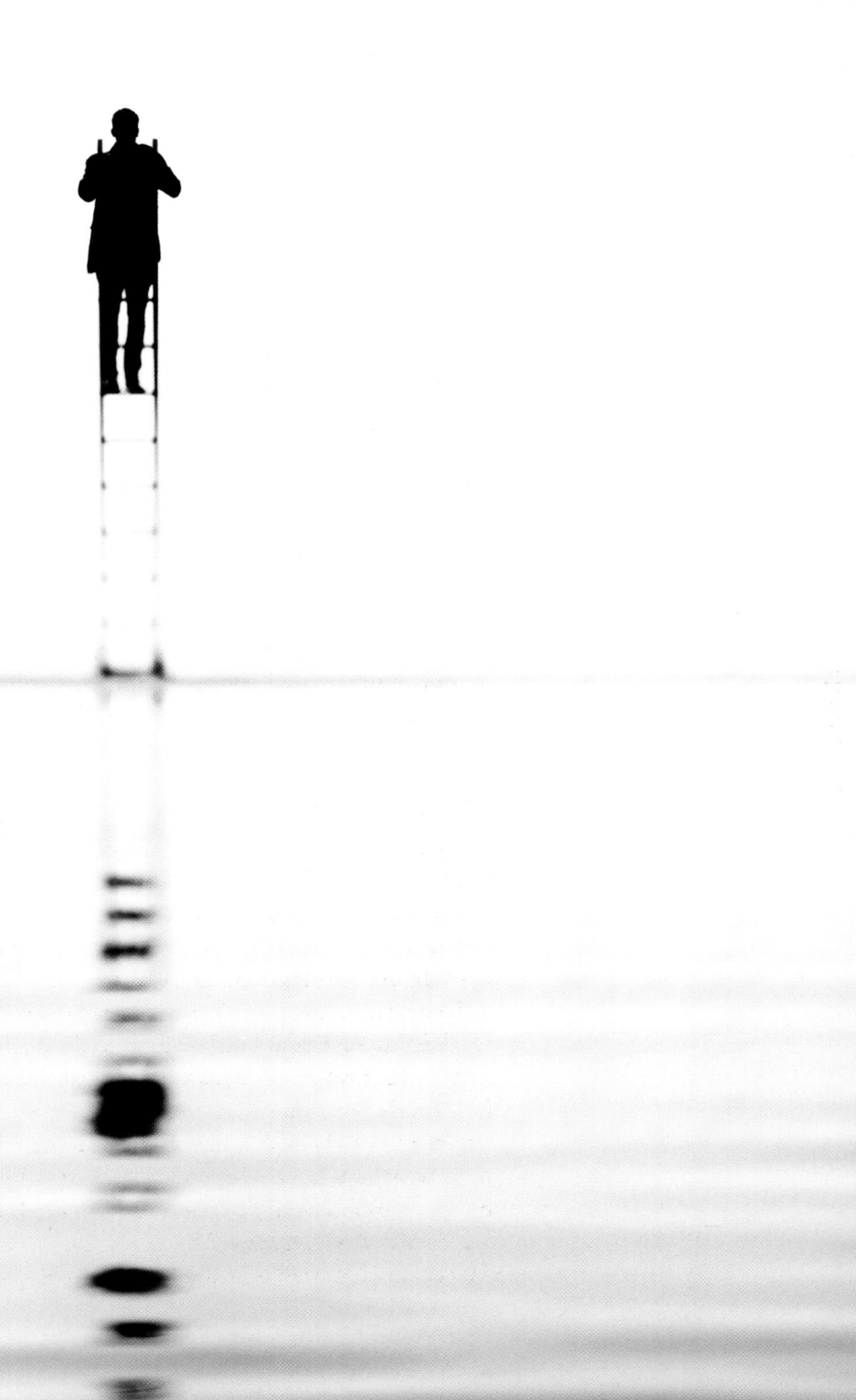

TO KNOW HOW TO GROW OLD IS THE MASTERWORK OF WISDOM, AND ONE OF THE MOST DIFFICULT CHAPTERS IN THE GREAT ART OF LIVING.

—HERMAN MELVILLE

THE OLD AND WISE KING This isn't only true for characters in a classic Charles Dickens tale. It's true for all of us who are open to learn from the brevity of it all. Like those of us who are friends with James, we cannot go on living the same way. Life and our relationship to time have now changed. And perhaps one of the best ways to honor his life is to live with him in mind and to choose the more noble path. With this in mind, I picked up an old book I hadn't read for years. I was searching for wisdom and happened upon the writings of an ancient king who had a lot to say.

The old king wrote as one looking back on a full life. He wrote about vanity, labor, and love. And he especially liked to write about time: "There is a time to live and a time to die… a time to weep and a time to laugh, a time to mourn and a time to dance." As I read deeper, it soon became clear that much of the narrative hinged on the theme of the brevity of time. So I flipped through the pages searching for the king's advice on how to live. I found shelter in his guiding words: "Whatever your hand finds to do, do it with all your might." Here was a mentor who understood the fight. The art of living a meaningful life requires mustering up and using every ounce of strength that we have. Might is a great way to live. *Might* is the perfect word. It implies urgency, effort, and force.

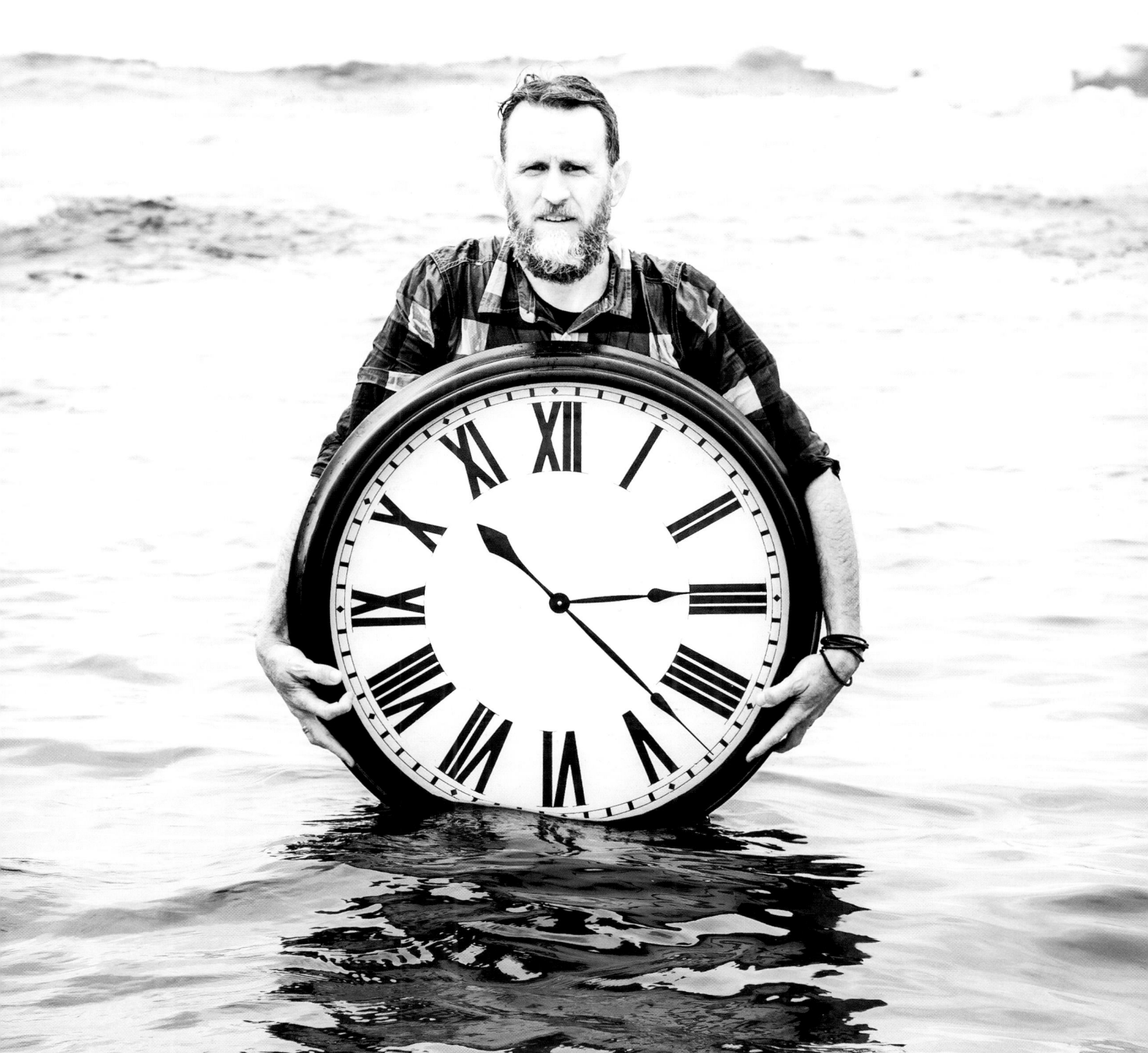

PAIN AND JOY When the poet Mary Oliver was diagnosed with cancer she said, "You could live a hundred years, it's happened. Or not. I am speaking from the fortunate platform of many years, none of which, I think, I ever wasted. Do you need a prod? Do you need a little darkness to get you going? Let me be urgent as a knife, then, and remind you of Keats, so single of purpose and thinking, for a while, he had a lifetime." Born in 1795, John Keats died when he was 25. Three of his poems are considered to be among the finest in the world. He wrote with such vitality, yet he had no idea. None of us do. We imagine a lifetime, but there is no guarantee.

Death may be inescapable, but we don't have to casually shake its hand. I've always been curious why certain people—like cancer survivors, kings, and poets—understand this so well. Maybe it's because they have paused long enough to let the reality sink in, and then they did something with their grief. In reflecting on the imminent death of his father, the poet Dylan Thomas wrote, "Do not go gentle into that good night. Rage. Rage against the dying of the light." These are wise words that I have taken to be a mantra for my own life. I invite you to consider doing the same. The fight to pursue life even as death looms large benefits from a little rage.

Death is inevitable, but we don't have to passively allow it to ruin our lives. We can choose how to respond. Fight, might, and rage are perfectly good responses, and so is joy. As one terminally ill patient said, "Part of the pain then is the joy now." Whatever strategy you choose, stop procrastinating and squandering time. It's your turn to live, and now is better than next week. Now is the time for joy. Now is the time to cherish the moments that remain. Now is the time to seize the day. Now is the time to honor those who have passed. Now is the time to live the life for which you were designed. Now is the time to stop worrying, complaining, and holding yourself back. Now is the time to pursue the forgotten dream. You can never change the cards you are dealt, but you can decide how to play the hand.

EXERCISE

STEP 1

Do an online search for "Dylan Thomas reads Do not go gentle into that good night." Click the link and press play. Then close your eyes and listen. After listening, open your journal and record your thoughts. Then create something that reflects the sentiment of how you feel. Whether a drawing, photograph, song, or poem, make something with the thread of these ideas.

STEP 2

The brevity of life is a teacher that you don't want to ignore. So take a walk in a nearby cemetery this week. Walk in silence and let the end of life be a light that guides how you pursue your dreams.

STEP 3

Ben Franklin once said, "Some people die at 25 and aren't buried until 75." Don't let that be you. Seize the day. Honor the gift of life by going out and doing something that invigorates your soul. Don't wait until tomorrow. Do it today.

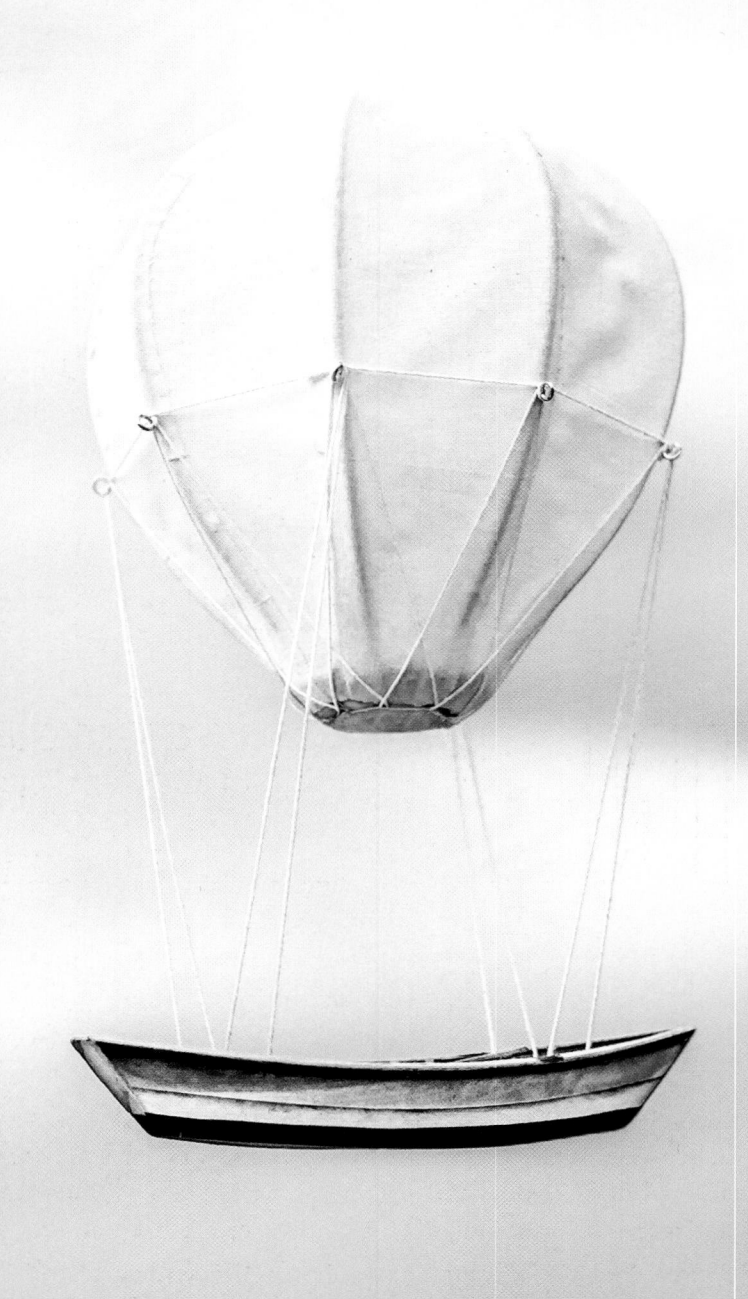

CHAPTER THIRTY-EIGHT

ITERATE AND INNOVATE

John knew what it was like to be poor. He was writer after all, and in the early 1900s, it was tough to get a job. John tried his luck in New York, but miserably failed. As he said, "I had a thin, lonely, hungry time of it. And I remember too well the cockroaches under my washbasin and the impossibility of getting a job. I was scared thoroughly. And I can't forget the scare." So John moved back to the comforts of California, where he was born. He picked up odd jobs, like working at a fish hatchery in Tahoe City, where he met his future wife. They got married and moved to Pacific Grove to live in a cottage owned by his dad. Still scraping by, John wrote even though funds were sparse. But they were in love, and that kept them afloat. As he wrote to a friend, "Financially we are a mess, but 'spiritually' we ride the clouds."

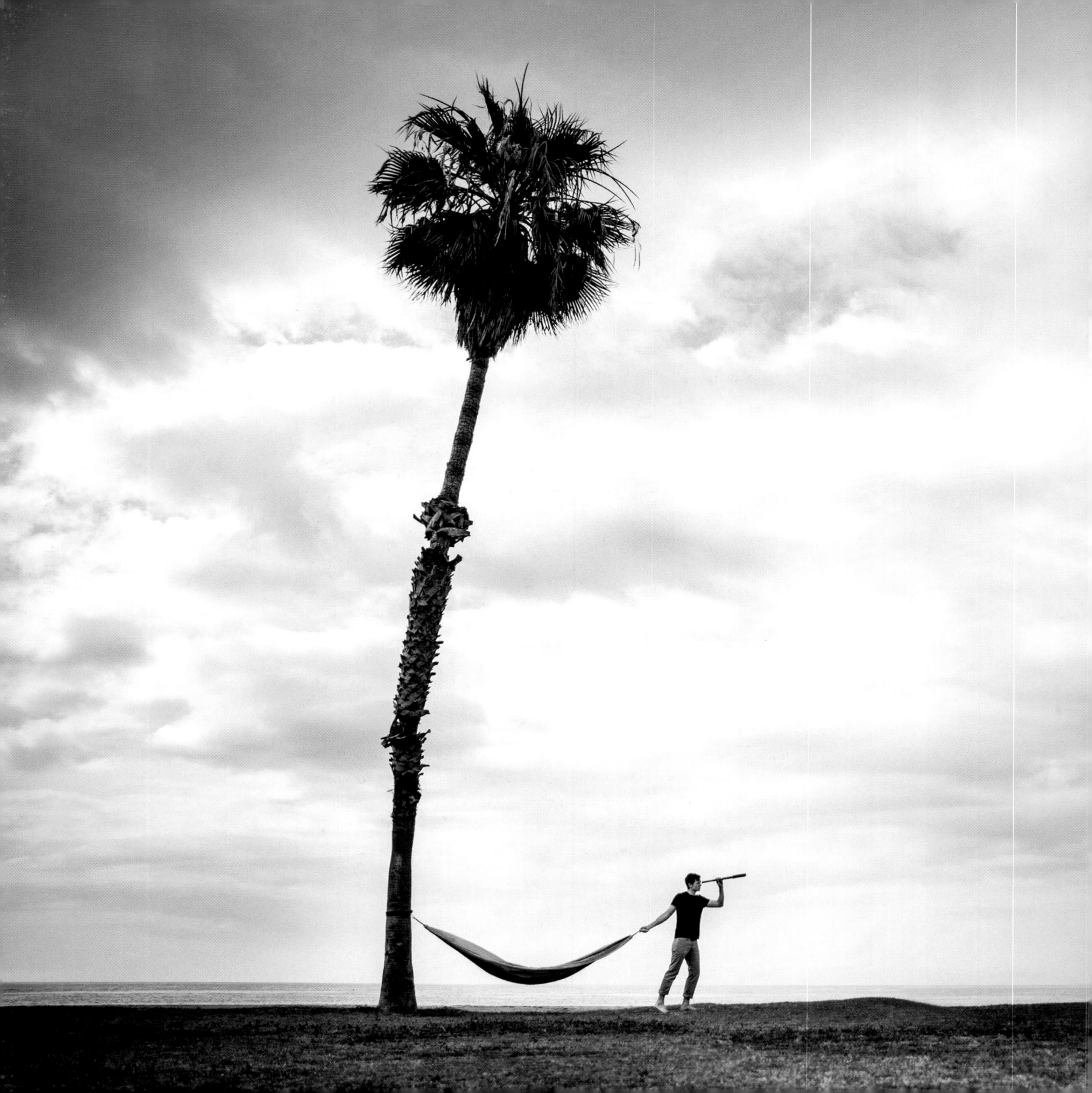

MIND THE GAP John was hungry for success. He wrote with a singular drive he called "monomania" for a few years. After completing his first novel, John and his wife waited patiently for the first reviews. It was a critical and commercial flop. Yet it wasn't as if he were a hack who didn't have strong writing skills. John went to Stanford and was sharp as a nail. But there was a gap—a gap between what he knew he could write and the writing he had done.

The gap is something that everyone who does creative work knows. The celebrated storyteller Ira Glass put it this way: "All of us who do creative work, we get into it because we have good taste. But there is this gap. For the first couple of years you make stuff, it's just not that good. It's trying to be good, it has potential, but it's not. But your taste, the thing that got you into the game, is still killer. And your taste is why your work disappoints you. A lot of people never get past this phase; they quit."

John wasn't willing to give up, so he fought with words for four more years—good work takes time. He finished another novel but felt depleted and alone. He wrote, "I need a dog pretty badly." Yet more than companionship, he needed some cash. The light company was scheduled to turn the power off in a few days. Fortunately, the novel was a very minor success. The electricity stayed on, and the gap diminished some more. He continued to write, and the following few novels closed the gap even more. When he published his book *Tortilla Flat*, the gap disappeared.

Tortilla Flat was a critical and commercial success. Now in his mid-thirties, John Steinbeck was getting his stride, and he continued to write at a quickening pace. Plus, Steinbeck finally had enough money to pay rent and fulfill a few dreams. One dream was getting a dog. So they adopted Toby, a small Irish setter pup. The puppy played around while Steinbeck sharpened his pencils and got to work.

MAN'S BEST FRIEND Steinbeck loved pencils, even though using them took more time. He began each day with twelve sharpened pencils sitting on his desk. This was his ritual to summon the muse. But once he picked up a pencil it was hard labor scratching out all those words. And using a pencil for so many hours built up calluses on his hand.

Steinbeck set out to write a new book about the place he grew up and the people who lived there—people who had callused hands from all their hard work. The book was turning out well. The plot was strong and filled with the intrinsic yet underestimated goodness and beauty of simple things. The sands of time seemed to be on his side.

One day after all twelve pencils were dull, he left his study and walked out the door. Seeing an opportunity to explore, Toby, the ever-inquisitive puppy, decided to take a look around. Finding a stack of papers, she quickly tore them to shreds. Months and months of work on the book was turned into trash. Steinbeck wrote to his publisher, "Minor tragedy stalked. There was no other draft. I was pretty mad, but the poor little fellow may have been acting critically." It was a painful blow, but Steinbeck didn't take offense. He even wondered if Toby knew what he was doing after all—maybe Toby was right and what had been written needed to be revised?

Steinbeck rewrote the book, and it turned out better the second time around. His experience of losing the book might just be what gave it its edge. And it was almost as if Steinbeck's own fight was hidden within his words. You can see it with quotes like these: "I know it's tough, but don't give up… I said I'd fight back, but I didn't say I'd fight fair…. And now we sing for everything that we've lost. And now we scream for everything that we've loved… Truth be told I would set my whole world on fire just to watch it burn in your eyes." But perhaps the most famous phrase gives it all away: "The best laid schemes of mice and men often go awry." Needless to say the book, *Of Mice and Men*, was a huge success.

Like most people who do creative work, Steinbeck wasn't an overnight success. Rather it was the endless hours, immense effort, and emotion that eventually led Steinbeck to create great work. All of the time spent on those

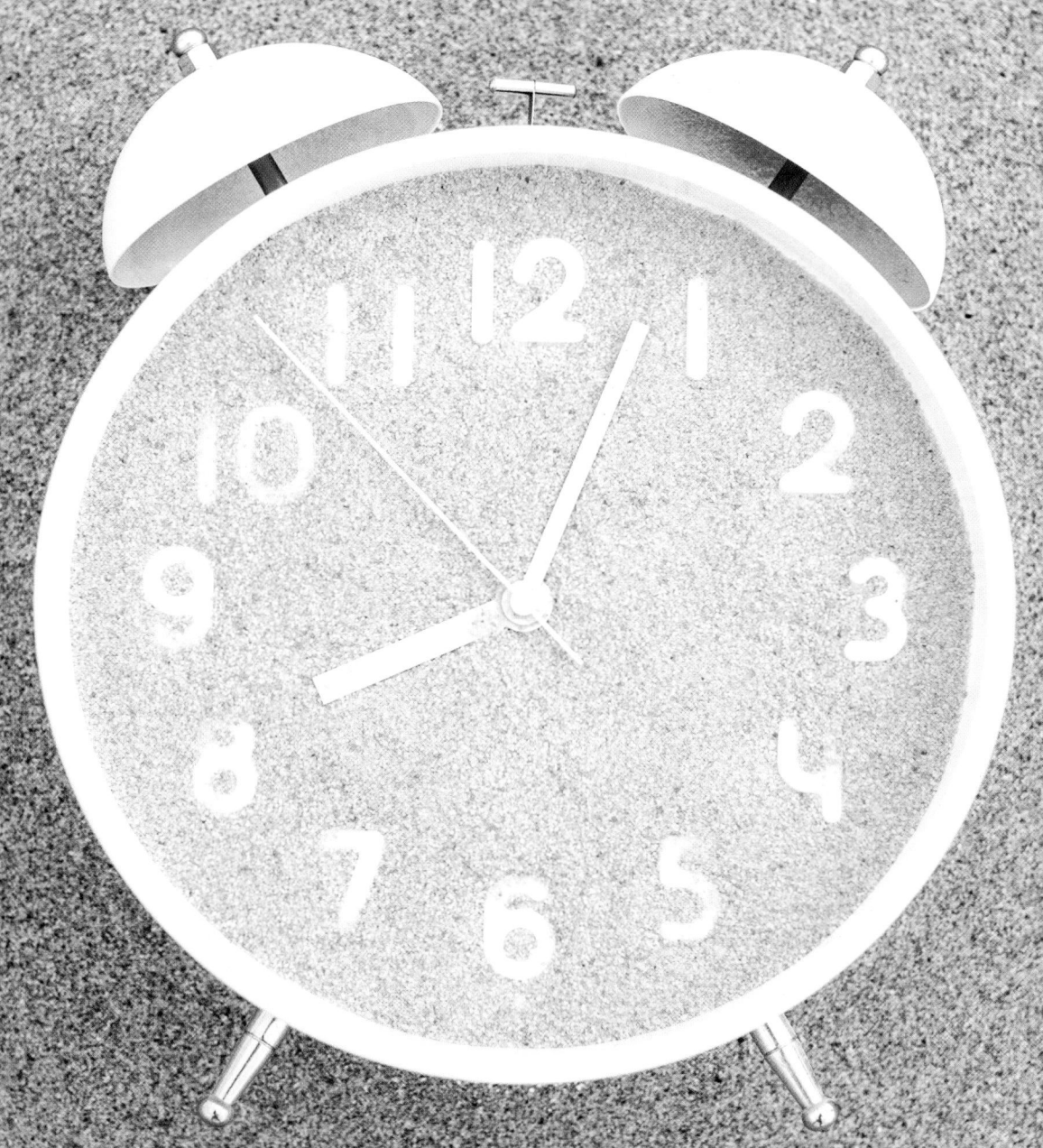

early unsuccessful books developed his skills and technique. Most of us want the skill (and the fame) but don't know where to start. And most of us don't start because we set our sights too high. We aim for the stars but can't even get off the ground.

Herein lies the problem with dreams that are big: they improve our vision but don't change our technique. Technique takes time, whether you're a writer working on rough drafts, a photographer shooting frames, or a musician practicing scales. The whole point is to start and persist; otherwise, procrastination sets in. As J. R. R. Tolkien said, "It's the job never started that takes the longest to finish." And whether you're a writer, photographer, poet, or martial artist, the journey to gain skill follows a similar path.

ENTER THE DRAGON Bruce's journey to greatness began when he was a kid. As a young boy he learned martial arts as a way to defend himself from other kids. Then in his teens he learned how to dance, becoming a cha-cha champion with all of his slick moves. After high school, he moved to Seattle to attend the University of Washington and pursue the higher mind. There he studied subjects like drama, psychology, and philosophy. Amidst the hard work of academic life, he discovered a love for poetry. And he wrote poems like this one, about Lake Washington: "The breeze on the bank. Already blows cool and mild. The distant merging of lake and sky."

Simultaneously, Bruce practiced martial arts, spending hours and hours refining his skills. And he trained with such discipline that he could do push-ups with only two fingers touching the ground. He was quick on his feet, strong in body, and growing in his mind. He would soon combine all these skills to create a version of martial arts that was completely his own. And Bruce Lee's fighting style wasn't just poetry in motion; it was art.

John Steinbeck and Bruce Lee are among some of the most creative people of their time. And if you look deeper into their stories, you'll discover that they both brought innovation to their trades. The innovation came from years of refining their craft. Their secret was to iterate and persist.

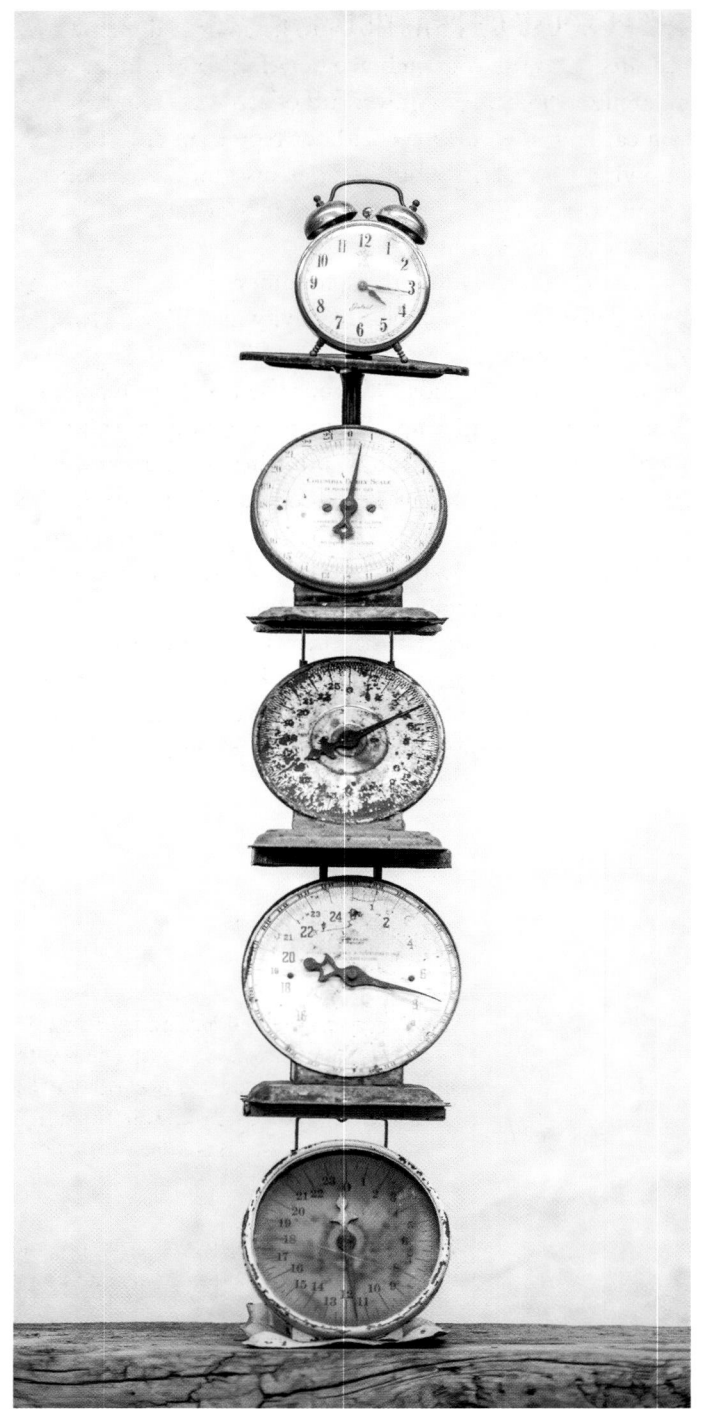

THE PURPOSE OF PRACTICE To iterate is to do something repeatedly. Those who embrace iteration approach craft like an archer who brings a quiver full of arrows—knowing that you can't hit the bull's-eye without repetition and skill, and knowing that a single bull's-eye is just good luck. But it's vision, patience, and persistence that provide the ability to hit it again and again.

It goes without saying that technique doesn't develop by itself. And without technique, creativity dies. That's why most kids stop drawing around the age of 12. It's the age when most art education ends. Without the training, repetition, and practice, they give up. Who wants to keep drawing bad pictures of the same old things? But when we learn new techniques, it feeds the creative fire. Technique is the lifeblood of all creativity that becomes art. But the point of developing technique is never simply the mastery of a technical skill. The point of learning technique is to transcend.

The popular image of Bruce Lee is an aggressive fighting machine. This image works because he was an indomitable force. Lee created his life with his own bare hands. As he said, "To hell with circumstances; I create opportunities." Lee was a force of nature and his ego was strong, but he was humble as well. As C. S. Lewis explained, "True humility is not thinking less of yourself, but thinking of yourself less." Bruce Lee thought highly of himself, but when was in the zone, all those thoughts disappeared. His technical skill transcended rational thought. It was as if his movement were a subconscious flow. And when he fought it was as if he walked on air.

Thinking can impede the creative flow. That explains why athletes, artists, dancers, and musicians put so much time into practicing their skill. As the French artist Edgar Degas said, "Only when he no longer knows what he is doing does the painter do good things." Yet to achieve such a state requires an immense amount of work. And it isn't just about mastery or skill. At the photography school where I taught, many of the graduating students were technical virtuosos but were expressively weak. These students had mistakenly confused technique as the end goal, gaining skills without emotional depth, heart, and soul. People like John Steinbeck and Bruce Lee combined technique with much more. The result was not a bag of tricks but a wild and prolific creative flow. The most creative pursue expertise with a higher and more noble goal.

EXERCISE

STEP 1
Set aside the time to develop your skill. Don't worry about writing a great novel or perfecting a martial arts move. That will come with time. Stop procrastinating because your dreams are so big. Begin where you are with what you have, and schedule the time to refine your craft. Select one skill that you want to learn, and schedule a fixed amount of time to practice and repeat your practice multiple times for the next month.

STEP 2
Technique combined with vision, heart, and soul leads to great things. Spend a few minutes in silence considering how you can add depth to the technique that you desire to learn.

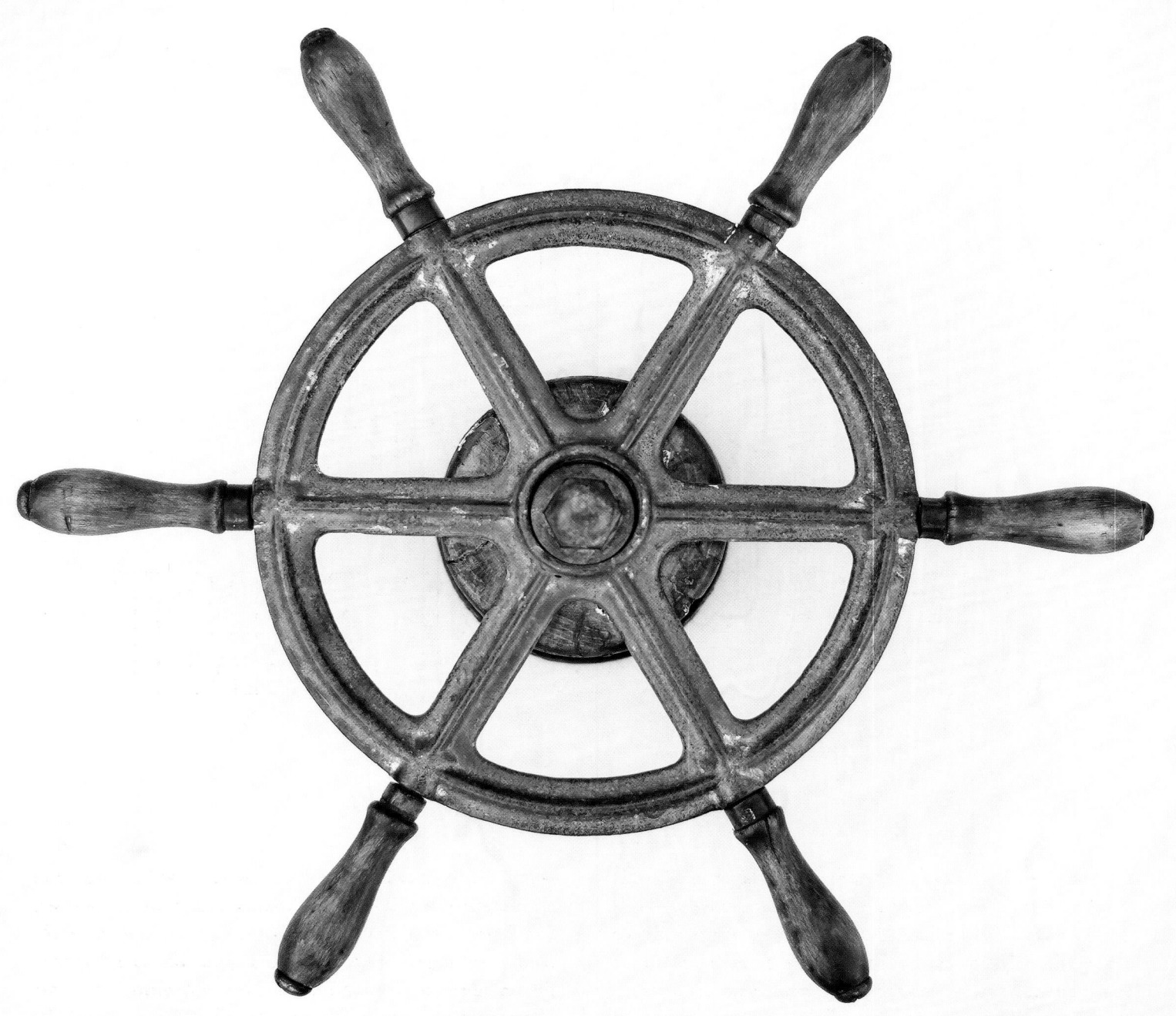

CHAPTER THIRTY-NINE

THE FREEDOM OF CONSTRAINT

Dr. Seuss's big break came when he was challenged with the idea of writing a book for young readers in an era when children's books were predictable and dull. This was his chance to steer the ship. But rather than give Dr. Seuss free rein, the publisher gave him a constraint— he could only use vocabulary from a list of 350 words. The first two words on the list were "cat" and "hat." This sparked an idea. Using only 225 words, Dr. Seuss wrote *The Cat in the Hat* and his reputation as the definitive children's book author and illustrator was set. Dr. Seuss took a year to compose what seems like a simple book. Creating within constraints is hard, but it can shape the final results into a more defined and desirable form. Dr. Seuss's efforts paid off, as the book was a huge hit. What seemed like a limitation was really an opportunity in disguise.

RULES. RULES. RULES. After the success of *The Cat in the Hat*, Dr. Seuss's editor, Bennett Cerf, made him a bet that he couldn't write a book using only 50 words. Dr. Seuss took on the challenge and wrote *Green Eggs and Ham*, one of his all-time bestsellers. It was the constraint that funneled his creative energy into creating such a good book. Yet when we think of Dr. Seuss, we don't tend to think of limited means. And we definitely don't associate Dr. Seuss with following the rules.

Although they look like free-flowing chaos, Dr. Seuss's books are more logical and consistent than they seem. As he explained, "If I start with a two-headed animal, I must never waver from that concept. There must be two hats in the closet, two toothbrushes in the bathroom, and two sets of spectacles on the night table." Such limits gave his work a "logical insanity," as he liked to say. And the logic and limitation is what gave the books their voice. The rules he imposed gave shape so that the stories didn't sprawl. The rules held the books together like tightly woven thread. And while the books are always a curious, quirky, and riotous read, they are cohesive and consistent as well. When a child picks up a Dr. Seuss book she smiles. She knows exactly what to expect, and still she's delighted and surprised.

Regardless of the type of book, Dr. Seuss held fast to certain self-imposed rules, like having only one illustration on a page and never using text to literally describe the illustrations. The copy and the illustrations had to hold their own. These rules made for a more interesting and sophisticated read. Rather than being pedantic and obvious, his work was subtle and suggestive. By letting the copy and illustrations stand by themselves, he elevated the reader, making her feel smart. And this approach ignited the imagination and made the reader more involved. Paradoxically, Dr. Seuss's rules made the books feel more open and free. Plus, it made them enjoyable for readers of any age.

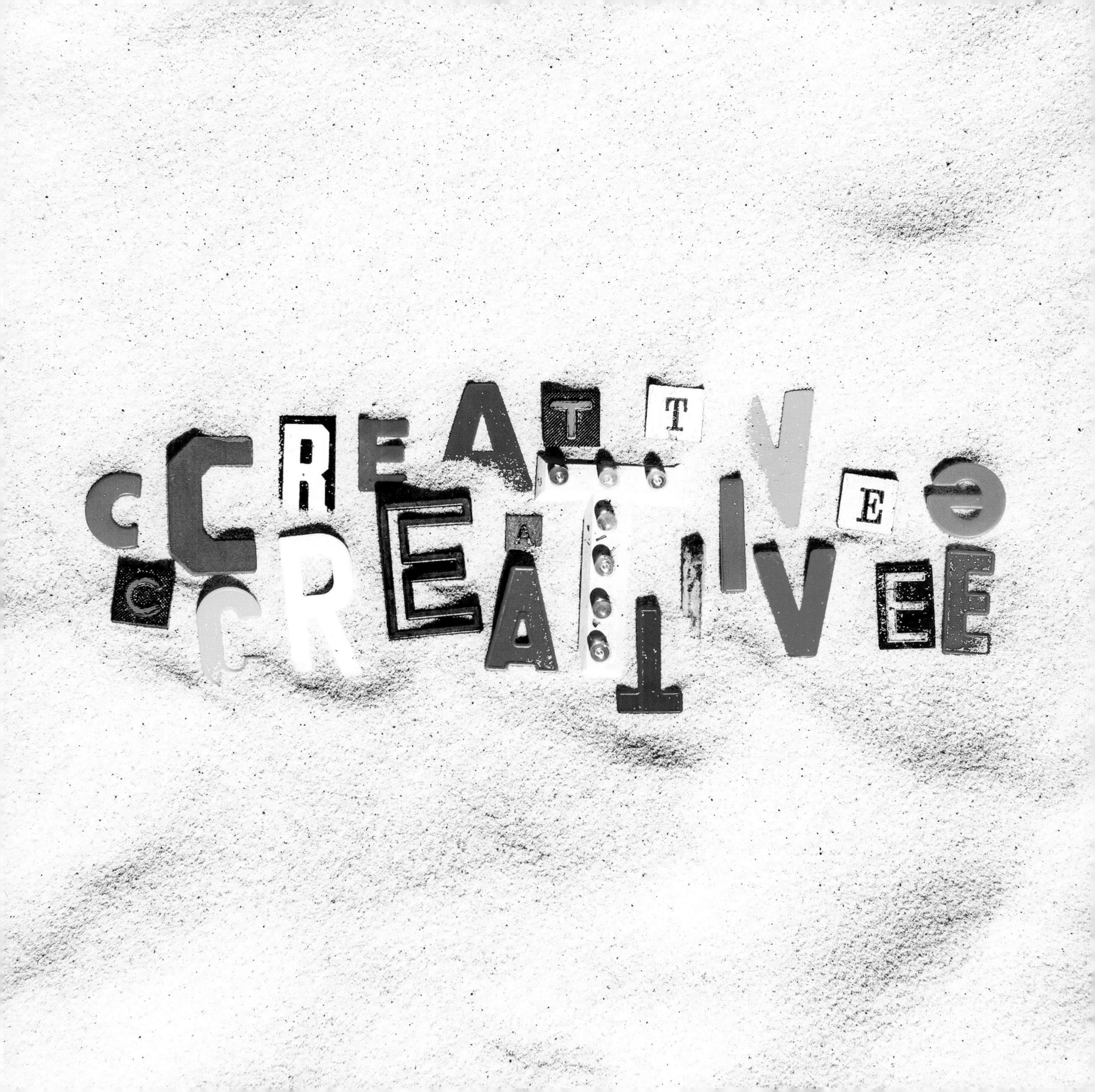

COMPOSITION WITH LIMITED MEANS The composer Igor Stravinsky wrote, "All art presupposes a work of selection." Like choosing the letters to arrange on the sand, it's impossible to be creative until we make a choice. And all art is limited and confined—Dr. Seuss with his words, the photographer with her frame, the musician with his notes, and the filmmaker with time. Imagine if a movie lasted all day or a song took six hours to hear. We would drift to sleep in the theater or tire of the endless harmonies, melodies, and tunes. What makes architecture, music, film, design, fashion, and every form of art beautiful is the break and the pause. It's the variation; it's the way the architect bends the rules or how the designer surprises us with simple and clean lines. And what makes any kind of art interesting is that it eventually stops. Art and time are closely connected, yet there's a persistent myth that creativity grows best without rules. But strange to tell, creativity likes limits, boxes, and walls. And it likes tension, problems, and stress. Without such limitations, it's unlikely to thrive.

Because of this, the quickest way to stifle an artist is to give her everything she needs. Without limits, problems, want, and hunger, she won't know what to do. Without challenge, creativity stops flowing. It's the difficulty that calls creativity to life. It's the fight that makes creativity so valuable and strong, like the tension of a string stretched between wood. Carefully wound, it gives the violin its voice. Without tension, the instrument is mute.

For the creative mind, the limit is a blessing and unlimited options a curse. Consider a composer who sits down to write an orchestral song. With unlimited options, it's nearly impossible to begin. That's why Stravinsky always started by defining the key. This self-imposed limitation set him free. It was the limitation of major or minor, sharp or flat, that provided somewhere to begin. The constraint makes art a possibility. In contrast, creativity dissipates and dissolves when we throw out structure, limits, and rules.

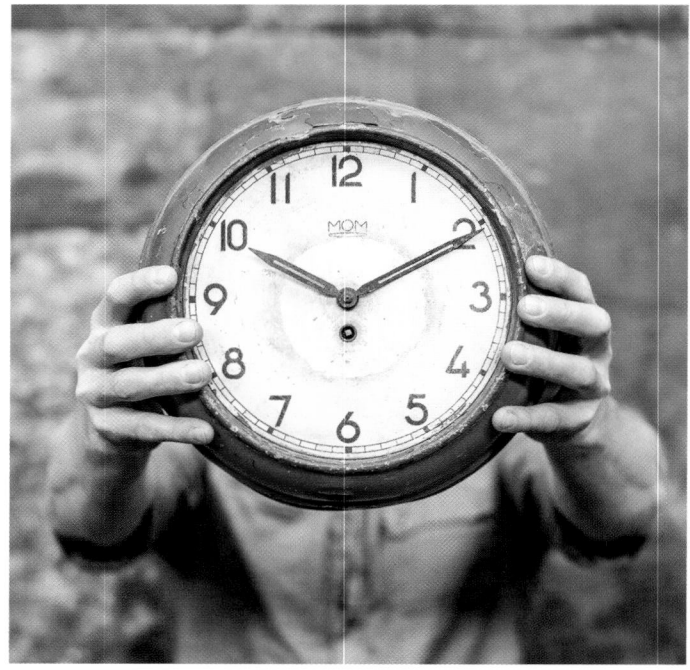

TOO MUCH GEAR When I first started taking photographs, I wished I had more time and more gear. My day job took up all my time, and my simple camera and single lens weren't as impressive as those of my peers. I felt like a fake, but I did my best. What I didn't realize then was that having less gear and not enough time helped me hone my craft. Without all the bells and whistles, I was nimble and free. Unencumbered by options, I was forced to create. It was a crucible for learning how to see, and having limited gear brought quick growth.

Although making photographs may not be your thing, we all have options to face. And it's easy to second-guess ourselves when we have too many choices to make. Worse, we become immobilized with so many different ideas. Yet the ones who thrive are those who embrace the freedom of constraints. So rather than setting out to be creative in a general way, get specific and impose some rules. Instead of trying to create "the best photograph ever," aim to create a photograph of a specific idea. Whatever the task or goal, add limits to funnel and focus your growth. Sometimes less truly is more.

WHEN FORCED TO WORK WITHIN A STRICT FRAMEWORK,
THE IMAGINATION IS TAXED TO ITS UTMOST—
AND WILL PRODUCE ITS RICHEST IDEAS. GIVEN TOTAL
FREEDOM, THE WORK IS LIKELY TO SPRAWL.

—T. S. ELLIOT

EXERCISE

STEP 1

Choose a creative task that you want to achieve. Select a few guidelines and limitations to give shape and definition to the project. Here's an example:

Creative task = Write a poem.

Guidelines = 1. Write about the ocean. 2. Include metaphors.

Limitations = 1. Use 25 words or less. 2. No rhymes. 3. No boats. 4. No fog.

Then set out to achieve the task.

STEP 2

The trouble with digital photography is that we capture too many frames. Excited about the moment, we push the shutter without taking the time to look. To counteract this trend, get out a sketchbook and camera. Travel to a location that interests you, whether your backyard or the city located hours away. Find a scene that interests your eye, but don't take the photograph. Sit down and sketch or draw the photograph that you would like to make. Even if you aren't good at drawing, that's OK. The point is to slow down, to sit, and to observe. Then after finishing the drawing, compose the shot and take a single frame.
Repeat this exercise three times on the same day.

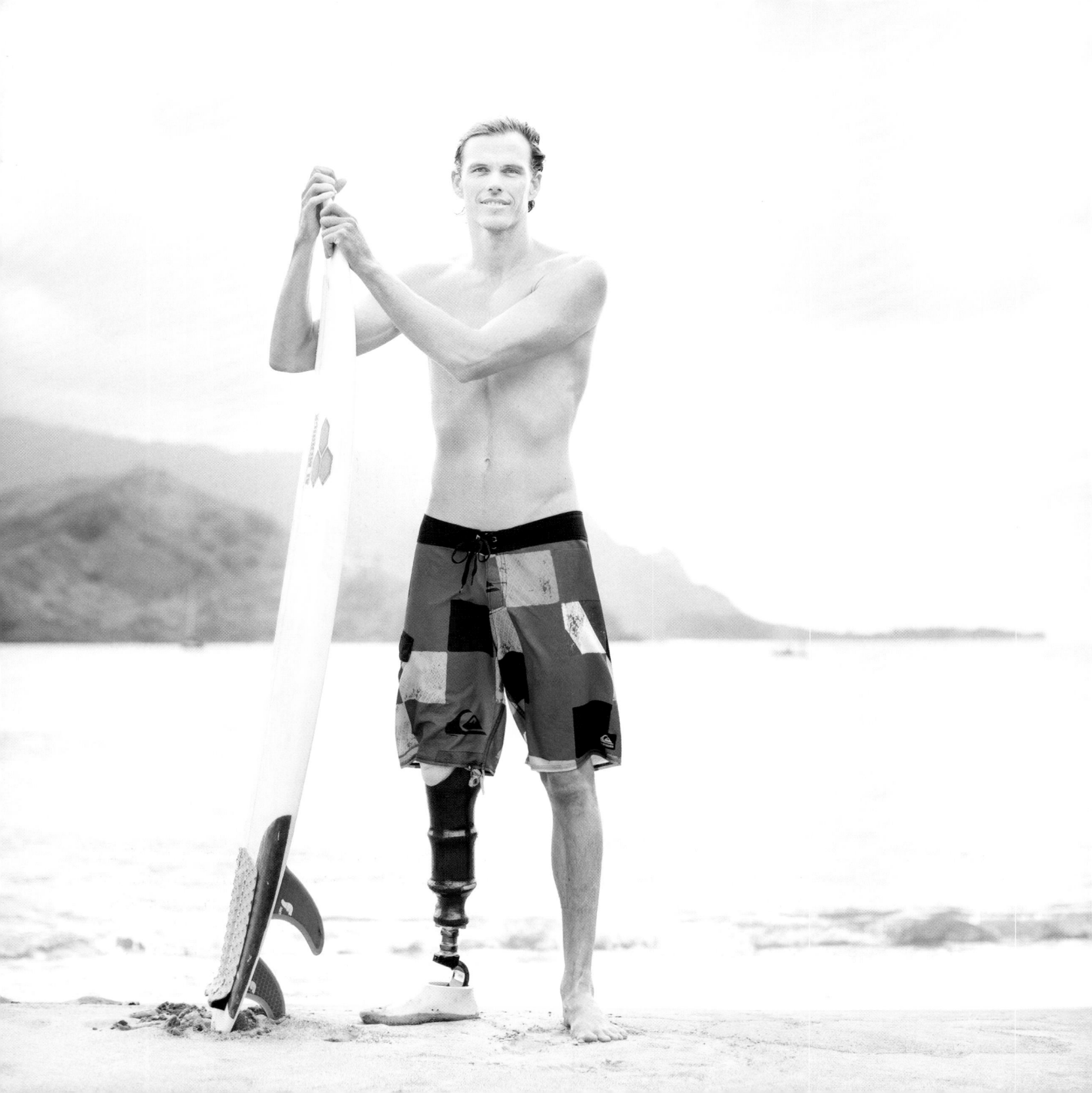

CHAPTER FORTY

GRATITUDE

When the shark sank its teeth into Mike's leg, he spun around in shock. What had started out as another perfect day turned into a gory scene. Mike was a senior in high school and had woken up early to go surfing with his buddies at one of their favorite local spots. He grew up on the north shore of Kauai and had been surfing his whole life. His family lived on a few acres that overlooked the sea. Pineapples grew in the garden; mangoes, papayas, and coconuts grew on the trees. Mike's family was warm, loving, and kind. It wasn't just paradise in a picturesque way—it was paradise in the true sense of the word. Mike's cares were small and his future was bright. On most mornings, he and his friends drove down to the beach to catch a sunrise surf before school. They paddled out into the water wearing big Hawaiian grins.

SALTWATER AND BLOOD When the shark bit, it began to thrash and drag Mike down. He furiously punched the shark, aiming for its nose but cutting his hands on its endless teeth. Finally, after a few solid blows the shark let go. Nowhere to be seen, the shark disappeared. In a frenzy, Mike yelled to his friends, "Shark! Shark! Shark!" and paddled toward land as fast as he could. Heart racing, adrenaline surging, he felt his leg shudder and convulse. "The shark is back for more," he said to himself. Turning to look over his shoulder, he bent his knee but nothing was there. The bleeding stump was a shock—just below his knee his leg was gone. Mike paddled hard and his friends got him to shore. The loss of blood was a life-threatening concern. His friends tied a tourniquet and drove as fast as they could. Miraculously, his life was saved.

I met Mike when he was a photography student in one of my classes. He was a bright-eyed student who carried himself with poise. Mike exuded kindness, generosity, and grace and always turned in the best work. It was obvious that he was living life like it was a sacred gift.

I knew Mike for over a year before he told me about the attack. One day I decided to ask about his slight limp. The story he told shook me to the core. I'm a surfer myself, and shark attack stories are something we all hear. And I've surfed in many places where other surfers have been taken down. Yet I had never heard someone recount such a story firsthand. At one point I said, "Wow. This must have really changed your life." I expected him to respond by telling me about fear, loss, and pain. But instead, in his warm Hawaiian accent, he said, "Yeah. It's really made me grateful." And then he went on to list all the things that he is grateful for: that the bite was below the knee, that his friends were there to help, that he was given a second chance, that he can still get out and surf, that it shaped the course of his life in such a positive way, that we get to live on a giant blue sphere, and that he's still alive. He went on and on. Mike's response was a life-changing moment for me. I had never witnessed gratitude in such a condensed and powerful form.

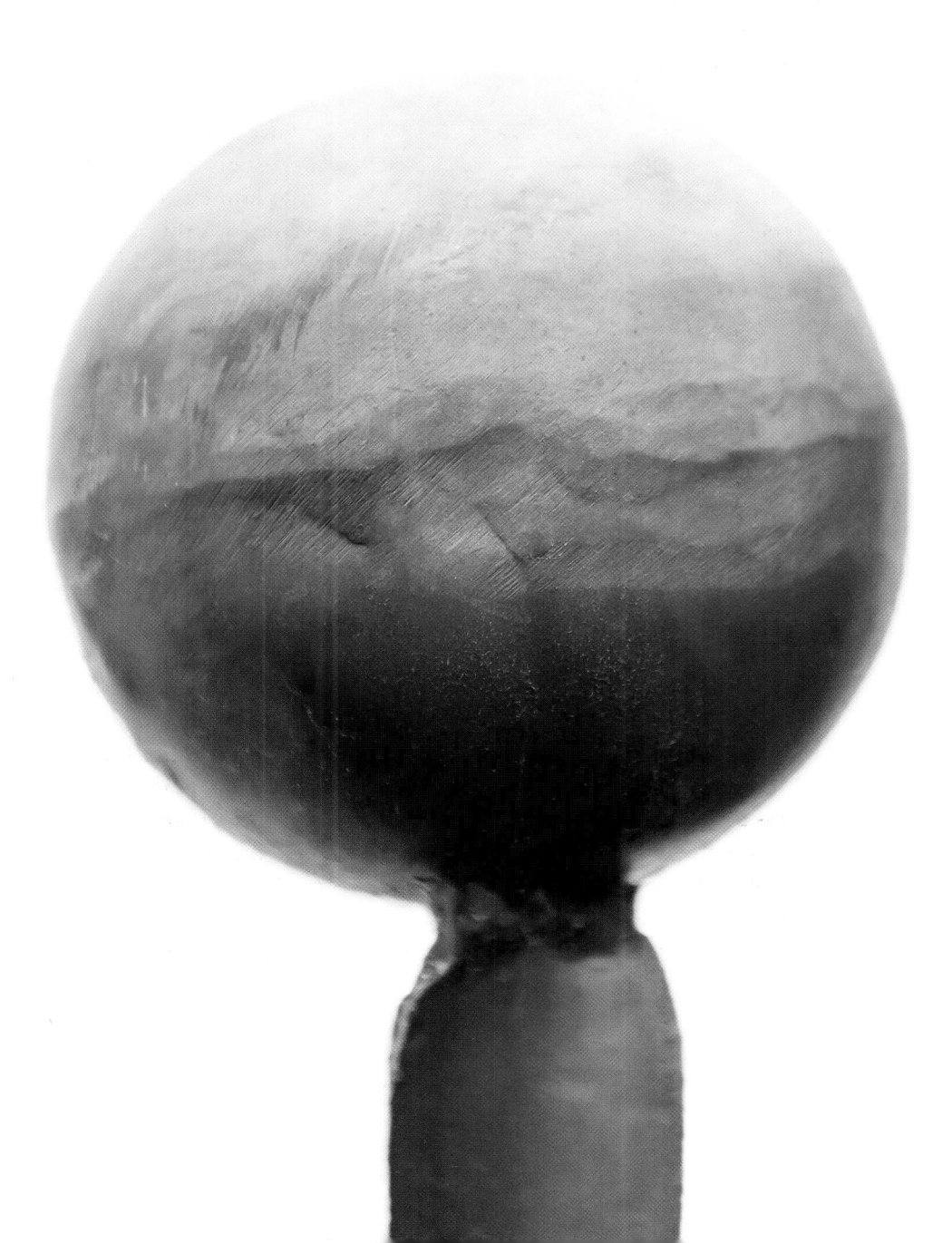

GRATITUDE THAT SAVES Since then, I've been lucky enough to consider Mike a friend. He's one of the most gracious and talented people I know. And he's become a professional photographer with worldwide acclaim. Last summer when my family went to Kauai, we met him at the beach, and Mike brought some boards for my kids, talked story, and showed us his prosthetic legs—one for walking and another for surfing. I captured a portrait of him (it's the opening image in this chapter) on that day. His mom stopped by the beach and invited us to his family home, where we made leis, picked pineapples, and watched a spectacular sunset light up the skies. I asked Mike how he got into photography and he said, "It was because of my leg."

After the accident, *National Geographic* sent a photographer to photograph Mike for a story in their magazine. The photographer and Mike became friends. This planted a seed that has since grown into a tree. And it all hinges on the response to the accident that Mike chose. Rather than fear, loathing, and self-pity, Mike selected gratitude, and this has turned him into a beacon of light—just ask anyone he knows. And his story isn't over yet; he still expresses gratitude every day, whether photographing or speaking out for the defense of the environment in Washington, DC.

When life bites, it's easy to respond in a pitiful and spiteful way. When we are wronged, it's easy to fly off the handle, complain, or lash out because of the pain. But the creative people among us find a different way. Rather than anger and distress, they spread grace. And their gratitude is like a lifering that saves.

THE THIEF WHO STOLE A GIFT Jean Valjean was orphaned and poor. In an attempt to feed his sister, he stole a piece of bread. Caught in the act, he was thrown in prison for five years. Upon his release, a desperate and wild animal-like look filled his eyes. Victor Hugo tells us the story in his timeless book *Les Misérables*. Once released from prison, Valjean is marked as a convict and cannot find shelter, food, or work. He is impoverished and utterly alone.

One cold and bitter night, he knocks on Monseigneur Bienvenu's manor door seeking shelter. Aware of the risk of housing such a man, the old bishop has pity and takes him in. He offers the man food, drink, and a place to sleep. The next morning Valjean has vanished, and so have the valuable silver forks and spoons.

The authorities catch the criminal and drag him back to the scene of the crime to confirm his guilt and send him back to prison again. Instead of being angry, the bishop seems grateful to see him again. The bishop greets Valjean with, "Ah! here you are!" Looking Jean Valjean straight in the eyes with a fierce gaze, he says, "I am glad to see you. Well, but how is this? I gave you the candlesticks too, which are of silver like the rest, and for which you can certainly get two hundred francs. Why did you not carry them away with your forks and spoons?" Valjean can't even respond.

The authorities leave, and Monseigneur Bienvenu grabs hold of the man. And as if peering into his soul he says, "Do not forget, never forget, that you have promised to use this money in becoming an honest man." Grateful beyond words, Valjean is forever changed.

THE MOST IMPORTANT CHOICE Whether as individuals or as communities, when we are grateful the world improves. Such was the case when the Danish stood up to protect the Jews during the Nazi invasion of World War II. Grateful to be able to help, the Danish resistance saved thousands of Jews by smuggling them to safety in the false bottoms of fishing boats. It was an amazing act of grace.

Do you get the point? In the face of tragedy and difficulty, you have a choice. One choice is creative and the other is not.

"When we choose gratitude, we see and live more deeply," as Robert Gupta told me one day. Gupta is a musician who is incredibly smart and equally kind. To give you a sense of his brilliance, he finished his master's degree at Yale and started playing for the Los Angeles Philharmonic when he was just 19. Gupta is a genius, and he believes strongly that music has the ability to change our lives.

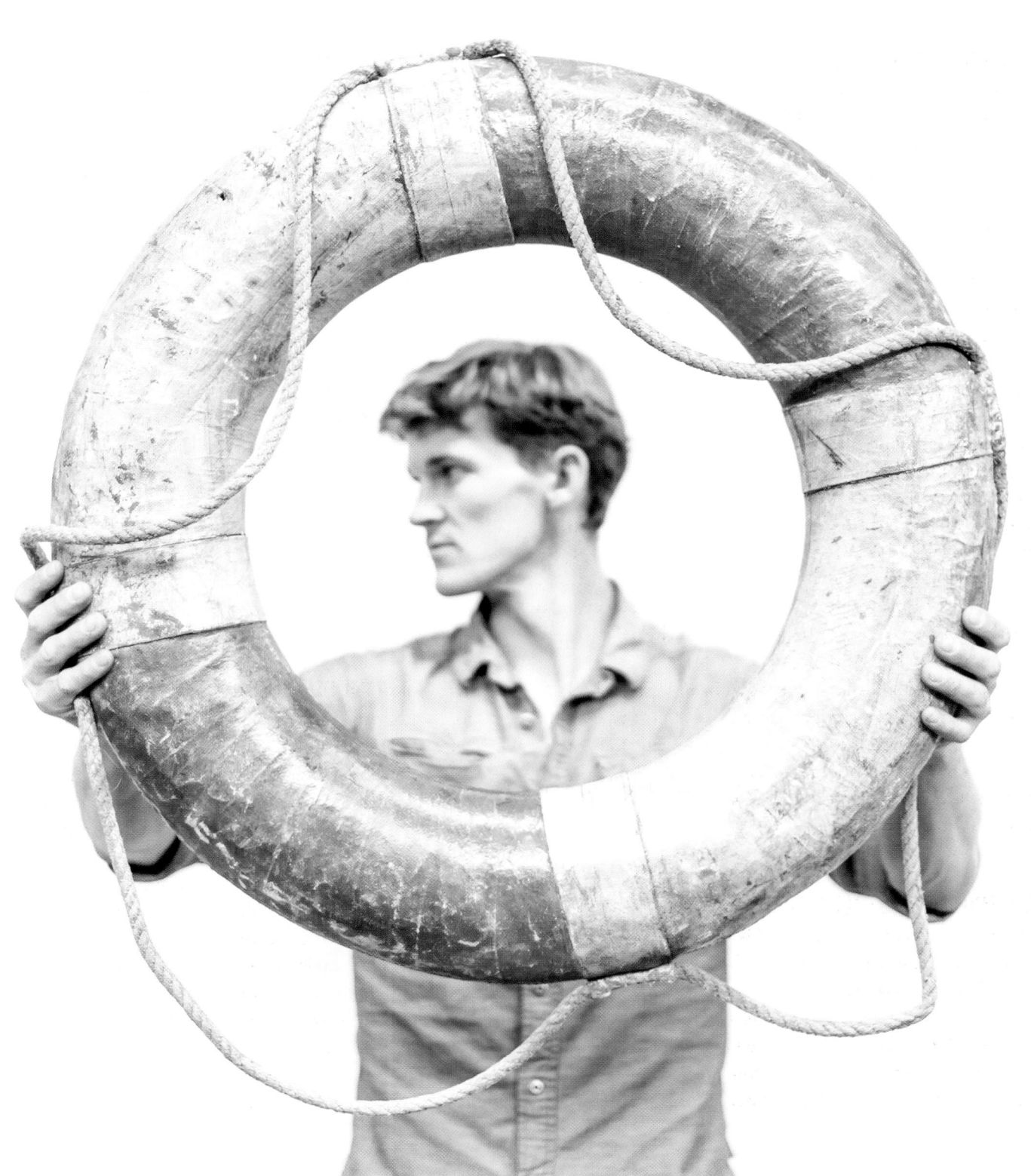

Gupta doesn't take his gift lightly and exudes gratitude for the skills he has. And so he shares the gift whenever he can, whether playing in a homeless shelter or on an international stage. He and I sat down to eat lunch, and I asked him what he's been up to these days. In a quiet tone he told me how he had started playing solo concerts in a hospice center for people during their final days. A few times, he explained, a patient died as he was playing a song. It was one of the most meaningful experiences of his life. And what a gift to give—to soften the pain of death and usher a soul from this life to the next.

Gupta, Bienvenu, and Valjean share a similar thread—they see the world through a gratitude lens. This lens makes their worlds come alive. As John Milton once wrote, "Gratitude bestows reverence, allowing us to encounter everyday epiphanies, those transcendent moments of awe that change forever how we experience life and the world." Gratitude is a lens, and it's also a tool. But it isn't a tool that helps you to achieve; it's more like one that shows you the way, like a compass.

But like all things, gratitude can be ignored, which leads to few questions for you: Will you carry it in your heart? Not as a way to become more creative or to make better stuff, but because the preciousness of life demands it be so. Will you allow gratitude to be central to your trade? Will you make gratitude central to your life? Will you choose gratitude today?

EXERCISE

STEP 1

Carry an index card in your pocket and put it next to your phone. Each time you reach into your pocket and feel the card, rather than checking your email or texting a friend, write down something that you are grateful for. Do this exercise for three days as a way to cleanse any ungratefulness in your heart. After accomplishing this for three continuous days, move on to step 2.

STEP 2

Over the long haul, it's easy to become ungrateful and to forget all the blessings you have received, as in the Old Testament story about how God provided manna (an edible substance like bread) so that His people wouldn't starve. Worried that they would forget, God asks them to create a jar and keep some manna inside. I love this idea so much that I created a "manna jar" of my own. It's pictured on the opposing page. The jar sits on my desk, and every morning (well, most mornings) I write three things that I'm grateful for. This habit helps me look at life through the gratitude lens. And it's really fun to go back and see what I have written. Consider creating your own jar, and fill it daily with three things that you are grateful for. Try this for three weeks.

STEP 3

Surround yourself with people who are grateful and who make you more grateful yourself. Take a few moments to think of people you know who exude gratitude, whether a fictional character like Jean Valjean or a person like Robert Gupta. Write down the names you come up with, and let these people be examples for you to lead a more gratitude-filled life.

CONCLUSION

Creativity is pure delight. It revitalizes the soul. But it isn't easy—at least not all the time. There are moments when the creative juices flow and the world seems beautiful, perfect, and serene. There are other moments of exasperation and defeat. All art, whether the art of living or the art of creating something new, is the echo of the delight and the struggle combined. Van Gogh once said, "Art demands dogged work." And so does pursuing your dreams. Yet it's in and through the difficult times that great art is born. And it's in these times that we are forged into something stronger than before.

Difficulty is the crucible that refines and strengthens at the same time. And it's in that place that we learn to appreciate life. For it's in the darkness that we learn to see light and in the cold that we value the warmth. Without challenge, we know not the full joys of life or the potential we have inside. As Albert Camus reflected, on his own experience, "In the depth of winter, I finally learned that there was within me an invincible summer." And my hope is that this book has helped you discover that there is an invincible summer within you as well.

Although sometimes hidden, the spark of this summer remains. It comes from the fact that you are unique and gifted in unparalleled ways. Yet this calling changes with the passage of time, and as a result, it's partially present and at the same time constantly being revealed. The nature of this ever-evolving call asks us to be aware, to become more, and to remember that life isn't as it first seems. There is more.

It's my hope that this book has given you reason to contemplate what that "more" might be. Yet it hasn't just been a book about ideas, but a book of action and of searching for that light that resides within. Finding this light is the key, and tending it might just be one of the most important activities you can pursue. Because when ignited, we create our best work and contribute in the most fascinating ways. And the path to igniting that spark isn't just imagination and dreams. Those elements are essential, but the secret is to use them as fuel. Creativity beckons you to try. Sitting still doesn't work. Neither does dreaming big dreams. Without action, creativity starts to fade and the power we once had is drained. The secret to the creative life is to do, to be, and to act—and to begin even though there is a gap between us and our ideal.

Crossing this gap takes hard work. As Michelangelo said, "If people knew how hard I had to work to gain my mastery, it wouldn't seem wonderful at all." In addition to hard work, it requires learning to see. As Van Gogh once wrote to his brother, "I see paintings or drawings in the poorest cottages, in the dirtiest corners." With a creative outlook, the mundane becomes magnificent and the ordinary becomes alive. Those who adopt such an approach see life not as it is but as it should be, so that even drudgery and difficulty become profound.

Yet as we've seen throughout this book, creativity isn't just for famous artists like Michelangelo and Van Gogh. We are all creative in our own unique ways. The most creative, whether artist, engineer, or chemist, have a common thread: they love what they do. Adopting a creative mind-set not only renews your mind but fills your heart and shapes who you will become. And my hope is that this book has brought this type of change.

After Michelangelo died, a note was found in his studio written in the handwriting of old age. It read, "Draw, Antonio; draw, Antonio; draw and don't waste time." It was written for his pupil but also for us. Now is the time to draw, dance, film, photograph, and write. Now is the time to live the life for which you were designed. Now is the time to pursue that dream and to fight. Fight like you have never fought before. A new life awaits for those who take up the charge.

THE CREATIVE FIGHT

THANKS

Thank you to my wife, Kelly, for your friendship, companionship, and love.
These last 19 years of marriage have been the best of my life. You are my best friend, soul
mate, and deepest love. And thank you to our three daughters, Annika, Sophia, and Elsie.
You are my inspiration and joy. I love you three more than you will ever know.

Thank you to those who inspired and encouraged me while writing this book:
Evan Chong, Michael Ninness, Shaun Walton, John Kelsey, Don Johnson, Bruce Heavin,
Rodney Smith, Julieanne Kost, Mitch Thomas, Keith Carter, Steven Tiller,
David duChemin, and Will Wallin.

Thank you to Susan Rimerman, who saw this book inside of me before I knew it was
there, and to Valerie Witte for adding your artistic touch to the pages of this book.
And thank you to the book design and production team: Cybele Grandjean, Kim Scott,
David Van Ness, Scout Festa, Liz Welch, and James Minkin.

Thank you to the creator, who has given me hope and a second chance at life.

Let's keep in touch! You can find me at: chrisorwig.com, Instagram (@chrisorwig),
and Facebook (Chris Orwig).

For more inspiration, visit: thecreativefight.com and carpediemsupplyco.com.

INDEX